# The Quest for Plausible Christian Discourse in a World of Pluralities

# Religions and Discourse

Edited by James M. M. Francis

Volume 35

PETER LANG

Oxford · Bern · Berlin · Bruxelles · Frankfurt am Main · New York · Wien

Younhee Kim

# The Quest for Plausible Christian Discourse in a World of Pluralities

## The Evolution of David Tracy's Understanding of 'Public Theology'

PETER LANG

Oxford · Bern · Berlin · Bruxelles · Frankfurt am Main · New York · Wien

Bibliographic information published by Die Deutsche Bibliothek
Die Deutsche Bibliothek lists this publication in the Deutsche National-
bibliografie; detailed bibliographic data is available on the Internet at
‹http://dnb.ddb.de›.

British Library and Library of Congress Cataloguing-in-Publication Data:
A catalogue record for this book is available from *The British Library*,
Great Britain, and from *The Library of Congress*, USA

ISSN 1422-8998
ISBN 978-3-03910-733-9

© Peter Lang AG, International Academic Publishers, Bern 2008
Hochfeldstrasse 32, Postfach 746, CH-3000 Bern 9, Switzerland
info@peterlang.com, www.peterlang.com, www.peterlang.net

Printed in Germany

# Contents

# Foreword

It is a pleasure to write a brief foreword to this fine work. Dr Kim possesses a first-rate mind for interpreting the often-shifting meanings in text after text. She also has finely wrought critical skills in her assessments, both positive and negative. After all, critical assessments of most texts are not, as some still think, confined to negative assessments but include both positive and negative critiques. I am very thankful for both the interpretations and the critiques.

As Hans-Georg Gadamer rightly teaches, the author's interaction cannot control the interpretation of the text. Once the text is written, it is on its own. The author becomes another reader. To be sure, it is often interesting and informative – to hear or read what the author intended. But the author's intention cannot be decisive. Just as in school, a student soon learns that it does not finally matter what he/she intended to say. What alone matters (for example, for a grade) is what is written.

Of course, given the nature of their subject-matter, philosophers and theologians can be rightly annoyed by bizarre readings (we have all endured them) or by a refusal by some critics to realize how simple and sometimes close to impossible the questions of philosophy and theology actually are. As John Henry Newman wisely stated, on some basic questions we should be thankful if the question is well-posed and the answer is meaningful and, at times, plausible, and at yet other times, true. This fact of philosophical and theological life is not, of course, an excuse for unnecessarily complex or vague writing on these almost impossible questions.

Alfred North Whitehead did not speak only for himself when he stated that he did not write more clearly on metaphysical questions because he did not think more clearly on them. Indeed, clarity is always desirable (pace the attack on clarté by some contemporary thinkers). But clarity is not, on some questions, always attainable. Whitehead's strength was to ask the "big" questions and to admit the often necessary vagueness of his answers. (The same can be said of Heidegger and many others.) Both Bertrand Russell (vis-à-vis Whitehead) and Rudolf Carnap (vis-à-vis Heidegger) insisted on clarity that illuminated many purely logical issues but either ignored or dismissed not only the "vague" answers but even the questions (e.g., on Being and Becoming) of a Whitehead or a Heidegger. Russell and Carnap were wrong.

Some thinkers – like my mentor, Bernard Lonergan, and many other enviable persons, including Dr Kim – write on the really difficult issues with both depth and clarity. Brava, I say. If you doubt, just read on in her fine work.

Perhaps it would be useful – as interesting and, to a limited extent, informative – to read from the author of the works interpreted in this work by Dr Kim. Hence, a very few observations on the trajectory those works take, as far as I can see now.

My texts are, I think, a series of sometimes stable, sometimes changing answers to a basic set of questions, of which the principal one is this: is the religious interpretation of human existence meaningful and true? This interpretation is found both as a religious dimension to our common existence (e.g., the limit-questions and limit experiences) and as particular religious experiences grounded in revelations and ways of life (e.g., revelation and redemptive ways of the life of justice and love; enlightenment and the compassionate way of life). Questions about the religious interpretation of human experience (both as a religious dimension to all life and as particular religions) are difficult, delicate, and important in any culture for which we have records. They are, therefore, questions that any thoughtful human being should ask. Without these questions human life is barely human.

If we can respond affirmatively to these "religious" questions, it follows that we would naturally ask whether the religious dimension to life and, distinctly but relatedly, any particular historical religion, articulates a referent to both a religious dimension (philosophy) and a revelatory religion (theology).

In my early work, I was hopeful for a positive answer to the religious questions from a strictly transcendental argument. I no longer have that hope – for reasons my books after *Blessed Rage for*

8

*Order* articulate. I now believe – as I argue in my forthcoming book based on my Gifford Lectures entitled *This Side of God* that the "answer" is beyond transcendental argument. The "answer" demands further attention – both philosophically and theologically – to the issues of temporality, historicity, and the meaning of revelation. One may find some ways (e.g., hermeneutical, and ethical-political) to assess namings of that religious referent: viz (in my present work), the names The Void, The Open, The Good, and God.

It is odd to me how the questions seem so much more complex and the answers more solid while being more tentative than they were viewed by my younger self. But what did I expect? The questions are the most difficult and important questions available to thought-ful persons. In my judgment, ultimately these questions define the almost impossible form of questioning named philosophy and always should define the even more impossible mode of questioning called theology.

With this fine book on my different attempts to answer these questions, Dr Kim has, by her probing interpretations and questions, also continued her own intellectual and spiritual journey. I look forward, deo volente, to watching her journey unfold.

David Tracy
November 2006
The University of Chicago

# Acknowledgements

This book is a revision of my doctoral dissertation which was written for the Faculty of Theology in Katholieke Universiteit Leuven (Catholic University of Louvain), Belgium in 2004. It is only right and fitting that I should express my gratitude for the support by various funding bodies and people who helped bring my doctoral research to fruition. The Institute of Missiology (Aachen, Germany) and the Katholieke Universiteit Leuven (by way of a Research Council Scholarship) financed my doctoral research. I am deeply grateful for their generosity and commitment to academic development. Amongst the many people who were consistently supportive over my doctoral years, my special thanks are due to Professor Terrence Merrigan, my supervisor, Professor Lieven Boeve, Professor Peter De Mey, Professor André Cloots, the Faculty of Philosophy in Katholieke Universiteit Leuven, Fr. Seo Kong-Seok, Professor Emeritus of Theology, Sogang University, South Korea, and Dr Richard Brosse, the Executive Director of the Institute of Missiology.

From November 2004 to August 2005, I was invited as a visiting staff member to the Milltown Institute of Theology and Philosophy in Dublin (NUI), Ireland. This gave me the opportunity to prepare my doctoral work for publication under the funding of the department of Mission Theology and Cultures of the Institute. I would like to express my sincere gratitude to Dr Brian Grogan, President of the Milltown Institute, Dr Patrick Roe, Head of the department of Mission Theology and Cultures, and many other staff members of the Institute.

For the publication of this book, I am also indebted to the research funding for the staff members of Mater Dei Institute of Education, Dublin City University, Ireland. A special word of thanks to Dr Dermot Lane, Rev. Michael Drumm, Dr Andrew McGrady, and Dr Gabriel Flynn of the institute.

I am very grateful to Professor David Tracy for writing a foreword to this book and giving his time to several private interviews which were very helpful and insightful for writing this book. My gratitude goes also to Dr Jim Francis, the Religions and Discourse Series Editor of Peter Lang, Dr Graham Speake, the Publishing Director of Peter Lang and Helena Sedgwick for all their assistance. Finally, I must mention that without the support of my parents, this project would have been impossible. For this reason, I dedicate this work to them.

# Abbreviations

## David Tracy's Books

| | |
|---|---|
| *AI* | *The Analogical Imagination: Christian Theology and the Culture of Pluralism* |
| *BRO* | *Blessed Rage for Order: The New Pluralism in Theology* |
| *DO* | *Dialogue with the Other: The Inter-Religious Dialogue* |
| *PA* | *Plurality and Ambiguity: Hermeneutics, Religion, Hope* |

## Journals

| | |
|---|---|
| *AJTP* | *American Journal of Theology and Philosophy* |
| *ATR* | *Anglican Theological Review* |
| *ChCent* | *The Christian Century* |
| *CrCur* | *Cross Currents* |
| *CTSAP* | *Catholic Theological Society of America Proceedings* |
| *HeyJ* | *The Heythrop Journal: A Quarterly Review of Philosophy and Theology* |
| *HTR* | *Harvard Theological Review* |
| *Int* | *Interpretation* |
| *JAAR* | *Journal of American Academy of Religion* |
| *JES* | *Journal of Ecumenical Studies* |
| *JR* | *The Journal of Religion* |
| *LS* | *Louvain Studies* |
| *Ph&Th* | *Philosophy and Theology* |
| *PhT* | *Philosophy Today* |
| *SR* | *Studies in Religion* |
| *TD* | *Theology Digest* |

| | |
|---|---|
| *Th* | *Theology* |
| *ThEd* | *Theological Education* |
| *ThT* | *Theology Today* |
| *TS* | *Theological Studies* |

# Introduction

"Jews demand signs and Greeks desire wisdom, but we proclaim Christ crucified, a stumbling block to Jews and foolishness to Gentiles, but to those who are the called, both Jews and Greeks, Christ the power of God and the wisdom of God" (1Cor 1: 22–4). This famous passage of St. Paul reflects, most pointedly, the self-understanding of the nascent Christian community that the proclamation of Christian faith is something that is not immediately intelligible, sensible or convincing for the surrounding world. However, what is interesting is that the early Christian community, as Matthew's Gospel proves,[1] had an astonishing desire and vision for evangelizing the outer world beyond Palestine with the conviction that the Christ-event had a universal significance for all humanity. Recent studies show that the early Christian missionary movements represented much more than a shift of content within the existent Jewish mission.[2] It is observed that Judaism never explicitly developed a mission to the Gentiles that had as its goal the conversion of the world as Christianity had. "Jewish missionary activity may have existed at times in Rome," but it was never specifically "a missionary religion" in character.[3] According to the Oxford scholar M. Goodman, mission understood as converting (proselytizing) the world is a phenomenon more or less invented by Christianity. Here, mission as converting means to "en-

---

1    "Now the eleven disciples went to Galilee, to the mountain to which Jesus had directed them. When they saw him, they worshiped him; but some doubted. And Jesus came and said to them, 'All authority in heaven and on earth has been given to me. Go therefore and make disciples of all nations, baptizing them in the name of the Father and of the Son and of the Holy Spirit, and teaching them to obey everything that I have commanded you. And remember, I am with you always, to the end of the age'" (Mt 28: 16–20).

2    For this information, see L.J. Lietaert Peerbolte, *Paul the Missionary* (Leuven: Peeters, 2003) 2–6.

3    S. McKnight, *A Light among the Gentiles: Jewish Missionary Activity in the Second Temple Period* (Minneapolis: Fortress Press, 1991) 116–17.

courage outsiders not only to change their way of life but also to be incorporated" within a new group whose teachings and rituals the converts had to come to share and practice.[4]

Certainly, this Christian missionary attitude including the conviction about the salvation of the world was not unrelated to the development of the apologetical endeavors to make Christian truth-claims intelligible to people in other religious, cultural, and intellectual worlds. These painstaking apologetical endeavors were most eminently carried out by Christian intellectuals who engaged with contemporary philosophical conceptualities and religious ideas. This endeavor to establish the intelligibility of Christian faith, that is to say, reflection on the relationship between Christian faith and reason, was, however, not just the imperative of the early Christian missionary community. Rather, this task has been a perennial work of Christian intellectuals in ever-new religious, cultural, intellectual, and social-political contexts, at least until they lose the conviction about the universal significance of Christian truth-claims. This endeavor of *fides quaerens intellectum*, however, never has been, nor will be, conclusive and exhaustive, but is in need of constant revision and renewal.

It can be said that what is known as fundamental theology today refers to a theological discipline which addresses and deals with, at a most radical level, this issue of constructing the intelligibility of Christian truth-claims in response to contextual challenges and exigencies:[5] in other words, the *border* problems between Christian faith and other significant human minds and the realities of the world. Indeed, according to Claude Geffré, since the specific function of fundamental theology is "to explain Christianity to the human mind, one will already expect its set of subjects and even its method to develop according to the historical development of the mind. We shall thus have to allow even more room for historical relativity in the

---

4   M. Goodman, *Mission and Conversion: Proselytizing in the Religious History of the Roman Empire* (Oxford: Clarendon Press, 1994) 4.

5   For an extensive analysis concerning the definition, history, goal, method, and content of fundamental theology, see Francis S. Fiorenza, *Foundational Theology: Jesus and the Church* (New York: Crossroad, 1985) 249–311.

structure and practice of fundamental theology than in the other sectors of theology."[6]

One of the most significant turning points in the structure and practice of fundamental theology (in Catholic circles) in recent times was the Second Vatican Council (1962–1965). In preconciliar days, Thomistic philosophy played an almost exclusive role as the dialogue partner of theology. However, since the Second Vatican Council, although this philosophical tradition is still influential in Catholic theology, its monopoly is no more. Since 1965 Catholic theologians have increasingly incorporated a broader spectrum of philosophies such as existentialism, hermeneutics, phenomenology, linguistic philosophy, process thought, Marxist philosophy, etc. In addition, theologians have engaged in serious interdisciplinary dialogue with sociologists, political scientists, psychologists, cultural anthropologists, biologists, physicists, and colleagues in other fields.[7] Catholic theologians' more active commitment to the ecumenical movement and much more serious dialogue with other great world religions have widely affected the way Catholics think, teach, and practice their theology today.[8]

David Tracy (1939–) is a leading contemporary Catholic theologian who has long been committed to developing fundamental theology. Tracy's fundamental theology, developed as it has been in

6    Claude Geffré, "Recent Developments in Fundamental Theology: An Interpretation," in *Concilium* 46 (1969) 6.

7    For example, a representative statement that endorses the pluralism of theological methodology and its dialogue partners is found in *Gaudium et Spes* (62): Theologians should engage in "new investigations" demanded by fresh questions coming from "science, history and philosophy." They "are invited to seek for more suitable ways of communicating doctrine" to the people of our time. Theologians are the ones who "possess a lawful freedom of inquiry and of thought, and the freedom to express their minds humbly and courageously about those matters in which they enjoy competence." For a more detailed analysis of the endorsement of the Second Vatican Council and later church documents for the pluralism of theological methods and approaches, see Gerald O'Collins, *Retrieving Fundamental Theology: The Three Styles of Contemporary Theology* (New York: Paulist Press, 1993) 7–9.

8    For the development of Catholic Theology (especially, fundamental theology) since 1965, see Gerald O'Collins, op. cit.

the wake of the so-called modern Catholic giants, Karl Rahner and Bernard Lonergan, reflects the significant transition between modernity and postmodernity. The benefit of studying his theological development is to witness a trajectory of methodological shifts from modernity to postmodernity. Tracy's theological development is eminently indicative of the fact that theology is a self-critical, and thereby, self-correcting discipline in line with ever-changing contextual demands and challenges.

As a postconciliar theologian, Tracy's theological practice has involved serious dialogues with other Christian denominational theologies, the wider range of philosophical traditions, and other great religions. Tracy is a renowned theologian who has shown a great sensitivity and openness to the shifts of theological context, and who has been unhesitating in incorporating the new achievements of philosophical, cultural, religious, and social-political scholarly enterprises into his theological practice. Such a keen receptivity has mainly to do with his acute concern with constructing and updating theological discourse as a public discourse which is accessible to, and plausible for, not only the Christian communities but also the outer world beyond these communities. Succinctly put, a key aim of Tracy's fundamental theology (from the 1970s up to the early 2000s) is to construct public theology, in response to two major themes: (1) 'pluralism' (whether theological, religious, philosophical, or cultural) and (2) 'otherness' (especially as this is reflected in the demand to do justice to the experience of long-marginalized groups such as the economic and politically down-trodden, ethnic and sexual minorities, other religious traditions, and even God as interruptive, shattering Other in postmodern philosophy and theology).

Our aim in this thesis, then, is to reflect critically on Tracy's achievement and on the limitations of his methodology in fundamental theology, especially as regards its success in addressing the concern with 'pluralism' and 'otherness.' More pointedly, our focal concern is to explore the suitability of Tracy's methodological program in light of the demand to do justice to our contemporary context of religious plurality. It is our contention that today the question of 'other religions' needs to be considered from the outset of one's theological practice, and can no longer be left for an addendum or afterthought to theology. Unless we deny the fact that Christianity today situates itself within a religiously pluralistic context, we cannot but acknowledge that religious plurality needs to be a point of departure for theological reflection.

The point of departure for our exploration of Tracy's theological development is his so-called "revisionist model" which is developed in his *Blessed Rage for Order*.[9] This work is the most important source for studying Tracy's fundamental theology. The extensive analysis of this work is an essential part of our thesis for two reasons: methodological and substantive. Firstly, in terms of the methodological aspect, this work is Tracy's fully fledged treatise on fundamental theology which deals with all the fundamentals of a theological system, that is, the principal theological sources, the methodology of investigation of these sources, the correlation of these sources, theological criteria for truth, etc. This work is a matrix of Tracy's fundamental theology from which his later methodological revisions have emerged. This means that without a thorough study of this work, it is rather difficult to spot and map out his later methodological development in a comprehensive and systematic way.

Secondly, in terms of the substantive aspect, Tracy's revisionist model is characterized as a 'modern' theology. It is true that modern methodology or modern epistemological presumptions have limitations as regards their ability to respond to today's postmodern and postmetaphysical questions and challenges. However, it is equally true that not all postmodern and postmetaphysical theological experiments are immediately convincing or plausible today. We agree with Tracy's view in his new preface to *Blessed Rage for Order* (1996) that "even those, like myself, who agree with the heart of the post-modern critiques [...] should still insist that there is no honest way around modernity. A thinker today can only go through modernity, never around it, to post-modernity."[10] In other words, our careful and critical reflection on modernity (and modern theology) is imperative for a

---

9    *Blessed Rage for Order: The New Pluralism in Theology* (San Francisco: Harper & Row, 1975).

10   "Preface," in *Blessed Rage for Order* (1996) xv.

fruitful envisioning of postmodern theology. Georges De Schrijver's comments are worth quoting here:

> Indeed, nowadays it has become modish to theologize in opposition to modernity, and by the same token to minimize, if not to reject, the achievements of theologians who critically dialogued with modernity. In terms of mediations, this means that 'modern ways of thinking' can no longer be viewed as valid or relevant instruments to reflect on revelation in accordance with the needs of the time. So part of my wager is that I am convinced that some basic patterns of 'modern theology' must be continued and transmitted to the next generations. For to do this is better, and more promising, than to engage in so-called postmodern theologies that covertly or overtly turn back to pre-modern thinking, and opt for a ghettoizing type of church life.[11]

Our thesis consists of four chapters. In the first chapter, we will examine Tracy's methodological exposition which serves as the

---

11    Georges De Schrijver, "The Use of Mediations in Theology Or, the Expanse and Self-Confinement of a Theology of the Trinity," in Jacques Haers, Edmondo Guzman and others (eds), *Mediations in Theology: Georges De Schrijver's Wager and Liberation Theologies* (Leuven: Peeters, 2003) 63. De Schrijver points out the positive values of modern theology as follows: "(i) the view that human beings are actors of their histories, and that this (collectively shared) responsible autonomy is part of their being created into the image of God; (ii) that religiosity is not just a matter of 'churchy-ness,' but rather demands that the deep concerns that religion stands for be extended to the whole of our 'being in the world.' The most deeply secular concerns are also the most deeply religious concerns. To try to stop the growth of abject poverty and illiteracy among the weakest sectors of the global village is an act of religiosity and not just of humanism; (iii) that modern theology possesses the instruments to perceive and to denounce the derailments and atrocities of modernity's calculating, instrumental reason (a calculation which constitutes the backbone of economic globalization today); (iv) that modern theology is not a monolithic bloc, but a basic way of thinking which can take on various forms in various continents. Latin American liberation theology is an offspring of modern theology (cross-fertilized by Marxism), but an offspring having its own character. And so is Dalit theology with its struggle against casteism, in the name of liberty, equality and fraternity; (v) that God's offer of grace has a universal ambit, and cannot be seen as confined to the solely baptized 'christo-fideles.' God's spirit also works elsewhere, outside the confines of the church, in the hearts and minds of people of other religions and of those having no affiliation to any religion at all." (De Schijver, op. cit., 63–4).

foundation of his revisionist model. This chapter consists of two sections. In the first section we explore the specific *contextual issues* that motivate Tracy's revisionist project. In the second section we examine his five *methodological theses* which guide his revisionist model.

The second and third chapters are concerned with how Tracy actually substantiates his revisionist project in accordance with his methodological exposition. Tracy describes his revisionist model as "philosophical reflection" upon two principal sources, viz., common human experience and the Christian tradition. By describing his approach as essentially a matter of "philosophical reflection," Tracy declares his intention to demonstrate the public intelligibility of the *religious* meanings present in both common human experience and the Christian tradition solely by means of a scientific methodology that is not dependent on any confessional tradition. In the second chapter we will examine Tracy's critical, scientific investigation of the above-mentioned two principal theological sources. We provide a detailed analysis of the sources (phenomenology and hermeneutical theories) that Tracy draws on for his investigation.

In the third chapter we reflect on Tracy's Christian theism which is the heart of his revisionist model. In Tracy's revisionist project the question of God is not an issue independent of his prior phen-omenological and hermeneutical investigation of two principal sour-ces. His theism is epistemologically grounded in this investigation of two sources. Tracy's aim in constructing Christian theism is to develop an understanding of God which avoids the pitfalls of both supernatural theism and atheistic secularism. We will take two steps. Firstly, we examine Tracy's attempt to defend the use of metaphysics (transcendental Thomism) to validate God's reality (God's *existence*). Secondly, we examine Tracy's metaphysical justification of God's *nature* (in what manner God exists and acts vis-à-vis the world), relying on the process thought of Charles Hartshorne. By using this source, Tracy endeavors to develop a vision of God which can make room for the positive values of modernity (including the legitimacy of critical inquiry, change, process, time, experiential, relational and social realities) and overcomes the problematic classical under-standing of God as immutable, changeless, and non-relative. In our critical assessment of Tracy's revisionist theism we discuss whether Tracy's argument, that his metaphysical validation of God demonstrates God as universally true and valid for *all* human religious experience, does justice to our contemporary experience of religious plurality.

In the final chapter we reflect on the shifts and continuities in Tracy's methodology of fundamental theology since his *Blessed Rage for Order* up to the early 2000s. We divide into two phases Tracy's methodological development after *Blessed Rage for Order*: (1) the 1980s; (2) from the 1990s to the early 2000s. Our analysis is directed by two key concerns. Firstly, we focus on what new methodological questions of fundamental theology addressed in new situations Tracy tries to grapple with, how he deals with those questions, and what his alternative proposals are. Secondly, we enquire whether Tracy's revised view of fundamental theology during this period, if it exists, can provide better methodological frameworks and insights for our contemporary context of pluralities.

In the course of our exploration of Tracy's theological development we do not forget that there is never a conclusive and exhaustive methodology which transcends the flux of ever-new contextual exigencies. One true thing, however, is that a good theology, like any other of the 'classic' oeuvres, contains rich resources and a profundity which is retrievable and utilizable by means of reinterpretation and re-evaluation in light of the newly demanding contexts. Tracy's theology, although its development is still underway, is certainly a valuable resource for envisioning a more prospective theological epistemology for today.

# Chapter One
# The Methodological Exposition of David Tracy's Fundamental Theology

The aim of this chapter is to examine Tracy's revisionist model of fundamental theology developed in his book, *Blessed Rage for Order*. Initially, Tracy planned to write a trilogy on the theological methodologies of three theological disciplines – viz., fundamental, systematic, and practical theology.[1] *Blessed Rage for Order* is the first volume of his projected trilogy and is devoted to fundamental theology. For Tracy, fundamental theology is a theological discipline that demands, at a foundational level, a public character. This is because fundamental theology's principal task is to articulate theological arguments in a scientific and public manner so that "any attentive, intelligent, reasonable and responsible person can understand and judge in keeping with fully public criteria for argument."[2] Hence, Tracy's project on fundamental theology can be considered as his attempt to establish the intelligibility of Christian theology as public discourse at a most radical level. Our concern is to investigate how Tracy's central argumentation concerning theology as a public

---

1    Tracy's treatise on systematic theology is *The Analogical Imagination: Christian Theology and the Culture of Pluralism* (New York: Crossroad, 1981). Tracy's third volume on practical theology has not been published. Tracy once said regarding this matter that, "I may never be ready to attempt that third volume of the projected trilogy: I know that I am not ready now. I make that unhappy admission not just because I still do not know my own mind clearly and systematically enough about four central issues of that practical theology – contemporary social theory, ethics, ecclesiology and the history of spirituality. It is also, indeed primarily, because I have changed the focus of my theological thought." Tracy, "God, Dialogue and Solidarity: A Theologian's Refrain," in *ChCent*, 107 (1990) 901.

2    *AI*, 63.

discourse is actualized in his methodological development of a fundamental theology.


# I. The Context of Tracy's Revisionist Model of Fundamental Theology


It is clear to Tracy that one's attempt to practise theology is, to a great extent, contextually motivated. Tracy's own fundamental theology is no exception.

Tracy describes the contextual exigency that propels his project as certain "crises" that confront every theologian, if he or she is committed simultaneously to both the modern critical human spirit, and the Christian vision. More concretely, Tracy describes these as "the crisis of meaning of traditional Christianity in the modern 'post-Christian' period and the present crisis of traditional modernity in the contemporary 'post-modern' world."[3] Here, two observations can be noted.

Firstly, Tracy delineates the crises onto two dimensions: on the side of Christianity and on the side of the world. On the one hand, his analysis points to the crisis that Christianity has undergone, namely the problem of the intelligibility of "traditional Christianity"[4] in the modern critical milieu. On the other hand, it designates the crisis that the Enlightenment ideal of human autonomous rationality is facing in view of the contemporary post-modern critique.

Secondly, Tracy diagnoses the situation in terms of conflicting values: "traditional" Christianity *vis-á-vis* the "post-Christian" world, and "traditional modernity" *vis-á-vis* the "post-modern" world. By describing the situation in terms of such conflicting values, Tracy

---

3    *BRO*, 4.

4    For Tracy, the term, 'traditional Christianity,' refers to a "supernatural" and "essentially positivist" understanding of Christianity based on classical metaphysics (*Ibid.*, 8–9).

intends to emphasize the exigency that a theological attempt to resolve this dual dilemma has to be made.

Tracy's project is a proposal of a theological model for resolving that dual dilemma. As the first step in his work, Tracy analyzes the crises in a more detailed manner. Tracy outlines the crisis that Christianity has undergone in the modern critical milieu under three aspects: the "cognitive, ethical, and existential crises."[5] Afterwards, he discusses the crisis of the Enlightenment ideal of autonomous human rationality operative in the post-modern context. We will now look at Tracy's analysis.

## 1. The Crisis of Christianity in the Modern Critical Milieu

In Tracy's analysis, the cognitive and ethical crises are closely related to each other. Tracy deals with the two crises from one particular point of view, namely, the perspective of the pursuit of knowledge or intellectual understanding. Therefore, we will examine these two crises together.

### The Cognitive and Ethical Crises

In his exposition of the cognitive and ethical crises that Christianity has undergone in the modern critical milieu, Tracy's chief concern is the struggle between traditional Christian claims and the modern autonomous, critical, rational mode of thought operative in various "natural and social sciences, the historical disciplines, the new philosophies, and the new ethical systems."[6] By *cognitive* crisis, Tracy means the reluctance to accept traditional Christian claims or beliefs over against "the findings of history and of the natural and human sciences."[7] For example, Tracy writes:

5    *Ibid.*, 4.
6    *Ibid.*, 5.
7    *Ibid.*

> To continue to uphold a literal interpretation of the Genesis account is simply and irrevocably impossible for anyone who accepts the findings of the modern physical and life sciences. To continue to believe a literalist theory of scriptural inspiration seems no longer an option to anyone who has investigated the results of modern historical study of the scriptures.[8]

Tracy points out that today such cognitive reluctance has been extended to include even the most central claims of Christianity, the beliefs in "revelation, God, and Christ."[9] The crisis is well designated by the "strange *pathos*"[10] that one experiences as a believer or a theologian, namely, that while one is still preoccupied with the import of the Christian faith for authentic human life, one is, nevertheless, estranged from the traditionally-held Christian beliefs at the cognitive level in view of modern critical intellectual exigencies. One cannot evade experiencing discordance between maintaining the Christian cognitive claims and taking up the modern critical modes of pursuit of knowledge which are chiefly characterized by "skepticism against unfounded assertions, the suspicion of irrational authority, the prizing of logical candor, the appeal to evidence, and the careful qualification of one's claims."[11]

This experience of discordance is also evident in Tracy's analysis of the *ethical* crisis that arises out of the basic clash of moralities underlying the cognitive struggle. In the discussion of the ethical crisis of knowledge, the central concept to be noted is the "morality of knowledge."[12] This concept is used to refer to an intellectual "con-

---

8   *Ibid.*
9   *Ibid.* Tracy does not offer any more explanation regarding this matter. However, in relation to his later discussion, we can think, for example, of the so-called "death of God" theologians who emerged from the sixties in America and negated the existence of God.
10  *Ibid.*, 4.
11  Van A. Harvey, "The Alienated Theologian," in Robert A. Evans (ed.), *The Future of Philosophical Theology* (Philadelphia: The Westminster Press, 1971) 118–19. Tracy's idea of this alienated pathos relies on Harvey's essay. We have consulted Harvey's essay for a clearer exposition of Tracy's view.
12  This concept is used by Van A. Harvey in his book, *The Historian and the Believer* (New York: Macmillan Publishing Co., Inc, 1966) 103. Tracy notes that his analysis is deeply indebted to Harvey's analysis (*BRO*, 18 n.28). In his own analysis, Tracy uses the concept in a more nuanced manner, such as

science" or a sense of "responsibility" for candor in the pursuit of knowledge.[13] According to Van A. Harvey, the ethical crisis of knowledge has emerged from a revolution in the morality of knowledge. There came about a "transformation of the intellectual ideal" since the Enlightenment, especially through Kant, which seems to be incompatible with the way to knowledge (or understanding) implicit in the traditional Christian conviction (e.g., *faith seeking understanding*).[14] The most essential characteristics of the modern morality of knowledge are the "will-to-truth more than the will-to-believe, investigation more than certainty, autonomy more than obedience to authority."[15] The revolutionary feature here is not so much the naïve promulgation of the human being's actual rationality as a call for the human being "to dare to think" critically, free from any authority that would restrict autonomous research and inquiry.[16] Whereas "the old morality celebrated faith and belief as virtues and regarded doubt as sin,"[17] "the new morality celebrates methodological skepticism and is distrustful of passion in matters of inquiry."[18] Tracy elucidates this disparity in the comparison between the "morality of belief" practiced by the traditional Christian theologian and the "new scientific morality" practiced by the modern historian and scientist in the natural and human sciences.[19] The fundamental loyalty of each is different. The traditional Christian theologian maintained a fundamental loyalty to the "church-community's beliefs" and had recourse to "whatever community of inquiry (usually philosophy) [which] aided him [sic] to defend and to reinterpret the tradition's beliefs for his contemp-

---

"morality of belief," and "morality of scientific knowledge." (*Ibid.*, 6 and 7). Since Tracy uses those concepts without spelling out their meanings, we shall consult Harvey's work when necessary.

13 Harvey, *The Historian and the Believer*, 104.
14 *Ibid.*, 39.
15 *Ibid.*
16 *Ibid.* See the idea in Immanuel Kant, "What is Enlightenment?" in Lewis W. Beck (ed.), *Critique of Practical Reason and Other Writings in Moral Philosophy* (Chicago: University of Chicago Press, 1949) 286–92.
17 Harvey, *The Historian and the Believer*, 103.
18 *Ibid.*
19 *BRO*, 6.

oraries."[20] The modern scientific inquirer, however, has *sole* recourse to "those methodological procedures which the particular scientific community of inquiry in question has developed."[21] In this disparity, Tracy sees the ethical crisis of the modern Christian theologian. For in the modern mind, one's cognitive claim is a matter of intellectual candor in accordance with the general canons of inquiry upheld by the scientific community, and not a matter of simply trading on traditional beliefs. In Harvey's words, the disparity that the modern Christian theologian faces implies not only a conflict of "two logics or two methodologies," but also a clash of "two ethics of judgment" between faith and modern critical inquiry.[22] In short, for the modern mind, intellectual integrity has to do with not only the will-to-truth, but also morality, namely, intellectual candor expressed in adherence to the methodological canons of inquiry, and not allowing these to be outstripped by the "whims of desire and sentiment."[23]

Tracy assumes that the modern Christian theologian *"ordinarily shares,"*[24] whether he/she admits it or not, the modern scientific morality of his/her contemporaries in other scientific disciplines. This means that, for Tracy, insofar as the modern Christian theologian shares the same ethical experience, as a scientific inquirer, with his/her contemporaries, he/she cannot but "challenge the traditional self-understanding of the theologian."[25] In other words, the modern ethical model of knowledge, *"critical inquiry,"*[26] is of crucial importance for the theologian's task, which cannot be reduced to a "simple defense of

---

20   *Ibid.* For the sake of consistency and to avoid interruptions to the text, we have decided to retain the now antiquated option for masculine terms (men, he, etc.) to refer to humankind which were used in *BRO* and in some other author's works.

21   *Ibid.* Tracy notes that, here, an important element to be pointed out is that, according to modern scientific morality, the reigning methods, paradigms, and conclusions can, in principle, be overthrown whenever the advancement of critical evidence for or against them takes place.

22   Harvey, *The Historian and the Believer*, 104.

23   *Ibid.*, 103.

24   *BRO*, 6 (italics mine).

25   *Ibid.*, 7.

26   *Ibid.*, 6 (italics mine).

28

or even [...] an orthodox reinterpretation of traditional belief."[27] Tracy writes:

> He [the modern theologian] finds that his ethical commitment to the morality of scientific knowledge forces him to assume a critical posture towards his own and his tradition's beliefs. He insists, to be sure, that the concept 'critical' does not bear a simply negative meaning. But critical does mean a fidelity to open-ended inquiry, a loyalty to defended methodological canons, a willingness to follow the evidence wherever it may lead. [...] The fundamental ethical commitment of the theologian *qua* theologian remains to that community of scientific inquiry whose province logically includes whatever issue is under investigation.[28]

According to the modern mind, the autonomy to pursue critical inquiry has as a correlate the intellectual responsibility to be open to public assessment. This is to say that the idea that theological claims should be based on "critical inquiry" cannot be detached from the idea that these claims must be publicly communicated and assessed. The idea of the public use of reason prevents our intellectual claims from degenerating into sheer subjectivism, and provides the possibility of public assessment of those claims.[29] The essential idea here is that the issue of autonomy cannot be isolated from the issue of rational assessment, "for both are but aspects of one activity aspiring to be knowledge."[30] Hence, "logical candor is not a rationalistic ideal; it is

27  *Ibid.*, 7. Tracy clarifies that the concept, 'orthodox,' here "is used throughout as a purely descriptive term. There is always the danger that 'orthodox' theologies can become the 'heresy' of 'orthodoxy'." (*Ibid.*, 18 n.34).

28  *Ibid.*, 7.

29  Harvey notes that Kant made it very clear in the same essay where he claimed the freedom from authority, that the public use of reason is an obligation in order to fulfill an intellectual inquirer's duty "to communicate to the public all his carefully tested and well-meaning thoughts." (Kant, "What is Enlightenment?," 288). Hence, Harvey writes, "the will-to-truth, which requires a protest against all restrictions on inquiry, is a correlate of the will-to-communication." (Harvey, *The Historian and the Believer*, 43).

30  Harvey, *ibid.*, 112. Harvey writes that the aspiration to be genuine knowledge "requires methodical skepticism, on the one hand, and a vigorous adherence to rational procedures on the other. The *sine qua non* of these procedures is the giving of reasons for one's conclusions. All rational claims are [...] appeals to other persons' minds, and one's respect for these persons is proportionate to the

the necessary condition for all responsible dialogue that aims at achieving genuine knowledge."[31] Put differently, the real question is "not how to make our assertions scientific, but how to make them so that they can be appropriately assessed."[32]

If this modern intellectual morality needs to be seriously considered, the ethical dilemma of the modern theologian is clear and painful. The dilemma reckoned by Tracy is how to reconcile or resolve the disparate moralities of faith (the will-to-believe) and of scientific mind (the will-to-truth and the will-to-communicate) in one's theological work. The question is how and where to locate faith in one's theological enterprise, while being loyal to modern morality of scientific knowledge. Tracy makes his position clear by saying that:

> In principle, the fundamental loyalty of the theologian *qua* theologian is to that morality of scientific knowledge which he shares with his colleagues, the philosophers, historians, and social scientists. No more than they, can he allow his own – or his tradition's – beliefs to serve as warrants for his arguments.[33]

The essential point Tracy wishes to make here is that, *in fact*, most theological practitioners, including himself, are Christian believers committed to explicit Christian faith. However, "*as a matter of methodological principle* such explicit faith is not required"[34] for one's scientific-theological work. For what allows theological argument to be scientific and thereby, available for public investigation and assessment, is not personal faith that cannot be tested, but "its mode of argumentation, its criteria, its evidence, its warrants, its methods"[35] which are open to other scientific communities. Hence,

degree that he gives them to understand what it would mean to accept or to reject these claims [...] It is to say that the claims we make in various fields ought to have the most relevant reasons brought forward on their behalf that we can bring." (*Ibid.*).

31    *Ibid.*, 43.
32    *Ibid.*, 112.
33    *BRO*, 7.
34    David Tracy, "Response to Professor Connelly–II," *CTSAP*, 29 (1974) 72 (italics mine). Tracy wrote this article as a response to John Connelly's article, "The Task of Theology," in the same issue, 1–58.
35    Tracy, "Response to Professor Connelly–II," 72.

Tracy affirms that, "In all properly theological inquiry, the analysis should be characterized by those same ethical stances of autonomous judgment, critical reflection, and properly skeptical hard-mindedness that characterize analysis in other fields."[36]

## The Existential Crisis

Tracy describes the *existential* crisis as the situation of the modern theologian disillusioned with two kinds of mystification. On the one hand, one finds oneself disenchanted with the mystifications constructed by the traditional "*supernatural*"[37] understanding of God and, on the other hand, disillusioned with the mystifications advocated by the "*secularist* self-understanding of the age."[38] In Tracy, the *supernatural* understanding of God refers to a supernatural theism based on classical metaphysics according to which God is the metaphysical absolute "who seems, in the end, indifferent to the ultimate significance of our actions."[39] The *secularist* understanding of the world here points to the "secular affirmation of the ultimate worth of our lives in nature and history," which, however, negates "any real ground

---

36   *BRO*, 7. A few points are relevant here. Firstly, Tracy's position here is the methodological posture of fundamental theology which, for him, demands a public character at a most radical level. However, as regards a systematic theology, Tracy acknowledges the role of the theologian's faith in his or her theological enterprise. He writes that, "*Systematic* theologies will be concerned principally with the ethical stance of loyalty or creative and critical fidelity to some classical religious tradition proper to its church relationship." He goes on to say that, "Both *systematic* and *practical* theologians will ordinarily assume personal involvement in and commitment to either a particular religious tradition or a particular praxis movement bearing religious significance." (*AI*, 57). Secondly, the issue of the relationship between faith and theology is a very important theme, and will be dealt with in our critique of Tracy's revisionist model for fundamental theology in chapter 3.

37   Tracy explains that "the use of the concept 'supernatural' here is the modern sense of religious studies where it is roughly equivalent to 'fundamentalism,' not in the more restricted medieval sense where it is a strictly theoretical concept for thematizing the Christian religion." (*BRO*, 19 n.40).

38   *Ibid.*, 10 (italics mine).

39   *Ibid.*, 8.

of meaning outside ourselves which assures us that our faith is not simply illusion."[40] In order to understand Tracy's exposition here, it is crucially important to note the distinction between *secular* and *secularistic* that Tracy employs, and which he draws from Schubert M. Ogden.[41]

According to Ogden's formulation of the distinction, *secular* (*secularity*) refers to the self-confident attitude of the modern spirit affirming that "it is our own secular decisions and finite processes of creative becoming which are the very stuff of the 'really real' and so themselves somehow of permanent significance."[42] It pronounces that "the world itself has an unconditioned worth and significance,"[43] and is disenchanted with supernaturalism's contempt of worldly reality. *Secularistic* (*secularism*), on the other hand, refers to the posture that is not merely content to affirm the autonomy and significance of human worldly life, but further "denies any transcendent reality in which the secular order has its ultimate ground and end."[44] There are purely immanent possibilities of the human being's self-understanding and destiny devoid of any transcendent authentication.

Basing himself on this distinction, Tracy elucidates the existential crisis of the modern theologian in the following manner. The modern theologian recognizes the two views as mystifications that are not adequate reflective accounts of the reality of God and the world. These are, in some sense, two extreme stances, namely, secularism (not secularity) and supernatural theism. The *secularism* cannot be maintained because it neither admits nor requires any transcendent reality so that there is no place for God at all. It is clear for the theologian that, no matter how uncanny talking about God might be in the modern post-Christian era, it could not be more uncanny than

---

40  *Ibid.*, 9–10.
41  For Ogden's formulation of the secular-secularistic distinction, see Schubert M. Ogden, *The Reality of God and Other Essays* (San Francisco: Harper & Row, Publishers, 1977) 6–20 and 44–70. There is a small difference of wording between Tracy (secularist) and Ogden (secularistic) for the same concept.
42  Ogden, *The Reality of God and Other Essays*, 64.
43  *Ibid.*, 69.
44  *Ibid.*, 15.

talking of Christianity without God.[45] The *supernatural theism* is hardly opted for because it does not seriously respect the worth of secularity (not secularism) that is the central claim of the modern spirit. According to Tracy, even the post-modern challenge to the optimistic rationalism of the Enlightenment does not necessarily lead to an anti-modern recapturing of the supernaturalism. It only serves to clarify at a deeper level the "full implications of the formerly 'modern' and now 'contemporary' secular struggle for authentic and full-scale human liberation."[46] Tracy goes on to claim that:

> It is true that the classical post-modern critiques of Enlightenment "illusion" expressed in the life-works of such thinkers as Freud, Marx, and Nietzsche called into serious question the naively rationalist claim of the Age of Enlightenment. These 'masters of suspicion' forever cast doubt on the belief that the solitary autonomous rational thinker could achieve, much less had already achieved, 'enlightenment.' What remains constant in the shift from modernity to post-modernity is the fact that such contemporary critiques of modernity deepen the fundamental commitment to those purely secular standards for knowledge and action initiated by the Enlightenment.[47]

In short, for Tracy, the locus of the existential crisis of the modern theologian lies in the dilemma of how to find the most adequate vision of the reality of God and the world: namely, on the one hand, while maintaining a fundamental commitment to the critical exigencies of the modern spirit, not falling into atheist secularism and,

45    Ogden notes that in the post-Christian era, in the so-called age of atheism, there has been in experiments a "theology without God" not only by some philosophers, but also by several modernist theologians. Their aim was to construct a tenable contemporary theology for the secularistic minds who "deny unequivocally that this world in any way points beyond itself." (Ogden, *The Reality of God*, 12). One examples in theology is Paul M. van Buren's *The Secular Meaning of the Gospel* (New York: Macmillan, 1963). According to Buren, "the empiricist in us finds the heart of the difficulty not in what is said about God, but in the very talking about God at all. We do not know 'what' God is, and we cannot understand how the word 'God' is being used [...] If it is meant to refer to an 'existential encounter,' a point of view, or the speaker's self-understanding, surely a more appropriate expression could be found." (Buren, *The Secular Meaning of the Gospel*, 84).

46    *BRO*, 8.

47    *Ibid.*

on the other hand, while upholding the Christian faith in the God of Jesus Christ, not retreating into supernatural theism.

In the course of his analysis, Tracy expresses his fundamental concern to resolve the dilemma by highlighting the idea of the "faith of secularity."[48] According to Tracy, the faith of secularity refers to our fundamental commitment to the "final worthwhileness of the struggle for truth and honesty in our inquiry, and for justice and even agapic love in our individual and social practice"[49] here and now in this world. Tracy's fundamental assumption is that the modern theologian who is disenchanted with the traditional supernatural conception does *share* this faith of secularity with his or her secular contemporaries as "*the* common faith."[50] In other words, the modern theologian can hardly share the traditional supernatural Christian self-understanding precisely because he or she believes that such understanding denies the faith of secularity "as that very faith is appropriately expressed in the true faith of Christianity itself."[51] Hence, Tracy explicates his central vision that, "A proper understanding of those central beliefs – in 'revelation,' in 'God,' in 'Jesus Christ' – can provide an adequate understanding, a correct 'reflective inventory,' or an existentially appropriate symbolic representation of the fundamental faith of secularity."[52] In short, he affirms that, "The Christian faith is at heart none other than the most adequate articulation of the basic faith of secularity itself."[53] Tracy explains the same vision from a different perspective: the modern theologian who holds the faith of secularity cannot share the secularist position because such a secularist understanding denies faith in God who is the necessary ground of our commitment to the final worth and meaning of existence. In

---

48    *Ibid.* Tracy notes that, throughout his work on fundamental theology, he is adopting the distinction between faith and belief. Faith refers to a "basic orientation and attitude (primal and often non-conceptual)" and belief refers to a "thematic explication of a particular historical, moral, or cognitive claim involved in a particular 'faith' stance." (*Ibid.*, 16 n.13).

49    *Ibid.*, 9.

50    *Ibid.*, 8.

51    *Ibid.*, 9.

52    *Ibid.*

53    *Ibid.*, 10.

other words, for Tracy, the affirmation of the ultimate 'worthwhileness' of our existence (faith of secularity) is a correlate of the affirmation of (the Christian) God's reality (the Christian faith) in the sense that faith in God is the necessary condition of our meaningful existence. The two affirmations are interlocked. Tracy insists that:

> only a coherent articulation of the reality of the Christian God can provide an adequate reflective account of both the unavoidable presupposition of our inquiry and our moral activity, and of the basic faith in the final meaningfulness of an authentic life which secularity itself has articulated with such power.[54]

In short, Tracy's fundamental vision for resolving the dilemma centers on his presupposition that, if the two faiths are *properly* and *adequately* understood and reinterpreted in a true sense, the faith of secularity and the Christian faith are not necessarily alienated and estranged from each other, but are in fact harmoniously interlinked.

*2. The Crisis of the Modern Secular Mind: The Demystification of the Modern Mystification*

As the final part of his whole analysis of the crises that the modern theologian is confronting, Tracy touches on the "post-modern (i.e., post-liberal)"[55] situation already operative in the modern context. Tracy delineates the essential feature of the present postmodern model

---

54  *Ibid.*
55  *Ibid.* Here, for Tracy, the "post-modern" situation refers to the situation in which new understandings of humanity and the world have been inaugurated by Karl Marx, Sigmund Freud, Nietzsche, and Kierkegaard (See *ibid.*, 11). Tracy uses the term, "post-liberal," (an equivalent of "post-modern" for him) to emphasize the specific feature of the postmodern situation. The feature is that postmodern critiques of modernity are not merely a dismissal of the modern liberal tradition. Rather, they are subtle expressions of the liberal spirit by means of a *critique* that is a typical posture of liberal tradition. Thus, for Tracy, the "post-liberal' situation refers to the situation in which the critical liberal tradition is radically continued, while exposing and negating the illusionary modern vision of humanity and the world. For the representatives of this "post-liberal" stance, Tracy adduces, among others, Hans-Georg Gadamer, the Frankfurt School, and Jürgen Habermas (See *ibid.*, 12–13).

for humanity as the exigency of "liberation" from the "illusions" of the Enlightenment ideal.[56] With a full recognition of the paradigmatic postmodern thinkers' criticism of the Enlightenment portrait of humanity's possibilities,[57] Tracy defines the spirit of "liberation" as an essential characteristic of the postmodern model for humanity. Whereas the Enlightenment modern model can be described as a model for "self-fulfillment" based on the autonomous, optimistic, and rationalist ideal of human and societal possibilities, the postmodern model can be described as a model for "self-transcendence" towards personal and societal "liberation."[58] Put more concretely, the postmodern demand for "self-transcendence" here refers to "a radical commitment to the struggle to transcend our present individual and societal states in favor of a continuous examination of those illusions which cloud our real and more limited possibilities for knowledge and action."[59]

However, Tracy wants to highlight his assumption that such postmodern commitment to self-transcending liberation is no other than the finest expression of the fundamental fidelity to the "radically critical and thereby emancipatory power of human rationality" initiated by the liberal spirit of the Enlightenment.[60] Tracy finds prominent examples of such commitment in several thinkers: Hans-Georg Gadamer, the Frankfurt School, and Jürgen Habermas. According to Tracy, Gadamer's critique of the Enlightenment's discrediting of prejudice and his defense of *Vorurteil* along with his hermeneutics of "rehabilitation of authority and tradition" is a good example of the

56   *Ibid.*, 11.
57   Tracy delineates the criticisms of Marx, Freud, Nietzsche, and Kierkegaard on the Enlightenment "illusion" as follows: "in Marxian terms, by the bourgeois intellectual's refusal to take note of or to struggle against the economic conditions which allow and enforce his privileges; in Freudian terms, by the disclosure of the subterranean forces of the unconscious which in fact motivate our presumably pure and autonomous conscious rationality; in the charges of Nietzsche and Kierkegaard alike, that our primary task is not the development of a finely tuned autonomous and sincere rationalism, but [...] becoming a self who realizes his or her own radical limitations and possibilities and yet struggles to become a human being of self-transcending authenticity." (*Ibid.*).
58   *Ibid.*
59   *Ibid.*
60   *Ibid.*, 13.

critique of the Enlightenment by means of a radicalization of the liberal critical spirit.[61] Another example is the critical social theory of the Frankfurt School that unveils the linguistic, intellectual, and socially oppressive structures disguised by the Enlightenment's instrumental rationality and technocracy.[62] Through dialectical analyses of the Enlightenment conformist ideal, critical social theory shows the power of critical rationality for unmasking "present illusions and reifications in a technological society," and also for enforcing the demand for personal and societal transformation.[63] In Jürgen Habermas (a member of the Frankfurt school), Tracy likewise finds the retrieval of the emancipatory power of human rationality. Tracy points out that the heart of Habermas' social theory is the claim that the problem of modernity is "one of a selective and one-sided use of a purposive rationality appropriate to social systems, but inappropriate to, indeed devastating to, the communicative rationality necessary for all social action in the 'lifeworld'."[64] Hence, Habermas' attempt of retrieval of the "fundamentally dialogical character of all reflective rationality" for communicative social action.[65]

According to Tracy, all these attempts show that the postmodern critiques of the Enlightenment conviction as "mythical" need not lead to a retreat to a merely conservative or antimodern or countercultural protest. Instead, they reassure the fact that only a truly critical rationality in its full radicality can unveil and counteract the present illusions, and "enforce in *praxis* human liberation on a personal and

61    Cf., Hans-Georg Gadamer, *Wahrheit und Methode* (Tübingen: J.C.B. Mohr, 1965, first published in 1960) 256–90; In the English edition, *Truth and Method* (New York: Crossroad, 1982, first published in 1975) 241–74. For a systematic interpretation of Gadamer's *Truth and Method*, see Georgia Warnke, *Gadamer: Hermeneutics, Tradition and Reason* (Cambridge: Polity Press, 1987).
62    See *BRO*, 13. For the critical theory of the Frankfurt School, see Martin Jay, *The Dialectical Imagination: A History of the Frankfurt School and the Institute of Social Research 1923–1950* (London: Heinemann Educational Books, 1973).
63    *BRO*, 13.
64    Tracy, "Theology, Critical Social Theory, and the Public Realm," in D. Browning and Francis S. Fiorenza (eds), *Habermas, Modernity, and Public Theology* (New York: Crossroad, 1992) 31.
65    *Ibid.*, 32.

societal scale."[66] Hence, he clarifies his fundamental assumption as follows:

> In sum, that fundamental faith in the ultimate worth of our life here and now which constitutes the basic faith common to the committed secular thinker and the committed Christian alike is maintained, clarified, and deepened by the post-modern critics of modernity.[67]

In accordance with this assumption, he foreshadows his basic posture for constructing his theological model in the following way: Firstly, basing himself on the conviction that the postmodern critiques of modernity are but the subtle expressions of a radical commitment to modern critical rationality, his theological model will uphold the "commitment to critical inquiry constitutive of the morality of scientific inquiry while exposing, negating, and transforming the reification of the human world which a merely Enlightenment attitude encourages and perhaps enforces."[68]

Secondly, the reinterpretation of Christianity attempted in his model is "an adequate critical articulation of, and symbolic representation for, *both* this secular faith and the basic meaning of the Christian faith itself."[69] Put differently, what he shall try to do is to search for a new prospect for conversation between secular faith and a Christian faith that is no longer caught up in traditional oppositions, such as "secularism vs. supernaturalism, liberalism vs. conservatism, science vs. poetry, concept vs. symbol, atheism vs. classical theism, religion vs. revelation, special revelation vs. original revelation, an exclusivist christology vs. the man Jesus as 'the man for others'."[70]

66    *BRO*, 13.
67    *Ibid.*, 14.
68    *Ibid.*
69    *Ibid.*, (italics mine).
70    *Ibid.*

# II. The Methodology of the Revisionist Theological Model

Our aim in this section is to examine the methodological construction of Tracy's revisionist model for fundamental theology by reflecting on Tracy's two methodological endeavors. Firstly, as the label of his model indicates, taking a "self-consciously revisionist attitude,"[71] he analyzes the achievements and limitations of the presently existing major theological models: the orthodox, liberal, neo-orthodox, and radical models, and finally presents the basic presuppositions of the revisionist model in comparison with the four models. Secondly, as methodological principles, Tracy presents the five theses of his revisionist model. In what follows, we will look at these two methodological endeavors respectively.

## 1. The Analysis of Major Models in Contemporary Theology

For the proper understanding of his analysis of the reigning theological models, Tracy makes a brief introductory remark on the focal angles in terms of which his analysis is conducted.

Firstly, Tracy clarifies that, for the notion of "model" used in the analysis, he employed the concepts developed by Ian Ramsey and Bernard Lonergan. This is to say, he adopts Ian Ramsey's notion of theological model as "disclosure," not as "picture."[72] Having recourse

---

71    *Ibid.*, 3.
72    A "picturing model" in Ramsey refers to a "model thought of as a replica, a copy picture, something which shares certain important properties with that which it models." Ian Ramsey, *Models and Mystery* (London: Oxford University Press, 1964) 2. A "disclosure model," which Ramsey advocates as a new alternative for theology, points to a model which arises not as pictorial replica, but from "some sort of structural similarity, some sort of echo between the model and the phenomena it enables us to understand." (*Ibid.*, 10). According to Ramsey, the disclosure model is generated from a "universe that discloses itself to us in a moment of insight. The disclosure which accompanies the birth of a model reveals to us what scientific models and theological models contrive in their various ways to understand." (*Ibid.*, 19–20). As regards the

to Ramsey's notion, Tracy expresses that, for him, theological models purport to "serve to disclose or re-present the realities which they interpret," rather than "provide exact pictures of the realities they disclose."[73] Hence, theologians, by using their models, cannot claim to provide pictorial descriptive replicas of theological realities (God, humanity, and the world), but "to disclose such realities with varying degrees of adequacy."[74]

From Lonergan's notion of model, Tracy takes on the idea that "models purport to be, not descriptions of reality, not hypotheses about reality but simply interlocking sets of terms and relations."[75] A model, as an interlocking set of terms and relations, is used functionally for "guiding investigations," "framing hypotheses," and "writing descriptions."[76]

Basing himself on Ramsey and Lonergan, Tracy explains his view in the following manner. Provided that our theological enterprise

deficiency of the model as "picture" for theology, Ramsey states that "a picture theology which is too taped and too cut and dried is self-condemned – leaving no place for the mystery and transcendence of God, leaving no place for wonder and worship." (*Ibid.*, 7). However, for Ramsey, this does not necessarily lead to the conclusion that in theology, the alternative to this descriptive picturing model is silence. The possible alternative can be the model as "disclosure." For the detail, see *ibid.*, 1–21.

73   *BRO*, 22.
74   *Ibid.*
75   Bernard Lonergan, *Method in Theology* (Toronto: University of Toronto Press, 1990; first published in 1971) 284.
76   Lonergan, *ibid.*, 285. Lonergan explains that, "Thus, a model will direct the attention of an investigator in a determinate direction with either of two results; it may provide him with a basic sketch of what he finds to be the case; or it may prove largely irrelevant, yet the discovery of this irrelevance may be the occasion of uncovering clues that otherwise might be overlooked." Hence, the important focus here is the *utility* of models, rather than the truthfulness or falseness of models. Lonergan goes on to say that, "When one possesses models, the task of framing an hypothesis is reduced to the simpler matter of tailoring a model to suit a given object or area. Finally, the utility of the model arises when it comes to describing a known reality. For known realities can be exceedingly complicated, and an adequate language to describe them hard to come by. So the formulation of models and their general acceptance as models can facilitate enormously both description and communication." (*Ibid.*, 285).

is *historically* situated and contextualized, contemporary theologians are not supposed to take the "usual alternatives of either trying to say everything [transhistorically or ahistorically] or of saying nothing at all" in their theological practices.[77] Hence, the need for developing models, which help us in "interpreting the basic factors present in concrete historical realities."[78]

Secondly, Tracy's analysis will focus on spelling out two fundamental realities, namely "the self," and "the object" of the theologian that are *disclosed* in the five major theological models.[79] More concretely, Tracy's central concern is to illuminate in each theological model the "self or subject-referent" of the theologian and the "object-referent" that the theologian investigates.[80] The reason for his focusing on these two realities lies in his own hypothesis that the most basic of interlocking sets of terms and relations provided by each model is, "those references to the self of the theologian and to the objects within that self's horizon which any given model discloses."[81]

Tracy assumes that all the theological models that he will analyze, share a general characteristic: they are attempting to interpret two fundamental phenomena, the "Christian tradition and contemporary understandings of human existence."[82] Tracy suggests that the most helpful way to deal with the question of how each theological model interprets these phenomena will be to investigate how each theological option construes the cognitive, ethical, and existential clashes between the modern critical spirit and Christianity. In sum, what he is going to highlight in his analysis is the "exact understandings each model has of the theological self and of the object of theological discourse in the context or horizon of that all-pervasive clash of beliefs, values, and faiths."[83] Thus, his analysis starts with a brief explanation of each model's general construal of both modernity

77    *BRO*, 23.
78    *Ibid.*
79    *Ibid.*, 22.
80    *Ibid.*
81    *Ibid.*, 23.
82    *Ibid.*
83    *Ibid.*

and Christianity and then moves on to specify the subject and object referents disclosed by each model.

### The Orthodox Model: Believers and Beliefs

According to Tracy, the orthodox theological model can be chiefly characterized as the model which takes its norms "in the 'authorities' affirmed by the particular church community, not by 'outside' communities of inquiry."[84] In this model, the theologian's principal task as theologian is to articulate an "adequate understanding of the beliefs" of one's particular church tradition in an *inner-theological* perspective.[85] The orthodox model does not seem impressed by the intellectual claims of other scholarly modern disciplines and the value claims of the wider culture, "except to suggest analogies for systematic reflection or to aid argumentation for strictly apologetic reflection."[86] The general attitude of orthodox theologians toward modernity is resistantly defensive. They argue that a solid commitment to "the perennial truths of traditional Christianity" is the best way of surviving the challenges of modern criticism.[87]

For the orthodox theologian, the subject-referent is an explicit believer in one's church tradition. The object-referent is an "analogous and systematic understanding" of the beliefs held out by one's tradition (dogmatic theology), and a "reasoned defense" of the beliefs

---

84   *Ibid.*, 35 n.12. This model includes "essentially fundamentalist positions," "Denzinger-theologies," and "most theologies labelled 'biblical'." (*Ibid.*, 24 and 35 n.13).

85   *Ibid.*, 24. As a classical example of orthodox theology in the Catholic tradition, Tracy points to the theological model elaborated in the First Vatican Council. The aim of theology in the First Vatican Council was not to "prove" the mysteries of the Catholic faith, but to "understand" those mysteries. That understanding is best achieved by following the classical medieval model: "(1) find analogies in nature for these beliefs; (2) use these analogies to provide a systematic understanding of the interconnection of [the] major mysteries of faith (Christ, Grace, Trinity); (3) try to relate that analogous understanding to the final end of man (Beatific Vision)." (*Ibid.*, 24).

86   *Ibid.*, 25.

87   *Ibid.*, 24.

(apologetic theology).[88] The major strength of this model, for Tracy, is its ability to "develop sophisticated models for providing systematic understanding of the basic beliefs" of the theologian's church tradition.[89] The major weakness is, in view of the relatively narrow scale of its subject and object-referents, its inability to make a wide and useful application of modern scientific scholarship to theological understanding, and more pointedly, its "theological inability to come to terms with the cognitive, ethical, and existential counter-claims of modernity."[90]

## *The Liberal Model: Modern Secularity and Christian Belief*

Tracy characterizes as "liberal"[91] those theologies that made an explicit commitment both to the cognitive, ethical, and existential experiments and values of modernity, and to the Christian vision. For Tracy, the kernel of liberal theology, in contrast to the orthodox model, is its deliberate acceptance of the distinctively modern spirit of free and open-ended inquiry, autonomous judgment, and critical investigation of all claims, even claims to religious truth.[92] More pointedly, the hub of liberal and modernist theologies was their candid and full admission of the modern challenges and keenness to "reformulate the very task of Christian theology in accordance with it."[93] In Tracy's judgment, the liberal model for the reformulation is principally the model of reconciliation, namely, to reflect on the "fundamental vision and values of traditional Christianity *in harmony with* the fundamental vision and values of modernity."[94] In other

---

88  *Ibid.*, 25.
89  *Ibid.*
90  *Ibid.*
91  Tracy notes that, in general, the term, "liberal," points to Protestant theologians, and "modernist" to Catholic theologians (*Ibid.*, 36 n.19).
92  See *ibid.*, 25–6.
93  *Ibid.*, 26.
94  *Ibid.* (italics mine). The representatives of this liberal model include Georg W.F. Hegel, Friedrich Schleiermacher, or Maurice Blondel (philosophical theology or philosophy of religion), Henry N. Wieman (ethical theology), Adolf van Harnack, Ernst Troeltsch, and Alfred Loisy (historical theology).

words, for liberal theologians, the principal way to maintain responsibly both commitments to the modern spirit and to the Christian vision is a reconciliation or harmonization of the two.

For liberal theologians, the self-referent is the theologian's own modern consciousness especially in its commitment to the modern critical spirit towards "all claims to meaning and truth, religious or otherwise."[95] The object-referent is the Christian tradition "as reformulated in accordance with such modern commitments and critiques."[96]

The strength and chief legacy of liberal theologies, in Tracy's assessment, are their inauguration of the "post-orthodox model" for the contemporary theological enterprise.[97] Tracy does not mention the major weakness of this model, because, for him, the theological task of this model has not yet been fully completed. The theological experiments of this liberal model, for him, should be continued, not in a modern but in a post-liberal context.

### The Neo-Orthodox Model: Radical Contemporary Christian Faith and the God of Jesus Christ

According to Tracy, neo-orthodox theology is an attempt at a corrective to the liberal model, rather than a radically new alternative theological model. Tracy understands that the neo-orthodox criticisms of liberal theologies fundamentally share the *liberal* and not regressively the orthodox understanding of theology. For him, the neo-orthodox attempt was not a sheer dismissal of the liberal enterprise, but a *continuation* of that enterprise by means of *critique* that is a typical posture of liberal tradition.[98] The neo-orthodox theologians' principal critiques of the liberal model are two-edged. With regard to the analysis of the human situation, the liberal model utterly neglected

---

95    *Ibid.*, 26.

96    *Ibid.*

97    *Ibid.*, 27.

98    In such an assessment, Tracy parallels the critical role of neo-orthodox theologians (viz., Karl Barth, Rudolf Bultumann, Paul Tillich, Richard Niebuhr, Reinhold Niebuhr) with that of the post-modern secular critics, such as Marx, Nietzsche, and Freud in terms of "both acceptance and negation of liberal modernity." (*Ibid.*; see also *ibid.*, 38 n.31).

to expose "those negative elements of tragedy, of terror, indeed, of sin in human existence."[99] With regard to the reinterpretation of the Christian faith (especially christology), the liberal model failed to explain adequately the essential belief of the Christian tradition, namely, that, "justification comes only from grace through faith in God's manifestation of self in the event of Jesus Christ."[100] In the assessment of the neo-orthodox, the liberal and modernist understanding of religious consciousness was not able to handle adequately the christological claim.

Based on these critiques, the central neo-orthodox corrective argument is that only a genuine recognition of "the unique gift of faith in the Word of God," which is fundamentally experiential and existential, can be a true foundation for an authentic Christian theology.[101] More pointedly, according to the neo-orthodox, the liberal theologies were unable to account for the fragile and precarious conditions of human existence. Thus, correlatively they failed to show the dialectical character of the experience of Christian faith, that is, the experience of the justifying and salvific power of the Christian faith in God who is wholly Other.[102]

For the neo-orthodox theologian, the subject-referent is the human being understood in a dialectical fashion. Tracy states that, "This subject-referent of the neo-orthodox theologian can also be said

---

99  *Ibid.*, 28. Tracy assesses the neo-orthodox analysis of the dialectical character of human condition as an achievement that gives a more accurate understanding of the actual human situation. For exemplary works on this, Tracy cites Reinhold Niebuhr, *The Nature and Destiny of Man I* (New York: Scriber, 1964), esp, 178–241; Paul Tillich, *Systematic theology II* (Digswell Place: James Nisbet & Co. Ltd., 1964, first published in 1957) 44–78.

100  *BRO*, 28.

101  *Ibid.*

102  In this regard, Tracy considers the following as positive elements that the neo-orthodox theologies achieved: the neo-orthodox interpretation of the irrevocably dialectical relationship between God and humanity which "serves to assure a firm grasp of an element of radical mystery"; the christocentric interpretation of the Christian faith which serves to explicate the christological claim "in a more adequate manner than liberal and modernist discussions of symbol, of history, and of religious consciousness were able to manage." (*Ibid.*, 28–9).

to include elements of an authentic post-modern contemporary consciousness as distinct from the modern" in the sense that the dialectical model of humanity is critical of the Enlightenment optimistic model of autonomous human possibilities.[103] The object-referent is the "wholly other God of Jesus Christ" disclosed in the dialectical experience of the Christian faith.[104]

The strength or the most lasting achievement of the neo-orthodox model, for Tracy, is its sensitivity to the essentially "hermeneutical aspect of the contemporary theological task," that is to say, its keen regard to the dialectical character of the Christian experience of faith in God.[105] More concretely, the lasting effect of neo-orthodox theologies lies in their profound recognition that contemporary Christian theology should cope with the post-modern understanding of the human condition, and should "develop more adequate hermeneutical tools to disclose the profoundly transformative meanings of the central Christian symbols."[106]

However, for Tracy, the neo-orthodox model, the finely reformulated corrective of the liberal model has a shortcoming. What Tracy sees as a deficiency in the neo-orthodox model is its underdeveloped *critical* analysis and reformulation of the central concepts and symbols of the Christian tradition. According to Tracy, neo-orthodox theologians seemed to take for granted that those Christian concepts and symbols had real existential impact on the contemporary human situation. Yet, however existentially meaningful those symbols may be, the neo-orthodox model did not seem sufficiently to "stand up to *critical* analysis of their coherence and their truth."[107] In other words, however paradoxical Christian faith may be, the concepts and symbols that formulate and represent the paradox did not seem to be "capable

---

103   *Ibid.*, 29–30.
104   Tracy states that this object-referent can be elaborated, in the major Protestant tradition (viz., neo-Reformation theology by Karl Barth), in terms of "God's Word operative in human existence as unexpected, unmerited, justifying Event." In Roman Catholic tradition, it can be formulated in terms of "the Radically Mysterious God" as explored by Karl Rahner (*Ibid.*, 30).
105   *Ibid.*, 29.
106   *Ibid.*
107   *Ibid.*, (italics mine).

of withstanding a critical experiential analysis of their truth."[108] For him, the neo-orthodox did not pursue their theologies to a genuinely critical conclusion.

## The Radical Model: Secular Affirmation and Theistic Negation

Tracy categorizes as the radical model the theologies that negate the central belief in God held by the Christian tradition. He considers as the representative of this theological model the so-called "death of God" theologies advocated by Thomas J.J. Altizer, William Hamilton, Paul van Buren, and Richard L. Rubenstein.[109] The principal tenet of the radical model is that the "Wholly Other God must die in order that the authentically liberated human being may live."[110] In other words, the traditional understanding of God as the Other held out by the orthodox, the liberal, and the neo-orthodox models alienates "human beings from one another, from the world, and from their authentic selves."[111] Thus, in order to salvage the "authentic conscience" of human beings committed to the struggle for human liberation, the God of the Christian tradition must be negated.[112] In the radical model, the God as Other in the Christian tradition and all human possibilities run counter to each other.

For the radical model, the self-referent is a subject committed to post-modern, secularist cognitive and moral values and convictions. The object-referent of this model is a radical reformulation of traditional Christianity by means of a crucial negation paired with an equally important affirmation. That is to say, while they are *opposed*

---

108  *Ibid.* Tracy asserts that the neo-orthodox theologies were too easily tempted to employ such concepts as, "paradox," "mystery," or "scandal," devoid of a critical argumentation (See *ibid.*, 39 n.46).

109  Thomas J.J. Altizer, *The Gospel of Christian Atheism* (Philadelphia: Westerminster, 1966); William Hamilton, *Radical Theology and the Death of God* (Indianapolis: Bobbs-Merrill, 1966); Paul van Buren, *The Secular Meaning of the Gospel* (New York: Macmillan, 1963); Richard L. Rubenstein, *After Auschuwitz* (Indianapolis: Bobbs-Merrill, 1966).

110  *BRO*, 31.

111  *Ibid.*

112  *Ibid.*

to the idea of God as Other in the Christian tradition, the radical theologians *affirm* "Jesus either as the paradigm of a life lived for others or as the decisive incarnational manifestation of a liberated humanity."[113] Tracy explains that, for the radical theologians:

> the central assertion of traditional Christianity which must be maintained is the Christian affirmation of a life which, in its commitment to liberation and to others, may serve to humanize the world: a life like that made present – perhaps even "contagious" – in Jesus of Nazareth and in the liberating event of the death of God in the contemporary world.[114]

Tracy reckons that this model of radical theology has been easily written off as simply "another fad or act of desperation from the sixties in America."[115] However, he advises that it is important to be aware of what the emergence of radical theologies means in the wider Christian tradition. For him, the appearance of the radical theologies is a call to rethink the question of the traditional Christian understanding of God. More concretely, he understands it as a challenge to reformulate the understanding of God in such a way that our new understanding should seriously concern both contemporary secular values and the Christian vision of human possibilities. The essential problematic point of this model, however, is quite apparent for him: its inability to provide a "meaningful way to affirm the reality of God."[116] For Tracy, it is clear that the possibility of practicing Christian theology can hardly be thought of, if there is no way to affirm the reality of God.

113  *Ibid.*
114  *Ibid.*
115  *Ibid.*, 41 n.58.
116  *Ibid.*, 32.

Finally, Tracy clarifies the fundamental presuppositions of the revisionist model for theology.[117] Systematically, the revisionist model can be characterized by two essential features.

Firstly, the revisionist model exploits fully and seriously the permanent achievements of the orthodox, the liberal, the neo-orthodox, and radical theologies. In this endeavor, the revisionist will also attempt to "rectify" the limitations of the four major models in the light of newly available resources: philosophical, historical, and social scientific research and reflection. For this revisionary process, the chief concerns and accomplishments of the later neo-orthodox and radical theologies will be taken seriously into consideration, since these theologies are regarded as "authentically self-critical moments in the larger enterprise of reconstructing an adequate model for contemporary Christian theology."[118]

Secondly, the revisionist model understands its task fundamentally as to *continue* "the critical task of the classical liberals and modernists in a genuinely post-liberal situation."[119] The revisionist model carries on the liberal task of critical scientific inquiry based on the faith of secularity, while having regard to postmodern concerns and critiques. The revisionist model is "post-liberal" in the sense that, rather than attempting to construct a new ideal for the theological task, it explores new methodological and substantive resources for ac-

---

117    In Tracy's view, some contemporary theologians belong to the revisionist theological camp: among Roman Catholic theologians, Leslie Dewart, *The Future of Belief* (New York: Herder and Herder, 1966); Gregory Baum, *Man Becoming: God in Secular Experience* (New York: Herder and Herder, 1970); Michael Novak, *Belief and Unbelief* (New York: Macmillan, 1965); idem, *Ascent of the Mountain, Flight of the Dove: An Invitation to Religious Studies* (New York: Harper & Row, 1971); among Protestant theologians, Langdon Gilkey, *Naming the Whirlwind: The Renewal of God-Language* (New York: Bobbs-Merrill, 1969); Van A. Harvey, *The Historian and the Believer*; Gordon E. Kaufman, *God the Problem* (Cambridge: Harvard University Press, 1972); and process theologians.

118    *BRO*, 33.

119    *Ibid.*, 32.

complishing the ideal of liberalism.[120] Tracy sums up this revisionist position in the following manner:

> Only a radical continuation of critical theory, symbolic reinterpretation, and responsible social and personal praxis can provide the hope for a fundamental revision of both the modern and the traditional Christian self-understandings.[121]

For the revisionist theologians, the self-referent is a subject committed at once to a reinterpreted post-liberal understanding of authentic secularity and to a reinterpreted Christian tradition. Here, the reinterpretations refer to "contemporary revisionist" understandings that challenge both an "anti-Christian secularism" and an "anti-secular, religious supernaturalism" in accordance with publicly available criteria.[122] The object-referent of revisionist theology is a critical and philosophical reformulation of both "the meanings present in common human experience and the meanings present in the Christian tradition."[123] More pointedly, it is a critical correlation between the two meanings manifested by the post-liberal reinterpretation of human experience and of the Christian tradition.[124]

---

120  *Ibid.*, 33.
121  *Ibid.*
122  *Ibid.*
123  *Ibid.*, 34.
124  According to Tracy, the critical correlation can be explained as: "the dramatic confrontation, the mutual illuminations and corrections, the possible basic reconciliation between the principal values, cognitive claims, and existential faiths of both a reinterpreted post-modern consciousness and a reinterpreted Christianity." (*Ibid.*, 32). Here, an important point should be mentioned. When we recall one of the central tenets of Tracy's revisionist theological model that was previously discussed, viz., "a revisionist reinterpretation of Christianity is an adequate critical articulation of, and symbolic representation for, both this secular faith and the basic meaning of the Christian faith itself" (*Ibid.*, 14), we find that Tracy does not seem to take up "the dramatic confrontation" in his critical correlation. Rather, his model seems to be conspicuously inclined to search for "the possible basic reconciliation" between meanings present in the secular faith and the Christian faith. In regard to this problem, we can find Tracy's brief explanation in a footnote. In his view, the need for "dramatic confrontations" is more congenial to a Christian dogmatics, than to a fundamental theology such as his present project. Tracy writes, "as the present exercise in fundamental theology will state in initial terms and as a full-fledged

## 2. Five Theses Proposed for the Revisionist Model for Theology

As his second methodological exposition, Tracy proposes five theses for the revisionist model for theology. Tracy states that the most succinct description of the revisionist model is "philosophical reflection upon the meanings present in common human experience and language, and upon the meanings present in the Christian fact."[125] The five theses are proposed to defend and to explicate this fundamental proposition. Let us look at the theses in detail.

dogmatics would articulate at length, there is often need for 'dramatic confrontations' between an authentic Christian view (e.g., on agapic love) and an authentic secular view (e.g., on Utopianism). [...] A Christian dogmatics would need to articulate all those dialectical possibilities. The present work is concerned only to articulate criteria for fundamental theology and their initial application to the questions of religion, theism, and Christology." (*Ibid.*, 42 n.66). We will evaluate this matter in our critique of Tracy's project.

125 *Ibid.*, 43. Two points are to be noted here. Firstly, note an addition of the term, "language," in the description above (cf., "the meanings present in common human experience" in *ibid.*, 34). Tracy's exposition of the five theses (*Ibid.*, 43–63) is the revised text of his previously published article, "The Task of Fundamental Theology," *JR*, 54 (1974) 13–34. In the same description in the article, the term, "language" is not seen. This addition seems due to Tracy's updated intention to employ the import of contemporary interpretation theory and linguistic philosophy (especially Paul Ricoeur's) in his theological methodology. We shall return to this in the next chapter. There is no significant difference in content between the article, "The Task of Fundamental Theology" and the revised one in *BRO*. Secondly, Tracy makes clear that his deliberate choice of the term, "Christian fact" (not Christian "message" or "kerygma" or "tradition") in the description above implies his stance that the fundamental theologian need *not* be a believing member of the Christian community (See *ibid.*, 57 n.3). However, throughout his work, Tracy is not consistent in using the term, the "Christian fact." Tracy freely and frequently uses the term, the "Christian tradition" as coterminous with the "Christian fact."

Thesis 1: *The Two Principal Sources for Theology Are Christian Texts and Common Human Experience and Language*

Tracy explains the first thesis in terms of *how* the two principal sources are *related* to the task of Christian theology, rather than *what* the two sources contain. Firstly, Tracy clarifies the relationship of the source, the "Christian texts,"[126] to the task of Christian theology. The central idea of this relationship is that Christian theology is required to show the "*appropriateness*" of one's theological statements to the "meanings of the major expressions and texts of the Christian tradition."[127] In other words, if one's theological statements are to be assessed as adequate, they ought to be *appropriate* to what is expressed by the charter symbols and discourses of the Christian tradition.[128] Tracy explains:

---

126   Tracy clarifies that although the "Christian fact" includes not only the Christian texts but also the Christian "symbols, rituals, events, witnesses," his present work limits this category principally to the "texts." He states that "the limitation seems appropriate for the present work insofar as Christianity as a religion of the word clearly involves written texts (the scriptures) as at least its charter document." (*Ibid.*, 15 n.5).

127   *Ibid.*, 43 (italics mine).

128   For this criterion of *appropriateness*, Tracy is indebted to Schubert Ogden's "What is Theology," in *JR*, 52 (1972) 22–40. According to Ogden, theology requires "dual criteria of adequacy." This means that "to be assessed as adequate, a theological statement must meet the two criteria of *appropriateness* and *understandability* as these may require in the given situation." (Ogden, *ibid.*, 25, italics mine). Concerning the criterion of *appropriateness*, Ogden states that, "No theological statement be deemed adequate unless it is *appropriate*, in the sense that it represents the same understanding of faith as is expressed in the 'datum discourse' of the Christian witness." (Ogden, *ibid.*). Concerning the criterion of *understandability*, Ogden explains that, "No theological statement be assessed as adequate which is not also *understandable*, in that it meets the relevant conditions of meaning and truth universally established with human existence." (Ogden, *ibid.*). Tracy also employs the same dual criteria for theological understanding, but with a slightly different terminology from Ogden's. Tracy terms the first criterion of *appropriateness* as "criteria of appropriateness" (Tracy uses the plural), and the second criterion of *understandability* as "criteria of adequacy." (*BRO*, 72).

This source of the theological task [the Christian texts] is variously labeled: 'the message' as with Paul Tillich, the 'kerygma' as with Rudolf Bultmann, the 'Christian witness of faith' as with Schubert Ogden, the 'tradition' as with most contemporary Catholic theologians. Whatever title is chosen, the recognition of the need for the Christian theologian to show just how and why his conclusions are *appropriate* to the Christian tradition remains as obvious in its demand as it proves to be difficult in its execution.[129]

Provided that the "scriptures remain the fundamental although not exclusive expression"[130] of that Christian tradition, a corollary of this assumption is that a principal theological task will involve an attempt at "contemporary formulations to state the meanings of Christian texts."[131] Put more concretely, the task is "to find appropriate interpretations of the major motifs of the scriptures and of the relationship of those interpretations to the confessional, doctrinal, symbolic, theological, and *praxis* expressions of the various Christian traditions."[132]

Secondly, Tracy explains the relationship of the second principal source, "common human experience and language," to the task of Christian theology.[133] The essential idea of this relationship is that Christian theology must demonstrate the *"adequacy"* of the central Christian theological claims to all human experience.[134] Tracy explains that:

---

129    *BRO*, 44 (italics mine).
130    *Ibid.* "This insistence is ordinarily formulated under the question of scripture as the *norma normans non normata.*" (*Ibid.*, 57 n.5).
131    *Ibid.*, 44.
132    *Ibid.*
133    Tracy indicates that here "common human experience" is coterminous with Paul Tillich's "situation," Rudolf Bultmann's "contemporary scientific world view," and Bernard Lonergan's contemporary phenomenon of a full-fledged "historical consciousness." (See *ibid.*).
134    *Ibid.*, (italics mine). Here, we notice that Tracy's view is aligned with the so-called "empirical" theology developed in the Anglo-American context. The "empiricism" that Tracy's theological position draws on here refers to a philosophical position that "it is from experience that philosophical reflection arises, and it is to experience that reflection must return for its justification." (Calvin O. Schrag, *Experience and Being: Prolegomena to a Future Ontology* (Evanston: Northwestern University Press, 1969) 17). Tracy's empirical po-

Insofar as the scriptures claim that the Christian self-understanding does, in fact, express an understanding of authentic human existence as such, the Christian theologian is impelled to test precisely that universalist claim.[135]

As a hypothesis of the theologian, rather than a thesis, the Christian universalist understanding of authentic human existence should be put to the test as regards its adequacy to actual human experience.[136] According to Tracy, the need to show the adequacy of Christian self-understanding to actual human experience is required primarily by the universalist assumption embedded in scriptures.[137] This is to say that the task is not demanded simply by the need to discover the "contemporary relevance" of the Christian understanding to human experience.[138] Rather, the task is essentially demanded by the "very logic of the Christian affirmations" that the Christian understanding of human existence is authentic and decisive for all human existence.[139]

sition is intimately reminiscent of Ogden's empirical theology. For Ogden, "to call theology 'empirical' means that even a theological kind of thinking would appeal somehow to our experience simply as men in providing the final justification for its claims." In other words, "it would acknowledge no final basis for its claims except our common human experience." (Schubert M. Ogden, "Present Prospects for Empirical Theology," in Bernard E. Meland (ed.), *The Future of Empirical Theology* (Chicago: The University of Chicago Press, 1969) 66–7). Tracy's "empirical" position will be fully detected only when Tracy's Christian theism is examined in chapter 3.

135   *BRO*, 44.

136   Tracy claims that, "One may continue to find Schleiermacher's slogan for the task of theology still accurate: 'The theses of faith must become the hypotheses of the theologian'." (*Ibid.*, 45). Here, we can see clearly that Tracy intends to take the "liberal" stance (critical investigation of all claims, even religious truth) for his theological model as he himself made clear in his previous analysis.

137   Tracy states that, "Rudolf Bultmann, for one, clarifies these reasons [inner theological reasons for the task] by his firm insistence that demythologizing is demanded not only by the contemporary world-view but also by the universalist, existential assumptions of the New Testament self-understanding itself." (*Ibid.*, 44). See Rudolf Bultmann, *inter alia.*, "New Testament and Mythology," in Hans W. Bartsch (ed.), *Kerygma and Myth: A Theological Debate* (New York: Harper & Row, 1953) esp. 10–16.

138   *BRO*, 44.

139   *Ibid.*

Thesis 2: *The Theological Task Will Involve a Critical Correlation of the Results of the Investigations of the Two Sources of Theology*

Provided that the two sources for theology are to be investigated, this thesis pronounces the need for a critical correlation of the results of the investigations. Regarding this thesis, Tracy limits his concerns to affirming the need for, and a basic principle of what he means by, a critical correlation. For this clarification, Tracy compares his standpoint to Paul Tillich's. The contemporary model of the method of correlation is indebted to Tillich. Tracy's intention here is to reveal his position in comparison to Tillich's.

Briefly speaking, Tillich's method of correlation is a methodical corollary of his notion of a theological system.[140] According to Tillich, theology is a constructive system complying with two essential needs: "the statement of the truth of the Christian message and the interpretation of this truth for every new generation."[141] This implies that there are two poles, "situation," and "message," between which theology moves back and forth in such a way that neither of them is sacrificed in the process of relation.[142] For Tillich, the method of correlation is a way of executing this theological task. For him, the method of correlation is a corrective to "three inadequate methods" of relating the "message" and the "situation": "supernaturalistic," "naturalistic," and "dualistic."[143] Let us look at briefly Tillich's assessment of these three methods.

According to Tillich, the "supernaturalistic" method does not do justice to the relationship between the two poles because the revealed truths are taken to "have fallen into the human situation like strange bodies from a strange world."[144] Thus, "no mediation to the human

---

140 Tillich writes that, "No method can be developed without a priori knowledge of the object to which it is applied. For systematic theology this means that its method is derived from a prior knowledge of the system which is to be built by the method." Paul Tillich, *Systematic Theology I* (Digswell Place: James Nisbet & Co. Ltd., 1964, first published in 1951) 67.
141 *Ibid.*, 3.
142 *Ibid.*, 8.
143 *Ibid.*, 72–3.
144 *Ibid.*, 72.

situation is possible."[145] In this method, human receptivity of the "message" is completely overlooked.

In the "naturalistic" or "humanistic" method, the relationship between the two poles is the very reverse way of the "supernaturalistic" method. In this method, the Christian truths are "explained as creations of man's religious self-realisation in the progressive process of religious history."[146] Thus, no mediation to the transcendental quality of the Christian "message" as revelation is possible. Since the Christian "message" is said to be derived from the natural human state, only the human is spoken to the human being.

Finally, by the "dualistic" method, Tillich means the method usually employed by so-called "natural theology."[147] According to Tillich, the method can be called "dualistic," insofar as "it builds a supernatural structure on a natural substructure."[148] On the one hand, it affirms the infinite gap between "man's spirit and God's spirit."[149] Yet, on the other hand, it believes that a relationship between them must be possible. The crucial problem of this method, for Tillich, is that it attempts to explain this relationship "by positing a body of theological truth which man can reach through his own efforts, in terms of a self-contradictory expression, through 'natural revelation'."[150] For Tillich, the theological arguments that are supposed to articulate this relation are true "in so far as they analyse human finitude and the question involved in it."[151] However, they are false in so far as they derive an answer from the human condition and human rational elaboration. In other words, the human "situation" can bring forth the questions implied in human existence, but is never able to provide the answers to them, which should be derived from the

145  *Ibid.*
146  *Ibid.*, 73. Tillich writes that, "Much of liberal theology in the last two centuries was 'humanistic' in this sense." (*Ibid.*).
147  *Ibid.*
148  *Ibid.*
149  *Ibid.*
150  *Ibid.*
151  *Ibid.*

Christian "message." For the answers are "'spoken' *to* human existence from beyond it."[152]

As the most adequate way of relating the "situation" and the "message," Tillich proposes the method of correlation. This is intended to remedy the afore-mentioned three methods. The method of correlation advocated by Tillich is a mutually interdependent relation between the *existential* questions raised by the human "situation" and the *theological* answers derived from the Christian "message."[153] The key point here is that the "answers" cannot be derived from an analysis of human existence. Since human existence itself is the question, it can never be the answer.[154] More concretely, Tillich states that in using the method of correlation, theology "makes an analysis of the human situation out of which the existential questions arise, and it demonstrates that the symbols used in the Christian message are the answers to these questions."[155] In that case, however, how can this correlation be characterized by a "mutually interdependent" relation? According to Tillich, it is a mutually interdependent relation in the sense that the human being asks questions, and that the Christian answers are "dependent on the structure of the questions" implied in human existence.[156] On the other hand, God answers human questions, and "under the impact of God's answers" human being asks them.[157]

---

152  *Ibid.*, 72.
153  *Ibid.*, 68.
154  See *ibid.*, 69.
155  *Ibid.*, 70.
156  *Ibid.*, 72. In other words, "the answers implied in the event of revelation are meaningful only in so far as they are in correlation with questions concerning the whole of our existence, with existential questions." (*Ibid.*, 69).
157  *Ibid.*, 73. For example, Tillich points out that existentialist analyses of the human situation of estrangement are indebted to classical Christian anthropology. He states: "Existentialism has analysed the 'old eon,' namely, the predicament of man and his world in the state of estrangement. In doing so, existentialism is a natural ally of Christianity. Immanual Kant once said that mathematics is the good luck of human reason. In the same way, one could say that existentialism is the good luck of Christian theology. It has helped to discover the classical Christian interpretation of human existence." (Tillich, *Systematic Theology II*, 30).

Tracy compares his standpoint to Tillich's on the method of correlation, and clarifies it as follows. Firstly, Tracy indicates that he shares with Tillich the view that the theological task works on (or correlates) two poles, namely, Tillich's "situation" and "message," or Tracy's own "common human experience" and "Christian texts."[158] According to Tracy, the implication of this view is that the theological task is understood as a hermeneutical reflection on "both 'message' and 'situation' (alternatively [...] the contemporary 'application' of the tradition to the contemporary situation)." [159] In contrast to the dogmatist and traditionalist theological stance which is characterized by the ahistorical and ahermeneutical repetition of earlier theological formulations, Tillich's method of correlation between two poles highlights the character of theology as constant new interpretation. Tracy states:

> Prior to the actual development of the technical resources of the postromantic hermeneutical theories of Gadamer and Ricoeur, Tillich's method of correlation already spoke to the need for every theological interpretation to include a moment of *application* to the situation and thereby prove to be a *new* interpretation.[160]

Hence, Tillich's method of correlation can be recognized as "one good way of rendering explicit the implicit matter-of-fact hermeneutical character of all theology."[161]

Secondly, Tracy assesses Tillich's aims for contemporary theology. As we mentioned above, Tillich's aim is to construct a the-

---

158 Tracy briefly remarks that there is, however, a difference between Tillich and himself concerning the two theological sources: whereas, for him, human 'experience' is a *source* for theology, it is a *medium* for Tillich (*BRO*, 57 n.12). This means that in Tillich, 'experience' is the medium through which the theological sources (the analyses of the human "situation" and the Christian "message") "speak to us," and through which we can understand them. In short, the correlation of the two sources for theology takes place within experience in Tillich's system (See Tillich, *Systematic Theology I*, 46).

159 Tracy, "Tillich and Contemporary Theology," in James L. Adams, Wilhelm Pauck and Roger L. Shinn (eds.), *The Thought of Paul Tillich* (San Francisco: Harper & Row, 1985) 263.

160 *Ibid.*, 262.

161 *Ibid.*, 264.

ological system that moves beyond "supernaturalistic," "naturalistic," and "dualistic" modes of understanding by using the method of correlation. Interestingly enough, Tracy agrees with Tillich's goal of moving beyond "supernaturalism" and "naturalism" but, he makes no mention of the third method, the "dualistic" mode of natural theology. When we recall Tracy's claims that his revisionist theological model aims to move beyond both an "anti-secular, religious supernaturalism" and "anti-Christian secularism,"[162] we can nevertheless see a significant interface between Tracy and Tillich (against "supernaturalism" and "naturalism" or "secularism"). Moreover, Tracy concurs with Tillich's proposition that the method of correlation can be a way for fulfilling this theological aim.

Thirdly, with regard to the specific method of correlation, Tracy explains his divergence from Tillich. Tracy judges Tillich's formulation of the method of correlation not to be a *critical correlation* of the "situation" and the "message" in full sense.[163] According to Tracy, Tillich's formulation is rather a juxtaposition between questions from the "situation" and answers from the "message." In other words, Tillich's correlation does not allow both questions and answers from *each* source. Tracy contends that, for instance, in the process of correlation, as far as the "questions" of the "situation" are to be taken with full seriousness, the "answers" provided by the "situation" should also be critically and seriously considered.[164] In short, the correlation process should involve a critical comparison of the answers provided by the Christian "message" and all other possible answers proffered by the "situation,"[165] According to Tracy, the theologian's com-

---

162   *BRO*, 33.
163   *Ibid.*, 46 (italics mine).
164   Tracy notes that this contention need not be applicable, if "the questions of both the 'situation' and the 'message' are of the logical type of fundamental philosophical questions whose very explication is a 'self-answering' one." (*Ibid.*, 57 n.14). Yet, Tracy claims that he does not see this aspect in Tillich's argument.
165   Tracy enquires, for example, "Why do we not find in Tillich a critical investigation of the claims that either Jean Paul Sartre's or Karl Jaspers' philosophies of existence provide a better 'answer' to the question of human estrangement than the Christian 'answer' does?" (*Ibid.*, 46). Here, we can see a

mitment to two sources does imply this full-scale correlation. Tracy contends that only the full-scale critical correlation of the questions and answers given by *"both* the 'situation' and the 'message'" can do justice to the twofold nature of the theologian's commitment.[166] Moreover, only this full-scale critical correlation can provide a successful prospect for fulfilling the theological aim of moving beyond both supernaturalism and naturalism.[167]

Thesis 3: *The Principal Method of Investigation of the Source "Common Human Experience and Language" Can Be Described as a Phenomenology of the "Religious Dimension" Present in Everyday and Scientific Experience and Language*

This thesis concerns the principal method for investigating the first source, "common human experience and language." For Tracy, the principal theological task at stake is to explain "how and why the existential meanings proper to Christian self-understanding are present in common human experience."[168] In order to undertake this task,

---

clue as to why Tracy categorizes Paul Tillich's theology into the neo-orthodox theological model in his previous analysis (See The Neo-Orthodox Model). Tracy's assessment of Tillich's method of correlation as juxtaposition, rather than a *critical* correlation, reflects his contention that "the neo-orthodox seemed unwilling at some inevitable final moment to follow to a truly critical conclusion the task which they themselves initiated." (*Ibid.*, 29).

166 *Ibid.*, 46.
167 In his later work, "Tillich and Contemporary Theology" (1985), though, Tracy makes a different evaluation regarding Tillich's method of correlation. Tracy points out that even though Tillich's own formulation indicates a juxtaposition between questions from the "situation" and answers from the "message," the way Tillich actually uses the method throughout his theological system is more faithful to a two-way correlation (correlation of the questions and answers of both sources). Tracy notes that, "The fact is that Tillich does allow the answers (not only the questions) of psychoanalysis, socialist theory, existentialism, and his own 'self-transcending' naturalism to provide answers, not only questions, in his theology. [...] In sum, the method of correlation is better formulated not as he usually formulated it, but as he actually employed it: an interpretative correlation of the questions and answers of the message with the questions and answers of the situation." (Tracy, "Tillich and Contemporary Theology," 266).
168 *BRO*, 47.

Tracy proposes a useful investigation: "to explicate a *pre-conceptual* dimension to our common shared experience that can legitimately be described as *religious*."[169] Here, Tracy uses a phenomenological concept, the "pre-conceptual" dimension of experience, referring to the "pre-reflective," or "pre-thematic" dimension of experience that is ordinarily blocked from sight by our routine, cultural preconceptions and prejudices.[170] The phenomenological objective of investigating this dimension of experience is to uncover the hidden or neglected aspect of experience by means of a conscious effort to untie the effect of conventional, cultural constructs or prejudgments.[171] For Tracy, this phenomenological investigation of the "pre-conceptual" dimension of experience dovetails with his theological aim of uncovering a realm of common experience that manifests itself as so ultimate that we cannot

---

169  *Ibid.*, (italics mine).

170  *Ibid.* As one of his main sources for phenomenological understanding, Tracy footnotes Herbert Spiegelberg's *The Phenomenological Movement: A Historical Introduction*, 2 vols. (The Hague: Nijhoff, 1969). According to Spiegelberg, "the first objective of the phenomenological approach is the enlarging and deepening of the range of our immediate experience. [...] Negatively, it expresses a revolt against an approach to philosophy that takes its point of departure from crystallized beliefs and theories handed down by a tradition which only too often perpetuates preconceptions and prejudgments. [...] It takes a determined effort to undo the effect of habitual patterns of thought and to return to the pristine innocence of first seeing." (Spiegelberg, *ibid.*, 656). For a more detailed explanation of this dimension of experience in relation to the theological task, see Langdon Gilkey, *Naming the Whirlwind: The Renewal of God-Language*, esp. 276–84. For the pre-conceptual dimension of experience in the perspective of phenomenology, see H.L. Dreyfus and S.J. Todes, *Discussion: The Three Worlds of Merleau-Ponty* in *Philosophy and Phenomenological Research* 22 (1961–1962) 559–65.

171  Regarding this point, Gilkey's explanation is helpful: "It is generally agreed that a most significant goal of the phenomenological movement has been to provide a method that will (*a*) eradicate or set to one side our normal, cultural prejudices in order that (*b*) new or neglected phenomena, aspects of experience as it actually is, may be seen, appropriated, and comprehended. For this purpose among others, the bracketing moves, especially those of the transcendental or phenomenological reduction of all questions of reality, existence, or causality, were devised, and thus the main slogan of the movement was 'to the things themselves'." (Gilkey, *Naming the Whirlwind*, 276).

but describe it as religious.[172] In other words, Tracy attempts to uncover this latent dimension of ultimacy for which religious discourse is adequate, through phenomenological investigation of the "pre-conceptual" or "pre-reflective" realm of our common human experience.

Furthermore, Tracy points out that a more recent phenomenological development, the so-called "hermeneutic phenomenology,"[173] can be a relatively adequate method for a theological inquiry. Hermeneutic phenomenology exhibits great interest in analyzing symbolic language which is expressive of our fundamental experience and which may also manifest a religious dimension.[174] Summarily stated, Tracy is talking about the two levels of the "religious dimension" elucidated by (hermeneutic) phenomenology.[175] The first level is the

172 Tracy states that, "Several major figures in the phenomenological tradition from Max Scheler through the recent work of Langdon Gilkey have demonstrated the effectiveness of phenomenological reflection in explicating that final or ultimate horizon precisely *as a religious one*." (*BRO*, 47). The relevant works are: Max Scheler, *The Eternal in Man* (New York: Harper, 1960); Louis Dupré, *The Other Dimension: A Search for the Meaning of Religious Attitudes* (New York: Doubleday, 1972); Langdon Gilkey, *Naming the Whirlwind: The Renewal of God-Language*.

173 Tracy indicates that, throughout his work, he is indebted to the representative proponents of hermeneutic phenomenology, among others, Hans-Georg Gadamer, *Truth and Method* and Paul Ricoeur, *inter alia.*, "New Developments in Phenomenology in France: The Phenomenology of Language," in *Social Research* 34 (1967) 1–30; "From Existentialism to the Philosophy of Language," in Charles E. Reagan and David Stewart (eds), *The Philosophy of Paul Ricoeur: An Anthology of His Work* (Boston: Beacon Press, 1978) 86–93, first published in *Criterion* 10 (1971) 14–18; "Philosophy and Religious Language," in *JR*, 54 (1974) 71–86.

174 For a good succinct discussion of this issue, see Paul Ricoeur, "From Existentialism to the Philosophy of Language," 86–93. Regarding the linguistic and symbolic character of experience, Ricoeur points out that, "We have a direct language to say purpose, motive, and 'I can', but we speak of evil by means of metaphors [symbolic language] such as estrangement, errance, burden, and bondage." (*Ibid.*, 87). In other words, we could speak of purposive action without symbolic language, but we could not speak of bad will or of evil without it.

175 Note that the phrase, "religious dimension," is deliberately used in preference to the concept, "religious experience" throughout Tracy's work "in order to indicate that 'religion' is not another human activity coordinate with such activities

"implicit" religious dimension appearing in the "pre-reflective" or "pre-symbolic" and unadulterated realm of experience, which was explored by the earlier phenomenological movement.[176] The second level is the "explicit" religious dimension manifested in explicit symbolic language and expressive of our fundamental (or "limit") experience, which has been analyzed by recent hermeneutic phenomenology. In short, for investigating the first source in his theological model, Tracy suggests employing (hermeneutic) phenomenology as a principal method without, however, limiting himself to this. The basic rationale for this suggestion lies in his assumption that phenomenology has shown its relative adequacy for elucidating the religious dimension of ultimacy operative in our common human experience and language, and with which religious discourses (e.g., those of the Christian texts) can be properly correlated.[177]

Thesis 4: *The Principal Method of Investigation of the Source, i.e., "The Christian Tradition," Can Be Described as an Historical and Hermeneutical Investigation of Classical Christian Texts*

This thesis identifies the two principal methods for investigating the "Christian texts" as the historical and hermeneutical methods. In this thesis, Tracy's concern is to explain the "particular understandings of the historical and hermeneutical methods that may prove helpful for this aspect of the theological task."[178] This implies that, for him, the

as art, morality, and science, but is rather a dimension of or horizon to *all* human activities." (*BRO*, 59 n.24).

176   Tracy is referring to "the earlier 'eidetic' formulations of Husserl and the Göttingen circle through the existential phenomenology of Sartre, Merleau-Ponty, Scheler, and the early Heidegger." (*Ibid.*, 47).

177   One important point to note: Tracy makes clear that phenomenology as a principal method for the first source should not be understood as one which can determine the "truth-value of the meanings uncovered." (*Ibid.*). For him, for determining this truth-value, another methodical process is necessary, namely, a "transcendental or metaphysical mode of reflection." (*Ibid.*, 52). This issue is going to be dealt with in the fifth thesis.

178   *Ibid.*, 49.

need for these methods is derived from the specific historical and hermeneutical character of the theological task.

Firstly, Tracy explains the need of the historical method in the search for the meanings present in the Christian texts. He writes:

> If the phenomenon labelled the "Christian fact" includes the significant gestures, symbols, and actions of the various Christian traditions, then the theologian must learn those historical methods capable of determining exactly what facts can be affirmed as probable. For the present investigation of texts, he must also learn historical methods in order to allow for the historical reconstruction of the basic texts of Christian self-understanding.[179]

According to Tracy, the attempt at the historical reconstruction of the Christian texts by contemporary historical scholarship is *imperative* for theology and distinguishes it from philosophy of religion. He explains that while philosophy of religion "would not involve determining the meanings and truth-status of the historical components of the 'Christian fact',"[180] theology should. For example, for understanding the Christian affirmation that "Jesus of Nazareth is the Christ," the theologian, unlike the philosopher of religion, needs to undertake the task to determine the meanings and truth-status of historical questions "about the person Jesus of Nazareth and about the belief of the Christian community that Jesus was the Christ."[181]

Secondly, on the historical basis of reconstruction, the next step for investigating the Christian texts is to interpret the "religious existential meanings" expressed by the metaphors, symbols, images, and concepts in the texts.[182] For this investigation, Tracy calls for the "hermeneutical task," as distinct from the historical one. In this thesis, Tracy limits his concern to explaining the *need* to employ the recent developments of hermeneutical theory on texts which seem "apt for illustrating the nature of the theologian's hermeneutic commitment."[183]

---

179  *Ibid.*
180  *Ibid.*, 59 n.29.
181  *Ibid.*, 50.
182  *Ibid.*
183  *Ibid.* In this fourth thesis, since Tracy's objective is simply to propose the *need* for the hermeneutical task of theology, his explanation of hermeneutical theory

The first hermeneutical development with which Tracy is concerned for interpreting the Christian texts, is the hermeneutical notion of "distanciation" which is a distinctive characteristic expressed in a written text.[184] For this idea, Tracy is indebted to Paul Ricoeur's interpretation theory as applied to a written text as distinct from a speech-act.[185] The idea of "distanciation" here has significant impli-

is minimal. We shall examine his specific use of the hermeneutical method in the next chapter.

184   For this notion, Tracy has recourse to the works of Paul Ricoeur: *Interpretation Theory: Discourse and the Surplus of Meaning* (Fort Worth: The Texas Christian University Press, 1976) esp. 25–44 and "Philosophy and Religious Language," 71–86. The former work was presented to a colloquium of the faculty at the University of Chicago Divinity School, in May 1971, and it was not yet published when Tracy wrote *BRO*.

185   According to Ricoeur, a text is defined as a discourse fixed by writing. Yet, this fixation by writing does not mean a mere transition of the same discourse from a speech-form to a textual form. This is to say that the birth of a text takes place when human thought is "*directly* brought to writing without the intermediary stage of spoken language." (Ricoeur, *Interpretation Theory*, 28). Writing takes the place of speech. In other words, by writing, "the fate of discourse is delivered over to *littera*, not to *vox*." (*Ibid.*, 29). The phenomenon that a discourse is directly inscribed in written form instead of being spoken generates several alterations in the relationships among the components of the communication process of the discourse. Firstly, there occurs a change in the referential function of discourse. In speech, the meaning of discourse is understood between interlocutors by the help of all the demonstrative and ostensive indicators, including gestures of pointing or further clarification of an unclear message directly with the speaker, etc. In short, "all references of oral language rely on monstrations [sic], which depend on the situation perceived as common by the members of the dialogue. All references in the dialogical situation consequently are situational." (*Ibid.*, 35). However, in a text, there are no more ostensive indicators as in speech. In the effacement of the ostensive reference, a new referential form emerges. The reference of discourse is severed from the situation of speech only to be configured through writing, which Ricoeur calls, the "quasi world of the text or *literature*." (Paul Ricoeur, "What is a Text?: Explanation and Understanding" in John B. Thompson (ed.), *Paul Ricoeur: Hermeneutics and the Human Sciences* (Cambridge: Cambridge University Press, 1988) 149. At the level of text, language undergoes a process of production within various textual formulations (e.g., narratives, parables, poems, essays, etc.) which is distinct from that of conversation. Thus, "text means discourse both as inscribed and wrought." (Ricoeur, *Interpretation*

cations for the "semantic autonomy of the text"[186] which the process of writing renders as an "objectification of discourse in a structured work."[187] Thanks to the writing process as a production, the text is constituted as an "autonomous object at a *distance* from the authorial intention, from its initial situation (its *Sitz im Leben*), and from its primitive audience."[188] Because of this distanciation, the text is open to unlimited new readings in different contextual conditions. In other words, the text must be able "to 'decontextualise' itself in such a way that it can be 'recontextualised' in a new situation."[189]

Tracy is convinced that this interpretation theory can help the theologian to overcome the theological interpretation of the Christian texts "in too psychological a direction."[190] The psychological way of interpretation here points to the "hermeneutical circle" which is pro-

*Theory*, 33). Owing to writing, the reader has the "world" of text which is the "ensemble of references opened up" by text (*Ibid.*, 36). Secondly, in speech, the referential intention of speaker and the meaning of discourse coincide each other because the "ability of discourse to refer back to the speaking subject presents a character of immediacy." (*Ibid.*, 29). However, with a text, the intention of the author and the meaning of the text do not coincide, because of the "disconnection of the mental intention of the author from the verbal meaning of the text" through the process proper to a work *wrought* by the "productive rules of literary composition." (*Ibid.*, 33). Now, the text is semantically autonomous from the mental intention of the author. Finally, the role of the hearer in conversation is transformed into that of reader. Whereas spoken discourse is addressed to someone, a text is addressed to an unknown reader, and potentially to whoever encounters the text. Ricoeur states: "this opportunity for multiple readings is the dialectical counterpart of the semantic autonomy of the text. [...] The right of the reader and the right of the text converge in an important struggle that generates the whole dynamic of interpretation. Hermeneutics begins where [interlocutory] dialogue ends." (*Ibid.*, 32). Summarily stated, a written text (work) obtains a new existence through three kinds of "distanciation": (1) distanciation from the situation of discourse; (2) distanciation from the author; (3) distanciation from the original audience.

186 *Ibid.*, 25.
187 Ricoeur, "The Hermeneutical Function of Distanciation," in *Paul Ricoeur: Hermeneutics and the Human Sciences*, 138. This article was first published in English in *PhT*, 17 (1973) 129–43.
188 Ricoeur, "Philosophy and Religious Language," 75 (italics of *distance* mine).
189 Ricoeur, "The Hermeneutical Function of Distanciation," 139.
190 *BRO*, 73.

duced by the "effort of one subjective consciousness (the interpreter) to understand another consciousness (the author)."[191] In such a psychological approach to interpretation, the interpreter will try to understand the meaning of the text in one of the following ways:

> Either by determining the author's original intention (for example, through redaction criticism); or by determining the original discourse situation (for example, Dodd and Jeremias on understanding the parables by finding the situation in the life of Jesus or of the primitive Christian community which the parables address); or by explicating the first historical addressee of that text (for example, social-cultural analyses of the communities at Corinth who received the Pauline letters).[192]

According to Tracy, these ways of interpretation are still legitimate and useful. However, concerning the deciphering of the "theological meaning" of the Christian texts, these psychological modes of interpretation have their limitations.[193] For Tracy, the limitation of the psychologizing conception of interpretation lies in its limited horizon with respect to the understanding of the meaning, namely, the intersubjectivity of the original author and the reader. The value of the interpretation theory which takes seriously the linguistic process of "distanciation," however, is that it allows the theologian to

191  *Ibid.*, 74. According to Ricoeur, the hermeneutical theories of Schleiermacher and Dilthey in the history of hermeneutics can be labeled psychological because they define the understanding of a text as the "recognition of an author's intention from the point of view of the primitive addresses in the original situation of discourse." (Ricoeur, *Interpretation Theory*, 22). Thus, their interpretation theories impose the "framework of intersubjectivity on hermeneutics." (*Ibid.*). The psychological character of Schleiermacher's hermeneutics is "Romanticist" because it attempts to reach the Romantic ideal of understanding – "to understand an author better than he understood himself." (*Ibid.*, 75). The psychological trait of Dilthey's hermeneutics can be found in his thought that every modality of our understanding implies a historical relation which is located in our primordial capacity to transpose ourselves into the mental life of others. Thus, the aim of his hermeneutics is to share a common dimension (the meaning of being as a human being) between the interpreter and the author. See Ricoeur, *From Text to Action* (London: Northwestern University Press, 1991) 59–62.

192  *BRO*, 74.

193  *Ibid.*

recognize the enlarged horizon of "the extra-linguistic referent of the text."[194] This referent of the text refers to a "world," or a certain "mode-of-being-in-the-world which the text opens up."[195] Ricoeur describes this dimension of meaning by saying that, "The text [not the author] speaks of a possible world and of a possible way of orienting oneself within it."[196] Tracy adopts this interpretation theory which allows the theologian to decipher the principal existential meanings of Christian texts and which also opens the possibility of a new possible way of looking at reality and a new mode of being.

The second development in contemporary hermeneutic and linguistic theory that Tracy intends to employ is the distinction between the meaning as the "sense" and the meaning as the "referent" of a text, and the distinct methods to explicate each.[197] Tracy presents the distinction between "sense" and "referent" in the following manner:

> The 'sense' of the text means the internal structure and meaning of the text as that structure can be determined through the ordinary methods of semantic and literary-critical inquiries. The 'referents' of the text do not pertain to the meaning 'behind' the text (e.g., the author's *real* intention or the social-cultural situation of the text). Rather, to shift metaphors, 'referent' basically manifests

---

194   *Ibid.*, 77.

195   *Ibid.*, 78.

196   Ricoeur, *Interpretation Theory*, 88.

197   BRO, 51. See Ricoeur, *Interpretation Theory*, 19–22. According to Ricoeur, the distinction between "sense" and "referent" in discourse was introduced into modern philosophy by Gottlob Frege in his article, "On Sense and Reference," trans. Max Black, in Peter Geach and Max Black (eds), *Translations from the Philosophical Writings of Gottlob Frege* (Oxford: Basil Blackwell, 1970) 56–78. According to Ricoeur, at the sentence level (discourse), the distinction between the meaning as "sense" and the meaning as "referent" is possibly made in accordance with the distinction between the meaning as "the 'what' of discourse" (sense) and the meaning as "the 'about what' of discourse" (referent) (Ricoeur, *Interpretation Theory*, 19). Put more pointedly, "whereas the *sense* is immanent to the discourse, and objective in the sense of ideal, the *reference* expresses the movement in which language transcends itself. In other words, the *sense* correlates the identification function and the predicative function within the sentence, and the *reference* relates language to the world." (*Ibid.*, 20).

the meaning 'in front of' the text, i.e., that way of perceiving reality, that mode of being-in-the-world which the text opens up for the intelligent reader.[198]

Tracy explains the distinct methods relevant to each. To discover the "sense," that is, the meaning immanent in discourse (e.g., in literary devices such as metaphors, symbols, images, and also genres), semantics and literary-critical methods are necessary. To discover the "referent," that is, the meaning directed toward the "extra-linguistic"[199] world by means of "sense," the "explicit hermeneutical" method is demanded.[200] In relation to the theological task to decipher the "religious existential meanings," Tracy highlights the importance of elucidating the meaning as the "referent":

> The meaning of major import to *the theologian* remains a concern that can be formulated by a question like the following: what is the mode-of-being-in-the-world *referred to* by the text? That question is not really answered until an explicitly hermeneutical enterprise is advanced.[201]

Summarily stated, for investigating the Christian texts, the revisionist theological model makes use of at least four connected methods. First, historical method is used for the historical reconstruction of the texts. Second, semantics is needed for determining the "linguistic

---

198  *BRO*, 51.
199  *Ibid.*, 76. Ricoeur explains that "only the sentence level allows us to distinguish what is said [sense] and about what it is said [reference]. In the system of language, say as a lexicon, there is no problem of reference; signs only refer to other signs within the system. With the sentence, however, language is directed beyond itself. Whereas the sense is immanent to the discourse, [...] the reference expresses the movement in which language transcends itself." (Ricoeur, *Interpretation Theory*, 20).
200  *BRO*, 76. According to Ricoeur, the two levels of meaning, "referent" and "sense," are in a dialectical relationship. They can only be distinguished, but do not exclude each other in an act of interpretation. Thus, the interpretation can mean the enterprise to relate the "inner or immanent constitution of the sense to the outer or transcendent intention of the reference." (Ricoeur, *Interpretation Theory*, 22).
201  *BRO*, 51–2. Tracy's assumption for this position is that all theological statements are related to the fundamental questions, meanings, and truth of human existence (*Ibid.*, 61 n.44 and n.45).

structure of the images and symbols involved in the text."[202] Third, literary-critical methods can help the theologian to discern the "particular character of the literary genres by means of which the images, metaphors, and symbols are structured, codified, and transformed."[203] Finally, the explicitly hermeneutical method is demanded for explicating the existential referent of the texts, namely, a "religious, Christian way of being-in-the-world."[204]

Thesis 5: *To Determine the Truth-Status of the Results of One's Investigations into the Meaning of Both Common Human Experience and Christian Texts the Theologian Should Employ an Explicitly Transcendental or Metaphysical Mode of Reflection*

As indicated earlier, Tracy defines his revisionist model for fundamental theology as "philosophical reflection upon the *meanings present* in common human experience and language, and upon the *meanings present* in the Christian fact."[205] In the third and fourth theses, he suggests to use phenomenological and hermeneutical analyses to uncover these meanings as *religious*. In this fifth thesis, Tracy addresses the need of metaphysical reflection by relating the religious meanings (or the religious dimension) uncovered by the above-mentioned analyses to the question of God. His central assumption is that it is possible and legitimate to formulate the question of God "as the question of the necessary referent (or object)" of such religious meanings (or religious dimension).[206] In other words, for him, God is the objective referent of the religious dimension present in human experience and Christian religious language. Now, his question is how to

---

202  *Ibid.*, 51.
203  *Ibid.*
204  *Ibid.*, 52. Tracy subdivides the two principal methods (historical and hermeneutical methods) into four methods. The second and third methods (semantics and literary-critical methods) belong to hermeneutical methods in a broad sense, insofar as they are related to the enterprise of interpretation (this is the case in Ricoeur). This is why Tracy uses the nuanced expression, "explicit hermeneutical" method for referring to the fourth method.
205  *Ibid.*, 43 (italics mine).
206  *Ibid.*, 54.

determine whether the meanings (or the dimension) uncovered as *religious* and *theistic* are *true*.[207] According to him, for determining the truth-status of *religious* and *theistic* meanings, a distinct mode of inquiry is needed, that is, a "transcendental or metaphysical mode of reflection."[208] Tracy explains the reason for this claim in the following way:

> Insofar as the 'meanings' uncovered by the earlier investigations are authentically religious and theistic ones, then their phenomenological and hermeneutic manifestation is also a manifestation of their truth-status. Yet, this insight is clearly affirmed, I believe, only when the metaphysical character of these phenomena as manifesting 'self-answering fundamental questions' is explicitly (i.e., transcendentally) formulated. Hence, the reason for the fifth thesis is actually more one of making explicit what is already present than it is a really new concern. But such is the character of all metaphysical and transcendental reflection: metaphysics mediates the most basic and, hence, most obvious presuppositions of all our thinking and living.[209]

Basing himself on the above argument, Tracy presents two essential reasons for the necessity of a transcendental or metaphysical reflection.

Firstly, in fundamental theology, the religious and theistic meanings "should be explicated with as much *conceptual* clarity as possible."[210] He explains that the analysis we need to attempt in a transcendental or metaphysical reflection "must depart from the properly metaphorical, proverbial, common-sense, and symbolic language of the originating religious language and must develop an explicitly conceptual language."[211] He goes on to say that, "Conceptual language does claim to articulate certain cognitive beliefs (or doctrines) that are either clearly implied by or even explicitly referred to by such [orig-

---

207 This question implies that Tracy employs, in his methodological system, the "analytic distinction between 'meaning' and 'truth'." Tracy intends to make the use of metaphysical reflection legitimate by adopting the distinction between "meaning" and "truth" and, thereby, differentiating the distinct mode of inquiry for each category.
208 *BRO*, 52.
209 *Ibid.*, 61 n.49.
210 *Ibid.*, 148.
211 *Ibid.*

inating religious] language."[212] For this task of a conceptual articulation, a metaphysical language is necessary. "Otherwise, the theologian can never be sure that he has avoided either incoherence or vagueness in determining the cognitive character of religious and theistic claims."[213]

Secondly, when he claims that God is the objective referent of the religious dimension present in common human experience and Christian religious language, the religious dimension in question here is not merely coordinate with other dimensions like the ethical, the aesthetic, or the cultural. Rather, the religious dimension "can be phenomenologically described as an ultimate or grounding dimension or horizon to *all* meaningful human activities."[214] Hence, the discipline which investigates the religious and theistic cognitive claims should be capable of accounting for not simply a particular dimension of experience, but all human experience as such. More concretely, the discipline should be capable of explicating the ground or the fundamental conditions in common human experience for having any notions of religion and God at all. Therefore, according to Tracy, the very nature of the religious and theistic cognitive claims requires "neither the disciplines of empirical science, nor ethics, nor aesthetics, nor general cultural analysis," but "one mode of analysis, metaphysical or transcendental analysis" for its validation.[215] This "metaphysical or transcendental" analysis provides "the explicit mediation of the basic presuppositions (or 'beliefs') that are the conditions of the possibility of our existing or understanding at all."[216]

---

212  *Ibid.*
213  *Ibid.*, 55. More specifically, in Ogden's words, metaphysics is necessary to explain how a theistic language "may be conceived precisely enough to avoid vagueness, while yet avoiding incoherence, either with itself or with our other general conceptions and experience." (Schubert M. Ogden, "The Task of Philosophical Theology," in Robert A. Evans (ed.), *The Future of Philosophical Theology* (Philadelphia: The Westminster Press, 1971) 71. According to Ogden, this task is critical especially in the cultural situation where the very notion of God is problematic.
214  *BRO*, 55 (italics mine).
215  *Ibid.*
216  *Ibid.*, 56.

Granting that the use of metaphysics for validating religious and theistic claims is necessary, Tracy is, however, well aware of the contemporary debate on the possibility of metaphysics as such since the emergence of historical consciousness.[217] He mentions that today "the claim for metaphysics is often under as great a suspicion of intellectual irresponsibility as is the claim for the objective reality of God."[218] The dilemma has to do with the fundamental suspicion of "classical philosophy's claim to be able to explicate the basic and ultimate presuppositions of reality."[219] Tracy perceives this crisis, however, not as a call for undoing classical philosophy's task and aim. Instead, he construes this crisis as a call for "a *purification, delimitation, and clarification of that* [classical philosophy's] *aim.*"[220] According to Tracy, insofar as philosophy is a discipline that has to do with every phenomenon or every "being" (universal) and with the quest for the ultimate ground and the fundamental presuppositions of that and every phenomenon or "being" (fundamental), its principal feature is its "transcendental" character.[221] He explains the meaning of "transcendental" by saying that "philosophy has always been transcendental in its self-understanding, precisely as a rising-above (to use one metaphor) or a going-beneath (to use another) any phenomenon to discover the most basic presuppositions or (more critically formulated) 'conditions of possibility' of that phenomenon."[222] Tracy argues that, for example, the Kantian transcendental philosophy, a

217  *Ibid.*, 148. For the background to this debate, Tracy indicates Langdon Gilkey, *Naming the Whirlwind*, 435–44; Gordon D. Kaufman, *Relativism, Knowledge and Faith* (Chicago: University of Chicago Press, 1960) 95–117.
218  *BRO*, 148.
219  *Ibid.*, 67.
220  *Ibid.* Tracy writes that, "For philosophy – at least among the great classical philosophers as distinct from their 'schools' – has always recognized itself as 'problematic' [...]. For that reason, a more accurate description of most of the major critical and post-critical philosophical movements does not concentrate simply upon their frequent distrust of classical 'systems' but rather recognizes their more disciplined understanding of philosophy's traditionally problematic status." (*Ibid.*).
221  For Tracy, the term, "transcendental" and the term, "metaphysical" are interchangeable.
222  *BRO*, 67.

representative modern critical philosophy, can be understood as a peculiarly modern formulation of such a classical transcendental task of philosophy, not as an elimination of it.[223] The phenomenological movements evident in Husserl or Heidegger also can be understood in the same way. These phenomenologists not only attempt to analyze phenomena, but also, in their own distinctive ways, go beyond the phenomena, and search for "the basic ground or presuppositions of every and all phenomena or any and all phenomenological re-flection."[224] Thus, in such phenomenological movements, the classical transcendental task itself persists, albeit in different approaches and formulations. Tracy claims that:

> In either philosophy's modern (critical) or its contemporary (post-critical) moments, therefore, the transcendental task of philosophy is both recognized and refined. Both the modern and contemporary reformulations of the philosophical task continue to involve themselves in the central aim of classical metaphysics: what are the basic *a priori* conditions of all human living and thinking? That task alone is properly transcendental – or, if one prefers, metaphysical. The accomplishment of that task will always remain 'proble-matic' in the exact sense that it can no more be indubitably 'proved' than it can be avoided by any serious philosophical thinking.[225]

223 *Ibid.* Tracy explains that the Kantian attempt is not an elimination, but a clarification of the classical transcendental task of philosophy in the sense that it is itself "the uniquely transcendental one: an explicit recognition that what one is reflecting upon is never merely 'given' for human consciousness. Rather every object – every phenomenon – has *a priori* conditions. Certain of such conditions are basic and universal for all human knowing and experience insofar as those conditions are conditions of possibility, i.e., they are so constitutive of any performance of cognition or experience that they can be reductively exhibited from it. Finally, the peculiarity of several major post-Kantian philosophies does not really deny this transcendental task. Rather these post-critical positions argue that the task can be executed adequately only when the Kantian exclusive attention to the centrality of 'understanding' or 'reason' is replaced. Instead, there must be an insistence upon the centrality and comprehensiveness of the originating lived 'experience' itself over its clear, distinct – and derivative – expressions in human 'understanding'." (*Ibid.*, 67–8).
224 *Ibid.*, 68.
225 *Ibid.* Tracy clarifies that this standpoint "remains accurate for three contemp-orary philosophical traditions: the phenomenological, the Anglo-American empirical, and the reformulated 'transcendental method' of Coreth, Lonergan,

74

In short, according to Tracy, the only choice is "not really between metaphysics or no metaphysics," but "between a self-conscious and explicit metaphysics or an unconscious yet operative one."[226]

In this first chapter, we have discussed Tracy's methodological exposition concerning his revisionist theological project. The next two chapters concern how Tracy carries actually out his revisionist theological project in accordance with his methodological exposition. In chapter 2, we shall explore Tracy's phenomenological and hermeneutical analyses of two principal sources, common human experience and Christian religious language. In chapter 3, we shall look at Tracy's transcendental (or metaphysical) reflection on God.

---

and Rahner." (*Ibid.*, 82 n.12). The anti-metaphysical philosophical tradition that Tracy has in his mind in this discussion is the analytical philosophy of positivism.

226   *Ibid.*, 68.

# Chapter Two
# The Key Structure of Tracy's Revisionist Model: The Correlation of Human Experience and the Christian Tradition

Our aim in this chapter is to examine Tracy analyses of two principal sources of fundamental theology: common human experience and the Christian texts. The focus of Tracy's analyses is to uncover the *religious* dimension present in these two sources. The importance of these analyses lies in the fact that Tracy's Christian theism (which will be dealt with in the next chapter) is grounded in or developed on the basis of the results of these analyses. In other words, without an exploration of these analyses, it is not possible to have a proper understanding of his revisionist validation of God. Moreover, in his new preface to *Blessed Rage for Order* (1996), he indicates that his analyses of common human experience and Christian religious language (by means of the category of "limit") still remain useful in contemporary postmodern situation.

This chapter consists of two parts. In the first part, we will examine Tracy's phenomenological investigation of human religious experience. In the second part, we will explore his hermeneutical investigation of Christian religious language.

# I. The Uncovering of the Religious Dimension of Common Human Experience

## 1. What is Meant by Human Experience?

Tracy explains that his notion of experience has not much to do with an "empiricist" notion of experience, but rather with a "phenomenological" one.[1] The "empiricist" notion of experience, in Tracy, refers to the "sensationalist" empiricism advocated by the classical British empiricist tradition of David Hume, or the so-called "logical" or "scientific" empiricism advocated by the logical positivists in the beginning of the twentieth century.[2] The key feature of this empiricist tradition is that an appeal to experience means an appeal to the content of "sense-impressions" or "ideas" (thoughts derived from sense-

---

[1]    Tracy clarifies the notion of experience germane to his own Anglo-American context by saying that, "The appeal to 'experience' in philosophies and theologies in the U.S. is a distinctive appeal which, in my observation, seems too often misunderstood by many European commentators. Part of the difficulty is, no doubt, merely semantic. For appeals to experience, from Jonathan Edwards through William James, Josiah Royce, John Dewey, Henry Nelson Wieman, the brothers Niebuhr, John Courtney Murray and beyond is *not* an appeal to an empiricist model of experience as verified sensations. Rather 'experience' is here understood as including also feeling, value, sociality and, in principle understood, therefore, as socially and historically mediated." David Tracy, "The Questions of Pluralism: The Context of the United States," in *Mid-Stream: An Ecumenical Journal* 22 (1983) 273.

[2]    The most important thinkers of the classical British empiricist tradition are John Locke, George Berkeley, David Hume, and John Stuart Mill. The representative proponents of logical positivism (the philosophical movement emanating from the Vienna Circle) are, among others, Moritz Schlick, Rudolf Carnap, Friedrich Waismann, A.J. Ayer, and Ludwig Wittgenstein. For a brief explanation of these traditions of empiricism, see Errol Bedford, "Empiricism" and P.L. Heath, "Logical Positivism," in J.O. Urmson and Jonathan Rée (eds), *The Concise Encyclopedia of Western Philosophy and Philosophers* (London: Unwin Hyman, 1960) respectively 88–90, 182–7. For a critique of the empiricist tradition in the American context, see John E. Smith, *Experience and God* (New York: Oxford University Press, 1974, first published in 1968) 21–45.

impressions) known from the observation of the human mind.[3] The major problem with this tradition, for Tracy, is its restriction of experience to the sensible data perceived by human consciousness and, thereby, its radical subjectivizing or psychologizing of human experience.[4] In other words, in this view, the terrain of experience is reduced to a collection of observable data present to, or found within, an individual consciousness. There is here a neglect of the dimensions or contexts of meaning in which human experience takes place but which belong to experience itself.[5] For Tracy, it is clear that this

3    According to Hume, the human mind consists of nothing but perceptions which are of two kinds, sense-impressions and ideas. The sense-impressions are sensations, feelings, and emotions, and ideas are what we call thoughts, but which are direct or indirect copies of sense-impressions. This means that we never have a simple idea which is not derived from our corresponding sense-impressions. Thus the objects of our thoughts are confined to what we have experienced or might experience through our senses and inner feeling (See D.G.C. MacNabb, "Hume, David," in *The Concise Encyclopedia of Western Philosophy and Philosophers*, 139). The "logical" empiricism advocated by logical positivists began by employing a more logically orientated version of classical empiricism. For the logical positivists, experience can be reduced to its decisive constituents, the "immediate and incorrigible sensory observations of which the observer's world consists. The structure so presented is reflected in language; more precisely, it can be shown by logical analysis that the propositions in which knowledge is expressed are similarly reducible to elementary propositions, corresponding one-to-one with actual or possible items of sense-experience." Hence, what the logical positivists count as sensical or meaningful is exhaustively those propositions "whose truth-or-falsity can be established on formal grounds (i.e., logic and mathematics)," and the propositions which are, or could be, "factually confirmed by verification (or falsification) through sense-experience." Thus, as in the classical empiricism, sense-experience is ultimate for the concept of human experience (P.L. Heath, "Logical Positivism," in *The Concise Encyclopedia of Western Philosophy and Philosophers*, 183).
4    See *BRO*, 64–5, 71, 173–4. For an explanation of this problem, see John E. Smith, *Experience and God*, 23–9. Smith points out that this subjectivizing or psychologizing of experience in classical empiricism is responsible for the inevitable "charge that experience is subjective and insubstantial." (See Smith, *ibid.*, 28).
5    Smith, *ibid.*, 36–9. Smith explains that, "The idea of experience as a succession of data given to and received by an individual mind served to identify the self

empiricist notion is too restricted. Human experience cannot simply be identified as a mere collection of momentary sense-reports recorded within the human mind, without reference to the social, cultural, and historical world which is its living context. For his theological model, Tracy seeks to employ a more integrative notion of experience, which he finds in the phenomenologists' concept of "lived experience."[6] As to their analyses of human experience, the phenomenologists are concerned with concrete, actual experience "as it is *lived in* the world and before it has received eidetic or essential form."[7] The difference between this approach and the empiricist tradition is its central focus on the way that a human being understands herself *in* the actual world within which any human experience subsists and which is its

largely as a theoretical knower of the world and, in turn, reduced the world to the status of a collection of phenomena waiting to be known and explained. Experience was considered solely in terms of content – qualities and their conjunctions as objects – and less attention was paid to the dimensions of experience, the different contexts of meaning within which the items of experience can be said to figure." (*Ibid.*, 36–7).

6   *BRO*, 66. Here, phenomenologists include the central figure in the development of the phenomenological movement, Edmund Husserl, and the so-called existential phenomenologists who were greatly influenced by Husserl, such as Martin Heidegger, Jean-Paul Sartre, and Maurice Merleau-Ponty. For a succinct explanation of these phenomenologists' approaches to experience, see Gilkey, *Naming Whirlwind: The Renewal of God-Language*, 278–82; for a more detailed history of these thinkers, see Herbert Spiegelberg, *The Phenomenological Movements*, 2 vols.

7   Gilkey, *Naming the Whirlwind*, 278 (italics mine). About this concern, Merleau-Ponty writes that, "Scientific points of view, according to which my existence is a moment of the world's, are always both naïve and at the same time dishonest, because they take for granted, without explicitly mentioning it, the other point of view, namely that of consciousness, through which from the outset a world forms itself round me and begins to exist for me. To return to things themselves is to return to that world which precedes knowledge, of which knowledge always *speaks*, and in relation to which every scientific schematization is an abstract and derivative sign-language, as is geography in relation to the country-side in which we have learnt beforehand what a forest, a prairie or a river is." Maurice Merleau-Ponty, *Phenomenology of Perception*, trans. by Colin Smith (London: Routledge, 1996, the first French edition from 1962 appeared under the title, *Phénoménologie de la Perception*) ix.

inalienable horizon.[8] Among existential phenomenologists (such as Heidegger, Sartre, and Merleau-Ponty), the notion of "existing" has replaced "pure consciousness" (the locus of experience in the empiricist tradition and idealism) in such a way that a self exists in the real world "where a contingent self discovers itself in interaction with real things around it."[9] The key mark of the phenomenological notion of experience can be identified as the awareness of the *facticity* (the inalienable presence) of the life-world of experience as its pre-given horizon. Summarily stated, the life-world which manifests itself in any immediate experience is "not what I think, but what I *live through*."[10] This means that the world as an all-inclusive horizon cannot simply be regarded as an objective, external entity.[11] Instead, the world as an all-

8  The development of this approach to human experience is deeply rooted in one of Husserl's central themes, developed towards the end of his life, "the life-world" (*Lebenswelt*). Husserl explains this concept as follows: "The life-world, for us who wakingly live in it, is always already there, existing in advance for us, the 'ground' of all praxis whether theoretical or extratheoretical. The world is pregiven to us, the waking, always somehow practically interested subjects, not occasionally but always and necessarily as the universal field of all actual and possible praxis, as horizon. [...] Waking life is being awake to the world, being constantly and directly 'conscious' of the world and of oneself as living *in* the world, actually experiencing [*erleben*] and actually effecting the ontic certainty of the world. [...] The world [...] does not exist as *an* entity, as an object, but exists with such uniqueness that the plural makes no sense when applied to it. Every plural, and every singular drawn from it, presupposes the world-horizon." Edmund Husserl, *The Crisis of European Sciences and Transcendental Phenomenology*, trans. by David Carr (Evanston: Northwestern University Press, 1970, the first German publication in 1954 under the title, *Die Krisis der europäischen Wissenschaften und die transzendentale Phänomenologie: Eine Einleitung in die phänomenologische Philosophie*) 142–3.

9  Gilkey, *Naming the Whirlwind*, 279 n.19. In addition, for the shift of the center of gravity of phenomenology in Heidegger, Sartre, and Merleau-Ponty from consciousness (Husserl) to existence, see Spiegelberg, *Phenomenological Movement*, vol.I. 271ff.; vol.II. 445ff., 516ff.

10  Merleau-Ponty, *Phenomenology of Perception*, xvi–xvii (italics mine).

11  Husserl claims that the history of our culture since the time of Galileo, prepared for by the creation of Euclidean geometry, reveals a gradual replacing of the world of immediate lived experience (*Lebenswelt*) by an objectively valid world of sciences. See Edmund Husserl, *Experience and Judgment: Investigations in a Genealogy of Logic*, trans. by James S. Churchill and Karl Ameriks (London:

inclusive horizon is the world as *experienced* as an "encompassing frame of reference, without which any account of even a single perception would be incomplete."[12] Therefore, "the theoretical scientific world must find its foundation in the life-world rather than the life-world finding its ultimate justification in scientific theory."[13]

Tracy tries to incorporate this continental phenomenological notion of experience of the life-world into his notion of experience within the Anglo-American context. Tracy describes this integrative concept of experience by such expressions as, "the self's non-sensuous experience of the self," or "experience as a self-in-a-world," or "the immediate lived experience of the self."[14] In these expressions, the concept, "self," represents a human subject as a whole existence, socially and historically related to the life-world, which is distinct from the empiricist, non-temporal, non-relational, pure consciousness endowed with senses. Tracy's concept of "common human experience," which serves as the principal source of his revisionist model, and as the basis of his Christian theism, should be understood in terms of this phenomenological background. Basing himself on this understanding of experience, Tracy attempts to elucidate the presence of the "autonomous *religious* dimension"[15] operative in common human experience. Put differently, the task is, for him, to explicate *religious experience* as an "immediate" or "lived" common human experience *without*, or *prior to*, appealing to any specialized experience of a particular explicit religious tradition. This suggests an important primary question, namely, how to *anthropologically* or *philosophically* define the meaning of "*religious*." Let us look at Tracy's criterion for the meaning of "*religious*."

Routledge and Kegan Paul, 1973, originally published in 1948 under the title, *Erfahrung und Urteil: Untersuchungen zur Genealogie der Logik*) 44.

12   Spiegelberg, *Phenomenological Movement*, vol.I, 161.
13   Joseph J. Kockelmans, Introduction to "IX. Life-World and World-Experiencing Life," in idem (ed.), *Phenomenology: The Philosophy of Edmund Husserl and Its Interpretation* (New York: A Doubleday Garden City, 1967) 196.
14   *BRO*, 66.
15   *Ibid.*, 143 n.72.

## 2. The Concept of "Limit" As a Key Criterion for the Meaning of "Religious"

For defining a characteristic of "religious," Tracy uses the concept of "limit" as a key anthropological or philosophical criterion. It is not an exaggeration to say that Tracy's whole analysis of the two main sources (common human experience and language, and the Christian texts)[16] hinges on the concept of "limit." Therefore, it is worthwhile, at first, to shortly discuss the philosophical background of Tracy's employment of this concept.

Tracy mentions that the concept of "limit" used in his analysis is related to the classical Kantian motif explaining religion.[17] He describes his analysis of the religious dimension as the "revisionist return to Kant via a reinterpretation of the category 'limit'."[18] However, in his own analysis, Tracy does not offer any detailed explanation of how his concept of "limit" is associated with the Kantian motif. The only way that we can understand this relationship is, first, to look at the Kantian motif of "limit," and, then, to examine how it is at work in Tracy's actual analysis. Our need to discuss this relationship lies in the fact that it sheds light on some important features of Tracy's understanding of the meaning of "religious." Let us begin by looking at the Kantian motif of "limit."

---

16    In his actual analysis of the first source, common human experience and language, Tracy's predominant concern is with human experience. The matter of language is quite minimally mentioned by Tracy, which is enough to be disregarded in our examination. Therefore, hereafter in our examination, the first source of Tracy's revisionist theology designates only common human experience.

17    Tracy mentions two relevant works of Kant: *Critique of Practical Reason and Other Writings in Moral Philosophy* (Chicago: University of Chicago Press, 1949); *Religion Within the Limits of Reason Alone* (New York: Harper and Row, 1960).

18    *BRO*, 115 n.51.

According to Kevin J. Vanhoozer, the "idea of limits may be the 'soul' of the Kantian philosophy."[19] It is well known that Kant is a representative Enlightenment thinker who attempts a critical inquiry into the *limits* of the competency of human reason. As to theoretical knowledge, the consequence of his limitation of the competency of human reason is to rule out virtually as unknowable the so-called principal, traditional, metaphysical questions such as 'the existence of God,' 'the immortality of the soul,' and 'the freedom' of will.'[20] In other words, those 'transcendent' questions are considered as insoluble within the competency of human cognition (pure reason) because they cannot be checked by our possible experience or *a priori* cognitive constitution.[21] An interesting element to be noted here,

19    Kevin J. Vanhoozer, "Philosophical Antecedents to Ricoeur's *Time and Narrative*," in David Wood (ed.), *On Paul Ricoeur: Narrative and Interpretation* (London: Routledge, 1991) 39.

20    Kant states that, "I cannot even assume God, freedom and immortality for the sake of the necessary practical use of my reason unless I simultaneously deprive speculative reason of its pretension to extravagant insights; because in order to attain to such insights, speculative reason would have to help itself to principles that in fact reach only to objects of possible experience, and which, if they were to be applied to what cannot be an object of experience, then they would always actually transform it into an appearance, and thus declare all practical extension of pure reason to be impossible. Thus I had to deny knowledge in order to make room for faith." Kant, *Critique of Pure Reason*, trans. by Paul Guyer and Allen W. Wood (Cambridge: Cambridge University Press, 1997) 117. On this point, cf. Henry E. Allison, "Kant, Immanuel," in Ted Honderich (ed.), *The Oxford Companion to Philosophy* (Oxford: Oxford University Press, 1995) 435–8, especially 436.

21    Kant writes that, "To cognize an object, it is required that I be able to prove its possibility (whether by the testimony of experience from its actuality or *a priori* [cognition] through reason)." (Kant, *Critique of Pure Reason*, 115). In this regard, Kant's famous phrase, "transcendental illusion" refers to the misuse of the faculty of human cognition, which "contrary to all the warnings of criticism, carries us away beyond the empirical use of the categories, and holds out to us the semblance of extending the pure understanding." (*Ibid.*, 385). Cf. P.F. Srawson, "Metaphysics" in J.O. Urmson and Jonathan Rée (eds), *The Concise Encyclopedia of Western Philosophy and Philosophers* (London: Unwin Hyman, 1960) 202–8.

however, one which is our focal concern in this discussion, is the double-dimensional character of Kantian thinking regarding the limit of human cognition. That is to say that Kant's critique of the capacity of human (pure) reason contains two dimensions. Namely, on the one hand, his critique has a *"negative* utility" in the sense that it clarifies and determines the *limits* of its use. On the other hand, his critique, affirms Kant, simultaneously serves a *"positive* utility."[22] Kant explains that:

> A critique that limits the speculative use of reason is, to be sure, to that extent *negative*, but because it simultaneously removes an obstacle that limits or even threatens to wipe out the practical use of reason, this critique is also in fact of *positive* and very important utility, as soon as we have convinced ourselves that there is an *absolutely necessary* practical use of pure reason (the *moral* use), in which reason unavoidably extends itself beyond the boundaries of sensibility, without needing any assistance from speculative reason, but in which it must also be made secure against any counteraction from the latter, in order not to fall into contradiction with itself.[23]

Interestingly enough, Kant explains this ambivalent character of his critique by using the metaphor of the police's job whose chief task is to "put a stop to the violence that citizens have to fear from other citizens [negative utility], so that each can carry on his own affairs in peace and safety [positive utility]."[24] In this metaphor, the police's *negative* utility signifies the usefulness of the critique of pure reason which functions as a critical safeguard against all transcendental adventures which overstep the limit of human cognition. However, at the very limit of this immanence, Kant, simultaneously, permits himself a glimpse of a *positive* way to think *beyond* the limit.[25] The

22 For the negative and positive utilities, see Kant, *Critique of Pure Reason*, 114–15.
23 *Ibid.*, 114 (italics mine). The issue of how the "absolutely necessary practical use of pure reason (the moral use)" is possible, is the central theme of Kant's second critique, *Critique of Practical Reason*.
24 Kant, *Critique of Pure Reason*, 115.
25 William Desmond portrays this ambivalent posture of Kant in the following manner: "Kant stands at the boundary of immanence, a forbidding angel with a flaming torch, and few have passed beyond his border post since that torch first blazed. I find some vacillation in his virtual dialectic. Kant may stand guard at

positive way is, for Kant, a way of morality which can open a path to think beyond immanence towards the ultimate end (*summum bonum*) and, eventually, God as its guarantor.[26] Ralf Meerbote explains this two-way thinking of Kant by saying that:

> The self-same reason which is operative in knowledge of nature ('theoretical reason') will now as ('practical reason') also be seen to be at work in such agency, in the moral character of some of our actions, and in non-theoretical justifications of religious beliefs such as faith in the existence of God.[27]

In Kant's moral use of reason, we can notice the return a transcendental adventure which he tries to deconstruct as "illusion" in his criticism of pure reason. A new breakthrough to the transcendent is attempted by another (moral) way of thinking. With regard to this double way of thinking in Kant, William Desmond comments in the following way:

---

> the boundary but he permits himself some furtive peeks across it, and with the illumination of his flame." William Desmond, *God and the Between* (forthcoming, Faculty of Philosophy, K.U. Leuven, Leuven, 2002) 92.

26  This way of justifying God, in Kant, does not amount to a theoretical proof. Rather, "Kant puts forward the ideas of immortality and God as postulates; they make no theoretical, cognitive claims; we have to think *as if*. [...] Kant is deeply diffident about making a direct and affirmative claim" of God (Desmond, *God and the Between*, 100). In short, Kant takes an indirect approach to justifying God in such a way that God has to arise as a necessary postulate relative to our *moral* being. Then, why is Kant deeply reserved to make a direct claim regarding God? According to Desmond, Kant is "so to say, a negative moral theologian, in letting God escape beyond our claims of necessary knowing." (*Ibid.*, 101). However, immediately, Desmond asks, "Does he [Kant] respect the reserve of God, release God from the idolizations of dogmatic reason? Even so, can Kant's *as if* argument escape being what he calls a transcendental 'subreption' – attributing to what is other what is more truly of ourselves?" (*Ibid.*). In other words, the question is whether "God is not to be measured on the scale of our moral justice." Desmond claims that Kant's postulated God is "the mirror image of the rationally self-determining moral agent who deserves to be rewarded because he [sic] has struggled and worked hard to be the good person he [sic] undoubtedly is." (Desmond, *ibid.*, 102).

27  Ralf Meerbote, "Kant," in Robert L. Arrington (ed.), *A Companion to the Philosophers* (Oxford and Malden: Blackwell Publishers Ltd., 1999) 345–6.

I see Kant as a philosopher of supreme tension: committed to respect what he saw at the limit, and yet impelled to think at the boundary of the limit, and indeed beyond. [...] He is *between* finitude and infinity, though he often masks that intermediacy in a manner more intent on securing coherent univocity *within* the between, and letting the equivocal darkness beyond take care of itself. In truth, however, these two sides cannot be kept from each other in an uncontaminated purity.[28]

Why, then, is the new way of breakthrough to the transcendent or the ultimate necessarily attempted by Kant? Even though Kant attempts to "purify" traditional metaphysics by means of the criticism of human reason itself, nevertheless, he cannot put a limit to the natural and inextinguishable metaphysical thrust of human reason. In other words, Kant cannot but acknowledge that human beings cannot resist the urge to think beyond, to think the ultimate, even though their theoretical knowledge of the nature and being of the ultimate is denied by an epistemic limit.[29] In short, there is an undeniable mindfulness of the transcendent beyond the limits of finitude and contingency of human reason. This tensile aspect is well represented by Kant's famous saying that, "Even if we cannot *cognize* these same objects as things in themselves, we at least must be able to *think* them as things in themselves."[30] Kant states:

I can *think* whatever I like, [...] as long as my concept is a possible thought, even if I cannot give any assurance whether or not there is a corresponding object somewhere within the sum total of all possibilities. But in order to ascribe objective validity to such a concept [...] something more is required.

28    Desmond, *God and the Between*, 97.
29    For an explanation of Kant's view of the insatiability of human reason's quest beyond limits, see Nicholas Rescher, *Kant's Theory of Knowledge and Reality* (Washington: University Press of America, Inc, 1983) 65–82.
30    Kant, *Critique of Pure Reason*, 115 (italics mine). As to the insatiability of human reason, Kant writes that, "The transcendental object lying at the ground of appearances, and with it the ground why our sensibility has it rather than another supreme condition – these are and remain inscrutable for us, even though the thing itself is given, only we have no insight into it. An ideal of pure reason, *however*, cannot be called *inscrutable*, because it has to display no further credentials for its reality than the need of reason to complete all synthetic unity by means of it." (*Ibid.*, 574, italics mine).

This 'more,' however, need not be sought in theoretical sources of cognition; it may also lie in *practical* ones.[31]

In short, for Kant, "metaphysics as knowing may be off limits, but morals as metaphysics takes us legitimately beyond the epistemic limit, and opens the way to God."[32] Desmond emphatically portrays this ambivalence of Kant's thinking that maintains both "deconstructive" and "reconstructive" moments as follows:

> Now Kant the destroyer of metaphysics, now Kant the reconstructer of metaphysics. Now Kant the destroyer of God, now Kant the defender of God. Now Kant is *as if* A, and now Kant is *as if non-*A. This is a mark of the equivocal: it feeds on a *two-way seeing*, or wavering or oscillation between them. Kant explicitly enjoins us to look in two ways, as if both could be assumed.[33]

### Tracy's Revisionist Interpretation of the Kantian Motif of "Limit"

Prior to examining Tracy's reinterpretation of the Kantian motif for his own purpose, we need to briefly mention an important qualification of the concept of "limit" that Tracy presupposes in his analysis.

As we already pointed out, Tracy employs the concept of "limit" as an essential category to define the meaning of "religious." Tracy qualifies the concept of "limit" in such a way that it is employed to be "*a* characteristic, not a universal definition of religion."[34] That is to say, the concept of "limit" does not preclude other possible categories characterizing the meaning of "religious." Aware of the difficulty and the illegitimacy of attempting a single universal definition of religion (or the religious perspective) in such a pluralistic situation as today,[35]

31     *Ibid.*, 115 (italics mine).
32     Desmond, *God and the Between*, 98.
33     *Ibid.*, 104.
34     *BRO*, 111 n.11.
35     According to Tracy, the main reasons for such difficulty and illegitimacy are: 1. the phenomenon of conflict in modern interpretations of religion (viz., the interpretations of religion as "illusion" and "projection" by Feuerbach, Marx, Nietzsche and Freud; religion as grounded in human universal experience by Schleiermacher, Otto, Tillich, Eliade, and Dupré; the sociological reality of religion in Weber, Durkheim, Mark and Troeltsch; the psychological reality of

Tracy explains that his aim here is to elucidate an essential factor which characterizes "a *religious* as distinct from a moral, an aesthetic, a scientific, or a political perspective."[36] Tracy states:

> I have come to believe that the concept "limit" can be used as a key (but not exhaustive) category for describing certain signal characteristics peculiar to any language or experience with a properly religious dimension. Whether that dimension be explicit or implicit is not, in fact, the central issue. My contention will be that all significant explicitly religious language and experience (the "religions") and all significant implicitly religious characteristics of our common experience (the "religious dimension") will bear at least the "family resemblance" of articulating or implying a limit-experience, a limit-language, or a limit-dimension.[37]

Regarding Tracy's reinterpretation of the Kantian motif of "limit" for his own purpose, the most notable element is Tracy's presentation of the concept of "limit" in *two* modalities. Tracy deals with the concept of "limit" as expressive of two dimensions, such as "limit-to" and "limit-of." By the "limit-to" dimension, Tracy means the human boundary situations which serve as limits to our ordinary experience, such as "finitude, contingency, or radical transience."[38] The "limit-of" dimension refers to "certain fundamental structures of our existence *beyond* (or, alternatively, grounding to) that ordinary experience (e.g., our fundamental trust in the worthwhileness of existence, our basic belief in order and value)."[39] Put differently, although Tracy uses the same term, "limit" in the two modalities, it represents different meanings. In the first modality ("limit-to"), the

religion in Freud and Jung, etc.); 2. the recognition that western definitions of religion are culturally bound to Christianity and cannot be "universally" applied to other religious traditions (See *AI*, 156–9).

36  *BRO*, 93 (italics mine). Tracy states that this modest posture is aligned with Wittgenstein's idea of "family resemblance" for characterizing something based not on common essence but a network of similarities which together sufficiently distinguish one cluster from another. For the explanation of religion as a family-resemblance concept, see John Hick, *An Interpretation of Religion* (New Haven and London: Yale University Press, 1989) 3–5.

37  *BRO*, 93.

38  *Ibid.*

39  *Ibid.*, (italics mine).

term, "limit," refers to a "boundary" or "limitation." In the second modality ("limit-of"), the same term, "limit," means "the fundamental" or "the final." As we shall see more clearly in discussing Tracy's Christian theism, God is, for him, explicated as the *referent* of the reality of "*limit-of*" by a transcendental or metaphysical formulation. In other words, God is affirmed as the sole *necessary reality* to account for (or the guarantor of) "our fundamental trust in the worthwhileness of existence" or "our belief in order and value" ("*limit-of*" dimension).[40] How, then, in Tracy, are these two dimensions ("limit-to" and "limit-of") linked in actual human experience? In other words, how does one move from one's finite boundary experiences ("limit-to" dimension) to thinking or experiencing the reality of "the final" or "the ultimate" ("limit-of" dimension)? According to Tracy, it is in our inextinguishable thrust towards "self-transcendence."[41] Tracy explains that we, human beings, live authentically insofar as we do not cease to allow ourselves an "expanding horizon."[42] "That expansion has as its chief aim the going-beyond one's own state," with the thrust at "some reality beyond ourselves, our desires, needs, fears, and even acts of understanding."[43] Thus, the reality beyond is not "constructed" by our own wishes, but "demanded" by our cognitive, moral, existential, and communal self-transcendence.[44]

---

40    Tracy claims that the task of fundamental theology is to state metaphysically "the abstract, general, universal and necessary features of the reality of God as the one *necessary existent* which can account for the reality of a *limit-of*, ground-to, horizon-to the whole disclosed in earlier phenomenological accounts." *AI*, 161 (italics mine).

41    *BRO*, 97. Concerning the concept of "self-transcendence," Tracy relies on Bernard Lonergan's notion which is indebted to Kant. See Lonergan, *Method in Theology*, 104–5. We will deal with the idea of "self-transcendence" in more detail in Tracy's reflection on "limit-questions" to our scientific enterprises.

42    *BRO*, 96.

43    *Ibid.*, 96–7. This view of Tracy (as shown in Kant) recalls William Desmond's remark that in our actual existence, the two sides, our experience of *finitude* and our inevitable mindfulness of *infinity*, "cannot be kept from each other in an uncontaminated purity." (Desmond, *God and the Between*, 97).

44    *BRO*, 97.

Summarily stated, concerning Tracy's reinterpretation of the Kantian motif of "limit," we can point out three related elements. Firstly, in Tracy's *two modalities* of the category of "limit," we can notice a reinterpretation of Kantian *two-way* thinking that oscillates between finitude and infinity.[45] With the concept of "limit," Tracy attempts to illumine not only human contingent boundary situations ("limit-to"), but also to elucidate the final or ultimate horizon without reference to which, for him, the question of human existence cannot be totally accounted for ("limit-of"). The distinctiveness of Tracy is that he regards the category of "limit" within a broader horizon than does Kant. Whereas the Kantian motif chiefly has an epistemological character, Tracy uses the category at a cognitive, moral, and existential level.

Secondly, Tracy's two-modality analysis, as reminiscent of Kant's two-way thinking, serves to show a path to an "ultimate" horizon and, eventually, God. Whereas, in Kant, the "ultimate" horizon is the ultimate good (*summum bonum*), in Tracy, it is our *fundamental* faith or trust in the worth of existence. Whereas, in Kant, God is the *necessary postulate* as the guarantor of the ultimate good, in Tracy, God is the *necessary referent* as the guarantor of our fundamental faith in the worth of existence. For Tracy, God is *demanded* as a *necessary existent* in order to explicate our fundamental faith in the final meaning and worth of human existence.[46] However, Tracy differentiates his ideas of the "ultimate" horizon and God from the Kantian ones which are restrictedly "moralized." For Tracy, the religious realm and God should be elucidated at a more

---

45   It should be noted that Tracy's two-modality reformulation is reminiscent of Kantian two-way thinking but contains its own distinctiveness which is not traced in Kant. This distinctiveness will be discussed in the next chapter.

46   We can see here that Tracy's understanding of God is aligned with the Kantian reasoning, viz., God is the *necessary postulate* as the condition of or ground to our (moral) being. An important question that should be raised here is whether Tracy's understanding of God can be free from the same kind of criticism of the Kantian understanding of God (viz., the criticism that the Kantian God is the "mirror image of the rationally self-determining moral agent") (Desmond, *God and the Between*, 102). We can ask here whether Tracy's God is not the "mirror image of the rationally self-determining" secular liberal agent.

integrative (cognitive, moral, existential, and communal) horizon than a purely ethical one.

Thirdly, for Tracy, the idea of the human thrust towards *self-transcendence* is essential for explaining the fundamental condition for our "thinking beyond," or the metaphysical exigence of the "ultimate" horizon and God. This idea is shown in Kant as an insatiable metaphysical impulse of human reason. For Tracy, human *self-transcendence* is vital to *mediate* the relationship between the finite realm and the ultimate realm. A key implication of this mediation is, for him, that the "religious" dimension mediated by self-transcendence falls within the human horizon, not within an other-worldly order.

Tracy is convinced that the use of the category of "limit" will serve to articulate the *religious* dimension of both common human experience and the Christian texts, without relying on any confessional, theological or dogmatic auspice.[47] He believes that the category of "limit" can be eminently useful to liberate a *religious* dimension from two inadequate perspectives: namely, on the one hand, by helping us to understand the religious dimension as an authentic human dimension free from a trans-worldly, super-natural, or ethereal world of fantasy; and, on the other hand, by warning us against any domestication of the religious dimension as a sheer ethical, aesthetic, or pseudo-scientific one as shown in the modern liberal tradition.[48] Our main concern with Tracy's analysis of the religious dimension of the two sources will be to examine how Tracy

---

47    It is in such a way that he intends to make his investigation of the two main sources meet his revisionist methodological principle presented in the preceding chapter, viz., taking a critical and scientific methodological procedure for public intelligibility, not trading on any confessional, authoritative, or dogmatic category. Recall Tracy's claim that the defense of the Christian understanding of God, "for the fundamental theologian at least, must be conducted on grounds other than his own or his community's vision of faith, or even his own or his community's defense of the continuing existential meaningfulness of religious experience and language." (*BRO*, 147).

48    This conviction recalls the aim of his revisionist theological model which intends to move beyond both an "anti-secular, religious supernaturalism" and "anti-Christian secularism." (See *ibid.*, 33).

actually demonstrates this possibility. We will first look at Tracy's analysis of the religious dimension of common human experience aided by his "limit" category.


## 3. "Limit-Questions" and "Limit-Situations" in Common Human Experience

Tracy's analysis of the religious dimension of common human experience consists in a three-dimensional investigation. Tracy intends to approach common human experience from three different aspects: cognitive, ethical, and existential. Accordingly, our investigation comprises: (1) reflection on "limit-questions" that arise within our scientific enterprises (cognitive aspect); (2) reflection on "limit-questions" that arise within our moral enterprises (ethical aspect); (3) reflection on "limit-situations" that arise within our everyday lives (existential aspect).

Tracy employs diverse sources (philosophical traditions) to analyze the religious dimension of each aspect. In fact, he relies on a different philosophical tradition for each analysis: the first analysis utilizes the transcendental method of Bernard Lonergan; the second analysis, the linguistic philosophy of Stephen Toulmin; and the third analysis, the existential phenomenology of Karl Jaspers and Martin Heidegger. Methodologically speaking, the employment of such a diverse range of philosophical traditions is, according to him, a way to make his analysis justified in a more public and convincing manner. Tracy writes that, "Such a pluralist choice [of philosophical traditions] may serve to provide more convincing evidence for the claim to a religious dimension that bears the logical meaning of limit and the existential weight of disclosive meaningfulness."[49] Let us look at the first analysis which concerns the religious dimension disclosed in our scientific enterprises.


49    *Ibid.*, 94.

*Reflection on Limit-Questions Disclosed in Our Scientific Enterprises*[50]

For this analysis, Tracy begins by thinking about the relationship between religion and science. Tracy observes that for describing the relationship between religion and science, variations of the so-called "two-language" approach have prevailed among most contemporary scientific and religious thinkers.[51] However, he wants to pay attention to a more recent position, the so-called "mediating" approach. The "mediating" approach claims that "there are significant similarities between the two disciplines," so much so that it argues "not only for the scientific study of religion (a commonplace) but also for a

50    Tracy notes that his term, "limit-questions," comes from Stephen Toulmin's expression, "limiting questions" used in Toulmin's book, *An Examination of the Place of Reason in Ethics* (Cambridge: Cambridge University Press, 1958, first published in 1950) 204–11. Toulmin characterizes "limiting questions" as "questions expressed in a form borrowed from a familiar mode of reasoning, but not doing the job which they normally do within that mode of reasoning. It is characteristic of them that only a small change is required, either in the form of the question, or in the context in which it is asked, in order to bring it unquestionably back into the scope of its apparent mode of reasoning. But it is equally characteristic of them that the way of answering suggested by the form of words employed will never completely satisfy the questioner, so that he continues to ask the question even after the resources of the apparent mode of reasoning have been exhausted. Questions of this kind I shall refer to as 'limiting questions'." (Toulmin, *ibid.*, 205).

51    The "two language" approach here refers to the position that "both fields [religion and science] have their own specific data, methods, and languages," based on Wittgenstein's theory of the "language game." (*BRO*, 94). Tracy explains two examples of the variation of the "two language" approach. "On the one hand, many linguistic philosophers argue that religious language is 'participant' or 'self-involving' language (Austin, Evans) in a manner which scientific language as 'spectatorial' cannot be. On the other hand, most religious thinkers influenced by neo-orthodox theology hold to their own variation of the two-language approach. Karl Barth, as the clearest exponent of this variously articulated position, held that theology is concerned only and solely with 'revelation' and is therefore neither encouraged nor distressed by the 'neutral' discoveries of science." (*Ibid.*, 95).

94

'religious dimension' to science itself."[52] Tracy focuses on the argument of Bernard Lonergan as the best example of the "mediating" approach. Lonergan's "mediating" approach is preeminently found in his development of the model of "self-transcendence." First, we will briefly look at Lonergan's model of "self-transcendence" which is essential for Lonergan's analysis of human scientific enterprises. Then, we will examine how Tracy incorporates it in his own analysis.

*Bernard Lonergan's Model of "Self-Transcendence"*

According to Lonergan, the human spirit has a "transcendental tendency" towards unrestricted questioning, granted that we are not confined to a habitat, but live in a universe, a world of meaning.[53] Lonergan's development of the model of "self-transcendence" based on the human transcendental tendency consists of three levels.

On the first level, "self-transcendence" is operative in our questions for *intelligence*. These are the questions of what, why, and how. Scientifically fruitful answers depend on our intellectual ability to "unify and relate, classify and construct, serialize and generalize" the relevant data.[54] In this process, we experience a "self-transcendence"

---

52   *Ibid.* Tracy points out some of the cultural factors which influence the emergence of this "mediating" position. "The gradual and steady reemergence of the positive need for symbol and even myth has rendered earlier discussions of demythologizing in accordance with the prevailing scientific world-view not so much incorrect as incomplete. The recurrent pattern of technological and ecological crises has rendered the curiously optimistic and manipulative 'end ideology' discussions of the 1950s as dated as other old-war rhetoric of that period." (*Ibid.*, 95–6). For the representative thinkers of this position, Tracy adduces Ian Barbour, Bernard Meland, Schubert Ogden (process philosophy); Bernard Lonergan (transcendental method); Michael Polanyi, Langdon Gilkey (general reflection on scientific method); Louis Dupré, Paul Ricoeur (phenomenology); Stephen Toulmin (linguistic philosophy).

53   Lonergan, *Method in Theology*, 103–4. Lonergan's idea of the human "transcendental tendency" recalls Kant's saying that "human reason has the peculiar fate in one species of its cognitions that it is burdened with questions which it cannot dismiss, since they are given to it as problems by the nature of reason itself." (Kant, *Critique of Pure Reason*, 99).

54   Lonergan, *Method in Theology*, 104.

in such a wise that we move "from the narrow strip of space-time accessible to immediate experience towards the construction of a world-view and towards the exploration of what we ourselves could be and could do."[55]

The second level of "self-transcendence" has to do with reflecting on "the nature of *reflection*."[56] The first level concerns a fruitful inquiry by means of the faculty of intelligence which results in certain definitions, formulations, or hypotheses. In this second stage, the question at stake is what our intellectual activities refer to? In other words, "to reflect on reflection is to ask just what happens when we marshal and weigh the evidence for pronouncing that this probably is so and that probably is not so."[57] What happens in our working on the evidence is a process of grasping "the sufficiency of the evidence for a prospective judgment."[58] Lonergan states that "to marshal the evidence is to ascertain whether all the conditions are fulfilled. To weigh the evidence is to ascertain whether the fulfilment of the conditions certainly or probably involves the existence or occurrence of the conditioned."[59] This process of reflection eventually elicits "judgments" by rational compulsion.[60] In his technical terminology, Lonergan calls the judgments elicited based on the sufficiency of the evidence, "virtually unconditioned."[61] "A virtually unconditioned is a conditioned whose conditions are all fulfilled."[62] According to Lonergan, in this reflective process to reach a "virtually unconditioned," we, in effect, enter into "self-transcendence" at another level. Lonergan explains:

---

55    *Ibid.*
56    *Ibid.*, 101.
57    *Ibid.* Tracy formulates the possible questions at this level in the following way: "Is it so? Why? For what reason? By what criteria? With what force of evidence?" (*BRO*, 97).
58    Lonergan, *Insight*, 279.
59    Lonergan, *Method in Theology*, 102.
60    Lonergan, *Insight*, 279.
61    *Ibid.*, 281. See also *Method in Theology*, 102.
62    Lonergan, *Method in Theology*, 102. According to Lonergan, since a "virtually unconditioned" fulfills its conditions, it is not *intrinsically* but "*de facto* absolute." (Lonergan, *Insight*, 378).

We move beyond imagination and guess-work, idea and hypothesis, theory and system, to ask whether or not this really is so or that really could be. Now self-transcendence takes on a new meaning. Not only does it go beyond the subject but also it seeks what is independent of the subject. For a judgment that this or that is so reports, not what appears to me, not what I imagine, not what I think, not what I wish, not what I would be inclined to say, not what seems to me, but what is so.[63]

The third (final) level of our questioning is concerned with deliberating on the *ethical* values of our scientific discoveries. The question at stake is "whether this or that is worth while [sic]."[64] Lonergan explains that "self-transcendence" at the first and second levels is only cognitive, that is, in the order of knowing. However, the final level of questioning is in the order of doing in which "self-transcendence becomes moral."[65] When we ask whether this or that is worthwhile, or truly good, we are searching not for our own needs, but for "objective value."[66] Lonergan states that, "Because we can ask such questions, and answer them, and live by the answers, we can effect in our living a moral self-transcendence."[67]

In his development of the model of "self-transcendence," Lonergan indicates an important element which is involved with it. According to him, at each level of "self-transcendence," the trans-cendental quality of our unrestricted questioning inevitably leads us to the question of God. Lonergan formulates the question of God which emerges at each level in the following way.

At the first level, we search for the possibility of scientifically fruitful inquiry which satisfies our intelligence. In this inquiry, we implicitly presuppose that the universe is intelligible. Lonergan claims that, "Once that is granted, there arises the question whether the universe could be intelligible without having an intelligent ground."[68] For him, this question is nothing but the question of God.

63    Lonergan, *Method in Theology*, 104.
64    *Ibid.*
65    *Ibid.*
66    *Ibid.*
67    *Ibid.*
68    *Ibid.*, 101.

At the second level, our questioning is concerned with reaching a judgment as "virtually unconditioned" viz., a conditioned that has no unfulfilled conditions. According to Lonergan, the process of our eliciting a "virtually unconditioned" judgment might impel us toward a further thrust. In other words, unless the "virtually unconditioned" is not self-substantiated, the scientific inquirer might ask about the possibility of a "formally unconditioned," viz., an unconditioned "which has no conditions at all, [which] stands outside the interlocked field of conditioning and conditioned."[69] Lonergan explains that the questioning regarding the "formally unconditioned" is the question of a necessary being, namely, the question of God.

At the third level, our questions concerning the ethical values of our scientific discoveries also lead to the question of a transcendent. According to Lonergan, our moral self-transcendence is "the possibility of benevolence and beneficence, of honest collaboration and of true love."[70] This moral "self-transcendence" leads us to ask the necessary *ground* of such possibilities of our moral consciousness. For him, such a question is the question of God.

In short, for Lonergan, the question of God is an inevitable consequence of the transcendental thrust of the human spirit. The human transcendental impulse drives us to ask about the intelligible, the unconditioned, the good of value, and, finally, the necessary ground of all these inquiries. Lonergan states:

> It [the question of God] arises out of our conscious intentionality, out of the *a priori* structured drive that promotes us from experiencing to the effort to understand, from understanding to the effort to judge truly, from judging to the

69  Lonergan, *Insight*, 378. Lonergan explains that whereas the virtually unconditioned is *de facto* absolute, the formally unconditioned is "intrinsically absolute." (*Ibid.*). The seminal idea of Lonergan's discussion of the virtually and formally unconditioned can be found in Kant: "for a given conditioned reason demands an absolute totality on the side of the conditions (under which the understanding subjects all appearances to synthetic unity). [...] Reason demands this in accordance with the principle: if the conditioned is given, then the whole sum of conditions, and hence the absolutely unconditioned, is also given, through which alone the conditioned was possible." (Kant, *Critique of Pure Reason*, 461).

70  Lonergan, *Method in Theology*, 104.

98

effort to choose rightly. In the measure that we advert to our own questioning and proceed to question it, there arises the question of God.[71]

According to Lonergan, insofar as the question of God is not a matter of knowing, but of intending by our *a priori* orientation, it is transcultural. The various ideas of God among atheists, agnostics, and humanists are the different expressions of God in different phases of historical and cultural development. Lonergan claims that however different the questions of God raised in different religious cultures, however different their answers, still, at the root of the human spirit, there is an undeniable native impulse towards the divine. Therefore, the question of God lies within the human reflective horizon, and, thereby, beyond cultural and religious differences.[72]

*Tracy's Reinterpretation of Lonergan's Model of "Self-Transcendence"*

Tracy observes, in Lonergan's model of "self-transcendence," the possibility to discuss the presence of the religious dimension operative in scientific enterprises. The key point of Tracy's reinterpretation of Lonergan's model is his translation of Lonergan's questions of God into the "limit-questions" of scientific enterprises. Tracy's funda-

---

71  *Ibid.*, 103.

72  Lonergan claims that, "The question of God, then, lies within man's [sic] horizon. Man's transcendental subjectivity is mutilated or abolished, unless he is stretching forth towards the intelligible, the unconditioned, the good of value. The reach, not of his attainment, but of his intending is unrestricted. There lies within his horizon a region for the divine, a shrine for ultimate holiness. It cannot be ignored. The atheist may pronounce it empty. The agnostic may urge that he finds his investigation has been inconclusive. The contemporary humanist will refuse to allow the question to arise. But their negations presuppose the spark in our clod, our native orientation to the divine." (*Ibid.*). Our problem here with Lonergan's claim is that he assumes that the divine or the ultimate intended by the human transcendental thrust is God. However, it is a known fact that human orientation to the divine or the ultimate is not necessarily formulated as the question of God in some other non-theistic religious traditions. For instance, Buddhism and Taoism are non-theistic traditions which do not presuppose any idea of God, but which are distinct from atheism in the western tradition.

mental claim is that unless a scientific inquirer deliberately refuses the urge to self-transcendence in his or her inquiries, he or she, at the final moment, cannot avoid the limit-question of the ultimate horizon which cannot but be called religious. Following Lonergan's model, Tracy reformulates the limit-questions of scientific inquiries at each level of "self-transcendence" in the following way.

At the first level of the questions for *intelligence*, according to Tracy, a scientific inquirer can ask the question of both a "limit-to" his or her inquiry and a "limit-of" his or her intellectual intending. For example, a "limit-to" question can be formulated as, "Can these answers work if the world is not intelligible?"[73] A "limit-of" question can be, "Can the world be intelligible if it does not have an intelligent ground?"[74] For him, the focal "limit-questions" at this "self-trans-cendence" level are the "conditions of possibility" for one's scientific inquiry.[75] According to Tracy, the limit-questions which touch on the issues of the condition of intellectual activity and of the *ultimate ground* for intelligibility manifest a *religious* dimension operative in our scientific inquiries.

With regard to the second level, Tracy reinterprets Lonergan's questioning for eliciting prospective judgments as "virtually uncon-ditioned" and "formally unconditioned" as limit-questions. For in-stance, once a scientific inquirer reaches a "virtually unconditioned" judgment [i.e., a conditioned whose scientific conditions are all fulfilled], he or she "might also ask whether there can be any virtually unconditioned judgments unless there exists also a formally uncon-ditioned (i.e., an unconditioned in the strict sense of no conditions whatsoever)."[76] For Tracy, such a question for a "formally uncon-ditioned" is a limit-question. For it concerns "an unconditioned 'yes' or 'no'" that we ought to presuppose to elicit any scientific judg-ment.[77] In other words, to ask such a question is to reflect on "a fact, a reality, a truth not constructed by our own needs but demanded by our

73    *BRO*, 98.
74    *Ibid.*
75    *Ibid.*
76    *Ibid.*
77    *Ibid.*, 97.

critical intelligence."[78] The self-transcending quality contained in this limit-question is, for Tracy, suggestive of the presence of the religious dimension in our scientific inquiries.

As to the questions at the third level, which concern moral "self-transcendence," Tracy very briefly reformulates them as limit-questions in the following way:

> Is it worthwhile to ask whether our goal, purposes, and ideals are themselves worthwhile (a limit-to question)? Can we understand and affirm such a demand for worthwhileness without affirming an intelligent, rational, responsible source and ground for them (a limit-of question)?[79]

In sum, Tracy's central argument is that no serious reflective inquirer can be free from the self-transcending process in his or her scientific inquiries in view of our human innate transcendental drive. This self-transcending impulse leads one to ask the limit-questions regarding "the ultimate intelligent, rational, and responsible grounds" of the scientific enterprise.[80] Such limit-questions are unmistakably disclosive of the religious dimension operative in those enterprises. Moreover, these limit-questions are raised within the process of scientific inquiry itself, not imposed extrinsically upon the inquirer by religiously-motivated force. In this sense, for Tracy, the religious dimension operative in our scientific inquiries has an *anthropological* character.[81]

Finally, there is an important question to be asked concerning Tracy's reinterpretation of Lonergan. What is implied by Tracy's reinterpretation of Lonergan's question of God into the "limit-question"? In other words, Lonergan directly draws forth the question of God from human questioning regarding the ground of intelligence,

---

78    *Ibid.*

79    *Ibid.*, 98.

80    *Ibid.*, 99. Tracy points out that when the need to seek the ultimate ground of scientific inquiries is denied, we shall meet a danger that some scientific theory is elevated to the level of a "scientific myth" as a final interpretation of all existence.

81    This position fundamentally concurs with Lonergan's stance that the question of God falls within the human horizon of unrestricted transcendental subjectivity.

unconditioned judgments, and moral values. However, Tracy intends to reformulate Lonergan's God-questions as "limit-questions" which stand for human religious experience in general. For Tracy, the question of the ground (limit-question) is a religious question in general, prior to the God-question. Therefore, instead of an immediate theological eliciting of the God-question in our questioning of the grounds, Tracy first insists on an expanded analysis concerning the justification of common human religious experience.[82] This expanded analysis is, for him, a foundational step for a critical fundamental theology. Lonergan's immediate eliciting of the question of God in the self-transcending process of human scientific inquiries seems to be, for Tracy, a *dogmatic* mediation that has not undergone a critical public methodological procedure.[83] Tracy's aim in this analysis is rather limited, namely, to show how the phenomenon of our inevitable thrust towards those limit-questions can shed light on the presence of the religious dimension within the scientific inquirer's own horizon. For him, to demonstrate the truth of the claim that God is the *necessary referent* of such a religious dimension is another task that should be also *critically* (not dogmatically) dealt with by a proper method.[84]

82   His three-dimensional analysis of common human experience is an attempt at the actualization of this insistence.

83   For example, from Tracy's viewpoint, the following critical questions are not taken into account in Lonergan's mediation of the God-question: how does one uncover the referent of the religious dimension present in the human reflective horizon as God? Is the Christian and theistic explication of that dimension *true*? For Tracy's criticism of Lonergan's methodology, see Tracy, "Method as Foundation for Theology: Bernard Lonergan's Option," in *JR*, 50 (1970) 292–318. For the discussion of Tracy's critique of Lonergan, see William M. Shea, "The Stance and Task of the Foundational Theologian: Critical or Dogmatic?," in *HeyJ*, 17 (1976) 273–92.

84   According to Tracy's methodological presentation in the preceding chapter (thesis 5), this task should be pursued by metaphysical-transcendental reflection. We will deal with this issue in his development of Christian theism.

Tracy's second analysis is concerned with elucidating the religious dimension in our moral discourse and experience. For this concern, Tracy's key question is "how one may best *distinguish* religious from moral discourse and experience."[85] Thus, this analysis deals with the well-known criticisms of the liberal theological tradition that fails to differentiate specifically the religious realm from the moral.[86] According to Tracy, the liberal tradition still has an influential effect upon secular culture at large in such a way that "religion is widely considered a reasonably useful if somewhat primitive way of being moral."[87] In other words, religion at best appears to provide paradigms, stories, and rituals which help to stimulate people into the ethical life.[88]

Tracy's assumption as a starting point for this analysis is that moral arguments are not wholly "self-contained."[89] This means that moral arguments, like the arguments of science, always presuppose some other assumptions, views, or faith. For example, "One ought to

---

85   *BRO*, 101 (italics mine).
86   Tracy explains that, "The fact remains [...] that (again with such notable exceptions as Schleiermacher, Otto, von Hugel, and Tyrrell) it is difficult to discover in either the classical Protestant liberals or the classical Catholic modernists an analysis that clearly and systematically differentiates the religious realm from the moral in other than narrowly neo-Kantian, i.e., basically ethical terms." (*Ibid.*, 100–1).
87   *Ibid.*, 101.
88   Tracy finds the reemergence of the liberal tradition in more contemporary terms in "the positions of such linguistic analysts of religious language as R.B. Braithwaite and R.M. Hare. In either case, the reader is hard pressed to find a qualitative difference between religious and moral language. In Hare's case, both such languages express our 'bliks' or basic attitudes towards the world. In Braithwaite's case, religious language is really moral 'attitudinal' language expressing the speaker's intention to act in a certain manner and articulating and internalizing that attitude through parable and story." (*Ibid.*). Cf. R.B. Braithwaite, *An Empiricist's View of the Nature of Religious Belief* (Cambridge: Cambridge University Press, 1955); R.M. Hare, "Theology and Falsification," in A. Flew and A. MacIntyre (eds), *New Essays in Philosophical Theology* (London: SCM Press, 1955) 99–103.
89   *BRO*, 102.

do what is right" is a moral truism. However, this pronouncement is not self-contained. This is evidenced by the fact that we can be driven further to ask a question like, "Why ought I to do anything that is right?" Tracy characterizes this kind of question as a "limit-question." The peculiarity of such a question is that it "still has the form of a moral question ('ought') but which does not actually function ethically."[90] He explains that, "In fact, there is no moral argument for answering that question [...] More summarily, we cannot really produce a moral argument for being moral."[91] This means that the limit-character of such a question appeals for an answer to a scope of reasoning which is different from the reasoning in which the question is formed. According to him, what a "limit-question" of morality implies or refers to does not have a bearing on morality *per se*, but on a *religious* dimension. For this fundamental argument, Tracy is indebted to Stephen Toulmin's analysis of "limiting questions" of morality.[92] In order to better understand Tracy's position, we will first look at Toulmin's analysis and, then, discuss how Tracy uses it for his own argument.

*Stephen Toulmin's Analysis of "Limiting Questions"*

According to Toulmin, the peculiarity of "limiting questions" can be identified by three major elements. Firstly, the meaning of "limiting questions" cannot be determined within the mode of reasoning in which the question is formed. In ordinary questions, Toulmin observes, the form of the question and the situation in which it is asked determine the meaning of the question. However, it cannot be so with "limiting questions." Toulmin explains that:

> our usage provides no standard interpretation of such questions [limiting questions]. Their form suggests a meaning of a familiar kind, but the situations in which they are asked are such that they cannot have that meaning. The form of words may therefore express any of a varied selection of personal pre-

90    *Ibid.*
91    *Ibid.*
92    Tracy's main source is Stephen Toulmin, *An Examination of the Place of Reason in Ethics* (London: Cambridge University Press, 1958).

dicaments, and we can only find out as we go along what is 'behind' the question.[93]

Toulmin's example is as follows: "If someone asks, 'Why ought I to give this book back to Jones today?,' and is given the answer, 'Because you promised to,' there is no room within the ethical mode of reasoning for him to ask, 'But why ought I to *really*?' – this question is a 'limiting question'."[94]

Secondly, a "limiting question" does not allow for "'alternative answers,' in the way in which there are to a typically ethical question."[95] Toulmin explains:

> Within the apparent mode of reasoning, all questions require a definite choice to be made – e.g., between two theories or social practices, between one moral decision and another, or between one scientific prediction and another. A 'limiting question,' however, does not present us with genuine alternatives to choose between.[96]

For example, to such a question, "Which ought I to do, *A* or *B*?," when there is nothing to choose between them on moral grounds, the only possible answer is "one taking account of the agent's own preferences – 'If you do *A*, then so-and-so, if you do *B*, then such-and-such.'"[97] However, if someone asks a question that insists on *the* answer independent of one's preference (e.g., "But which ought I *really* to do?"), such a question is a "limiting question."

Thirdly, in terms of the mode of forming the questions, "limiting questions" do not show any "extra-rational" or super-rational trait of reasoning. They are, in fact, rational questions. Therefore, there is always the thrust to answer to these questions in the way that the form of questions appears to demand. However, either to answer or to decline to answer in this way would leave the questioner equally discontented. "If you refuse, his [the questioner's] desire for such an answer remains unstilled: if you answer, there is nothing to stop the

---

93   Toulmin, *An Examination of the Place of Reason in Ethics*, 205.
94   *Ibid.*, 217–18.
95   *Ibid.*, 207.
96   *Ibid.*, 205–6.
97   *Ibid.*, 218.

question from arising again about your reply."[98] In short, a question is called a limiting question when it cannot be resolved "by any literal answer to his [sic] question, or by any rational analysis of the question itself."[99]

Summarily stated, the peculiar characteristics of the "limiting questions" analyzed by Toulmin hinge on the idea of an impasse or a *cul-de-sac* which our apparent mode of rationalist or moral reasoning cannot get through in order to allow for an exact answer. Given this character of "limiting questions," Toulmin asks whether "limiting questions" are, then, meaningless or non-sensical utterances as the so-called positivist linguistic philosophers claim?[100] Toulmin's answer is

---

98    *Ibid.*, 206.
99    *Ibid.*, 207.
100   In fact, Toulmin's discussion of "limiting questions" is purported to refute the claim of the so-called positivist linguistic philosophers. According to them, apart from the formal, literal, or analytic statements of mathematics and logic, and the statements which can be verifiable by observation, no statements are meaning-ridden. Consequently, metaphysical, religious, and theological discourses are rejected, not as unproved, but as meaningless or non-sensical. The representative positivists whom Toulmin refers to are A.J. Ayer, Moritz Schlick, and Bertrand Russell, etc. Against empiricist and positivist claims, Toulmin's fundamental argument is that "every mode of reasoning, every type of sentence, and (if one is particular) every single sentence will have its own logical criteria, to be discovered by examining its individual, peculiar *uses*." (*Ibid.*, 83; italics mine). Toulmin goes on to say that, "Speech is no single-purpose tool. It is, in fact, more like a Boy Scout's knife (an implement with two kinds of blade, a screw-driver, a corkscrew, a tin-and-bottle opener, a file, an awl, and even a thing for taking stones out of horses' hooves); and, further, it is one which we continually shape and modify, adding new devices (modes of reasoning, and types of concept) to perform new functions, and grinding old ones afresh, in the light of experience, so that they shall serve their old, familiar, well-tried purposes better." (*Ibid.*). We can see here that Toulmin's position is akin to a later Wittgensteinian approach to the use of language. Based on this view, Toulmin comments on the positivist position by saying that, "Provided that we remember that religion has functions other than that of competing with science and ethics on their own grounds, we shall understand that to reject all religious arguments for this reason [for the difficulty of logical justification] is to make a serious logical blunder – an error as great as that of taking figurative phrases literally, or of supposing that the mathematical theory of numbers (say) has any deep, religious significance. There are two such

that this is not so. How, then, does Toulmin appraise the value or significance of "limiting questions"? In his consideration of the significance of "limiting questions," Toulmin focuses on the boundary sphere between ethics and religion in which reason moves towards a religious dimension. According to Toulmin, a "limiting question" becomes significant or "alive," only when it is approached as a "religious question." In other words, Toulmin assigns questions described as "religious" to the category of "limiting questions." He states that "limiting questions" are "expressions, not of any desire for exact knowledge, or for the ability to anticipate and predict particular future events."[101] Rather they reflect our fundamental "desire for reassurance, for a general confidence about the future" against fearful uncertainty.[102] Much imbued with existential philosophies, Toulmin sees the fundamental human condition as being under an unpre-

---

errors, as Pascal points out – 'first, to take everything literally; secondly, to take everything spiritually'." (*Ibid.*, 212).

101    *Ibid.*, 216.

102    *Ibid.* Toulmin takes two famous examples of "limiting questions" reflecting our fundamental desire for a confidence about the future against uncertainty. The first one is from Blaise Pascal's writing: "When I consider the briefness of my life, swallowed up in the eternity before and behind it, the small space I fill, or even see, engulfed in the infinite immensity of spaces which I know not, and which know not me, I am afraid [...] Who has set me here? By whose order and arrangement have this place and this time been allotted me? [...]" (G. Michaut (ed.), *Les Pensées de Pascal, disposées suivant l'ordre du cahier autographique* (Fribourg, 1896) no.188, p.70, cited in Toulmin, *ibid.*, 209–10). The second example is from the questions Dmitri Karamazov asks in his dream recorded in Dostoevsky's *The Brothers Karamazov*: "Tell me why it is those poor mothers stand there? Why are people poor? Why is the babe poor? Why is the steppe barren? Why don't they hug each other and kiss? Why don't they sing songs of joy? Why are they so dark from black misery? Why don't they feed the babe? [...] And he felt that, though his questions were unreasonable and senseless, yet he wanted to ask just that; and he had to ask it just in that way. And he felt that a passion of pity, such as he had never known before, was rising in his heart, that he wanted to cry, that he wanted to do something for them all, so that the babe should weep no more, so that dark-faced, dried-up mother should not weep, that no one should shed tears again from that moment. [...]" (Dostoevsky, *The Brothers Karamazov*, trans. by Garnett (1912) 546–8, cited in Toulmin, *ibid.*, 210).

dictable threat to a meaningful existence. For him, our most urgent problem under such a situation is to accept and maintain the conviction that the future will finally be trustworthy in spite of fearful uncertainty. Such a faith, for him, points to a religious dimension operative in our existence. For him, a religious dimension means a spiritual dimension of faith which is above all "concerned with 'the confidence of things which are hoped for, and the certainty of things which are not seen'" (Heb. 11: 1).[103] In short, it is in the limiting questions that such a fundamental confidence (expressive of a religious dimension) finds explicit expression. Therefore, the significance of "limiting questions" lies in their *mediating* effect: to disclose a latent religious dimension in our common reflective activities such as moral questionings.

*Tracy's Understanding of "Limit-Questions" in Morality*

Tracy draws on two elements of Toulmin's analysis of "limiting questions" to illuminate the religious dimension operative in our moral enterprises.

Firstly, Toulmin's analysis demonstrates the peculiarity of the religious dimension as distinct from the moral one by uncovering the *paradoxical* presence of the religious dimension in our moral questioning. That is to say, our continual moral questioning, at its limit, cannot but contain "limiting questions" of morality. The paradoxicality of a "limiting question" of morality is that although it still

---

103   Toulmin, *ibid.*, 216. Toulmin writes that, "Over those matters of fact which are not to be 'explained' scientifically, like the deaths in the Jones family, the function of religion is to help us resign ourselves to them – and so feel like accepting them. Likewise, over matters of duty which are not to be justified further in ethical terms, it is for religion to help us embrace them – and so feel like accepting them. [...] Ethics provides the *reasons* for choosing the 'right' course: religion helps us to put our *hearts* into it." (*Ibid.*, 218–19). In Toulmin's current discussion, his explanation of religion or the religious dimension is not more specific than this. We know that this view is very minimal. For the moment, our only focus is Toulmin's attempt to explicate what the religious use of language can peculiarly manifest by using Wittgenstein's theory of the use of language.

maintains the form of a moral question (e.g., Why *ought* I stand for justice anyway?), its actual questioning goes beyond the moral dimension. "In fact there is no moral argument for answering that question."[104] Thus, such a "limiting question," for Toulmin, cannot but be approached as a religious question. In short, a "limiting question" of morality is expressive of a religious dimension in such a way that it is not solved or subdued by moral arguments despite its linguistic form of moral discourse. Tracy writes:

> Given that insight, an analyst of religious and theological language may recognize that this language, when used properly, is neither a simple misuse of scientific language (as implied by Flew in the 'Theology and Falsification Debate'), nor simply reducible without remainder to moral language as implied by the classical 'liberal' analyses or by E.B. Braithwaite's linguistic analysis. Religious and theological language, on the contrary, is a language of limit-questions and, to extend Toulmin's point, limit-answers.[105]

Secondly, Tracy observes that, following the later Wittgenstein's approach to the use of language, Toulmin's analysis unpacks "the differing uses of argument (and hence of 'truth') present in the distinct uses of everyday language (aesthetic, moral, religious, scientific, etc.)."[106] In other words, Toulmin argues for the linguistic need to uncover the distinct "forms of life" which the distinct uses of language disclose. For example, the "form of life" or the situation of human existence that religious language functions to disclose is, for him, a "desire for reassurance, for a general confidence about the future" in the face of uncertainty and distress.[107] By explicating the distinct "form of life" disclosed by religious language, which is different from what moral or any other language aims to express, Toulmin tries to safeguard the religious dimension as an autonomous realm operative in human existential situations.

Tracy then examines Schubert Ogden's interpretation of Toulmin. According to Tracy, Ogden develops Toulmin's analysis in the direction of the Anglo-American empirical tradition. Ogden reform-

104   *BRO*, 102.
105   *Ibid.*, 102–3.
106   *Ibid.*, 102.
107   Toulmin, *An Examination of the Place of Reason in Ethics*, 216.

ulates Toulmin's key idea of "reassurance" in such a way that it can be understood as a "re-presenting assurance."[108] By this expression, Ogden means that "religious assertions can serve to re-assure us only because they themselves are the re-presentation of a confidence somehow already present prior to their being made."[109] According to Ogden, religious assertions, like ethical and scientific ones, rest on certain presuppositions that we already take for granted in our existence as human beings. The presupposition that religious assertions represent is, for Ogden, "our ineradicable confidence in the final worth of our existence."[110] This confidence is "a faith common to us all."[111] A rather long statement of Ogden which explains the re-

---

108   Ogden, *The Reality of God*, 32.

109   *Ibid.*

110   *Ibid.*, 37. Ogden writes that, "The one thing for which none of us can rationally decide, whatever his particular choices, is the eventual nullity of any of his decisions. Even the suicide who intentionally takes his own life implicitly affirms the ultimate meaning of his tragic choice." (*Ibid.*, 36).

111   *Ibid.* The seminal idea of Ogden's notion of a "common human faith" can be found in John Dewey's work, *A Common Faith* (New Haven and London: Yale University Press, 1970, first published in 1934). Although Ogden does not follow Dewey's naturalistic (in Ogden's terminology, "secularistic" which is connotative of the modern atheistic approach) position, his "secular" (not necessarily atheistic) approach to religious faith seems to be influenced, in a sense, by Dewey's notion of a "common faith" of human beings. One of the important implications of Ogden's secular approach to religious faith is that religious faith never falls within a supernatural realm, but within the realm of common human experience. In this position, we can see a trace of Dewey's understanding of religious faith developed in his *A Common Faith*. As a background of Ogden's notion of "a faith common to all," we will briefly look at Dewey's notion of human religious faith.

In his book, *A Common Faith*, Dewey attempts to work out a "conception of the nature of the religious phase of experience, one that separates it from the supernatural and the things that have grown up about it." (John Dewey, *A Common Faith*, 2). For him, all derivations from the supernatural understanding of religion are encumbrances to what is genuinely religious on its own account. What he tries to lighten is "the religious quality of experience" which is hampered to come to consciousness by "conceptions of supernatural that were imbedded in those cultures wherein man had little control over outer nature and little in the way of sure method of inquiry and test." (*Ibid.*, 56). According to Dewey, "the religious attitude signifies something that is bound through

lationship between a common faith and religious assertions is worth quoting:

imagination to a *general* attitude" inherent in natural experience (*Ibid.*, 23). Thus, the faith that is religious can be described as "the unification of the self through allegiance to inclusive ideal ends, which imagination presents to us and to which the human will responds as worthy of controlling our desires and choices." (*Ibid.*, 33). This faith is not specially bound up with a particular authorized channel of belief. Instead, it is a common human faith in the ideal values which have their roots not outside of nature, but "in natural conditions" through human creative embodiment. Dewey states that "the ideal ends to which we attach our faith are not shadowy and wavering. They assume concrete form in our understanding of our relations to one another and the values contained in these relations [...] Here are all the elements for a religious faith that shall not be confined to sect, class, or race. Such a faith has always been implicitly the common faith of mankind. It remains to make it explicit and militant." (*Ibid.*, 87). John H. Randall comments on Dewey's conception of religious faith in the following way. Dewey's conception of religious faith reflects a practical idealism embedded in the American temper of Dewey's time which was directed toward humanitarian zeal and social good with a distaste for the concern with any particular religious creed or dogma. "That urge expresses the vague religious life of the 'unchurched,' of that great body of Americans who, while continuing to feel Christian sentiments, feel also a deep distrust of all institutionalized religion, all 'churchianity'." (John H. Randall, "The Religion of Shared Experience," in (no indication of editor) *The Philosopher of the Common Man: Essays in Honour of John Dewey to Celebrate His Eightieth Birthday* (New York: G.P. Putnam's Sons, 1940) 106–7). This tendency results in "the emergence in them all of what may well be called a distinctly American form of religion." (Randall, *ibid.*, 107). Randall explains that the twin sources of Dewey's notion of religious faith are the experiences of democracy and science. These two sources serve as a ground of "the common man's religion of common-ness" based on common life in a common world freed from "monopolized, protected, private, and special" religion (*Ibid.*, 121). Randall states that Dewey is convinced that a genuine democratic community "most fully realizes the possibilities inherent in man's fundamentally social nature [...] To be captured morally and imaginatively by such an ideal, to acknowledge its rightful claim over our desires and purposes, to live in its light, is to live religiously [...] Democratic experience is thus for Dewey not only, with all the overtones he manages to put into the term, a *common* experience in which the common man can take part: it is literally a religious *communion* in which men find themselves at one and in unity with their fellow men and with the natural conditions of human achievement." (*Ibid.*, 110–11).

111

They [religious assertions] are not so much the *cause* of our general confidence that existence is meaningful as its *effect*. By this I mean that the various 'religions' or 'faiths' of mankind, including what may be called the 'Christian religion,' are one and all expressions or re-presentations of a yet deeper faith that precedes them. Logically prior to every particular religious assertion is an original confidence in the meaning and worth of life, through which not simply all our religious answers, but even our religious questions first become possible or have any sense [...] Because all religions are by their very nature re-presentative, they never originate our faith in life's meaning, but rather provide us with particular symbolic forms through which that faith may be more or less adequately re-affirmed at the level of self-conscious belief.[112]

In sum, Ogden's argumentation is that religious assertions are, in a way, attempts to express the answers to limiting questions at the level of particular beliefs, aiming at providing the needed reassurance (or "re-presenting assurance").

Tracy concludes that the analyses of Toulmin and Ogden help to "clarify the fact that when we use the word 'religion' we mean the use of language to re-present certain limit-answers to certain limit-questions."[113] Put differently, when we use the expression, "our fundamental confidence," (as a "limit-of" dimension of our existential experiences), "we mean that 'form of life' (that mode-of-being-in-the-world) manifested by religious as re-presentative language."[114] The most important implication here, for Tracy, is that "we are dealing

---

112 Ogden, *The Reality of God*, 33–4. Ogden's argument that particular religious assertions or beliefs are not the cause but the effect of our intrinsic general confidence echoes John Dewey's idea. Dewey asserts that, "It is the claim of religions that they effect this generic and enduring change in attitude ['a change *of* will conceived as the organic plenitude of our being']. I should like to turn the statement around and say that whenever this change takes place there is a definitely religious attitude. It is not *a* religion that brings it about, but when it occurs, from whatever cause and by whatever means, there is a religious outlook and function. As I have said before, the doctrinal or intellectual apparatus and the institutional accretions that grow up are, in a strict sense, adventitious to the intrinsic quality of such experience." (John Dewey, *A Common Faith*, 17).

113 *BRO*, 104.

114 *Ibid.* Tracy's endorsement of the idea of the "representative" function of religious language, which is indebted to Schubert Ogden, will be critically examined at the end of this chapter.

with a language and an experience whose logically limit-character distinguishes its use [as *religious*] from other uses of language and from other dimensions of experience or forms of life."[115]

*Reflection on "Limit-Situations" in Our Everyday Experience*[116]

Tracy's final analysis of the religious dimension of common human experience, concerns the phenomenon of "limit-situations" in our everyday lives. Since Tracy's analysis of limit-situations" is far less complicated than the previous ones, we will deal with it briefly.

For explicating "limit-situations," Tracy uses existentialist philosophers' analyses of human existence, especially those of Karl Jaspers, Martin Heidegger, and Gabriel Marcel.[117] Basing himself on existentialist analyses, Tracy characterizes a "limit-situation" in the following manner:

> [It is] a situation wherein we find ourselves not the masters of our fate but radically contingent or limited (boundary-situations). At the same time, we may also find ourselves radically out-of-our-everyday-selves as ecstatic, as gifted, even as 'graced'.[118]

More concretely, this description points to two different kinds of "limit-situation," a negative and a positive one. They are "either those 'boundary' situations of guilt, anxiety, sickness, and the recognition of death as one's own destiny [negative], or those situations called 'ecstatic experiences' – intense joy, love, reassurance, creation [positive]."[119] Tracy's analysis of the religious dimension in these "limit-

---

115   *Ibid.*

116   The same text concerning this theme in *BRO*, 105–9 is also found in Tracy, "Religious Language as Limit-Language," in *TD*, 22 (1974) 292–6.

117   In his explanation, Tracy simply employs some of the key terms from these philosophers' analyses, rather than delving into their analyses.

118   *BRO*, 107.

119   *Ibid.*, 105. Tracy draws on the following sources: for the negative mode of limit-situations as "boundary-situations," Karl Jaspers, *The Perennial Scope of Philosophy* (New York: Philosophical Library, 1949) 85–7, 168–80; idem, *Philosophy*, vol.2 (Chicago: University of Chicago Press, 1970) 177–218; for positive "ecstatic experiences," among others, Gabriel Marcel, *Being and*

situations" hinges on two main ideas. With the positive "limit-situations" ("ecstatic experiences"), Tracy identifies a religious implication in their "*self-transcending*" quality. With the negative "limit-situations," Tracy focuses on the idea of "*radical contingency*" to identify the religious dimension. We will look at the essential feature of each kind of "limit-situation" respectively.

Firstly, concerning the self-transcending quality of positive "limit-situations," Tracy explains in the following way:

> When in the grasp of such experiences [experiences of positive "limit-situations" such as 'ecstatic experiences'], we all find, however momentarily, that we can and do transcend our usual lackluster selves and our usual everyday worlds to touch upon a dimension of experience which cannot be stated adequately in the language of ordinary, everyday experience.[120]

Moreover, the self-transcending character of "ecstatic experiences," by their "limit-disclosing" power, may lead us to sense "the possibilities of an existential grounding for those everyday experiences of self-transcendence which disclose the most deeply held meanings of our lives."[121] In short, for Tracy, such "self-transcending" (or "limit-disclosing") experiences are expressive of a final world of meaning beyond the everyday. And this ultimate horizon of meaning may manifest itself as a *religious* dimension or horizon to our lives. Tracy writes that such ecstatic experiences "may [...] disclose to us, however hesitantly, the character of that ultimate horizon of meaning which religious persons call 'gracious,' 'eventful,' 'faithful,' 'revelatory'."[122] Tracy claims that the religious character of authentic

*Having* (London: Dacre, 1949); Abraham H. Maslow, *Religions, Values and Peak Experiences* (New York: Viking, 1970).

120 *BRO*, 105. Tracy explains that such an experience, in the words of Lonergan, "as religious mystics remind us, may be a taste of that self-transcending experience of a 'being-in-love-without-qualification' familiar to the authentically religious person." (*Ibid.*). For the reference to Lonergan, see Lonergan, *Method in Theology*, 101–10.

121 *BRO*, 106.

122 *Ibid.* In his own reformulation of the category of "limit," Tracy expresses the religious character of such experiences by saying that, "that *limit-to* the everyday [...] seems to disclose – in the same *ec-stasis* – a *limit-of* whose

experiences of ecstacy is, therefore, not something to be necessarily understood in explicitly religious terms embedded in a particular religious tradition. Yet, those experiences can be well described as "religious" in view of the self-transcending or limit-disclosing character which surfaces in the experiences themselves.

Secondly, to illuminate the religious implication of negative "limit-situations," Tracy takes the example of the phenomenological analysis of *anxiety* (*Angst*) attempted by Heidegger.[123] Tracy's focal concern here is how *anxiety* emerges as a qualitatively different phenomenon from that of fear in human experience, and how it eventually points to a religious quality.

Tracy sums up the key idea of Heidegger's analysis by explaining that whereas fear appears as a fear of something (e.g., a fear of crowds, of heights, of the dark, of war, etc.), *anxiety* is a "fear of *no-object*-in-the-world-alongside-other-objects."[124] In other words, it is a "fear of No-thing."[125] Heidegger describes this unique and strange phenomenon by saying that:

> Nothing which is ready-to-hand or present-at-hand within the world functions as that in the face of which anxiety is anxious [...] Accordingly, when something threatening brings itself close, anxiety does not 'see' any definite 'here' or 'yonder' from which it comes. That in the face of which one has anxiety is characterized by the fact that what threatens is *nowhere*. Anxiety 'does not know' what that in the face of which it is anxious is [...] In that in the face of which one has anxiety, the 'It is nothing and nowhere' becomes manifest.[126]

Put differently, anxiety is a dimension of human existence disclosive of "our often forgotten but never totally absent consciousness of our

---

graciousness bears a religious character." (*Ibid.*; italics of 'limit-to' and 'limit-of' mine). Here, although Tracy explicates the religious character of ecstatic experiences in general, his expressions are reminiscent of Christian experiences.

123   See Martin Heidegger, *Being and Time*, trans. by John Macquarrie and Edward Robinson (Oxford: Basil Blackwell, 1967) 228–35.

124   *BRO*, 107.

125   *Ibid.*

126   Heidegger, *Being and Time*, 231.

own radical *contingency*."[127] Tracy emphatically describes this undeniable radical *contingency* by saying that:

> In anxiety, we do not merely consider, we know that we neither create ourselves nor can we assume the continuance of existence. Instead we find ourselves – as the metaphors of the existentialists and the mystics alike remind us – poised over an abyss, a chasm, whose exact nature we do not know but whose experiential reality we cannot deny.[128]

Tracy portrays this feature of radical contingency a dimension of our human existence which is grounded by "no other thing in the universe, but rather by No-thing."[129] Here, the expression, "No-thing" can be understood as a symbolic expression that describes the "literally unspoken, and perhaps unspeakable, final dimension to the end of our lives."[130] For explicating such experiences, at a certain point, a conceptual language begins to falter. Then, a symbolic language comes into play. Tracy writes that, "Such language, as symbolic, involves a double intentionality which expresses both a literal meaning [...] and a non-literal meaning which otherwise remains unsaid and unspoken (in this case, the disclosure of an other, a final dimension, which serves as limit-to our experience of the everyday and limit-of the rest of our existence)."[131] Here, the unutterable final dimension or horizon, for Tracy, can be described as a "religious dimension" inherent in human existential situations.

## 4. Conclusion

Tracy's three-dimensional analysis of common human experience is an attempt to clarify his definition of a revisionist theological task in view of its first source, namely, a "philosophical reflection upon common human experience."[132] Here, "philosophical reflection" dis-

---

127    *BRO*, 107 (italics mine).
128    *Ibid.*
129    *Ibid.*
130    *Ibid.*, 107–8.
131    *Ibid.*, 108.
132    *Ibid.*, 109.

tinctly suggests the concern of his project: to critically reflect upon common human experience (specifically religious experience) without any confessional, dogmatical or theological auspice. For him, this reflection is a foundational step for constructing a critical fundamental theology. The focal concern of his fundamental theology is to demonstrate that the understanding of God (Christian theism) is a critical reflection which is not only Christian but is also true of every human being. It is therefore essential to Tracy's project that he critically exhibits the legitimacy of the undeniable presence of a religious dimension in *common* human experience.

Against this backdrop, his use of a philosophical (not theological) category such as "limit" to characterize the meaning of "religious" appears to be a deliberate option. His revisionist return to the Kantian motif of "limit" shows his reinterpretation of the motif from within his own Anglo-American tradition. For example, in the two modalities of the category "limit" (*limit-to* and *limit-of*), his explanation of "*limit-of*" dimension clearly reflects that fact. He explains the *limit-of* dimension as the fundamental structure of our existence beyond (or grounding) our everyday experience. For him, the fundamental structure can be best described as "our fundamental trust in the worthwhileness of existence, [or] our basic belief in order and value."[133] This idea noticeably echoes the optimistic humanitarian conviction of secularity developed by John Dewey and Schubert Ogden in the Anglo-American context. As we will see in Tracy's revisionist theological model as a whole, this idea of the fundamental faith of secularity plays a basic role in his correlation of human experience to the Christian tradition, and also in his understanding of God.

For Tracy, the most eminent merit of the category of "limit" is that it serves to identify the *religious dimension* of human experience as a *common* and *autonomous* one. Tracy is convinced that his analysis demonstrates this possibility by employing the diverse philosophical analyses of human scientific, moral, and everyday experiences. For Tracy, the religious dimension is elucidated as a *common* human dimension in the sense that it is not a "supernatural" realm out-

133    *Ibid.*, 93.

there, but a *mediated* dimension within the human reflective horizon (aided by Lonergan's analysis). It is, however, an *autonomous* dimension distinct from any other human activity such as science, morality, or culture because it is not subdued by or reduced to any of those realms (aided by Toulmin's analysis). According to Tracy, insofar as the *religious* dimension is understood as neither a supernatural realm, nor an ethically and culturally domesticated realm, but rather as a final, a limit-dimension to the whole of everyday existence, religion can continue to authentically operate in our secular lives.

Tracy clarifies that his analysis of common human experience can be described as a phenomenological one in a broad sense. This means that, in terms of his three sets of criteria (meaning, meaningfulness, and truth), this analysis is conducted according to the first two sets of criteria. Namely, firstly, he analyzes the *meaning* of the religious dimension as a meaning with a "limit" character (*limit-to* and *limit-of*). Secondly, he illuminates the existential *meaningfulness* of a religious dimension (e.g., reassurance) present in common human experience. For fulfilling the final set of criteria of "truth," however, he asks for another necessary methodological procedure (a metaphysical-transcendental reflection) which leads to the explicit question of God as the objective referent of such a human religious reality. For him, the question of truth is only clarified by the conceptual explication of the cognitive claims involved in such (limit) human religious experience. [134] The principal cognitive claim involved in human religious experience and in explicitly religious language (e.g., Christian language), argues Tracy, is "the explicitly *theistic* claim: that the objective referent of all such language and experience is that reality religious human beings mean when they say 'God'." [135] Basing

---

134   More concretely, in clarifying the question of truth, he will deal with not only the cognitive claims involved in human religious experience (first source), but also those claims involved in explicitly Christian religious language (second source). Therefore, his discussion of the issue of truth which is related to the question of God will come after his phenomenological analysis of the *meaning* and *meaningfulness* of Christian religious language, which we will examine in the following section.

135   *BRO*, 109 (italics mine). Granted that the issue of how Tracy uncovers the referent of religious experience and language as God will be examined later,

himself on this fundamental assumption, he calls for a metaphysical-transcendental reflection as the *necessary* way for determining the truth value of such a cognitive claim.[136] Prior to this final metaphysical-transcendental reflection on God, however, he undertakes another phenomenological analysis: the analysis of Christian religious

two important questions need to be mentioned here. The first question is how to appraise Tracy's above theistic assumption concerning human religious experience. Is it a pre-theological or *philosophical* reflection (as the definition of his revisionist theology says: "*philosophical* reflection on common human experience")? Or is it an already theological consideration impregnated with an apologetic concern. If the former is the case, the philosophical tradition he uses for his reflection must be explicitly theistic. Then, his philosophical reflection on human religious experience (as *common*) precludes non-theistic human religious experience. It prejudges the character of human religious experience as *theistic*. If the latter is the case, the definition of his revisionist theology, viz., *philosophical* reflection on common human experience, is not suitable. We will explore this problematic issue in Tracy's development of Christian theism. A follow-up question is, more specifically, whether the religious experience which involves a theistic cognitive claim can be a *common* human experience. Can this theistic assumption be a common core to religious experience that transcends the boundaries of different religions and cultures? This question is vital since, a fundamental theology, as Tracy argues, aims at a public discourse at a most radical level which is understandable to "any attentive, intelligent, reasonable and responsible person." (*AI*, 63). We will deal with these issues in our critique of Tracy's revisionist theology in the next chapter.

136  Tracy points out that for the Wittgensteinians and most phenomenologists, phenomenological analysis (disclosing the meaning and meaningfulness of the religious dimension) manifests truth. A good example is Heidegger's insistence upon truth as *a-letheia*. In other words, according to Tracy, most phenomenologists and linguistic analysts will advocate the "softer" claim that a "limit-of" dimension and the referent of that dimension, God "may be displayed, disclosed or shown but cannot in principle be *stated*." (*AI*, 161, italics mine). However, for those, like himself, who "argue the so-called 'hard' (i.e., the metaphysical or transcendental) line," a fundamental theology is supposed to "*partly state* – more exactly, to metaphysically state – the abstract, general, universal and necessary features of the reality of God" as the referent of what is disclosed as religious realities in earlier phenomenological investigation (*Ibid.*, italics mine). The question of how Tracy includes this in his fundamental theological system will be discussed in the next chapter on his development of Christian theism.

119

language (the second source). Let us examine his analysis of the religious dimension disclosed in the Christian texts.


## II. The Analysis of the Religious Language of Christian Texts


In this examination, we will explore Tracy's "philosophical reflection" upon the meanings present in Christian texts (the second source). As in his previous analysis of common human experience, his concern with "*philosophical* reflection" here needs to be noted. For him, this concern indicates that his analysis shall be critical and scientific in keeping with fully public methodological criteria.[137] Hence, he is convinced to show the public intelligibility of the meanings disclosed by Christian *religious* language in correlation with human *religious* experience. In working toward this goal, Tracy wants to take a critical stance which is not committed to the Christian texts as anything more than data for analysis. This means that he does not intend to approach the meanings of the Christian texts either dogmatically or kerygmatically.[138] In view of this methodological con-

---

137  According to the fourth thesis of his revisionist methodological principles, the scientific method he suggests for this analysis is "an historical and hermeneutical investigation." (*BRO*, 49). In his actual analysis, Tracy focuses on the New Testament scholarship which is based on contemporary literary and hermeneutical theories.

138  Here, we need to recall his methodological principle on the role of the faith of the theologian in his/her theological work. He explains that most theological practitioners, including himself, *in fact*, are Christian believers committed to explicit Christian faith. However, in the case of *fundamental* theology, "*as a matter of methodological principle* such explicit faith is not required." (Tracy, "Response to Professor Connelly–II," 72, italics mine). He states that, "In principle, the fundamental loyalty of the theologian *qua* theologian is to that morality of scientific knowledge which he shares with his colleagues, the philosophers, historians, and social scientists. No more than they, can he allow his own – or his tradition's – beliefs to serve as warrants for his arguments."

cern, he adopts the following scientific methodological procedure for his analysis: firstly, he sets up the central hypothesis of the analysis; secondly, he circumscribes the area of his analysis in accordance with the hypothesis; finally, he tests the legitimacy of the hypothesis by means of the new developments of the New Testament scholarship of his time. In this analysis, as shown in the previous one, the philosophical (theologically neutral) category of "limit" will be used as a key criterion for elucidating the *religious* dimension disclosed by the Christian texts.

Tracy's fundamental hypothesis is that the distinctiveness of explicitly religious language "lies in its character as a limit-language disclosive of certain limit-experiences."[139] On the basis of this funda-

---

(*BRO*, 7). In our examination, we will pay attention to how Tracy conducts his actual analysis in keeping with this principle.

139  *BRO*, 119. For the background of this hypothesis of Tracy, Ian Ramsey's work, *Religious Language: An Empirical Placing of Theological Phrases* (London: SCM Press Ltd., 1969) plays an important role. Ramsey's key argument is that unlike poetic, ethical, or scientific language, religious language represents a peculiar kind of human situation which cannot be literally described but whose reality cannot be denied. The distinguishing human situation that religious language expresses involves an "odd discernment" of reality and a "*total* commitment" as a response to that discernment (Ramsey, *ibid.*, 28 and 37). Such a peculiar situation is the "empirical place" for religious language. Correlatively, according to Ramsey, religious language will be constructed as an "odd" language invested with strange qualifications, which is evocative enough of an "odd discernment" and a "total commitment." (See *ibid.*, 49). To illustrate and develop this view, Ramsey investigates the linguistic functions of the traditional qualifiers centered on God (such as "immutable," "unity," "perfection," "*first* cause," "creator *ex nihilo*," and "*eternal* purpose," etc.). In his analysis of Christian religious language, Tracy intends to translate Ramsey's expression of "odd" language into the expression of "limit-language." Tracy states that, "If it be correct to say that the 'empirical placing' of religious language involves an odd personal discernment, a total commitment, and a universal significance, then a simpler, less ambiguous expression than 'oddness' is to designate religious language a limit-language disclosive of certain limit-experiences." (*BRO*, 131–2). See also Ricoeur's assessment of Ramsey's discussion of religious language as an "odd" language in his "The Specificity of Language." There, Ricoeur prefers the concept of "limit" to the concept of "oddness" of Ramsey for articulating the peculiar character of religious language. Tracy's position seems to echo Ricoeur's standpoint.

mental hypothesis, he puts forward the claim that the New Testament's use of some important language forms legitimately testifies to this characteristic. Thus, reformulated more concretely, his central hypothesis is that some language forms in the New Testament can be properly described as a limit-language disclosive of human limit-experiences, which represent "our most basic faith" and are "disclosive of an authentically human mode-of-being-in-the-world."[140]

The specific areas of his analysis are three literary genres of the New Testament: proverbs, proclamatory sayings, and parables. Tracy's focus on these genres is related to an important discovery of New Testament scholarship aided by the new literary and hermeneutical theories of his time. According to these new studies, the New Testament uses these genres in a unique way. It makes some modifications of the typical traditional usages of these genres, which serve those language forms identified as limit-language.[141] Tracy explains this feature as follows:

---

140  *BRO*, 119 and 124. Tracy adds that "the present study is not restricted in principle but only in fact to the limit-character of Christian religious language. To repeat our consistent insistence, even the limit-character of Christian religious language is, I believe, an important but not exclusive characteristic of that language." (*Ibid.*, 138 n.24).

141  Tracy lists the representative works for this contribution as follows: Robert Funk, *Language, Hermeneutic and the Word of God* (New York: Harper and Row, 1966); Dominic Crossan, *In Parables* (New York: Harper and Row, 1973); Norman Perrin, "The Parables of Jesus as Parables, as Metaphors and as Aesthetic Objects," in *JR*, 50 (1970) 340–6; idem, "The Modern Interpretation of the Parables of Jesus and the Problem of Hermeneutics," in *Int*, 25 (1971) 131–48; idem, *The New Testament: An Introduction* (New York: Harcourt, Brace Jovanovich, 1974) 3–39; Dan O. Via, *The Parables: Their Literary and Existential Dimension* (Philadelphia: Fortress, 1967); Amos N. Wilder, *Early Christian Rhetoric: The Language of the Gospel* (New York: Harper and Row, 1964); William A. Beardslee, "The Uses of the Proverb in the Synoptic Tradition," in *Int*, 24 (1970) 61–76; idem, *Literary Criticism of the New Testament* (Philadelphia: Fortress, 1970); Paul Ricoeur, "The Specificity of Language," in *Semeia* 4 (1975) 107–48. Note that Paul Ricoeur's essay is the last section of his work on biblical hermeneutics published in the same issue of *Semeia* (pp.29–148). This work consists of four major sections: "Outline" (pp.29–36); "The Narrative Form" (pp.37–73); "The Metaphorical Process" (pp.75–106); "The Specificity of Language" (pp.107–48). When Tracy uses the

The New Testament consistently modifies the traditional use of language of proverbs, eschatological sayings, and parables through such procedures as intensification, transgression, and 'going to the limits' of language; these modifications allow the interpreter to propose that the sense of this language should be described as a limit-language of a genuinely religious character.[142]

As a means of testing his central hypothesis, Tracy investigates each of the three literary genres in two ways. Firstly, he examines the "limit" character of the religious language of each genre (literary concern). For this examination, Tracy relies on the relevant New Testament studies.[143] Secondly, he elucidates the visions of human possibilities that the "limit" language of each genre discloses (hermeneutical concern). After our exposition of Tracy's analysis of all three genres, we will look at Tracy's correlation between the visions of the Christian religious language, and the human religious experiences examined in the preceding analysis.

---

final essay, "The Specificity of Language," he refers to an unpublished text (with the slightly different title, "The Specificity of Religious Language") since the published version was not available when he wrote *BRO*.

142  *BRO*, 124. This explanation seems to be indebted to Paul Ricoeur's description contained in his "The Specificity of Language." In this essay, Ricoeur analyzes the same three genres of the New Testament, incorporating some of the New Testament scholarship mentioned above. Ricoeur writes there that, "I propose to show how religious language [in this analysis, specifically, proverbs, proclamatory sayings, and parables] *modifies* poetic language by various procedures such as intensification, transgression, and going to the limit, which make it, according to Ian Ramsey's expression, an 'odd' language. I will place the study of these diverse procedures under the general title of 'limit-expressions.'" (Ricoeur, "The Specificity of Language," 107; hereafter this work will be referred to as "Specificity"). In our examination, we will see how each of the three genres exhibits the literary trait of "intensification," or "transgression," or "going to the limit" as the modification of the traditional usage.

143  In his investigation, Tracy's handling of the New Testament studies which support his arguments is very brief. Hence, for a better understanding of how legitimately New Testament scholarship serves for backing up Tracy's arguments, we will explore in detail the relevant New Testament studies that Tracy utilizes.

*1. The "Limit" Character of Christian Religious Language and Its "Limit-Visions"*

*The Proverbs*

For his examination of the limit character of proverbial language in the New Testament, Tracy draws on William A. Beardslee's works.[144] The key note of Beardslee's interpretation of the proverbs in the New Testament is "intensification." According to Beardslee, proverbial wisdom "shows itself to be a very flexible form, capable of expressing very different sorts of ideas and styles of faith" in accordance with different literary purposes and settings.[145] In its usual form, the proverb expresses a "project of making a unified whole of one's life," or "an orderly tract of experience which can be repeated."[146] However, the peculiarity of the use of proverbial sayings in the Synoptic Gospels can be described as "the intensification of proverbial insight."[147] Beardslee explains that, in the Synoptic Gospels, this intensification of proverbial insight is primarily attempted by means of the literary devices of "paradox" and "hyperbole."[148]

According to him, paradox is usually related to "antithetical formulations."[149] The antithetical formulations attempted by the Synoptic paradox are the ones that express "a *reversal* of situation," as

144 William A. Beardslee's relevant works here are "The Uses of the Proverb in the Synoptic Tradition," in *Int*, 24 (1970) 61–76; *Literary Criticism of the New Testament* (Philadelphia: Fortress Press, 1970) 30–41.

145 Beardslee, *Literary Criticism of the New Testament*, 40. Hereafter, this work will be referred to as *Literary Criticism*.

146 Beardslee, *Literary Criticism*, 41 and idem, "Uses of the Proverb in the Synoptic Gospels," 65. Hereafter, the latter work will be referred to as "Uses of Proverb."

147 Beardslee, *Literary Criticism*, 39. Beardslee explains that, "Though there are in Mark and Q (and in material peculiar to Luck and Matthew) examples of proverbs which express a rather general folk wisdom, with its rather relaxed and sometimes even resigned attitude toward the making of choices, it is evident that in the most characteristic Synoptic sayings this wisdom is immensely concentrated and intensified." (Beardslee, "Uses of Proverb," 66).

148 Beardslee, "Uses of Proverb," 66.

149 *Ibid.*

shown in proverbs such as "Whoever seeks to gain his life will lose it, but whoever loses his life will preserve it" (Lk 17: 33; cf. Mk 8: 35 and Jn 12: 25).[150] Here, says Beardslee, the intensification is embodied in the sharp overturning of fortune in which "the imagination is jolted out of its vision of a continuous connection between one situation and the other."[151] In other words, the intensified proverbial insight disorients the ordinary project of "making a continuous whole out of one's existence."[152]

Hyperbole, another distinctive literary device of intensification, is generally related to "a kind of sardonic humor."[153] However, the hyperbole in the Synoptics, like paradox, is used to upset common sense: e.g., "Love your enemies, do good to those who hate you" (Lk 6: 27; Mt 5: 44); "It is easier for a camel to go through the eye of a needle than for a rich man to enter the kingdom of God" (Mk 10: 25). The use of exaggeration provokes the reader to break through the familiar vision of life by means of an abrupt rupture.[154] In sum, the intensification of the Synoptic proverbs by means of paradox and hyperbole:

> has to do with the shifting of its function from that of identifying some repeatable tract of experience, useful to know about when engaged in the project of striving to make a coherent whole out of one's existence, to that of jolting the hearer out of this hoped-for continuity into a new judgment about his existence.[155]

Tracy claims that Beardslee's analysis effectively demonstrates how the intensified proverbial sayings of the Synoptics exhibit the

---

150  *Ibid.*, 67 (italics mine).
151  *Ibid.*
152  *Ibid.*, 71.
153  *Ibid.*, 68.
154  In his analysis of Beardslee's interpretation of proverb, Ricoeur expresses this provocative effect of hyperbole as "*re-orientation by disorientation.*" Ricoeur says that the proverb takes the round-about way of "an impossible possibility." (Ricoeur, "Specificity," 114).
155  Beardslee, "Uses of Proverb," 72.

character of a limit-language disclosive of a limit-sense.[156] The intensified proverbs challenge or question "our everyday way of being in the world – our moral projects, our intellectual strivings, our traditional proverbial wisdom, our hopes, and struggles" which appear to suffice for a meaningful existence.[157] Tracy explains that, "Its sense is the sense of all authentically religious language: the strange, jarring, paradoxical, and unnerving sense of a limit-language" which points us beyond the banal meaning of life.[158] Put differently, in order to disclose such a limit-sense, the ordinary form of proverbial sayings needs to be shifted to an intensified form characteristic of paradox or hyperbole. Next, Tracy considers what unique vision can be gleaned from the proverbial language of the Synoptics. Tracy explicates this with two examples. First, from the proverb, "Whoever seeks to gain his life will lose it, but whoever loses his life will preserve it" (Lk 17: 33), Tracy elucidates the following vision. This proverb of paradox does not encourage us to give up making a continuous whole of our life project. Instead, it manifests the insight that:

> the everyday with all its ambiguity including all its wisdom and goodness must be 'intensified' to the point where we reach the limit of all present efforts, where we are jarred into 'letting go' of even our best struggles: to 'lose our life' in order to gain it.[159]

With another example, the proverb, "Let the dead bury the dead," Tracy writes as follows:

> 'Let the dead bury the dead' does not give us common-sense advice for orienting us toward grief and loss. Such a proverb deliberately disorients us, disconnects us from the ordinary, the acceptable, the 'respectable.' If we allow New Testament proverbial language to disclose its genuinely religious mean-

---

156 Tracy explains that the "intensification of ordinary proverbial language by the linguistic strategies of paradox and hyperbole alerts one to the limit of the ordinary use of such language and thereby discloses the properly limit-sense of New Testament proverbs." (*BRO*, 125).
157 *Ibid.*
158 *Ibid.*
159 *Ibid.*

ing, such proverbs can reorient us to that dimension of life which restores a wholeness of meaning to all our basic activities.[160]

## The Proclamatory Sayings

Tracy's second analysis focuses on the proclamatory sayings of the New Testament as another representative example of a language form which reveals the limit character of religious language. For this investigation, Tracy has recourse to Norman Perrin's study of the proclamatory sayings of Jesus. Although he bases himself on Perrin's study, he does not offer a detailed explanation of it. Therefore, first, we will briefly look at Perrin's study as far as it is relevant to Tracy's concern. Then, we will examine Tracy's use of it for his own argument.

## Norman Perrin's Analysis of Proclamatory Sayings

Perrin explains that, according to the contemporary scholarly opinion of his time, the following proclamatory sayings can be counted among Jesus' authentic sayings. The common theme of the sayings is the "Kingdom of God."[161]

(i) Lk 11: 20: "But if it is by the finger of God that I cast out demons then the Kingdom of God has come upon you."

(ii) Lk 17: 20–1: "The Kingdom of God is not coming with signs to be observed; nor will they say, 'Lo, here it is! or 'There!' for behold, the kingdom of God is in the midst of you."

(iii) Mt 11: 12: "From the days of John the Baptist until now, the Kingdom of Heaven has suffered violence, and men of violence plunder it."

---

160  *Ibid.*, 134.
161  Norman Perrin, Jesus and the Language of the Kingdom: Symbol and Metaphor in New Testament Interpretation (Philadelphia: Fortress Press, 1976) 41. Hereafter, this work will be referred to as *Jesus and Language*.

A noteworthy element in Perrin's interpretation of these sayings is his linking of them to modern linguistic theories of *symbol*.[162] According to Perrin, the scholarly investigation of this literary genre of proclamatory sayings, ever since Johannes Weiss through Albert Schweitzer, Rudolf Bultmann, Charles H. Dodd, and Joachim Jeremias,[163] has focused on two common issues. The first issue is what the *idea* or *conception* of the "Kingdom of God" in these sayings is. The second issue is the temporal order of the coming of the "Kingdom of God. In other words, the issue is whether the temporal order of the "Kingdom of God" is future ("consequent eschatology" of Schweitzer) or already here ("realized eschatology" of Dodd) or both present and future ("proleptic eschatology" of Weiss, Bultmann and Jeremias). Over against these two main concerns, Perrin attempts a new approach to these sayings inspired by modern linguistic theories of symbol. His interest is to demonstrate how modern linguistic developments can contribute to a corrective interpretation of Jesus' proclamatory sayings concerning the "Kingdom of God."

The first contention of Perrin is that the "Kingdom of God" is not an *idea* or a *conception*, but *a symbol*. Here, Perrin's notion of symbol is aided by the theories of *symbol* developed by Philip Wheelwright and Paul Ricoeur. In order to understand Perrin's argument, we need to see in brief the key ideas of these theories of symbol.

According to Wheelwright, "a symbol, in general, is a relatively stable and repeatable element of perceptual experience, standing for some larger meaning or set of meaning which cannot be given, or not fully given, in perceptual experience itself."[164] He distinguishes two

---

162  Perrin's main sources are Philip Wheelwright, *Metaphor and Reality* (Bloomington: Indiana University Press, 1975, first published in 1962) and Paul Ricoeur, *The Symbolism of Evil*, trans. by Emerson Buchanan (Boston: Beacon Press, 1969).

163  Johannes Weiss, *Die Predigt Jesu vom Reiche Gottes* (Göttingen: Vandenhoeck and Ruprecht, 1964, first published in 1892); Albert Schweitzer, *Geschichte der Leben-Jesu-Forschung* (Tübingen: J.C.B. Mohr, 1913); Rudolf Bultmann, *Jesus* (Tübingen: J.C.B. Mohr, 1926); Charles H. Dodd, *The Parables of the Kingdom of God* (London: Nisbet and Co. Ltd., 1935); Joachim Jeremias, *Die Gleichnisse Jesu* (Zürich: Leemann and Co., 1947).

164  Philip Wheelwright, *Metaphor and Reality*, 92.

different kinds of symbols in terms of their relationship to what they represent. There are the symbols which have a one-to-one relationship to what they represent such as mathematical symbols. Such symbols are called, in Wheelwright's terms, "steno-symbols" which aim at "a public exactitude, an uncompromising identity of reference for all who use them correctly."[165] Another kind of symbol is the one that represents a set of meanings that can neither be "stipulative" (or exhaustive) nor be "exact" in a one-to-one referential relationship. Wheelwright calls these symbols "tensive symbols."[166] "Tensive symbols" are, thus, lively and dynamic inasmuch as their essential tension rests on their multiple-semantic potential. The "tensive" symbol does not stipulate a meaning, but triggers a meaning.

Another discussion of symbol that Perrin finds important is Paul Ricoeur's theory. According to Ricoeur, broadly speaking, the symbol is a sign which "aims at something beyond itself and stands for that something."[167] Yet, more specifically, the symbol is not just a sign. The difference is that while the reference of a sign is exhausted by its "first or literal intentionality," the symbol "conceals in its aim a double intentionality."[168] In other words, signs are transparent of meanings inasmuch as they "say only what they want to say in positing that which they signify."[169] However, symbols are "opaque, because the first, literal, obvious meaning itself points analogically to a second meaning which is not given otherwise than in it."[170] He explains the distinctiveness of symbol as follows:

> Unlike a comparison that we *consider* from outside, the symbol is the move-
> ment of the primary meaning which makes us participate in the latent meaning
> and thus assimilates us to that which is symbolized without our being able to
> master the similitude intellectually. It is in this sense that the symbol is dona-

---

165 *Ibid.*, 94. Wheelwright explains that, "There are also steno-symbols of a more casual sort, where a metaphor has become rigid not through stipulation but through human inertia." (*Ibid.*).
166 Wheelwright, *ibid.*
167 Paul Ricoeur, *The Symbolism of Evil*, 15.
168 *Ibid.*
169 *Ibid.*
170 *Ibid.*

tive; it is donative because it is a primary intentionality that gives the second meaning analogically.[171]

Ricoeur states that the "opacity" underlying its referential mode "constitutes the depth of the symbol, which, it will be said, is inexhaustible."[172]

In view of these modern linguistic theories of *symbol*,[173] Perrin suggests that we can see the "Kingdom of God" as a fundamentally "tensive symbol" (or a symbol, not a sign in Ricoeur) whose meaning can "never be exhausted, nor adequately expressed by any one referent." Perrin claims that:

> 'Kingdom of God' is not an *idea* or a *conception*, it is a *symbol*. As a symbol it can *represent* or *evoke* a whole range of or series of conceptions or ideas, but it only becomes a conception or idea if it constantly represents or evokes that one conception or idea, and we then take the step of creating a kind of verbal shorthand in speaking of the 'conception of the Kingdom.'[174]

In view of these theories of symbol, Perrin contends that if we consider the "Kingdom of God" as *an idea* or *conception*, we are compelled to understand it as a steno-symbol or a sign on the lips of Jesus. Then, we are obliged to search for *the* most adequate referent of the "Kingdom of God" in the proclamation of Jesus in a one-to-one referential relationship. This approach cannot but "prejudge" by one fixed referent the whole range of meanings that 'Kingdom of God' can trigger as a *symbol*.[175] Concerning the reference of the "Kingdom of God," Perrin suggests that it needs to be elucidated in relation to the ancient Jewish "*myth* of the activity of God as king on behalf of his people."[176] Against this backdrop of meaning, the reference of the

171  *Ibid.*, 15–16.
172  *Ibid.*, 15.
173  Perrin understands that "what for Wheelwright is a distinction between a 'steno-symbol' and a 'tensive symbol' is for Ricoeur a distinction between a 'sign' and a 'symbol'." (Perrin, *Jesus and Language*, 30).
174  *Ibid.*, 33.
175  *Ibid.*
176  *Ibid.*, (italics mine). Perrin presents three background elements to bear in mind when we approach the Kingdom sayings of Jesus: "In the first place, 'Kingdom

activity of God needs to be understood in many and varied ways.[177] Since God's activity for his people is manifest in diversified forms in different times and places, the evoked meaning of the symbolic language of the "Kingdom of God" should be approached as "plurisignificant."[178] In short, the "Kingdom of God" can never be fixed in any one referent.[179]

If this new approach to "Kingdom of God" as a symbol is accepted, according to Perrin, an important question can be raised as

of God' is a symbol with deep roots in the Jewish consciousness of themselves as the people of God. Then, secondly, it functions within the context of the myth of God active in history on behalf of his people; indeed by the time of Jesus it had come to represent particularly the expectation of a final, eschatological act of God on behalf of his people. Thirdly, it could be understood and used either as a steno-or as a tensive symbol, to use a modern but nonetheless appropriate distinction. It is against this background that we must view the message of Jesus." (*Ibid.*, 32).

According to Ricoeur, *myths* are regarded "as a species of symbols, as symbols developed in the form of narrations and articulated in a time and a space that cannot be co-ordinated with the time and space of history and geography according to the critical method." (Ricoeur, *The Symbolism of Evil*, 18). He explains that, "By its triple function of concrete universality, temporal orientation, and finally ontological exploration, the myth has a way of *revealing* things that is not reducible to any translation from a language in cipher to a clear language." (*Ibid.*, 163). Perrin's idea of myth appears to rely on Ricoeur's theory.

177 Perrin explains that, "Even in ancient Jewish apocalyptic the hope by the use of the symbolic language [Kingdom of God] could vary enormously; it could take many varied forms. Moreover, it was pointed out that even in the time of maximum apocalyptic influence the Kaddish prayer [e.g., 'May he establish his kingdom in your lifetime and in your days and in the lifetime of all the house of Israel, even speedily and at a near time'] was in regular use, which means that the symbolic language could evoke other and different forms of the hope for the kingly activity of God on behalf of his people." (*Ibid.*, 33–4).

178 Perrin, *ibid.*, 29.

179 Perrin claims that, "To speak of Jesus' *conception* [not *symbol*] of the Kingdom is to imply that for Jesus Kingdom of God evoked a consistent well-defined understanding of the nature and form of the activity of God represented by that symbolic language. This is to set limits to the discussion within the confines of which it could never be settled, limits, moreover, which it constantly strove to break." (Perrin, *ibid.*, 34).

to the second common concern of scholarly investigation, namely, the exact nature of the temporal order of the coming of the "Kingdom of God." For Perrin, the problematic aspect of this concern is that it is tied to the *literal* interpretation of the "when" of the coming of the Kingdom. This "when" issue is usually conjoined to the question of which eschatology ("consequent" or "realized" or "proleptic") is *the* most correct one. In the light of the theories of symbol used above, this concern to determine the *literal* "when" (in Ricoeur's words, "a first or literal intentionality") cannot be the real focus of interpretation. For the real focus of the interpretation of a symbol should be the "latent meaning" or the "second intentionality" donated by the literal or first meaning.[180] Having left behind the concern of resolving the literal, temporal character of the eschatological occurrence, Perrin attempts to offer a new interpretative perspective on Jesus' proclamatory sayings concerning the "Kingdom of God."[181] As an example, let us look at his commentary on Lk 17: 20–1: "The Kingdom of God is not coming with signs to be observed; nor will they say, 'Lo here it is!' or 'There!' for behold, the Kingdom of God is in the midst of you."

According to Perrin, this saying implicitly alludes to the "apocalyptic practice of 'sign seeking'" attempted by both ancient Judaism and primitive Christianity.[182] In this "sign seeking," what is sought is a powerful and convincing 'symptom' that can be identified as part of the event of the apocalyptic drama of God's kingly activity. Perrin claims that this "sign seeking" is "dependent upon the treatment of the myth of the activity of God on behalf of his people as *allegory* and its

---

180　See Ricoeur, *The Symbolism of Evil*, 15–16.
181　Perrin's book, *Jesus and the Language of the Kingdom* is devoted to a new interpretative perspective on Jesus' sayings relating to the "Kingdom of God" based on modern theories of symbol. In this book, he deals with four different categories of Jesus' sayings regarding the "Kingdom of God": the proclamatory sayings (or the Kingdom sayings); the Lord's prayer; the proverbial sayings; the major parables. In relation to Tracy's concern, our focus in this examination is only his interpretation of the first category, the proclamatory sayings.
182　Perrin, *Jesus and Language*, 44.

132

symbols as *steno*-symbols."[183] For this seeking supposes a one-to-one referential relationship between the myth of the kingly activity of God and *a* relevant sign.[184] However, in this saying of Lk 17: 20–1, Jesus rejected the traditional apocalyptic "sign seeking" for the coming of Kingdom of God. This indicates, claims Perrin, that Jesus "rejected the treatment of the myth [God's kingly activity for his people] as *allegory* and its symbols as *steno*-symbols."[185] In short, in Jesus' saying, there occurs a "transgression" of the traditional apocalyptic language of "sign seeking" and a new perspective on the "Kingdom of God" is opened. Perrin explains that:

> In the message of Jesus the myth is true myth and the symbols of God's redemptive activity are tensive symbols. This is the meaning I would now give to the enigmatic 'the kingdom of God *entos hymon estin* [is in the midst of you].' It means that the symbol of the kingly activity of God on behalf of his people confronts the hearers of Jesus as a true tensive symbol with its evocation of a whole set of meanings, and that the myth is, in the message of Jesus, true myth with its power to mediate the experience of existential reality.[186]

183   *Ibid.*, 45 (italics mine). Here, Perrin places allegory and steno-symbol on the same footing in terms of their modality of communicating a meaning in a one-to-one relationship. Perrin's understanding of allegory seems to incorporate Paul Ricoeur's theory. According to Ricoeur, "in an allegory what is primarily signified – that is to say, the literal meaning – is contingent, and what is signified secondarily, the symbolic meaning itself, is external enough to be directly accessible. Hence, there is a relation of *translation* between the two meanings." (Paul Ricoeur, *The Symbolism of Evil*, 16, italics mine). Therefore, Ricoeur goes on to say that, "Symbol and allegory, then, are not on the same footing: symbols precede hermeneutics; allegories are already hermeneutic. This is so because the symbol presents its meaning transparently in an entirely different way than by translation. [...] It [symbol] presents its meaning in the opaque transparency of an enigma and not by translation. Hence, I oppose the *donation of meaning in trans-parency* in symbols to the interpretation by *translation* of allegories." (*Ibid.*).

184   Perrin writes that, "Typically the apocalyptic seer told the story of the history of his people in symbols [steno-symbols] where...for the most part each symbol bore a one-to-one relationship to that which it depicted. The thing was Antiochus Epiphanes, that thing was Judas Maccabee, the other thing was the coming of the Romans, and so on." (Perrin, *Jesus and Language*, 44).

185   *Ibid.*, 45 (italics mine).

186   *Ibid.*

Perrin's argument is that, as Jesus indicates in the saying, if the reference of the "Kingdom of God" cannot be exhausted by any one apprehension of reality as *a* sign, the interpretation of "the Kingdom of God is in the midst of you" is not necessarily limited just to the determination of the *literal* meaning of its *temporal* coming. Instead, beyond that issue (the first literal intentionality), the second intentionality, in which the real depth of the symbolic reference abides, should be the chief concern. Perrin leaves open the discussion of what the symbolic reference of the "Kingdom of God" (the second intentionality) might be. Perrin asserts only that Jesus' proclamatory sayings about the Kingdom are "a challenge to the hearers to take the ancient myth with renewed seriousness, and to begin to anticipate the manifestation of the reality of which it speaks in the concrete actuality of their experience."[187]

*Tracy's Understanding of Proclamatory Sayings*

Tracy assesses that Perrin's study of Jesus' proclamatory sayings in terms of the theories of symbol shows how such sayings are a limit-language disclosive of a limit-vision. Tracy appraises Perrin's symbolic approach to Jesus' Kingdom sayings in the following way:

> I interpret the significance of Perrin's discovery as follows: only when the interpreter recognizes *linguistically* that he is dealing here with an authentically religious use of language, will he be willing to abandon both an interpretation which ties that language to traditional apocalyptic usage and an interpretation which has as its chief concern the determination of the literal "when" of the eschatological occurrence.[188]

Tracy's observation has two implications. Firstly, Perrin's interpretation of Jesus' Kingdom sayings in terms of the notion of symbol sheds light on the *religious* dimension of those sayings. The new religious perspective on those sayings denotes something other than the conventional apocalyptic "sign seeking" and the literal temporality of the Kingdom's coming. Tracy wants to reformulate this new

187   *Ibid.*, 43.
188   *BRO*, 126 (italics mine).

religious perspective in terms of his pivotal category, "limit." Secondly, Perrin demonstrates this possibility only by appealing to a *linguistic* approach which is a dogmatically or kerygmatically neutral approach. Thus, Perrin's analysis helps to elucidate the intelligibility of the *religious* dimension of Christian religious language in a scientific (public) manner.

With regard to the first implication, Tracy explains the corrective perspective illuminated by Perrin's study in the following way. "The proclamatory sayings of Jesus break the traditional apocalyptic usage by transgressing altogether its literal temporal character."[189] For example, the proclamatory language, "The Kingdom of God is in the midst of you" in Lk 17: 20–1 does not speak of the Kingdom's coming in a temporal sense of "an everyday 'when'."[190] Instead, it breaks all conventional concern with the literal sense of time as regards the Kingdom's coming. According to Tracy, "that language intensifies the recognition that the everyday, even at its most significant, is utterly unable to disclose the final meaning of the everyday. It brings the listener/reader to a point which can only be described as beyond the limits of the everyday."[191] In other words, in this proclamatory saying, we find a "limit-language" which overturns "our finest temporal predictions and our most significant temporal events."[192] However, Tracy guards against any misunderstanding of this saying in terms of a super-natural view of time. "Literalize that language and that super-everyday world of supernaturalism called fundamentalism emerges."[193] Rather, in this saying, we need to recognize "a religious use of language which challenges, provokes, jars alike our wisdom, our morality, and our sense of everyday time."[194] In this provocation, there occurs a disclosure of a new world of meaning. There opens up "another" world which is "not an apocalyptic, super-everyday world; but a 'limit' dimension to *this* world, *this* experience,

189    *Ibid.*
190    *Ibid.*
191    *Ibid.*
192    *Ibid.*
193    *Ibid.*
194    *Ibid.*

*this* language."[195] In sum, Jesus' proclamatory sayings do not offer us any temporal plan for the occurrence of the "Kingdom of God" as past, as future, or as present. Rather, these sayings reveal to us the authentic meaning of time "as the e-vent [sic], the happening, for the disclosure of God's gracious and trustworthy action to happen now."[196]

*The Parables*

In his analysis of parabolic language, Tracy's fundamental interest remains consistent, namely, whether the parabolic language of the New Testament can be *linguistically* appraised as a "limit-language" disclosive of "limit-visions" for human possibilities.[197] In other words, his concern is whether we can elucidate the "religious" reference of parabolic language simply by appealing to a literary-hermeneutical analysis of its *literary form*. To explore this issue, Tracy employs new approaches to parable-interpretation over against traditional studies.[198] The notable trait of these new studies is that they make use of modern literary theories of metaphor.[199]

195  *Ibid.*
196  *Ibid.*, 134.
197  Tracy expresses his focal question in this analysis as follows: "With the intensification-process which Beardslee found in the New Testament use of proverbs, with the overturning of chronological time which Norman Perrin discovered in the eschatological proclamation sayings, there seemed solid linguistic reason to suggest that these New Testament uses of language were legitimately described in limit-language terms. Can the parable also be properly described as involving a limit use of language?" (*Ibid.*, 129).
198  For the new approaches to parable-interpretation, see *inter alia*, Dominic Crossan, *In Parables*; Norman Perrin, "The Parables of Jesus as Parables, as Metaphors and as Aesthetic Objects"; idem, "The Modern Interpretation of the Parables of Jesus and the Problem of Hermeneutics"; Dan O. Via, *The Parables: Their Literary and Existential Dimension*; Paul Ricoeur, "The Specificity of Language."
199  Regarding the leading theories of metaphor which influenced the new approaches to parable-interpretation, see *inter alia*, I.A. Richards, *Philosophy of Rhetoric* (New York: Oxford, 1936) esp. 90–4 on the "transaction theory" of metaphor; Monroe Beardsley, "The Metaphorical Twist," in Warren Shibles (ed.), *Essays on Metaphor* (Whitewater, Wisc.: The Language Press, 1972) 73–

According to Tracy's brief sketch, traditionally, the earliest and the most typical interpretation of the parables of the New Testament was an allegorical one.[200] A remarkable turning point with regard to the traditional allegorical interpretation, however, was made in the work of Adolph Jülicher.[201] Jülicher's key argument is that parables are not allegories, but a unique literary genre recounting a moral teaching by a story of ordinary life. The limitation of this work is, however, the strong moralism in its interpretation of parables, an interpretation imbued with the religious liberalism of his time. The next important contribution to modern parabolic interpretation was the work of Charles H. Dodd and Joachim Jeremias.[202] The major accomplishment of these works consisted of two elements. Firstly, these works attempted a historical reconstruction of the parables by the employment of historical-critical method which analyzed "the actual life-situation (*Sitz im Leben*) of either Jesus, or of the early Christian community, or of the redactor of the various parables."[203] Until recently, this *Sitz-im-Leben* approach has been very influential. What we cannot resolve by this historical-critical method is, however, the explication of the meaning of the *world* of the reconstructed texts

93; Max Black, *Models and Metaphors* (Ithaca: Cornell University Press, 1962) esp. 25–48; Philip Wheelwright, *Metaphor and Reality*; Paul Ricoeur, "The Metaphorical Process"; idem, "Word, Polysemy, Metaphor: Creativity in Language," in Mario J. Valdés (ed.), *A Ricoeur Reader: Reflection and Imagination* (Hertfordshire: Harvester Wheatsheaf, 1991) 65–85, already published in *PhT*, 17 (1973) 97–128; idem, *Interpretation Theory: Discourse and the Surplus of Meaning*.

200   Tracy writes that, "In the New Testament itself, in the exegeses of Alexandria, Antioch, and Augustine, in the Medieval tradition of the 'four senses' of scripture, parables, until fairly recently, have been widely interpreted as allegories." (*BRO*, 127). For the historical development of interpretation of scripture in terms of the "four senses," see Henri de Lubac, *Exégèse mèdiévale* (Paris: Aubier, 1959–1963).

201   Adolph Jülicher, *Die Gleichnisreden Jesu* (Tübingen: J.C.B. Mohr, 1910, first published in 1888).

202   Charles H. Dodd, *The Parables of the Kingdom* (London: Nisbet and Co. Ltd., 1935); Joachim Jeremias, *Die Gleichnisse Jesu* (Zürich: Leemann and Co., 1947).

203   *BRO*, 127. For a succinct explanation of the parabolic interpretations of Dodd and Jeremias, see Perrin, *Jesus and Language*, 91–107.

(the referents of the texts).[204] For this task, we need another method of analysis, such as "a properly hermeneutical" investigation.[205] Secondly, these works rediscovered the eschatological-religious, not ethical, vision of the parables. This rediscovery could allow "a reinterpretation of the religious-as-eschatological vision of Christianity," which departed from the sheer moral interpretation inspired by modern liberalism.[206] Tracy remarks that, "in that sense, this stage of parable-interpretation already discloses the unique 'limit-vision' of Christian eschatology as a religious not merely ethical vision for the contemporary reader."[207] However, Tracy intends to move beyond these works for his analysis. To repeat, his prime concern is to show "how the actual *language form* of the New Testament parables linguistically discloses the limit-vision of Christian eschatology."[208] Put differently, his concern is to demonstrate "how that limit-vision in

---

204 Tracy explains that, "To what aspects of reality, ordinary or perhaps extra-ordinary, do these texts refer the reader? These referents of the text do not refer to the meaning 'behind' the text (such as the author's real intention or the social-cultural situation of the text [what the *Sitz-im-Leben* approach can explicate]). Rather, [...] the referent of the text expresses the meaning 'in front of the text.' More exactly, we can determine both an object-referent of some existential import (viz., that way of perceiving reality, that mode of being-in-the-world which the text opens up for the intelligent reader) and a subject-referent (viz., the personal vision of the author implied by the text)." (*BRO*, 78).

205 For his own analysis, Tracy relies, to a great extent, on Paul Ricoeur's hermeneutical theories.

206 *BRO*, 127.

207 *Ibid.*

208 *Ibid.*, 128 (italics mine). As to this concern, Tracy seems to incorporate Ricoeur's argument. Ricoeur writes that, "What Jeremias has not shown is how that eschatological vision is expressed in the very *form* of the parables. His interpretation passes directly to a theological interpretation, indeed to a theological interpretation presented in a language very near to that of the traditional preaching of German Lutheranism [...] And this short-circuit between a historical critique and a theological interpretation makes us miss an essential trait which would appear for a *literary* analysis placed between the historical critique and the theological interpretation." (Ricoeur, "Specificity," 115).

turn can be adequately articulated only in a limit-language" such as parables.[209]

To achieve this, Tracy utilizes the so-called "third" stage of New Testament scholarship on parables.[210] Tracy observes that the distinctiveness of the third-stage approaches to parable-interpretation is, internal differences among the scholars notwithstanding, the insight that "the fundamental linguistic form operative in the narrative genre of parable is the metaphor."[211] Among the scholars of this position, Tracy is, in particular, indebted to Paul Ricoeur's interpretation of parables. Ricoeur characterizes the literary form of parable as the "conjunction of a narrative form and a metaphorical process."[212] As this characterization suggests, the modern theory of metaphor plays a crucial role in the interpretation of parabolic language. Moreover, Paul Ricoeur's theory of metaphor and his parabolic interpretation based on that theory involve a profound *hermeneutical* concern. The hermeneutical concern, for Ricoeur, refers to the task of interpreting the *referential* meaning of the *world* of a text.[213] This hermeneutical approach is essentially adopted in Tracy's interpretation of the parables.[214]

Tracy's analysis of parables presents us with a difficulty. That difficulty lies in that he utilizes Ricoeur's literary-hermeneutical theories in his own discussion, presupposing that we already have a

209   *BRO*, 128.
210   *Ibid.*, For the major works of this group, see *supra*.
211   *Ibid.*
212   Ricoeur, "The Metaphorical Process," 75.
213   For Ricoeur, the hermeneutical interpretation concerns the interpretive "movement of the internal structure of the work toward its reference, toward the sort of world which the work opens up *in front of* the text." (Ricoeur, *ibid.*, 82). We will look in detail at how this hermeneutical concern is an essential element in Paul Ricoeur's theory of metaphor and his interpretation of the parabolic language in the following examination.
214   More accurately speaking, the hermeneutical approach is shown in Tracy's analysis of all three literary genres: proverbs, proclamatory sayings, and parables. In our examination of his analysis of proverbs and proclamatory sayings in the preceding sections, we already indicated his hermeneutical construals of the "limit-visions" disclosed in those sayings. In this section, this issue will be more clearly illuminated.

knowledge of those theories. Thus, prior to examining Tracy's discussion, we need to spell out the key features of Ricoeur's theories to which Tracy's analysis is indebted. Accordingly, in what follows, our examination consists of three points. Firstly, we will look into Ricoeur's theory of metaphor which is requisite for understanding his interpretation of parables. Secondly, we will investigate Ricoeur's interpretation of parables. Finally, we will examine how Tracy uses Ricoeur's work for his own analysis.[215]

215 There is another important reason that we need to examine Ricoeur's literary-hermeneutical theories here. In his analysis of the Christian texts and his correlation of common human experience and the vision of the Christian texts, Tracy incorporates, to a great extent, Ricoeur's literary-hermeneutical theories. However, for the matter of how the cognitive claims involved in human religious experience and the Christian texts are *conceptually* mediated, Tracy diverges from Paul Ricoeur's position. Whereas Paul Ricoeur maintains a phenomenological-hermeneutical mediation (hermeneutics as a philosophical reflection), Tracy takes on a "transcendental-metaphysical" reflection (note thesis 5 in the preceding chapter). Tracy states that, "A revisionist theologian, moreover, may well find this recent hermeneutical theory [most importantly the theory of Paul Ricoeur in his analysis] particularly helpful for his/her own enterprise. This theory allows the theologian to employ a method capable of explicating the principal existential meanings of Christian texts *without* involving one in the difficulties of either psychologizing those meanings or of expecting 'hermeneutics' to carry *the impossible burden of ethical and metaphysical analysis.*" (*BRO*, 79; italics mine). It is clear that, in his revisionist model, Tracy intends to use hermeneutics only as an interpretation theory to investigate the Christian texts, not to use it further as a way of conceptual (philosophical) mediation. He states that, "The tendency in contemporary theology to imply that hermeneutics can encompass the entire field of theology is eliminated by this understanding of the limited but highly important task of hermeneutics (namely, to determine the sense and the referents of texts)." (*Ibid.*, 78).

Ricoeur's theory of metaphor begins by calling into question the traditional view of metaphor in view of modern semantics. In traditional rhetorics,[216] the metaphor was considered as "a trope by resemblance or by analogy," having the effect of "stylistic ornament."[217] The decisive trait here is to replace the conventional word with another one which seems to be more pleasant or to provide a name for the unnamable by analogy.[218] Since the main role of metaphor here is to *substitute* a word by a word, modern scholars call this traditional treatment a substitution theory.[219] Through substitution, metaphor provides refreshment by breaking commonplaceness in deviating from the use of conventional words. In short, metaphor, in the traditional view, neither offers any new information nor generates any creative meaning. Rather, it only "gives color to speech" to please or to attract the audience.[220]

In contrast to the traditional view, Ricoeur elaborates his theory of metaphor in terms of two focal aspects: (1) the semantic innovation

216  The traditional view on metaphor "begins with the Greek sophists, moves through Aristotle, Cicero and Quintillian, and [...] ends with the last treatises on rhetoric of the 19th century." (Ricoeur, "The Metaphorical Process," 76).
217  Ricoeur, "Word, Polysemy, Metaphor: Creativity in Language," in Mario J. Valdés (ed.), *A Ricoeur Reader: Reflection and Imagination* (Hertfordshire: Harvester Wheatsheaf, 1991) 76. Hereafter, this work will be referred to as "Word, Polysemy, Metaphor."
218  For example, old age is to life what evening is to day, and so we can call evening 'the old age of the day,' and call old age 'the evening of life' for pleasure. Another example for providing a name for the unnamable by analogy: scattering seed is called 'sowing,' but there is no term for the scattering of light by the sun; but as this is related to the sun as sowing is to the scatterer of seed, we may have the expression 'sowing the god-created flame.'
219  Ricoeur calls this manner of substitution "denomination" or "displacement." (Ricoeur, *Interpretation Theory*, 49). Ricoeur explains that the important step for the contemporary theory of metaphor which departed from the traditional rhetorics of metaphor as substitution was initiated by scholars such as I.A. Richards, Max Black, Colin Turbayne, Monroe Beardsley, Douglas Berggren, and others (See Ricoeur, "Word, Polysemy, Metaphor," 76).
220  Ricoeur, "Word, Polysemy, Metaphor," 77.

of metaphor; (2) the referential function of redefining reality of metaphor.

## The Semantic Innovation of Metaphor

The central hypothesis of Ricoeur's theory of metaphor is that "metaphor is more than a figure of style, but contains *semantic innovation*."[221] This hypothesis indicates that there is a shift of perspective regarding metaphor, from "a rhetoric of the *word* to a semantics of *discourse* or of the sentence."[222] This means that, according to Ricoeur, the impact of metaphor on a production of meaning occurs at the level of the sentence or of discourse as a whole, not at the level of the word. He states that, "Metaphor depends on a semantics of the sentence before it concerns a semantics of the word. Metaphor is only meaningful in a statement."[223] In this sense, metaphor is a "phenomenon of predication, not denomination."[224] For instance, "nature is a temple where living columns…," is a metaphorical utterance. Here, the metaphorical occurrence first proceeds from a tension at the level of predication, not from a tension between the two terms, "nature" and "temple." This means that the verb "is" is not just used to relate two words, "nature" and "temple," but contains a tension between a literal and a metaphorical predication. Namely, the "is" involves a tension between "both a literal 'is not' and a metaphorical 'is like'."[225] The tension is "in the *relation* itself, in the copular."[226] This implies that the semantically 'impertinent' relation between the two terms creates "*what is* in a certain way."[227]

---

221   Ricoeur, "The Metaphorical Process," 75.
222   *Ibid.*, Ricoeur explains that this is the first discovery of a semantic view of metaphor.
223   *Ibid.*, 77.
224   Ricoeur, *Interpretation Theory*, 50.
225   Ricoeur, "The Metaphorical Process," 88.
226   Ricoeur, "Word, Polysemy, Metaphor," 81 (italics mine).
227   Ricoeur, "The Metaphorical Process," 88. Ricoeur explains that, "The tension in a metaphorical utterance is really not something that occurs between two terms in the utterance, but rather between two opposed interpretations of the

According to Ricoeur, the metaphorical meaning is generated from the semantic absurdity which arises where a literal interpretation breaks down. Ricoeur states that the self-destruction of meaning in a literal interpretation, "by means of the semantic impertinence or the inconsistency of the statement, is only the reverse side of an innovation of meaning on the level of the entire sentence."[228] It is by this semantic innovation that a living metaphor is constituted.[229] The essential trait to be noted here is that the semantic impertinence is a "calculated error."[230] In other words, it is a purposive misplacement in the "play of resemblance."[231] This means that the metaphorical function is to disclose a rapprochement of meaning, hitherto unperceived, between things that were conventionally classified as incompatible. Ricoeur claims that, "What is at stake in a metaphorical statement is making a 'kinship' appear where ordinary vision perceives no mutual appropriateness at all."[232] In short, in a metaphorical utterance, the resemblance and the disparity are not merely conflated. Instead, the resemblance works "*in spite of*" disparity.[233]

From this analysis, Ricoeur draws two conclusions over against traditional rhetorical views on metaphor. Firstly, a living metaphor is "*untranslatable*" because its meaning is emergent, so that it does not

---

utterance. It is the conflict between these two interpretations that sustains the metaphor." (Ricoeur, *Interpretation Theory*, 50).

228  Ricouer, "The Metaphorical Process," 84.

229  Ricoeur explains that we do not recognize this phenomenon of semantic innovation, "if we only consider dead metaphors which are no longer true metaphors, for example, the foot of a chair, or the leg of a table. True metaphors are *metaphors of invention* in which a new extension of the meaning of the words answers a novel discordance in the sentence. It is true that the metaphor of invention tends through repetition to become a dead metaphor. Then the extension of meaning is noted in the lexicon and becomes part of the polysemy of the word which is thereby simply augmented. But there are no living metaphors in the dictionary." (*Ibid.*, 80).

230  *Ibid.*, 79.

231  *Ibid.*, 78.

232  *Ibid.* Ricoeur writes that, "To see sameness in the difference is the genius of metaphor." (Ricoeur, "Word, Polysemy, Metaphor," 80).

233  Ricoeur, "Word, Polysemy, Metaphor," 81.

fall into the conventional category of signification.[234] Ricoeur claims that, "In this respect, metaphor is an instantaneous creation, a *semantic innovation* which has no status in established language and which exists only in the attribution of unusual predicates."[235] Secondly, a living metaphor is not a rhetorical ornament which only gives color to speech, but has the "referential function" to say something new about our reality.[236] Ricoeur expresses this function as metaphor's "extraordinary power of redescribing reality."[237] According to him, this function of metaphor means that metaphor includes an existential-referential dimension. Let us focus on this second aspect of metaphor.

*The Referential Function of Redefining Reality of Metaphor*

Ricoeur's reflection on the metaphor's referential function is related to the first characteristic of metaphor: the meaning of a metaphorical statement is emergent and *innovative* in the breakdown of a literal interpretation.[238] According to Ricoeur, this element suggests that "the

---

234  Ricoeur, "The Metaphorical Process," 80.
235  *Ibid.*, 79.
236  Ricoeur, "Word, Polysemy, Metaphor," 84.
237  *Ibid.*
238  Ricoeur clarifies that the reflection on the referential function of metaphorical statements bases itself on an important semantic hypothesis. That hypothesis is the distinction between the meaning as "sense" and the meaning as "reference." In a statement, "sense" refers to what is said and "reference" designates that about which something is said. More pointedly, "what a statement says [sense] is immanent within it – it is its internal arrangement. That with which it deals [reference] is extra-linguistic. It is the real insofar as it is conveyed in language; it is what is said about the world." (Ricoeur, "The Metaphorical Process," 81). For Ricoeur, two implications are to be noted in relation to this hypothesis. Firstly, insofar as he takes seriously this distinction between "sense" and "reference," his interpretation of a metaphorical statement breaks with "structuralism where language functions purely internally or immanently, where an element refers only to another element of the same system." (*Ibid.*). Secondly, where the meaning as "reference" is concerned, it contains a "hermeneutical conception" in the sense that it says something about the world disclosed by a metaphorical statement. Ricoeur explains that the distinction between "sense" and "reference" invites us to a movement, "that is, the movement of the internal structure of the work toward its reference, toward the

metaphorical interpretation gives rise to a re-interpretationof reality itself, in spite of, and thanks to" the breakdown of the ordinary reference.[239] The essential idea here is that the strategy of a metaphorical statement is "neither to improve communication nor to insure univocity in argumentation, but to shatter and to increase our sense of reality by shattering and increasing our language."[240] The metaphorical meaning consists in grasping "a new vision of reality [...] which is resisted by ordinary vision tied to the ordinary use of words."[241]

Ricoeur calls this referential function of metaphor its "heuristic function."[242] He attempts to explain the heuristic function of metaphor by relating it to a model developed by Max Blake.[243] The similarity between metaphor and model in terms of the referential function is "to describe an unknown thing or a lesser-known thing in terms of a

sort of world which the work opens up *in front of* the text." (*Ibid.*, 82). For the more detailed explanation of the distinction between sense and reference, see a footnote in our examination of Thesis 4 in the preceding chapter.

239  *Ibid.*, 84.
240  Ricoeur, "Word, Polysemy, Metaphor," 85. In this claim, Ricoeur implicitly contrasts metaphorical language with "ordinary language" which "aims at communication by cleverly reducing ambiguity," and "scientific language" which "aims at univocity in argumentation by suppressing equivocity." (*Ibid.*, 83).
241  Ricoeur, "The Metaphorical Process," 84.
242  Ricoeur, "Word, Polysemy, Metaphor," 84.
243  For the heuristic function of model, Ricoeur uses Max Blake's *Models and Metaphors*. According to Ricoeur's reading of Max Blake, there are three different kinds of models. They are "scale models, which materially resemble the specimen, for example, a model boat; analogical models, which conserve only the structural identities, for example, a diagram; and theoretical models, which consist in constructing an imaginary object more accessible to description and in transposing the properties of this object onto a domain of more complex reality." (Ricoeur, "The Metaphorical Process," 85). In terms of the referential function, the metaphor can be compared to the "theoretical models" among these three types. Ricoeur explains that, "Now, says Max Blake, to describe a domain of reality in terms of an imaginary theoretical model is a certain manner of seeing things 'otherwise,' by changing our language on the subject of these things. And the change of language goes through the construction of a *heuristic fiction* and the transposition of this heuristic fiction to reality itself." (*Ibid.*). Ricoeur finds that this function of a "theoretical model" can be applied to metaphor.

better-known things thanks to a similarity of structure."[244] Max Black describes the (theoretical) models that introduce new connections among disparate things, by analogy, as *"heuristic fictions."*[245] This means that these models serve as instruments to describe the unknown or lesser-known domain of investigation in an *as if* relationship. That is to say, the models themselves are not the *actual* constructions of the postulated properties to be investigated. Yet, the models are *fictitious* devices to describe an obscure complex domain in an intelligible manner by suggesting the presumed isomorphism between the models and the domain of application. Ricoeur attempts to apply this function of models to metaphors.[246] He says that, "Metaphor is nothing other than the application of a familiar label to a new object which first resists and then surrenders to its application."[247] By breaking through

244 Ricoeur, "Word, Polysemy, Metaphor," 84. Max Blake sees the referential function of (a living) metaphor as "to bring two separate domains into cognitive and emotional relation by using language directly appropriate to the one as a lens for seeing the other; the implications, suggestions, and supporting values entwined with the literal use of the metaphorical expression enable us to see a new subject matter in a new way." (Max Black, *Models and Metaphors*, 236–7). Black explains that the same function applies to the role of (theoretical) models. He says, "they [theoretical models], too, bring about a wedding of disparate subjects, by a distinctive operation of transfer of the *implications* of relatively well-organized cognitive fields. And as with other weddings, their outcomes are unpredictable. [...] It [the use of a model] may also help us to notice what otherwise would be overlooked, to shift the relative emphasis attached to details – in short, to *see new connections*." (*Ibid.*, 237). He goes on to say that the "use of theoretical models resembles the use of metaphors in requiring analogical transfer of a vocabulary. Metaphor and model-making reveal new relationships; both are attempts to pour new content into old bottles." (*Ibid.*, 238–9).

245 *Ibid.*, 228. Note the different expressions of "heuristic function" and "heuristic fiction" in this discussion.

246 Ricoeur states that, "Metaphor is to poetic language as model is to scientific language." (Ricoeur, "The Metaphorical Process," 85). In short, Ricoeur sums up two essential characteristics of model which can be applied to metaphor. Firstly, a model is "a fiction, that is, it is a way of making an object easier to handle." Secondly, "this fiction is heuristic fiction inasmuch as we may transfer the description of this better-known object to the field to be described on the basis of a partial isomorphism." (Ricoeur, "Word, Polysemy, Metaphor," 85).

247 Ricoeur, "The Metaphorical Process," 86.

146

the conventional structures of our language, metaphor also shatters the ordinary structures of what we call reality. Thus, there is a resistance. However, the *epoché* of ordinary reference in such resistance is the "negative condition for the disclosure of new aspects of reality."[248] Ricoeur says that, "With metaphor we experience the metamorphosis of both language and reality."[249] And the reality, "as redescribed, is itself novel reality."[250] In sum, Ricoeur's conclusion is that metaphor is a strategy of discourse through which "language divests itself of its ordinary descriptive function in order to serve its extraordinary function of re-description" of reality.[251] Moreover, Ricoeur indicates that "the metaphor comes closest to this heuristic function when the metaphorical process is channelled by a fictional narrative."[252] According to Ricoeur, a good example of this combination is the *parables*. Let us look at Ricoeur's analysis of the *parables*.

*Paul Ricoeur's Interpretation of Parables*

As we have already pointed out, Ricoeur characterizes the parable as "the mode of discourse which applies to a *narrative form* a metaphorical process."[253] Because of this literary character, claims Ricoeur, "in the parables the narrative has to be taken metaphorically and not literally."[254] The question is how the metaphorical process is at work in the parables. In other words, what clues compel us to interpret the parables as metaphoric narratives? In order to answer this question, Ricoeur, first, specifies a distinctive feature of the metaphorical process operative in fictional narratives. Ricoeur explains that, in fictional narratives such as parables, "the bearers of the metaphor are not the individual sentences of the narratives, but the

248   Ricoeur, "Word, Polysemy, Metaphor," 84.
249   *Ibid.*, 85.
250   *Ibid.*
251   Ricoeur, "The Metaphorical Process," 88.
252   *Ibid.*, 95.
253   *Ibid.*, 88.
254   *Ibid.*, 89.

whole structure, the narratives as a whole."[255] And the metaphoricity of the whole structure of the parable consists in the *plot* of the narrative. This is to say, the metaphoricity finds itself not locally in the words or sentences, but in what *happens* in the narrative. Ricoeur explains:

> The 'plot' is not, like the forms and the codes of the followers of Propp, an underlying structure which makes the *told* story unessential, as a mere epiphenomenon of the codes themselves; the plot is the very structure *of* the narrative. [...] As Jeremias has convincingly shown, if the kingdom of God is *like* something, it is not like the man who..., the woman who..., the year which..., the pearl which..., but the kingdom is like what *happens* in the story. The Kingdom of God is not as *who*, but as *when*. In other words, it is the 'plot' as such which is the bearer of the metaphoric process.[256]

Ricoeur explicates the peculiar character of the "plot" of the New Testament parables in the following way. They are, on the one hand, narratives of normalcy. They are radically profane stories: selling and buying, sowing a seed, letting down a net into a sea, and so on. Yet, on the other hand, in these commonplace stories, there is an element of extravagance which heightens the eccentricity of the modes of behavior. For instance, the extravagance of the landlord in the "Parable of the Wicked Tenants," who after having sent his servants, sends his son; the host in the "Parable of the Great Feast" looks for substitute guests in the street; in the "Parable of the Prodigal Son," the father oversteps all bounds in greeting his son; in the "Parable of the Laborers in the Vineyard," the employer pays the employees of the eleventh hour the same wages as those hired first, an so on. We have extraordinary behavior in ordinary stories. Ricoeur expresses this paradox as "the *extraordinary* is *like* the *ordinary*."[257]

---

255  *Ibid.*, 94. In other words, the metaphorical process is operative "at the level of 'composition' (Aristotle spoke of *taxis*) which is characteristic of a *work*." (*Ibid.*, 93).

256  *Ibid.*, 97–8.

257  Ricoeur, "Listening to the Parables of Jesus," in Charles E. Reagan & David Stewart (eds), *The Philosophy of Paul Ricoeur* (Boston: Beacon Press, 1978) 239.

Ricoeur discovers in this paradoxical character of the plot ("mixing the 'extraordinary' with the 'ordinary'") the metaphorical tension.[258] The extraordinary within the ordinary in the dynamism of a narrative structure provokes tension, in which the parabolic meaning is created. Ricoeur attempts to show this procedure with an example, one of the most condensed parables, Mt 13: 44: 'The Kingdom of Heaven is like treasure hidden in a field, which someone found and hid; then in his joy he goes and sells all that he has and buys that field.' In this parable, the first layer of the plot consists of ordinary human activities: finding, hiding, selling, and buying. It is a radically profane story. A paradoxical implication of this feature is that the "Kingdom of Heaven" is compared to such ordinary things. Despite the religious theme of the parable (the "Kingdom of Heaven"), "there are no gods, no demons, no angels, no miracles, no time before time, as in the creation stories, not even founding events as in the Exodus account."[259]

Besides this first layer, there is another layer of the plot which forms a contrast to the first. There is an extravagance of behavior: after finding a treasure hidden in a field, *selling everything else* and *buying the field*. The overall plot of the narrative bears a tension between these two different layers. It can be said that this tension is between "the kind of thing *about* which it is spoken – the Kingdom of Heaven – and the kind of thing *to* which it is compared."[260] It is with this tension that our search for the meaning of the parable begins. With his hermeneutical concern, Ricoeur attempts to interpret a

---

258  Ricoeur, "The Metaphorical Process," 99. Ricoeur applies to the parables his 'tension theory' of metaphor. In metaphorical sentences, the meaning of metaphor proceeds from the tension between two opposed (a literal and metaphorical) interpretations at the level of sentence. In the parables, the metaphorical meaning proceeds from the tension between two opposed (ordinary and extraordinary) layers of plot at the level of the whole structure of the narrative.

259  Ricoeur, "Listening to the Parables of Jesus," 239. Ricoeur explains that, in the parables, "the first thing which may amaze us is that at the very moment we were expecting the language of the myth, the language of the sacred, the language of mysteries, we receive the language of our history, the language of the profane, the language of open drama." (*Ibid.*, 240).

260  *Ibid.*

possible meaning ("reference") disclosed in the metaphorical process of this parable as follows.

In our parable, there are three essential movements: *finding* the treasure, *selling* everything else, *buying* the field. At the level of meaning as "sense," these movements denote ordinary agricultural, practical, and commercial activities. However, the extravagant behavior in those movements manifests something other ("reference") than what those movements simply indicate. According to Ricoeur's interpretation, *finding* the treasure signifies that something fundamental happens in our life-situation. Finding the treasure is an "event" that "encompasses all the kinds of *encounters*" which we can neither create nor expect.[261] Ricoeur says, "Something happens. Let us be prepared for the newness of what is new. Then we shall 'find'."[262] This first critical moment brings forth two other decisive moments: *selling* all possessions and *buying* the field. *Selling* all possessions symbolizes a "reversal" or "conversion."[263] It means much more than making a new or better choice, but denotes a *shift* "in the vision, in the imagination, in the heart, before all kinds of good intentions and all kinds of good decisions and good actions."[264] From this reversal, there comes an action: *buying* the field. Ricoeur sums up the "reference" disclosed in the dramatic structure of our parable in the following manner:

> First, encountering the Event, then changing one's heart, then doing accordingly. This succession is full of sense: the Kingdom of God is compared to the chain of these three acts: letting the Event blossom, looking in another direction, and doing with all one's strength in accordance with the new vision.[265]

261  *Ibid.*
262  *Ibid.*, 241.
263  *Ibid.*
264  *Ibid.*
265  *Ibid.* Note an important claim of Ricoeur here. Ricoeur calls our attention to the procedure of the two critical movements: reversal and decision (or action). He asserts that, "Decision does not even come second. Before Decision; Reversal." (*Ibid.*). Ricoeur claims that it is a hasty reduction to understand the parable as simply a moral teaching with the emphasis on action. Before action, the critical moment of reversal or conversion should be recognized. However, this claim

In the beginning of this analysis, we pointed out that Ricoeur characterizes the parable as the combination of a narrative form and a metaphorical process. Now, highlighting the referential function of the parable, Ricoeur describes this conjunction in a more specified manner. The parable is the combination of "the *closure* of the narrative form" and "the *openness* of the metaphorical process."[266] Here, "the closure of the narrative form" indicates that the parable as a narrative is a *formed* literary composition. It has an internal structure of meaning. "The openness of the metaphorical process" designates the dynamic *referential* process which moves beyond immanent linguistic meaning ("sense") toward extra-linguistic meaning ("reference"). In the parables, it is the dimension of extravagance in the plot that "delivers the *openness* of the metaphorical process from the *closure* of the narrative form."[267] Ricoeur explains that, "The parabolic message proceeds from this *tension* between a form which circumscribes it and a process which transgresses the narrative boundaries and point to an

does not mean to underestimate the idea of action implied in the parable. Rather, Ricoeur is apprehensive of the attenuation of the first two critical moments (*encounter* and *reversal*) that actually engender the final moment of *action*. Ricoeur points out that if the parable is reduced to simply a message for action or a good deed, it "seems to be nothing more than a moral fable, a mere call to 'do the same.' Thus reduced to a moral teaching, the Parable ceases to be a Parable of the Kingdom of God to become an allegory of charitable action. We have to replace it within the inclusion of the Parables of Event, Reversal, and Decision, if the moral fable is to speak once more as a Parable." (*Ibid.*, 242). For him, parabolic discourse is always "more" than our projection of it to a practical, ethical, or political teaching. It has the quality to disorient and dislocate our project of making a whole of our life before reorientation (decision and action). Ricoeur concludes that "to listen to the parables of Jesus, it seems to me, is to let one's imagination be opened to the new possibilities disclosed by the extravagance of these short dramas. If we look at the Parables as at a word addressed *first* to our imagination rather than our will, we shall not be tempted to reduce them to mere didactic devices, to moralizing allegories. We will let their poetic power display itself within us." (*Ibid.*, 245, italics mine).

266  Ricoeur, "The Metaphorical Process," 99.
267  *Ibid.*

'outer,' to a 'beyond'."[268] In other words, "the specific *narrative inconsistency* [the extraordinary within the ordinary] tends to break up the narrative pattern and to generate the transgression from 'inner' sense to 'outer' reference."[269] The parabolic discourse, then, has nothing to do with the question of the truth or falseness of a statement. Rather, it provides a "disclosure model" that leads us to see something other or more than what we normally look at. Ricoeur portrays this hermeneutical recognition in such a way that "the course of life is broken, the surprise bursts out. The unexpected happens; the audience is questioned and brought to think about the unthinkable."[270]

*Tracy's Understanding of Parables*

For Tracy, Ricoeur's interpretation of parables, based on the theory of metaphor, is an important source for backing up his hypothesis that, in the New Testament parables, the "religious 'limit' use of language [is] operative."[271] Tracy pays attention to the linguistic-existential element of Ricoeur's interpretation. According to Tracy, in Ricoeur's inter-pretation, the limit-character of the parables is elucidated by showing that "*linguistically*, the underlying metaphor of the parable explodes by means of the extraordinary elements" in the ordinary narrative form.[272] Furthermore, Ricoeur's analysis shows the process by which

---

268 Ricoeur, *ibid*. Ricoeur states that, "The metaphorical process [...] 'opens' discourse toward the outside, namely toward both the infinity of life and the infinity of interpretation." (*Ibid.*).
269 *Ibid.*
270 *Ibid.*, 103.
271 *BRO*, 130. In the concluding part of his analysis of the three literary genres, proclamatory sayings, proverbs, and parables, Ricoeur writes that these literary forms "present a similarity of function, namely the type of *abuse* which shatters the very form of discourse employed. I have tried to call attention to this by calling them *limit-expressions*." (Ricoeur, "Specificity," 121–2). More ac-curately speaking, this analysis of Ricoeur seems to serve for not only backing up but also setting up Tracy's hypothesis that those three New Testament language forms are a "limit-language."
272 *BRO*, 130 (italics mine). In other words, for Tracy, the clue to justify parabolic language as a "limit-language" is detected "in the 'extravagant' behavior of several of the characters which clash with the ordinary narrative." (*Ibid.*).

152

the very tension of this linguistic clash (the metaphorical tension) delivers the *existential*-referential dimension of meaning of the parables. For Tracy, this referential function of parables has to do with disclosing a "limit-vision of human possibilities" in the breakdown of everydayness.[273] Tracy describes the existential-referential power of the parables in the following way:

> The parables, as stories, take the reader to the point where the course of ordinary life is broken; an intensification of the everyday emerges; the unexpected happens; a strange world of meaning is projected which challenges, jars, disorients our everyday vision precisely by both showing us the limits to the everyday and projecting the limit-character of the whole.[274]

Tracy perceives this existential-referential dimension of meaning as the *religious* dimension disclosed by the New Testament parables. For him, the contribution of Ricoeur's analysis is its ability to demonstrate the parables' referential power for a *religious* dimension by exploring their own peculiar *literary-hermeneutical* traits. Tracy explains:

> In linguistic terms, one need not appeal merely to an additional 'theological' interpretation of the parables after a 'literary' interpretation has been completed. [...] One need not appeal only to the general eschatological religious vision enunciated by Jeremias, Dodd, or Bultmann as the parabolic horizon of meaning in order to understand that eschatological, limit horizon. Rather one may note that, even linguistically, these narratives, for all their ordinariness, force the underlying metaphor to a limit which can be described as a 'religious' use of language.[275]

Tracy also draws attention to the significance of the metaphoric referential function of the parabolic language explicated by Ricoeur. The peculiar character of that function is that the referential meaning of parabolic language is *emergent*, so that it cannot be simply reduced or translatable to a fixed idea or a maxim. The important implication of this theory, for Tracy, is that we can never – morally, politically, or culturally – subjugate the *religious* meaning of parabolic language. He

273   *Ibid.*
274   *Ibid.*
275   *Ibid.*

states that, "The parables do not merely tell a pleasant (or unpleasant) story to evoke a moral maxim."[276] For example, the central meaning of the parable of the Prodigal Son (Lk 15: 11–32) can be taken as the "Father's love without limit" (Jeremias). According to Tracy, this interpretation is feasible but not sufficient. For the meaning of the parable *emerges* in an *innovative* manner from the impact of the *shock* that is created by the metaphorical tension embedded in the narrative. In other words, since the *emergent* meaning from the impact of *astonishment* points to an extra-linguistic meaning ("reference") in the breakdown of ordinary narrative consistency, it cannot be directly translated into a fixed idea or a maxim. Where this does happen, the parable can easily degenerate into a dead metaphor. Tracy explains:

> To read the story, to watch the intertwining of the sub-plot of the elder son and the plot of the prodigal son is to await and receive the surprise of an ordinary story become extraordinary; to witness a common, possibly now dead metaphor explode with a linguistic power that discloses possibilities for human existence which seem and are beyond the limit of what our ordinary language and experience might imagine.[277]

Thus, Tracy describes the *emergent* meaning at best as a "limit-vision of human possibilities" or a "new and extraordinary, but possible mode-of-being-in-the-world."[278] The point here is that we should bear in mind that the extra-linguistic meaning opened up by the metaphorical tension of the parables can never be exhausted by our projection of a meaning.[279] The "limit" or odd use of language in the parables is the expression of this difficulty. For Tracy, this approach to parabolic language contributes to safeguard and highlight the autonomous and unique realm of the *religious* dimension of a Christ-

---

276  *Ibid.*, 134.
277  *Ibid.*, 131.
278  *Ibid.*, 130 and 134.
279  In other words, the parables are models of disclosure. "They are fictions. As with all good fiction, they redescribe ordinary reality in order to disclose a new, an extraordinary possibility for our lives. In the peculiar limit-use of narrative and metaphor in the parables these fictions redescribe the extraordinary in the ordinary in such manner that the ordinary is transgressed and a new and extraordinary, but possible mode-of-being-in-the-world is disclosed." (*Ibid.*, 134).

ian religious language which resists any moral, political, or cultural domestication of its referential meaning.

## 2. Conclusion: The Correlation Between Christian Religious Language and Common Human Experience

We have examined how Tracy conducted a "philosophical reflection" upon the meanings present in Christian religious language. His "philosophical reflection" here aims to substantiate the legitimacy of his hypothesis that Christian religious language is expressive of human "limit-experiences" as religious. The point is how to demonstrate the *universal significance* or *public intelligibility* of the meanings present in Christian religious language in correlation with human *religious* experiences. Tracy's strategy for fulfilling this task is to focus on the *linguistic* dimension of Christian religious language in keeping with the development of modern linguistic philosophy. Christian religious language in his investigation is approached as a peculiar use of human language, to which scientific linguistic inquiries apply, rather than as an inventory of revelation pervaded with extraordinary meanings not ordinarily conveyed by the language itself. In other words, he attempts to investigate the *religious* meanings of Christian texts by focusing on their peculiar linguisticality. It should be noted here that the feasibility of this attempt rests on the development of the modern linguistic philosophy of discourse. The most important development in relation to Tracy's attempt is the interpretation theory relevant to a discourse or text.[280] The kernel of this theory is that the meaning of a text (a bigger unit than words) has to be considered at two different levels: its immanent structure (semiotic level) and the level of manifestation (semantic level).[281] The former refers to the level of "sense," and the

280  See thesis 4 in the preceding chapter where, in a footnote, we already explained the interpretation theory of a written text elaborated by Paul Ricoeur which Tracy adopts in his investigation of the Christian texts.

281  Ricoeur explains this modern linguistic theory in the following way: "language aims at something, or, more exactly, it has a double direction; an ideal direction (to say something) and a real reference (to say about something)." (Ricoeur, "Structure, Word, Event," in Don Ihde (ed.), *The Conflict of Interpretations:*

latter designates the level of "reference."[282] These two levels are not necessarily to be dealt with in antinomy. Our linguistic experience occurs in the relationship of these two levels, specifically, in the movement from the level of "sense" toward the level of "reference." According to Ricoeur (and Gottlob Frege as well), the essential aspect of language can be found in its signifying intention that breaks the closed *immanent* structure of "sense" and advances toward the other *external* "reference." In other words, the "sense" is "what wishes to be applied, in order to express, grasp, apprehend, and finally to show, to manifest" the "reference" ("the thinkable and the sayable in our experience").[283] This movement is described as the "transcendence" of language.[284] Ricoeur states, "in this movement [of transcendence], language leaps across two thresholds: the threshold of ideality of meaning and, beyond this meaning, the threshold of reference. Across

*Essays in Hermeneutics* (Evanston: Northwestern University Press, 1974) 84). Ricoeur describes this double-level approach to language as the "understanding of the hierarchical levels of language." (*Ibid.*, 86). At the first level, "a language is taxonomy, a body of already emitted texts, a repertory of signs, an inventory of units, and a combinatory system of elements. The hierarchy of the levels of language includes something more than a series of articulated systems: phonological, lexical, and syntactic. We actually change levels when we pass from the units of a language to the new unit constituted by the sentence or the utterance. This is no longer the unit of a language, but of speech or discourse. By changing the unit, one also changes the function, or rather, one passes from structure to function. We then have the opportunity of encountering language as saying [...] This large unit is properly semantic, [...] which is not solely to signify in general but to say something, to refer the sign to the thing." (*Ibid.*).

282   We already explained in the preceding chapter (thesis 4) that this distinction is derived from Gottlob Frege's distinction between *Sinn* and *Bedeutung* (Max Black translated these expressions as "sense" and "reference"). Ricoeur explains that, "Frege showed precisely that the aim of language is double: the aim of an ideal sense or meaning (that is, not belonging to the physical or psychic world) and the aim of reference. If the meaning can be called inexistent, insofar as it is a pure object of thought, it is the reference – *Bedeutung* – which roots our words and sentences in reality. '[...] it is the exigency of truth (*das Streben nach Wahrheit*) which drives (*treibt*) us to advance (*vordringen*) toward the reference.' This advance of (ideal) meaning toward the (real) reference is the very soul of language." (*Ibid.*, 87).

283   *Ibid.*, 91.

284   *Ibid.*, 87.

156

this double threshold and by means of this movement of transcendence, language *'means'* [*veut dire*]; it has taken hold of reality and expresses the hold of reality on thought."[285] The important point in relation to Tracy's concern is this "expressivity" of language "not in the sense of expressing emotion, that is, in the sense in which the speaker expresses himself, but in the sense in which language [by itself] expresses something, says something."[286] In other words, at the level of manifestation ("reference"), language finds its expressivity "in relation with reality, with experience, with the world, with existence."[287]

Provided that this theory of "expressivity" of language is accepted, Tracy's concern is with the peculiar linguisticality (or distinctive uses of language) of Christian texts and their "expressivity" of certain experience, the world, and existence.[288] Here, the pivotal category of his revisionist investigation, "limit," is at work. Tracy applies the category of "limit" to the peculiar linguisticality of three important genres of the New Testament: proverbs, proclamatory sayings, and parables. Tracy's selection of these three genres has to do with the recognition that they exhibit, *par excellence*, the character of "limit-language" by means of various literary devices (such as hyper-

285  *Ibid.*, 84 ("[*veut dire*]" is editor's insertion.).

286  Ricoeur, "The Problem of Double Meaning," in *The Conflict of Interpretations*, 77. More specifically, this theory is elaborated in the form of three kinds of "distanciation" that a written text obtains: (1) distanciation from the situation of the discourse; (2) distanciation from the author; (3) distanciation from the original audience (See Ricoeur, *Interpretation Theory*, 37).

287  Ricoeur, "The Problem of Double Meaning," 63. Ricoeur explains that, at the level of manifestation ("reference"), the "ontology" of language finds its place. He writes that, "There is a mystery *of* language, namely, that language speaks, says something, says something about being. If there is an enigma of symbolism, it resides wholly on the level of manifestation, where the equivocalness of being is spoken in the equivocalness of discourse." (*Ibid.*, 77–8).

288  This theory of the "expressivity" of the text apart from the author, the original audience, and the situation of the text (the so-called the autonomy of text) plays a vital role in the development of Tracy's theory of the "classic" in his *The Analogical Imagination*. A basic concern there is with defending the public character of Christian texts as a "religious classic" which asks for an on-going risk of interpretation beyond time and space.

bole, paradox, symbolic and metaphoric components). Correlatively, the "reference" of such "limit" uses of language is, for him, human "limit-experiences." In other words, the linguistic "expressivity" of the three genres has to do with the "limit-experiences" of human beings which we discussed in the preceding section. This claim shows that his correlation between Christian texts and human religious experience already underlies his linguistic-hermeneutical investigation of the New Testament.

Tracy's principal claim in his correlation is that "the limit-experience described in the New Testament language remains within the realm of authentically *human* experience."[289] Christian religious language does not express an outlandish or an extraterrestrial world that demands our *sacrificium intellectus* to understand and accept it. Rather, such language unmistakably discloses human reality. Summarily, Tracy portrays this correlative relationship in the following way. The limit-language as shown in the New Testament discloses the "final realm of meaningfulness to our lives, that 'other' trusting faithful dimension to our existence, which may adequately allow the explicit acknowledgment that the whole of our existence is other than a 'getting and spending,' other than absurd, other even than the real, the 'everyday' world."[290] Correlatively, this "other" or "religious" dimension to our existence may be perceived in our "limit-situations," and in our reflection upon the "limit-questions" of scientific and moral enterprises. In these instances of perception, "we may find ourselves turning to the limit-language of religion in order to see how they try to re-present that 'other,' that limit-dimension of our lives."[291] Based on this correlation, Tracy concludes that "the categories limit-language and limit-experience, therefore, seem useful,

289   *BRO*, 131.
290   *Ibid.*, 132.
291   *Ibid.* More concretely, Tracy describes this correlative relationship in the following way: "If we could hear – or 'over-hear' – the limit-language of the Christian gospel anew, we might experience again a dimension to life which renders it whole. If we could at least listen to the 'hints and guesses' disclosed to us in limit-situations, we might have some intimation of the odd, mysterious, indeed scandalous limit-experience which that gospel proclaims as an authentic human possibility." (*Ibid.*, 133).

158

tentative, and admittedly revisionist formulations of the genuinely religious dimension of both our common faith and our explicitly Christian faith."[292]

With regard to Tracy's correlation, two characteristics need to be pointed out. Firstly, the chief concern of his correlation in this fundamental theological enterprise is, and this is an undeniably apologetic intention, to *reconcile* the religious vision disclosed in the Christian texts with human religious experience. Thus, although he presents various modes of correlation as revisionist possibilities such as "the dramatic confrontation," "mutual illuminations and corrections," and "basic reconciliation" between the two sources, his correlation, in effect, exhibits only the mode of "basic reconciliation."[293]

Secondly, Tracy employs a double-faceted principle for elucidating the relationship between Christian religious language and human religious experience. On the one hand, Tracy takes up Ogden's view of the *representative* character of religious language. As we have already seen, Ogden's position is rather extreme to the extent that religious assertions, by their very *representative* character, "never originate [as a cause] our faith in life's meaning," but rather reassure or reaffirm an already present deeper faith in the worth of existence (human common faith with a natural religious quality) "as its *effect*."[294] Hence, this viewpoint does not allow religious language any possibility to provoke or project a *new* vision that disorients or upsets our existing conviction or faith.[295] In other words, this position pre-

---

292    *Ibid.*
293    Moreover, Tracy does not attempt a full range of critical correlations as he clarifies them earlier in comparison to Paul Tillich (See Thesis 2 in the preceding chapter). There, he claims that a critical correlation means a critical comparison of questions and answers given by *both* sources, human experience and the Christian texts (for instance, the comparison between existential philosophical answers and the Christian answer to the question of human estrangement). However, Tracy does not attempt this full range of critical comparison in his actual correlation. It is presumed that, in this fundamental theological project, his apologetic concern prevails, which leads him to focus predominantly on the need for "basic *reconciliation*" between two sources.
294    Ogden, *The Reality of God*, 33–4.
295    With regard to the relationship between Christian religious language and human experience, in Ogden's viewpoint, human experience has a privileged place to

cludes the *"redescriptive"* function of religious language that we find in Ricoeur's theory of religious language.[296] The double-faceted aspect of Tracy's correlation means that he tries to bring together these two seemingly discordant theories of Ogden and Ricoeur in a complementary way. Basically, Tracy maintains Ogden's standpoint by saying that "religious language in general *re-presents* that basic confidence and trust in existence which *is* our fundamental faith, our

the extent that Christian religious language is almost a passive reflection of it. At the opposite pole to Ogden is George Lindbeck. For Lindbeck, on the contrary, the authority of Christian religious language is such that the Bible "absorbs the world." Lindbeck's position can be clearly seen in his argument that, "It is important to note the direction of interpretation. Typology does not make scriptural contents into metaphors for extrascriptural realties, but the other way around. It does not suggest, as is often said in our day, that believers find their stories in the Bible, but rather that they make the story of the Bible their story." Lindbeck states that, "It is the religion instantiated in Scripture which defines being, truth, goodness, and beauty, and the nonscriptural exemplifications of these realities need to be transformed into figures (or types or antitypes) of the scriptural ones. Intratextual theology [Lindbeck's theological program] redescribes reality within the scriptural framework rather than translating Scripture into extrascriptural categories." (All quotations from Lindbeck, *The Nature of Doctrine*, 118). We can observe dangers in both extreme positions. Lindbeck's position exposes the danger of fideism, and Ogden's position reveals the danger of banalizing religion. Regarding the danger of banalizing religion, Lieven Boeve's remarks are relevant here: "As Metz has noted, it is not naivety that is a threat to the future of religion but banality. Religion becomes banal when it is nothing more than a reduplication of what is going on already, what is being said and done in spite of religion." Lieven Boeve, "God Interrupts History: Apocalypticism as an Indispensable Theological Conceptual Strategy," in *LS*, 26 (2001) 212; for Metz's reference, see Johann Baptist Metz, "Unterwegs zu einer nachidealistischen Theologie," in Johannes B. Bauer (ed.), *Entwürfe der Theologie* (Graz & Vienna and Cologne: Styria, 1985) 227ff.

296 We may explain Ogden and Ricoeur's different theories of religious language in the following way. Ricoeur's theory allows the hermeneutical circle between human experience and religious texts in such a way that human experience interprets religious texts and religious texts also interpret human experience. In Ogden's theory, however, there is only one direction of interpretation (not a hermeneutical circle of two-way communication): human experience interprets religious texts as its representations, but religious texts do not add anything new to human experience and only reassure us about what we already know.

basic authentic mode of being in the world."[297] More concretely, he explains that religious language "*re-presents* our always threatened basic confidence and trust in the very meaningfulness of even our most cherished and most noble enterprises, science, morality, and culture. That language discloses the reassurance needed that the final reality of our lives is in fact trustworthy."[298] However, at the same time, by incorporating Ricoeur's hermeneutical theory, Tracy asserts that religious language, such as the parabolic language of the New Testament, "does not merely *re-present* such faith [the fundamental faith in existence]," but also does "*redescribe* ordinary existence to show how authentic existence itself may occur."[299] In other words, he claims that, "Religious language, whenever it is authentically related to a religious insight of extraordinary force as in the New Testament, employs and explodes all our ordinary language forms in order to jar us into a recognition of what, on our own, can seem only a desirable but impossible possible mode-of-being-in-the world."[300] In the above descriptions, we can clearly see that Tracy utilizes the theories of both Ogden and Ricoeur in a complementary way. However, it should be noted that Ogden's theory does not allow any room for a position like Ricoeur's where religious language can *cause* or provoke something *new* in our existing conviction of faith. For Ogden, it is very clear that religious language never gives rise to a new conviction, since it does nothing but represent or reassure our already existing faith. A perplexing point is that although Tracy explicitly recognizes Ogden's position (in another discussion), he uses it complementarily with Ricoeur's theory here.[301] Tracy does not seem disturbed by the discordance between these two theories here.

---

297  *BRO*, 134 (italics of *re-presents* mine).
298  *Ibid.*, 135 (italics mine).
299  *Ibid.*, 134 (italics mine).
300  *Ibid.*, 136.
301  In the following statement, we can clearly observe that, on this point, Tracy endorses Ogden's position. "In initially linguistic terms, Ogden develops Toulmin's own insistence that we use religious language to 'reassure' ourselves that the 'whole' and the 'future' are trustworthy in order to argue that all religious *language* thereby bears the linguistic form of *re-presentation*. We misunderstand the function of religious language if we claim that it *causes*

Why, then, does Tracy take both theories into account in his correlation? This might be understood in the following way. There is no doubt that Tracy takes the hermeneutical import of Ricoeur's theory of religious language seriously.[302] He takes up Ogden's theory, too, however, because its key implication supports his fundamental standpoint. The chief implication of Ogden's theory is that religious faiths, including the Christian faith, encoded in religious assertions, are not something estranged from the fundamental faith of *secularity* (not secularism).[303] Rather, they are the "expressions" or "re-presentations" of the faith of secularity as the *common* faith. This idea significantly supports the basic standpoint of Tracy's revisionist model which declares, "the Christian faith is at heart none other than the most adequate articulation of the basic faith of secularity itself."[304]

> (presents) our general confidence or trust in the meaningfulness of existence. We understand such language correctly only when we recognize that the use of religious language is *an effect* (a *re*-presentation) of an already present basic confidence or trust [...]. In Ogden's words, religions 'provide us with particular symbolic forms through which that faith [i.e., our basic confidence and trust in the meaningfulness of existence] may be more or less adequately re-affirmed at the level of self-conscious belief'." (*Ibid.*, 103).

302   For example, in his concluding part on correlation, Tracy sums up the power of the New Testament language in following way: "As proverbial, that religious language disorients us and forces us to see another, a seemingly impossible way of living with authenticity. As parabolic, that language redescribes our experience in such manner that the sense of its meaning (its now limit-metaphor) discloses a limit-referent which projects and promises that one can in fact live a life of wholeness, of total commitment, or radical honesty and agapic love in the presence of the gracious God of Jesus the Christ." (*Ibid.*, 136).

303   Ogden calls for disenchantment with supernaturalism's contempt of worldly reality by affirming that "the world itself has an unconditioned worth and significance" as pronounced by the Christian doctrine of creation (Ogden, *The Reality of God*, 69). Ogden writes that, "Even the ethos of modern science must be understood against the background of the Christian doctrine of creation, with its claim that the world is utterly secular and therefore open to the most probing inquiry, and yet is also sufficiently significant to be worthy of our most careful attention." (*Ibid.*). For the idea of secularity in contrast to secularism, see *ibid.*, 6–20 and 44–70.

304   *BRO*, 10. More concretely, Tracy states that, "A proper understanding of those central beliefs – in 'revelation,' in 'God,' in 'Jesus Christ' – can provide an adequate understanding, a correct 'reflective inventory,' or an existentially

In his methodological exposition, he clarifies the faith of secularity as our fundamental commitment to the "final worthwhileness of the struggle for truth and honesty in our inquiry, and for justice and even agapic love in our individual and social practice."[305] Therefore, for him, the limit-vision of human possibilities projected in Christian religious language is none other than the articulation of a way of being that finds form in this fundamental commitment. In sum, Tracy seems to adopt the theories of both Ogden and Ricoeur for his own purpose despite their incongruity.

In his investigation of Christian texts, what Tracy attempts to demonstrate is how Christian religious language can be referential and reality-depicting prior to and without articulating its cognitive claims. This suggests that there still remains an important task to undertake: the justification of the truth of the cognitive claims involved in Christian religious language. For example, according to him, the expression, "Kingdom of God," a central theme of the New Testament, however it is used (as a metaphor, a symbol, or a myth), "includes cognitive claims (e.g., there is a God and he has some relationship with humanity)."[306] Thus, this religious expression calls for a conceptual articulation. According to him, the kernel of the cognitive claims involved in Christian religious language is the question of "God." Moreover, for him, this question of "God" is also associated with human "limit-experiences" as religious. Historically, argues Tracy, the principal cognitive claim of Christianity is that the Christian God is "the sole and single objective ground of all reality."[307] Hence, Tracy claims that, "Given the prior analysis of religious language and experience, it seems fair to conclude that, for the Christian religion at least, the word 'God' has a primary use or function to refer to the objective ground in reality itself for those limit-experiences of a final confidence and trust disclosed in Christian God-

appropriate symbolic representation of the fundamental faith of secularity." (*Ibid.*, 9).

305  *Ibid.*, 9.
306  *Ibid.*, 142 n.67.
307  *Ibid.*, 147.

language."[308] In short, from the perspective of Christianity, "God" is the referent of the cognitive claims involved in human religious experience in general and Christian religious language. Basing himself on this assumption, Tracy argues that the task of articulating the cognitive claims involving the God-question demands another methodological reflection apart from the "phenomenological" or the "hermeneutical" investigation. He argues that these claims "can be specified and should be examined on *metaphysical* grounds."[309] In the next chapter, we shall examine how Tracy deals with this dimension of the question of God.

308   *Ibid.*, 148.
309   *Ibid.*, 142 n.67 (italics mine).

# Chapter Three
## The Heart of Tracy's Revisionist Model: The Question of God

Our aim in this chapter is to examine the most essential concern of Tracy's revisionist theological project, the question of God.[1] For Tracy, a critical reflection upon God is the most demanding task in terms of fulfilling his revisionist methodological goal: to construct a theological discourse (here, to explicate the reality of God) to a level of conceptual clarity and public intelligibility solely by means of a scientific methodology.[2] The question at stake, for him, is how to

1    The question of God has been one of the most central concerns of Tracy's theological project. In the 1970s, Tracy's goal was to explicate the reality of God to a level of conceptual clarity based on objective argumentation (the revisionist goal). Later, especially in the 1990s, Tracy's major writings were still devoted to the God-question but via a different approach from his revisionist one. The major reason for the shift of his understanding of God has to do with the "quintessential turn of much contemporary thought – the turn to the other" of so-called post-modern awareness (Tracy, "The Hidden God: The Divine Other of Liberation," in *CrCur*, 46 (1996) 5). For him, this new awareness disabuses the modern project of a clear-cut schematization of God (e.g., articulated by various kinds of "ism"). Tracy asserts that "God enters contemporary history not as a consoling 'ism' but above all as an awesome, often terrifying, hope-beyond-hope. God enters history again not as a new speculation – but as the unpredictable, liberating, Hidden God. For this God reveals Godself in hiddenness: in cross and negativity, above all in the suffering of all those others whom the grand narrative of modernity has too often set aside as non-peoples, non-events, non-memories, in a word, non-history." (*Ibid.*, 7–8). In the next chapter, we will deal with the major content and significance of the shift in Tracy's understanding of God.

2    Tracy describes the character of this task as follows: "if there is any issue that requires clear-headed reflection by anyone, either deeply or marginally in church, in theology or even, as most serious religious thinkers argue, in the human enterprise itself, that issue remains the reality of God. If one has not come to terms with this issue then the rest – church reforms, new theological

rationally and critically articulate the reality of God based on objective argumentations.[3] In Tracy's revisionist project, this question of God is not an issue independent of his prior analyses of human religious experience ("limit-experience") and Christian religious language ("limit-language"). Thus, the burden of his task includes the question of how to rationally substantiate God's reality in relation to the religious ("limit") dimension of human experience and of Christian religious language. That is to say, he needs to show how the dimension of religion is mediated to theism (i.e., God as the referent of the human religious dimension).[4] In short, his goal is to rationally demonstrate that Christian theism is a theological reflection which is not only *Christian* but also *true* to every human being. This is why the starting point to develop his understanding of God is not specifically Christian experience but human experience as such (as attempted by his prior investigation of human religious experience and its relation to Christian religious language). His central assumption is that some ineluctable, common, experiential aspect of what it is to be a human being (i.e., "limit-dimension" as religious) can provide the rational grounding for the fundamental affirmation of God.[5] In other words, in

articulations, Christian involvement in the world – are, in the final analysis, whistling in the wind." Tracy, "God's Reality: The Most Important Issue," in *ATR*, 55 (1973) 218.

3    *BRO*, 147. This description does not imply, however, that his revisionist reflection upon God attempts a philosophy of God (as a part of a philosophy of religion), which is distinct from a theological enterprise. In a section of this chapter, we will discuss how Tracy characterizes his reflection upon God as a *theological* endeavor by applying his own criteria ("criteria of appropriateness").

4    Tracy states that "the logical order [...] is also of some importance: from religion to theism, not vice versa." (*Ibid.*, 83 n.27).

5    Maurice F. Wiles characterizes this move of seeking for an anthropological basis (especially in human experience) for the fundamental belief in God as an important trait of twentieth-century theological works. The major representative theologians of this trait in recent years, among others, include Karl Rahner, Wolfhart Pannenberg, and Schubert Ogden. For a summary explanation of these three theologians in terms of this issue, see Maurice F. Wiles, "Can Theology Still Be About God?," in Sheila G. Davaney (ed.), *Theology at the End of Modernity: Essays in Honour of Gordon Kaufman* (Philadelphia: Trinity, 1991) 221–32. Philip Clayton identifies David Tracy as one of the theologians who

this mode of reasoning, "the reality of God is something that can, by a process of deep and careful reflection, come to be seen to be genuinely entailed in our practical existence as human selves."[6] Tracy states:

> The centuries-long effort to articulate in explicitly cognitive terms the correct understanding of Christian religious experience and language has resulted in the development of certain "doctrines" or explicit articles of belief. Such doctrines are not in fact peculiar to an understanding of religious experience and language. Rather, any understanding of any experience – moral or aesthetic, for example – inevitably *gives rise to* the development of explicit cognitive doctrines for a given ethical, scientific, aesthetic, or religious tradition.[7]

This statement indicates an essential principle underlying the development of Tracy's reflection on God: namely, that the cradle of *particular* Christian doctrines (including Christian theism) is a *universal* human experience in a particular religious context or tradition. Basing himself on this principle, Tracy asserts that the defense of Christian theism, "for the fundamental theologian at least, must be conducted on grounds other than his own or his community's vision of

understands God-talk as a "particularly effective way of expressing aspects of human experience of the world." Philip Clayton, *The Problem of God in Modern Thought* (Grand Rapids and Cambridge: William B. Eerdmans Publishing Company, 2000) 14.

6    Wiles, *ibid.*, 227.

7    *BRO*, 146 (italics mine). Such an argument indicates an approach which leads George Lindbeck to describe Tracy's position as typical of the "experiential-expressive" model, one of four models with regard to the theory of religion and doctrine including: the "propositionalist" model, the "experiential-expressive" model, the "two-dimensional" model combining both propositionalist and experiential-expressive aspects, and his own "cultural-linguistic" model. Lindbeck describes the "experiential-expressive" model by saying that "whatever the variations, thinkers of this tradition ['experiential-expressivism'] all locate ultimately significant contact with whatever is finally important to religion in the prereflective experiential depths of the self and regard the public or outer features of religion as expressive and evocative objectifications (i.e., non-discursive symbols) of internal experience." Lindbeck, *The Nature of Doctrine: Religion and Theology in a Postliberal Age* (Philadelphia: The Westminster Press, 1984) 21. For Tracy's response to this labeling, see Tracy, "Lindbeck's New Program for Theology," in *Thomist* 49 (1985) 460–72.

faith."[8] This chapter is devoted to exploring how Tracy undertakes this task.

This chapter is divided into two parts. In the first part (I), we will examine Tracy's justification of his hypothesis: God is "the objective *referent*" of the cognitive claims involved in human religious experience in general and Christian religious language in particular.[9] For this task, Tracy draws on a "metaphysical or transcendental reflection." Our examination in this part is subdivided into two sections. The first section (1) will focus on his hypothesis itself. We will analyze the underlying principles which are conducive to his *theistic* hypothesis. In the second section (2), we will look at what Tracy means by his "metaphysical or transcendental reflection," and how Tracy attempts his justification of God by using it. In the second part (II), we will examine Tracy's option for a prospective Christian theism for the revisionist model: the God of process thought.

## I. The Metaphysical (Transcendental) Justification of God's Reality

Tracy's prior "philosophical reflection" upon human religious experience and Christian religious language aims at one principal issue: the elucidation of the *meaningfulness* and *meaning* of the religious dimension of these two sources.[10] By using phenomenological and

---

8    *BRO*, 147. This statement recalls Tracy's position, pointed out in the preceding chapter, that fundamental theologians, as distinct from systematic and practical theologians, in fact, ordinarily share the commitment to a particular Christian tradition, but "in principle will abstract themselves from all religious 'faith commitments' for the legitimate purposes of critical analysis of all religious and theological claims." (*AI*, 57; see also *BRO*, 6–7; Tracy, "Response to Professor Connelly – II," 72).

9    *BRO*, 109 (italics mine).

10   Recall Tracy's three sets of criteria, namely, the criteria of *meaningfulness*, *meaning*, and *truth*.

hermeneutical analyses (methodological thesis 3 and 4), Tracy attempts to demonstrate that:

> In terms of criteria of existential *meaningfulness* there seem good reasons to affirm the reality of both a religious dimension of our common experience and the existential significance of the originating language of the Christian religious heritage. In terms of the criteria of coherent logical *meaning*, there also seem solid reasons to affirm that the category "limit" is a useful if merely initial index to religious meaning.[11]

Now, there remains the final task in order to fulfill the aim of his revisionist model for fundamental theology: the conceptual clarification of cognitive claims involved in human religious experience and Christian religious language. For Tracy, with this issue, two essential elements are associated. Firstly, there is the question of God that comprises the kernel of the cognitive claims involved in human religious experience and Christian religious language. This element informs Tracy's central *hypothesis* of the issue of God, viz., God is the ultimate *referent* of the cognitive claims involved in human religious experience ("limit-experience") and Christian religious language ("limit-language"). Secondly, Tracy considers this *theistic* understanding of the religious cognitive claims as that which pertains to the question of truth (distinct from that of meaningfulness and meaning), for which "an explicitly metaphysical (or transcendental) analysis" is demanded.[12] This element informs Tracy's methodological proposition for the *justification* of the reality of God. Let us look at these two elements in more detail.

11   *BRO*, 136.
12   *Ibid.*, 147.

*1. God as the Referent of Religious Cognitive Claims:*
*The Underlying Principles*

As we mentioned above, Tracy's hypothesis concerning the issue of God is that God is "the objective *referent*" of the cognitive claims involved in human religious experience and Christian religious language. This hypothesis involves a double statement: namely, God is not only the *referent* of the cognitive claims contained in the originating, religious "limit-language" of the Christian texts, but also the *referent* of those implied in human "limit-experience" as religious. In short, as a basic assumption, he opts for the fundamentally "theistic self-understanding presupposed by common human experience and language and explicitly referred to in representative Christian texts."[13] The most problematic aspect in this correlation may be his *theistic* assumption concerning human religious experience in general. Interestingly enough, he is aware of the fact that this theistic assumption is not immediately applicable to the religious experiences in other non-theistic religious traditions.[14] However, at this point, Tracy does not yet express his keen, postmodern concern with "otherness" and "difference" that is evident in his later works.[15] Instead, he is strongly

13   *Ibid.*, 54. In the preceding chapter, we examined Tracy's correlation between two sources (common human experience and Christian religious language) conducted at the level of *religion*, in which the category of "limit" is pivotal: viz., the categories of "limit-experience" and "limit-language" are "revisionist formulations of the genuinely religious dimension of both our common faith and our explicitly Christian faith." (*Ibid.*, 133). Now, Tracy attempts a correlation at another level, the level of theism. By this correlation, Tracy addresses the question of the theistic referent of both human religious experience and the Christian experience, namely, the question of God.

14   Tracy writes that, "It is well to remember that not only can other authentically religious traditions – such as Buddhism – deny the need to maintain the theistic claim; even some Christian theologians – and, one suspects, many Christians in practice if not in theory – effectively deny that claim." (*Ibid.*, 147).

15   Most importantly, *Plurality and Ambiguity* (San Francisco: Harper and Row, 1987); "The Uneasy Alliance Reconceived: Catholic Theological Method, Modernity, and Postmodernity," in *TS*, 50 (1989) 548–70; "Beyond Foundationalism and Relativism: Hermeneutics and the New Ecumenism," in his *On Naming the Present* (Maryknoll: Orbis Books, 1994); "Theology and the Many

convinced that his "metaphysical or transcendental" reflection upon God will demonstrate the truth of his theistic claim as adequate to *all* human experience.[16] Since this issue of how Tracy demonstrates this possibility pertains to the section concerning his justification of God, we will examine it there. For the moment, we will focus on what reasoning or principles are operative (i) in his *theistic* assumption concerning human religious experience, and, further, (ii) in his *theistic* correlation between human religious experience and the Christian experience.

## The Theistic Prospect Assumed in the Religious Dimension of Human Experience

In his initial analysis of the religious dimension present in common human experience, Tracy's aim is to show that this dimension is neither a supernatural realm, nor an ethically and culturally domesticated realm, but an ultimate, a "limit" dimension to our scientific and moral enterprises, and existential situations. In that analysis, although Tracy is reticent about the affirmation of God in relation to such a "limit" dimension,[17] he intimates his theistic perspective on this matter. Tracy's theistic prospect regarding the human religious dimension can be glimpsed *par excellence* in his *schematic* reinterpretation of the Kantian notion of "limit." Tracy schematizes this notion into two modalities ("limit-to" and "limit-of") in such a way that each modality refers to a reality which can be conceptually delineated: viz., "limit-to" refers to a "boundary" or "limitation";

Faces of Postmodernity," in *ThT*, 51 (1994) 104–14; "The Hidden God: The Divine Other of Liberation," in *CrCur*, 46 (1996) 5–16.

16  His revisionist aim to defend Christian theism "on grounds other than his [the theologian's] own or his community's vision of faith" assumes this conviction.

17  In the preceding chapter, we already indicated that Tracy expresses his position over against Lonergan's. Tracy critiques as a dogmatic (not critical) inference Lonergan's immediate affirmation of God in the "self-transcending" process of human scientific inquiries. For Tracy, the affirmation of God as the necessary referent of such a religious dimension (the dimension of "self-transcendence") should be critically conducted by a proper method (metaphysical or transcendental reflection), as another task.

"limit-of" refers to "the fundamental," "the final," "horizon-to" or "ground-of." This schematization is distinctive to Tracy, and not found in Kant. For Kant, the category of "limit" does not represent a conceptually determinable reality. Rather, for him, it represents a *motive* which mediates between finitude and infinity in human thinking.[18] In short, for Kant, the category of "limit" is "not a fact, but an act."[19] In contrast with Kant, however, Tracy embodies that category in conceptual realities ("limit-to" and "limit-of"). This conceptual embodiment is not unrelated to his theistic concern as regards the human religious dimension.[20] For this concern, his conceptualization of the modality of "limit-of," in particular, deserves our attention. As we mentioned, in his two-modality schema, "limit-of" refers to the reality disclosed as "the fundamental," "the final," or the "ground-of" our existence in our "limit-to" situations. We note here that Tracy's conceptualization of the modality of "limit-of" bears upon a certain metaphysical reality which is "beyond (or, alternatively, grounding to)" our ordinary experience. For him, this metaphysical reality is unmistakably associated with the God of theism. Tracy states that this association is the case "in the Western tradition,

---

18  In the preceding chapter, we explained the double-dimensional character of the Kantian critique of human cognition: viz., the "negative" and "positive" utilities of the Kantian *limitation* of the competency of human pure reason which oscillates between finitude and infinity. And we also indicated there that Tracy's two-modality interpretation of the Kantian motive of "limit" is reminiscent of Kant's two-way thinking. Granting this, there is a crucial discrepancy between them, which we are going to illuminate in this section.

19  Ricoeur, "Specificity," 142. According to Ricoeur, the worth of the Kantian category of "limit" as an *act* lies in its function "as a warning against a new scholasticism." (*Ibid.*, 143). In relation to the question of God, it reminds us of the important "tension between the *objective* claim of knowledge and the *poetic* [metaphorical, symbolic, or limit] presentation of the Unconditioned" as shown in Christian religious language, which should be preserved for overcoming objectivism concerning God (*Ibid.*). In the conclusion of this chapter, we will discuss this issue in relation to Tracy's revisionist position.

20  Concerning this observation, see Gerald M. Boodoo, *Development and Consolidation: the Use of Theological Method in the Works of David Tracy* (unpublished doctoral dissertation, Faculty of Theology, K.U. Leuven, Leuven, 1991) 153–61.

when the metaphysical reality of God as the one necessary existent grounding all reality is explicated as *the referent* of just such limit-experiences of a religious dimension to our lives."[21] The reality of God is, for him, a strict necessity to account for the reality of "limit-of" disclosed in our "religious-as-*limit-to* experiences and questions."[22] In sum, it is not inappropriate to say that his theistic prospect is deliberately assumed in his analysis of the religious dimension of common human experience. Notwithstanding that the analysis is claimed as a *phenomenological* analysis aided by a theologically neutral category, "limit," it is worked in the light of a recognizable theological agenda. Put differently, his (hidden) theological agenda (a theistic prospect for human religious experience) plays an essential role in his distinctive conceptual schematization of the Kantian category of "limit." That is to say that, whereas, in Kant, the category of "limit" is a mediating motive which serves to open a path to think beyond immanence towards the ultimate or the ground,[23] in Tracy, that category is conceptually embodied as a metaphysical reality, the ground itself ("limit-of"), which is unambiguously associated with the reality of the theistic God. More specifically, in his hypothesis, this God as the referent of the "limit-of" dimension is *correlated* with the God referred to by Christian religious "limit-language." In the following section, we will search for the underlying principle that is operative in this *theistic* correlation.[24]

---

21    *AI*, 160.

22    *Ibid.*, 161.

23    Recall Kant's statement that, "A critique that *limits* the speculative use of reason is, to be sure, to that extent negative, but because it simultaneously removes an obstacle that limits or even threatens to wipe out the practical use of reason, this critique is also in fact of positive and very important utility, as soon as we have convinced ourselves that there is an absolutely necessary practical use of pure reason (the moral use), in which reason unavoidably *extends itself beyond the boundaries of sensibility*..." Kant, *Critique of Pure Reason*, 114: Bxxv (italics mine).

24    Here, we use the expression, "underlying," because Tracy does not offer any detailed explanation of how he draws forth such a theistic correlation, but merely assumes it.

In the very beginning of this chapter, we indicated in a footnote that Tracy himself differentiates his fundamental theological project from a philosophy of religion. This differentiation, which crucially comes to the fore in his discussion of God, provides a key to understand Tracy's *theistic* correlation between human religious experience and the Christian experience.

For an understanding of this differentiation, we need to recall the two sets of criteria which he presents in his first thesis regarding the methodological principles related to the two theological sources (common human experience and the Christian tradition). The two sets of criteria are the "criteria of appropriateness" and the "criteria of adequacy."[25] Tracy proposes these criteria for explaining how the task of fundamental theology can be characterized by its relationship to the two theological sources. Tracy's argument is that these two sets of criteria are "succinct expressions of the twofold demand upon what I call the 'fundamental theologian' [as distinct from a philosopher of religion]."[26] Let us briefly look back at these criteria and see how they function as underlying principles for Tracy's *theistic* correlation.

According to Tracy, the "criteria of appropriateness" address the responsibility of the fundamental theologian, as distinct from that of a philosopher. The fundamental theologian is required to show how his/her theological categories (or formulations or conclusions) are *appropriate* to "the meanings of the major expressions and texts of the Christian tradition."[27] In other words, the theologian's categories should be *appropriate* to the Christian self-understanding as this is expressed in the charter symbols and discourses of the Christian tradition. Tracy claims:

> If this responsibility is not addressed, then Christian theology becomes without remainder a philosophy of religion. Comforting though that thought may be to all those justifiably wary of the hazards of hermeneutics and history, a purely contemporary philosophy of religion is not a fundamental theology in either the

25 See *BRO*, 43–5 and 70–3; see our examination of Thesis 1 in the first chapter.
26 *Ibid.*, 57 n.4.
27 *Ibid.*, 43.

traditional or even revisionist sense of the term. The theologian's task is neither to invent a new religion nor to leave his interpreters the task of determining the appropriateness of his categories to the Christian tradition. Rather the theologian must himself assume this responsibility.[28]

As for the "criteria of adequacy," Tracy claims that a fundamental theology has to demonstrate "the adequacy of the major Christian theological categories for all human experience."[29] Insofar as it is held that the Christian self-understanding expressed in the Christian tradition claims to be an understanding of authentic human existence as such, the fundamental theologian is obliged to validate this universalist claim as true. Tracy argues that this task is asked for by the universalist Christian self-understanding itself.

In view of the above descriptions, we can draw forth how Tracy understands the fundamental character of a fundamental theology: fundamental theology takes the "*theses*" of the Christian faith ("criteria of appropriateness") as its "*hypotheses*" to be validated as the truth-as-adequacy-to-all human experience ("criteria of adequacy").[30] It is against this backdrop that we may understand Tracy's *theistic* correlation between human religious experience and the Christian experience. His theistic correlation is his *hypothesis* formulated out of a *thesis* of the Christian faith in God (or the Christian self-understanding of God). He points out that "from the viewpoint of historical investigation, a secure conclusion would seem to be that whatever else Christianity has been it has also been (and ordinarily understood itself to be) a theistic religion."[31] More concretely, he states that "to many contemporary analysts of Christian experience and language, [...] the central, indeed the constitutive cognitive claim of that religion is its articulation of the Christian God as the sole and single objective ground of all reality."[32] Tracy relates this *universalist* Christian *thesis* concerning God to the result of his prior investigation of human religious experience ("limit-to" and "limit-of" dimensions) *from the*

---

28    *Ibid.*, 72.
29    *Ibid.*, 44.
30    See *ibid.*, 57 n.10.
31    *Ibid.*, 54.
32    *Ibid.*, 147.

*vantage point of the Christian universalist claim.* This means that he subsumes the unnamed "ultimate" reality disclosed in the human religious dimension (in his schematization, "limit-of") under the *universalist* Christian God. For him, this subsumption seems to be legitimate in view of his "criteria of appropriateness." Hence comes his *theistic* correlation as follows: "Given the prior analysis of religious language and experience, it seems fair to conclude that, *for the Christian religion at least,* the word 'God' has a primary use or function to refer to the objective ground in reality itself for those limit-experiences of a final confidence and trust disclosed in Christian God-language."[33]

## 2. The Metaphysical Justification of Theistic Claims

### The Meaning of the "Metaphysical-Transcendental" Reflection

Our concern in this section is to examine how Tracy attempts to justify his theistic hypothesis discussed above. Tracy's goal here is to demonstrate the possibility and necessity of a *metaphysical* validation of his theistic claim. In order to understand the metaphysical validation of his theistic hypothesis, we, first, need to know what Tracy means by a "metaphysical-transcendental" reflection. Given the fact that "metaphysics" as such is too vast and too general a concept,[34] it would be better to begin by pointing out what particular metaphysical system Tracy takes on for his purpose.

Tracy's option is the so-called "transcendental method" developed in Neo-Thomism. Neo-Thomism began in the middle of the nineteenth century and retained its dominance until the middle of the twentieth century, predominantly through the philosophers and

---

33    *Ibid.,* 148 (italics mine).
34    For this difficulty, see Theodor W. Adorno, *Metaphysics: Concepts and Problems,* in Rolf Tiedemann (ed.) and trans. by Edmund Jephcott (Stanford: Standford University Press, 2000) 1–9 (Lecture One of 11 May 1965: *What is Metaphysics?*).

theologians of the Roman Catholic tradition.[35] It puts forward its aim as the creative recovery of the metaphysics of Thomas Aquinas in a conversation with contemporary culture and modern philosophical traditions. The "transcendental method" (or "transcendental Thomism") can be identified as one of the significant attempts at this conversation. The most important thinker who inaugurated the "transcendental method" is widely considered to be the Belgian Jesuit philosopher, Joseph Maréchal (1878–1944).[36] Afterwards, this tradition was developed in various ways by other philosophers and

35   Although, in the beginning, Neo-Thomism was faced with a conflict with some leaders of the Church, it was eventually endorsed by Pope Leo XIII's encyclical, *Aeterni Patris* in 1879 as a means of providing the philosophical resources for theology to meet the needs of the time. The pope believed that "the wisdom of St. Thomas could restore the bond between European thought and its Christian past which the Enlightenment and the French Revolution had severed, and restore to life the continent's intellectual and religious tradition. Furthermore, since, in Leo's eyes, the philosophy of St. Thomas was the most rigorous, coherent, and inclusive of the high medieval systems, he was confident that it would measure up to the systematic exigencies of modern philosophy, while its openness to the Christian faith would keep it from falling victim to the religious and moral narrowness of modern thought." Gerald A. McCool, *The Neo-Thomists* (Milwaukee: Marquette University Press, 1994) 2. The most important Roman Catholic Neo-Thomists are Jacques Maritain, Etienne Gilson, and Austin Farrer, etc. For an introduction to these Neo-Thomists, see Eugene T. Long, "Neo-Thomism," in idem, *Twentieth-Century Western Philosophy of Religion 1900–2000* (Dordrecht: Kluwer Academic Publishers, 2000) 338–48; for a general survey of Neo-Thomism, see John F.X. Knasas, *Being and Some Twentieth-Century Thomists* (New York: Fordham University Press, 2003) 1–31; Mark Schoof, *A Survey of Catholic Theology 1800–1970* (New York: Paulist Newman Press, 1970).

36   Joseph Maréchal inaugurated the transcendental Thomism with his five-volume work, *Le point de départ de la métaphysique: Leçons sur le développement historique et théorique du problème de la connaissance* (Louvain: Museum Lessianum, 1926–1947). For a thorough and systematic study of Joseph Maréchal, see Otto Muck, *The Transcendental Method* (New York: Herder and Herder, 1968); see also, John F.X. Knasas, *Being and Some Twentieth-Century Thomists*, 45–61 and 93–100.

theologians, such as, Emerich Coreth, Karl Rahner, Bernard Lonergan, etc.[37]

The transcendental Thomists attempt a conversation between Kant's transcendental philosophy and Thomistic metaphysics. The chief goal of this conversation is to restore a metaphysics of realism (Aristotelian-Thomistic metaphysics) by means of remedying the Kantian failure in this regard, but on Kant's own presuppositions.[38] In other words, utilizing the Kantian transcendental logic as a useful tool, the transcendental Thomists attempt to revalidate classical metaphysics (Aristotelian-Thomistic) by overcoming the Kantian agnosticism concerning the constitutive knowledge of being as such (*An-sich-Sein*).[39]

---

37   For a succinct introduction to these transcendental Thomists, see Long, "Neo-Thomism," 348–58; Knasas, *Being and Twentieth-Century Thomists*, 93–107; Muck, *The Transcendental Method*, 184–306.

38   Otto Muck writes that "Maréchal was the first to see the connections between the Thomistic metaphysics of knowledge and transcendental philosophy. Furthermore, he was able to develop the transcendental method to such an extent that it served as a means of demonstrating these connections, thus overcoming deficiencies in Kant and the idealists with their own method. This is the aim of his five-volume work, *Le point de départ de la métaphysique: Leçons sur le développement historique et théorique du problème de la connaissance*" (Muck, *The Transcendental Method*, 26).

39   According to Emerich Coreth's brief explanation of the history of western metaphysics, a fully fledged form of the agnosticism concerning the constitutive knowledge of being as such (being as real) is evident in Christian Wolff's (1679–1754) metaphysical system. Wolff understands metaphysics as "*theoretical philosophy.*" This means that, for him, the real task of metaphysics is "to deduce, from clearly defined concepts and axioms, the statements which apply to every *possible* object of thought. In this way, metaphysics no longer is a real study of being, but a mere formal doctrine of axioms or principles. It is no longer rooted in being." (Emerich Coreth, *Metaphysics*, translation and edition by Joseph Donceel (New York: Herder and Herder, 1968) 21). According to Coreth, this Wolffian understanding of metaphysics had an influence upon the development of Kant's thought. Coreth explains that although Kant's transcendental turn in philosophical thinking made a pioneering contribution to modern philosophy, his transcendental philosophy is "but the self-critique of a metaphysics without being, of a metaphysics of essence and of subjectivity." (Coreth, *ibid.*, 24).

Granted that the transcendental Thomists indicated above had an influence on Tracy's revisionist model in one way or another, the most important source for Tracy's metaphysical reflection is Emerich Coreth. Tracy relies on Coreth's transcendental method for what he refers to as his own "metaphysical or transcendental" reflection. Hence, in order to understand Tracy's position, it is imperative to look at Coreth's transcendental method. In what follows, we will first look at the basic structure of Coreth's transcendental method. After this examination, we will illuminate how Tracy incorporates this source for building his position.

*The Basic Structure of Emerich Coreth's Transcendental Method*

*The Starting Point of the Transcendental Method*

Coreth distinguishes the transcendental method over against two other existing methods applied in metaphysics: "the synthetic-inductive and the analytic-deductive."[40]

The "synthetic-inductive" method refers to the way of reasoning which "passes from the multiplicity of concrete data of experience to general laws which apply to absolutely all forms of experience."[41] The problem with this method, according to Coreth, lies in its un-reasonable assumption that the generalization of concrete data of experience can lead to the establishment of universal, necessary truths. It can at best lead to "increasing probability, not to absolute necessary truth, and metaphysics is not satisfied with anything less."[42] The "analytic-deductive" method refers to the way of reasoning which derives "the whole of metaphysics from a simple self-evident starting point."[43] The essential assumption involved here is that the starting

---

40  *Ibid.*, 32.
41  *Ibid.*, 33.
42  *Ibid.* Coreth writes that "other sciences are allowed to presuppose the validity of the process of induction; but metaphysics can presuppose nothing and should be able to justify the method of induction, something which can certainly not be done inductively. Therefore, the synthetic-inductive method is unable to lead us into real metaphysical knowledge." (*Ibid.*).
43  *Ibid.*

point of metaphysics is a certain primary axiom which does not demand any further logical and critical presuppositions. In other words, metaphysics proceeds from a certain primary principle which is, in its very nature, self-evident, thus, indemonstrable. Coreth points to the drawback of this method as follows: the presupposition in this method is that "the starting point precontains virtually the full extent of all our knowledge of beings as beings. But how can the truth of this presupposition be established beyond the possibility of any doubt, in an analytical or deductive way?"[44] An important element to be clarified here is that, for Coreth, "induction" and "deduction" as such cannot be the problem. Rather, the problem consists, as shown in the above descriptions, in the unreasonable assumptions that both methods make in the shaping of metaphysical knowledge.[45] As we shall see later, his "transcendental method" uses "induction" and "deduction" as methodical devices but under different conditions.

Since metaphysics can start neither with the concrete data of experience ("synthetic-inductive" method), nor with a certain axiomatic principle or abstract idea ("analytic-deductive" method), Coreth's fundamental question is "how then can we start to build the science of metaphysics?"[46] Coreth's solution is the use of the "transcendental method" which starts with a special kind of experience, namely, "an intellectual experience."[47] This experience refers to a self-reflective or a transcendental experience which has to do with reflecting upon our having an experience. Coreth explains that "when we know an object (sense experience), we are also aware of knowing

---

44    *Ibid.*
45    Coreth describes the dangers involved in both methods as follows. The "synthetic-inductive" method may induce a "dogmatic empiricism," which is reflected "in claiming to derive from mere sense experience something which is not really contained in it, which is affirmed without real justification, dogmatically. Here one claims to derive from a few particular experiences that which applies to all experience, from the observation of a few contingent facts that which is absolute and necessary." (*Ibid.*, 34). The "analytic-deductive" method may issue in an "essentialism" which "would confine us within the domain of possibility, of mere ideas or essences," thus, not into reality (*Ibid.*).
46    *Ibid.*, 34.
47    *Ibid.*, 42.

this object (intellectual intuition). In other words, every instance of sense experience contains elements which transcend that experience. The limits of sense experience can be transcended, because we always have already transcended them."[48] In short, in the transcendental method, the attention is given not so much to objects as to our object-oriented *act* as such. Hence, objects are considered insofar as they are in relation to our object-oriented *act*, rather than in themselves.[49] For Coreth, the most essential reason for taking this self-reflective (transcendental) *act* of our thinking as the starting point of metaphysics is that it can provide a presuppositionless, undeniable, and therefore, firm basis of metaphysics. In what sense, then, is this so? Coreth attempts to demonstrate this possibility through the phenomenon of *questioning* which represents, *par excellence*, the self-reflective *act* of human thinking. Coreth explains:

> Every starting point [of metaphysics] which we may consider can and should be challenged and questioned for its validity. This very fact suggests the answer to our inquiry. The correct starting point is *the question itself*. The question itself cannot be challenged or questioned, it presupposes nothing, it takes nothing for granted. Should we nevertheless question it, then the question by which we challenge it will be the starting point. If we wonder about the very possibility of questioning, we will do so by questioning.[50]

It is impossible, without contradiction, to deny our possibility of questioning. Here, it is the *act* of questioning, not the *content* of questioning, that is undeniable. In Coreth's transcendental method, a "presuppositionless metaphysics, accordingly, begins from questioning: not from the appearance of it, nor from the concept of it, nor from judgments about it, but from the performance, the *Vollzug*."[51]

---

48  *Ibid.*, 34–5.
49  Regarding this trait of the transcendental method, see Muck, *The Transcendental Method*, 312.
50  Coreth, *Metaphysics*, 38–9.
51  Lonergan wrote a critique of Coreth's *Metaphysics*, first published in *Gregorianum* 44 (1963) 307–18; reprinted in *The Current* 5 (1964) 6–23. The title of his critique is "Metaphysics as Horizon," which is appended to the end of Coreth's *Metaphysics* (the English edition) in 197–219. The above quotation is from Lonergan's critique, "Metaphysics as Horizon," 201.

The transcendental method, in its system, consists of a double movement: "reduction" and "deduction." The movement of "reduction" is concerned with uncovering the conditions of possibility of the very act of questioning. Coreth calls these conditions "*transcendental conditions.*"[52] He explains that "reduction" is a movement of "return from that which is thematically known to that which is unthematically co-known in the act of consciousness, to that which is pre-known as a condition of the act."[53] The essential point here is that "the transcendental conditions are not properly *presupposed*, but *co-affirmed*" unthematically and implicitly in the act of questioning itself.[54] By analyzing the fundamental structure of questioning, Coreth attempts a further explanation of this fact.

According to Coreth, in order for a *question* to be asked, there must be two underlying principles in combination: *Fraglichkeit* and *Fragbarkeit*. The former refers to "the possibility of asking the question because we do not know the answer as yet."[55] The latter refers to "the possibility of asking the question because we know enough to ask a pertinent question."[56] So, for example, when we ask about a science that encompasses everything, this questioning suggests that we have already in some way encompassed everything. When we question the possibility of a science of being as being, this inquiring suggests that we have in some way a knowledge of being as being. In short, we cannot ask about that about which we know nothing. Hence, questioning is possible when there is a combination (not a juxtaposition) of knowing (*Fragbarkeit*) and not-knowing (*Fraglichkeit*). Coreth describes this combination as "a knowing not-knowing, a knowing ignorance, aware of its own ignorance, hence

---

52    Coreth, *Metaphysics*, 51.
53    *Ibid.*, 37.
54    *Ibid.*, 51 (italics mine). Coreth states that "ontic or logical conditions are presupposed, either as actually fulfilled or as known, while transcendental conditions are conditions of the possibility of the act, unthematically co-affirmed in the act." (*Ibid.*).
55    *Ibid.*, 53.
56    *Ibid.*

proceeding beyond the limits of its own knowledge, and anticipating, in some kind of pre-knowledge, that which it does not know as yet."[57] He goes on to explain that "such a knowing ignorance begets the desire to know and evokes the question. We may call it the *pre-knowledge of the question*."[58] According to Coreth, this unthematic, implicit *pre-knowledge* co-affirmed in the very act of questioning is the transcendental condition of questioning.

Another movement of the transcendental method, "deduction" is concerned with making explicit in cognitive concepts the unthematic, implicit pre-knowledge uncovered by the movement of "reduction." These two movements, "reduction" and "deduction" are not separated but in "constant interaction, they influence each other" in the fashion of a dialectical relationship.[59] Coreth explains that "whereas reduction proceeds from a particular experience to the conditions of its possibility, deduction goes from these conditions to the *essential* structures of the same experience," namely, "its nature, its possibility, and its necessity."[60] According to Coreth, the *pre-knowledge* implicitly co-affirmed in our questioning can be "called its [our questioning's] *horizon*, since it is the background against which the question stands out."[61] For Coreth, the task of the movement of "deduction" is a

---

57    *Ibid.*, 54.
58    *Ibid.*
59    *Ibid.*, 37.
60    *Ibid.*, 37.
61    *Ibid.*, 54. For a better understanding of this pre-knowledge (more specifically in his terms, "pure pre-knowledge"), we need to clarify some terminology. Coreth distinguishes the pre-knowledge of questioning into three levels: "modifying co-knowledge," "constitutive co-knowledge," and "pure pre-knowledge." The "modifying co-knowledge" refers to a pre-knowledge which we have heard, read, or thought at an empirical level concerning a particular question. This knowledge influences the question and modifies its meaning differently for different people according to their different backgrounds. This knowledge is "not a condition of the possibility nor a constitutive element of the question, it merely modifies the meaning of the question for the questioner." (*Ibid.*, 55). The "constitutive co-knowledge" refers to a pre-knowledge which enters more deeply in the act of questioning in such a way that it is a condition of the possibility of this or that particular question, but not the condition of the possibility of the questioning as such. For example, Coreth explains, "when we

thematic explication of this *horizon*. In effect, this task is unmistakably related to his concern with the revalidation of the possibility of a metaphysics of being (in his own terms, "transcendental-metaphysical *ontology*"). In what follows, we shall look at how Coreth undertakes that task of "deduction."

inquire about the starting point of metaphysics, we must know what metaphysics is or wishes to be, what a starting point is, that metaphysics has a starting point. This kind of knowledge is a condition of the possibility of this question, it can be derived from it reductively. We call this knowledge *constitutive co-knowledge*." (*Ibid.*, 56). Finally, "pure pre-knowledge" has to do with a constitutive element of the question as question, namely the "movement of the question beyond what is known, into the unknown." (*Ibid.*). Coreth writes that "it is a pure pre-knowledge, a pure transcending of what is already known, a pure anticipation of what is not known yet. We call it *pure* because it does not derive from any empirical content of the question, nor does it contain any content of that kind. For such contents do not explain why the mind strives past them towards something else. This pure pre-knowledge, as the movement of pure surpassing and pure anticipation, is *the constitutive condition of the possibility of any question whatsoever.*" (*Ibid.*, 57). An important element to be noted here is that these three kinds of pre-knowledge are not operative in separation, but in combination in every single question. Concerning this combinatorial relationship, Coreth explains as follows. "The single concrete question is conditioned by constitutive co-knowledge and is accompanied by modifying co-knowledge [...] This [horizon made up of both types of co-knowledge] is a limited, partial horizon of possible questions, an empirical horizon constituted by the questioner's own past experience. Every single question possesses such an empirical horizon. These partial empirical horizons presuppose, however, a previous encompassing total horizon of all questioning and of all knowledge, which is no longer empirical, but purely *a priori* [pure pre-knowledge]." (*Ibid.*). It should be clearly noted that concerning the movement of "deduction" of his transcendental method, Coreth's focus is on the *pure pre-knowledge as a priori total horizon* of any question as question. Hence, what we mean by "pre-knowledge" or "horizon" without any further distinction in the text refers to the pure pre-knowledge or the *a priori* total horizon.

In the preceding section, we noted that what makes questioning possible is a "knowing not knowing" or a "knowing ignorance" (a combination of *Fraglichkeit* and *Fragbarkeit*). Here, the "knowing not knowing" points to the fact that our knowing is limited. Coreth explains that it is also the case, however, that "to know a limit as limit is already to be beyond this limit" in the sense that it involves our anticipation of further knowledge, of something more to be known.[62] Coreth calls this anticipation the "pure anticipation of the questionable as such."[63] According to him, the final goal of questioning is the questionable as such. The issue here is how to explicate "the questionable as such."

Coreth explains that, firstly, "the questionable as such" has no limits. He states that "if there were limits, we would ask questions about them, and, by so doing, we would pass beyond them, do away with them. Hence the questionable as such is simply everything."[64] Secondly, as far as "the questionable as such" has to do with our inquiry about *everything*, not in the sense of every thing in particular, but everything at once, it has to do with "the unity of all that we may inquire about, the unity of all the questionable."[65] From this argument, Coreth draws forth his pivotal proposition: the unity of all the *questionable* is "the unity of *being*."[66] In other words, the questionable as such, anticipated in the act of questioning, is *being* as such. He explains that "whenever we inquire, we inquire about the being of things. What IS this, that, everything? Hence being as such is the ultimate aim, the unlimited *horizon* of every question."[67] In short, "this totality of being is not the sum of all previously known beings, but the anticipation of the totality and of the unity of all beings,

---

62    *Ibid.*, 59.
63    *Ibid.*, 60.
64    *Ibid.*, 61.
65    *Ibid.*, 62.
66    *Ibid.* Coreth states that this unity of being is a condition of the possibility of questioning as such. Every single question is always comprised within this horizon of being.
67    *Ibid.*, (italics mine).

present to the human mind as the unthematic pre-knowledge of every question."[68] Coreth clarifies that what he means by *being* here is *esse* (not *ens*), namely, what makes beings exist as beings, the act of being.[69] More importantly, this understanding of *being* as *esse* is reached not by *induction* from prior partial knowledge but by *anticipation* impelled by unlimited human inquiring, the human desire for unity and totality.[70] In sum, the transcendental method understands *being* (*esse*) as "the previous total *framework* in which every partial knowledge fits. It is the *horizon* within which every particular act of knowledge occurs."[71]

---

68    *Ibid.* Coreth explains that even when we do not know the answer to such a question as, "Is there anything like *being*?" or "Is there really something which possesses *being* as such?," our question itself cannot be possible without the pre-knowledge of *being*. Such questions concerning *being* as such, moreover, "get their answer in the very *act* of questioning. When we inquire whether anything really is, we are aware that our act of inquiring and that we, the inquirer, really *are*. This awareness is implied in our awareness of the act of inquiring, in our lived or exercised knowledge. Here again the explicit question is answered by the implicit lived knowledge." (*Ibid.*, 63).

69    In the text, whenever we refer to being as such (*esse*), we will use italics: *being*.

70    Put differently, Coreth clarifies that, in the transcendental method, uncovering *being* as such is reached not by *induction* from some particular knowledge or experience, but by *induction* from the self-transcending experience which presupposes nothing. This is the difference of his use of *induction* from that of the "synthetic-inductive" method which we already saw. He states that "we use induction, since we start from experience. But this experience is not mere sense experience, it is an intellectual experience. And we do not, as is done in the other sciences, generalize from a few contingent instances, but we look for the *a priori* conditions of possibility." (Coreth, *Metaphysics*, 42). With respect to the understanding of *being* as such by *anticipation*, Coreth explains that "we know about being in its totality and that we do not know everything about it. We know about it, otherwise we could not inquire about it [*Fragbarkeit*]. We do not know everything about it, we want to know more about it, otherwise there would be no need and no sense inquiring about it [*Fraglichkeit*]. This shows that man is congenitally a metaphysical being, who cannot help inquiring – at least implicitly – about the totality of being, since he cannot go through life without asking questions." (*Ibid.*, 63–4).

71    *Ibid.*, 63 (italics mine).

## The Characteristics of Being

Basing himself on the idea that *being* as such is the pre-knowledge, the horizon, and the condition of the possibility of questioning (or self-reflective thinking), Coreth explicates more specific characteristics of the reality of *being*. This explication of the characteristics of *being* provides a preparatory foundation for his metaphysical demonstration of God's existence.

1. *Being (esse) as the unconditioned*: Coreth characterizes *being* as the unconditioned in the sense that "it is the unconditioned condition of all questioning, it is the absolutely necessary."[72] Coreth argues that when we ask questions, we do not only ask how things are phenomenologically in relation to us, but also how they *are* absolutely in themselves. As long as we have only answers about things within a restricted phenomenological horizon of validity, we continue to ask questions about that which really *is*. Thus, in our questioning, there is always operative an absolute horizon of *being* against which the relative phenomenological horizon stands. He says that "we would not even be able to inquire about an unconditioned validity, if our question were basically locked up within the scope of conditioned and limited validity."[73] In other words, the very act of questioning testifies to the necessary presence of the horizon of *being* as the unconditioned. He explains:

> We do not begin by presupposing finite beings which are conditioned and contingent and argue from the conditioned to the unconditioned, from the contingent to the necessary. For it is impossible to know the conditioned or the

72  *Ibid.*, 65.
73  *Ibid.*, 64–5. Coreth contends that "we can speak of 'validity for me' only because we contrast it with 'validity in itself.' There is a contradiction latent in all forms of idealism and of relativism, in their claim that our knowledge is valid only for us, not in itself. They make a distinction between that which is valid for us and that which is valid in itself, and they imply that this difference is valid in itself, not merely for us. In other words, merely subjective validity is limited validity [...]. The relativist can assert the limited validity of human knowledge only by transcending it. He affirms that it is absolutely valid to say that human knowledge is only relatively valid, and thus he contradicts himself." (*Ibid.*, 65).

contingent as such, except against the horizon of the unconditioned and of the necessary. We start by establishing the unconditioned and absolute nature of being as a whole, which is presupposed and co-affirmed in every question, as a condition of its possibility.[74]

2. *Being (esse) as the unlimited*: According to Coreth, the unconditionedness of *being* implies that *being* "cannot be transcended, that there is no going beyond it, that it is unlimited, infinite."[75] This is to say that *being* is the all-encompassing horizon in which everything is open to question without limitation. In other words, *being* is the condition of possibility for the fact that particular beings, regardless of what they are, can be posited and asked. Coreth states that "that which constitutes the ultimate, unconditioned reality of things is *being*, and that which affects absolutely everything, without any limitation, is likewise *being*. Being is therefore the ultimate reality, both intensively and extensively. And the horizon of being, within which we ask the question as question, is simply unlimited."[76]

As a whole, Coreth sees the two characteristics of being, intensively "unconditioned" and extensively "unlimited," in integration. He states:

> The horizon of unconditioned validity is necessarily the unlimited horizon of being as such. Only an unlimited horizon can give rise to absolute validity. But the beings which we reach in knowledge and inquiry within this horizon are *finite*. As such, they can never exhaust the infinity of the horizon of being. The dynamism of our mind proceeds necessarily beyond every finite object, beyond the sum of all possible finite objects, towards the infinite itself. It can reach its fulfillment only in the unlimited.[77]

74    *Ibid.*, 66.
75    *Ibid.*
76    *Ibid.*, 67.
77    *Ibid.*, 173–4.

## The Restoration of a Metaphysics of Realism in the Transcendental Method

At the outset, we mentioned that the chief goal of the "transcendental method" is a restoration of a metaphysics of realism in modern terms by means of the conversation between Kant's transcendental philosophy and Thomistic metaphysics. Otto Muck explains that the transcendental Thomists try to show that:

> A complete disclosure of the total order of reality is possible from the transcendental point of view. The exponents of the transcendental method in neo-scholasticism attempt to work out a proof of this fact. They show that the faithful pursuit of this method leads not only to answers to questions which are drawn from transcendental reflection, but that these answers are arrived at primarily through a transcendentally grounded metaphysics which agrees in its essentials with the Aristotelian-Thomistic metaphysics.[78]

In our previous examination, we looked at how Coreth conducts a dialectical conversation between the two movements of "reduction" (aided by Kant's transcendental philosophy) and "deduction" (aided by Thomistic metaphysics). In this section, we will briefly discuss how the philosophical traditions of Kant and Thomistic metaphysics are operative in each movement of "reduction" and "deduction." This observation will help us to see how these operations are employed in view of the goal of the transcendental method, viz., a restoration of a metaphysics of realism.

Concerning the use of Kant's transcendental philosophy in the movement of "reduction," two elements can be pointed out. Firstly, the transcendental method aims at reflecting upon not so much objects as our *way* of knowing objects, as shown in Kant. The central focus here is on the *reflectivity* of our knowledge on knowledge. Coreth writes that "for Kant it meant a passage from the conditioned to the condition, from the object of experience to pure reason which determines this object. Thus metaphysics turns into transcendental philosophy."[79] Coreth, however, utilizes and develops the Kantian

---

78    Muck, *The Transcendental Method*, 20.
79    Coreth, *Metaphysics*, 23.

transcendental reflection for his own purpose, viz., building a meta-physics. Coreth lays down his metaphysics on this reflectivity of the human intellect (i.e., questioning) as its starting point because of two crucial traits of this reflectivity. Firstly, it does not restrict our consciousness to any particular domain, but touches on the infinitely transcending horizon of all the knowable in view of its unlimited thrust. Secondly, it presupposes nothing in its actuation by its very nature and its capacity for asking everything: namely, it takes nothing for granted. Hence, for Coreth, human reflection as such (questioning) can be the starting point for building a metaphysics which is in turn the most universal and foundational science.

Secondly, the transcendental method incorporates the Kantian transcendental philosophy in that it aims at reflecting upon the *a priori* conditions which make possible our knowledge. For Kant, knowledge is to be understood from the previous, *a priori* conditions of its possibility. This claim is his solution for overcoming both rationalism and empiricism as regards the question of the possibility of universal and necessary knowledge. Coreth explains:

> Against rationalism, he [Kant] maintained that universal and necessary prin-ciples cannot be merely analytic, that they must be synthetic, if they are to increase our knowledge; in other words, they must not merely explain what we know already, they must add something to our knowledge. But synthetic judgments, Kant saw, which must be universally and necessarily true, cannot derive from sense experience, cannot be, in the sense of empiricism, synthetic judgments *a posteriori*. Sense experience refers only to the singular and to the contingent. Kant solved this problem by stating that there must exist judgments which are synthetic *a priori*, previous to experience, yet yielding really new knowledge. Thus the problem of the possibility of metaphysics becomes the problem of the possibility of judgments which are synthetic *a priori*.[80]

Although the transcendental method is indebted to Kant's trans-cendental philosophy in terms of the two preceding aspects (focusing on the reflectivity of the human intellect and on the transcendental conditions of knowledge), it endeavors to overcome Kant's agnos-ticism on the total order of reality, the objective domain of meta-physics. As we have already seen, for Coreth, as distinct from Kant,

80    *Ibid.*

the *a priori* (transcendental) conditions serve as the key for building his metaphysics.[81] For Coreth, the limitation of Kant's philosophical system is that it does not blend the objective ontological question into its transcendental reflection. Rather, it is restricted to the domain of human transcendental subjectivity. Coreth explains:

> For Kant, the concepts and principles of pure reason are valid only within the domain of sense experience. Even within this domain they cannot determine the object as it is 'in itself,' but only as it appears to us. Such a metaphysics has no longer an objective, but only a subjective function; thinking is locked up in a mere 'metaphysics of subjectivity.' All this results from the fact that, long before Kant, metaphysics had lost its foundation in being. Kant's critique of pure reason is but the self-critique of a metaphysics without being, of a metaphysics of essence and of subjectivity.[82]

Coreth finds the reason for this limitation of Kant's system in the fact that Kant considers only the transcendental conditions of the *content* of knowledge, not those of the *act* of knowledge which transcends a particular content of knowledge. Consequently, for Kant, insofar as knowledge is only possible in the phenomenal order, "he shut himself up in the phenomenal order, he was unable to reach the domain of metaphysics."[83]

Over against such a limitation of Kant's transcendental reflection, what Coreth attempts to do is to recover the domain of metaphysics, the horizon of *being* as such, by means of focusing on the transcendental conditions of the *act* of knowledge (more specifically, the *act* of questioning).[84] This attempt is what the movement

81  We already demonstrated that, for Coreth, the transcendental condition of the possibility of questioning is *being* as such, upon which his metaphysics is built. However, this uncovering of *being* as such is not yet explicit in the movement of "reduction," but only in the movement of "deduction." This means that Coreth's transcendental method incorporates the Kantian transcendental philosophy only to the extent that it reflects upon the transcendental conditions of our knowledge. Accordingly, Coreth makes clear that his concern to make the transcendental condition thematically explicit in *being* as such is not Kantian.

82  Coreth, *Metaphysics*, 24.

83  *Ibid.*, 52.

84  In his critique of Coreth's transcendental method, Lonergan points to two elements of difference between Coreth and Kant. Lonergan says that, firstly,

of "deduction" is all about. A key aspect of the movement of "deduction" that Coreth wants to highlight is the fact that, in that movement, the order of *being* is not appended to the *act* of questioning from without, but is *disclosed* in the *act* itself as the horizon of the act. In other words, the objective order of *being* is not postulated, but is disclosed in the *act* (not in the *content*) of questioning.[85] Hence, the dialectic of the transcendental method is described as "the dialectic of *act* and *content*" (not of *content* and *content*).[86] Coreth explains this dialectic as follows:

> Coreth's transcendental inquiry is "not into the *a priori* conditions of cognitional objects, but into the *a priori* conditions of questions. Kant wrote an *Erkenntniskritik*: the conditioned is the objective pole, the condition is the subjective pole. Fr. Coreth is writing a metaphysics: his subjective pole, questioning is the conditioned; and his objective pole, being is the condition. Hence Fr. Coreth's transcendental inquiry is just the inverse of Kant's." (Lonergan, "Metaphysics as Horizon," 217). Secondly, according to Lonergan, since Kant's cognitional perception is "not of noumena, there cannot arise within the Kantian approach any question of the *existence en soi* of the objects known in Kant's world as appearance. But what follows from Kant's *a priori*, does not follow from Fr. Coreth's. Fr. Coreth's is being as unrestricted, the whole of all that is; within being there is already included *An-sich-Sein* [being-in-itself] [...] For Kant cognitional operations can be related to objects only through *Anschauung* [intuition], so that perception has to be the constitutive principle of objectivity. For Fr. Coreth the constitutive principle of objectivity is the question: questioning immediately intends being; data are referred to being as what questions are about; answers are referred to being as answers to questions." (*Ibid.*, 217–18).

85   Since we have already examined Coreth's argument concerning how the order of *being* is disclosed in the *act* of questioning, we will not repeat it here. Let us look at Lonergan's explication of the disclosing process of the order of being in Coreth's transcendental method. He explains: for example, "I am stating what really and truly is so when I state that we are under an illusion whenever we claim to know what really and truly is so. However, the content of the explicitly contradictory statement adds to the content of the first what is found implicitly in the first, not as content, but as performance. Now to bring to light such contradictions is the operative moment in Fr. Coreth's use of transcendental method." (*Ibid.*, 204).

86   Coreth, *Metaphysics*, 53. Lonergan comments this dialectic of Coreth that, according to Coreth, "we should learn that questioning [act] not only is about being [content] but is itself being, being in its *Gelichtetheit* (luminousness),

192

The *act* and that which is unthematically co-affirmed in it must be expressed in concepts, transformed into *content*. Yet this conceptual thinking, the *content*, must never lose touch with the *act*, which always transcends it, which can never be exhaustively expressed in it. The *concept* must stay rooted in the *act*, explicit knowledge must feed on the knowledge implied in the *act*, on what we have called *exercised or lived knowledge*.[87]

In short, it can be said that the dialectic between the movements of "reduction" and "deduction" involves the dialectic between *act* and *content*.

We mentioned before that, in the movement of "deduction," Thomistic metaphysics is operative. The movement of "deduction" refers to the process of mediating into content (or concepts) the unthematic knowledge co-affirmed in the act of questioning. We saw that, for Coreth, this process serves for building his *ontology* (the domain of *being* as such). In what sense, then, does this movement of "reduction" incorporate Thomistic metaphysics?

For Coreth, *being* as such is not what can be, but what *is* as real, which is maintained in Aristotelian-Thomistic metaphysics.[88] Coreth explains that the "deduction" of the transcendental method does not start from a mere idea or principle, but from a real, existential experience of self-transcending human spirit, which discloses itself to us "as endowed with a pre-reflexive metaphysical knowledge of being."[89] Coreth goes on to say that "this is not idealism, for we hold

being in its openness to being, being that is realizing itself through inquiry to knowing that, through knowing, it may come to loving. This being of the questioning questioner is the latent metaphysics from which explicit metaphysics is derived; and in explicit metaphysics it is the primary analogate through which other being as being is understood." (Lonergan, "Metaphysics as Horizon," 203–4).

87  Coreth, *Metaphysics*, 53 (the italics of act and content are mine).

88  Lonergan explains that, "for Fr. Coreth, being is precisely what St. Thomas meant by being. For as intended in questioning, being is unrestricted. In that premise there is already included the conclusion that *esse de se est illimitatum* (being of itself is unlimited), whence it will follow that finite being is a compound of essence and existence and that every *ens* is an *ens* by its relations to *esse*." (Lonergan, "Metaphysics as Horizon," 213–14).

89  Coreth, *Metaphysics*, 42. Lonergan clarifies this aspect of Coreth's trans-cendental method as follows: "When one states that a statement is merely

that reality cannot be deduced with logical necessity from a first principle, that it can be known only from experience. This is not essentialism, for our deduction does not stay within the realm of mere possibility. Our metaphysics considers real being, the totality of all that which really is. It is in touch with reality because it starts from the reality of the self-actuation of our inquiring spirit, from which it proceeds to the rest of reality." [90] For Coreth, the transcendental subjectivity is not a closed, inner domain, because, in its very *act* (*Vollzug*) towards infinity, subjectivity is already in the objective realm of *being* as such which transcends it. He concludes that "hence, in metaphysics, we never discover or demonstrate anything which is really new or unknown," but uncover the implicitly co-affirmed *"knowledge implied in the act*, or more simply, *lived knowledge or exercised knowledge"* which is revealed to our self-actuating spirit.[91] This means that, as far as this lived knowledge of being is implied in a real experience, metaphysical knowledge of being is not merely possible, but real.

*Emerich Coreth's Arguments for the Existence of God*

Finally, we would like to look briefly at Coreth's arguments for the existence of God based on his metaphysics of *being* (in his own terms, "transcendental-metaphysical *ontology*"). According to Coreth, metaphysics is a science which consists in a plurality of aspects. Firstly, metaphysics may refer to "transcendental-metaphysical *anthropol-*

logical, one means that really and truly it is merely logical. It follows that one cannot suppose that all statements are merely logical, for then it would be merely logical that they are merely logical, and it would be impossible to say that any [sic] really and truly is merely logical. The same holds for the merely hypothetical, the merely phenomenal, and any other restricted or qualified realm. By the same stroke any and every form of idealism is excluded. The possibility of questioning is being, and this being is being in its unqualified sense, *An-sich-Sein* (being-in-itself)." (Lonergan, "Metaphysics as Horizon," 203).

90    Coreth, *Metaphysics*, 42–3. In the context of the above statement, Coreth distinguishes his use of "deduction" from that of the "analytic-deductive" method which he had critiqued earlier.

91    *Ibid.*, 44, 40.

*ogy*," insofar as it investigates the *a priori* structure and laws of human self-transcending thinking. Secondly, metaphysics may refer to "transcendental-metaphysical *ontology*," insofar as it discovers the *being* of all that is in the *a priori* structure of the self-actuation of human thinking. Finally, metaphysics may refer to "transcendental-metaphysical *theology*," insofar as it shows that human self-transcending thinking and the knowledge of *being* implied in it are intelligible only against the background of the Absolute. However, "these three aspects constitute an indivisible unity; none of them can be investigated without taking into account the two others."[92] This statement indicates that his doctrine of God is the final component of his metaphysics. This is to say that his "transcendental-metaphysical *anthropology*" and his "transcendental-metaphysical *ontology*" serve as the metaphysical foundation for his philosophical theology. The following statement indicates his position more clearly:

> The doctrine of being has its peak in the doctrine of God, as the latter finds its foundation in the doctrine of being. Metaphysics as the science of beings as beings finds its fulfillment only when it turns into a science of the divine Being. And metaphysics as the science of the divine Being is possible only when it derives from the science of beings as such. Both aspects are complementary, they possess – as Aristotle has said – their unity in metaphysics.[93]

In what follows, we will discuss Coreth's argument for the existence of God which is a part of his "transcendental-metaphysical *theology*." In his work, *Metaphysics*, Coreth's "transcendental metaphysical *theology*" involves three issues: (1) the existence of God; (2) God's essence; (3) God and human being. Coreth's arguments concerning these issues are basically Thomistic. In relation to Tracy's God-discussion, it is important to look at how Coreth connects his metaphysics of *being* and God's existence. For this concern, Coreth's discussion on (1) the existence of God is most essential. Therefore, we will only focus on this topic. Another reason for this limited focus is that for the issues of (2) God's essence and (3) God and human beings, Tracy does not adopt Coreth's Thomistic position. Instead, for

92   *Ibid.*, 44.
93   *Ibid.*, 170.

those issues, Tracy opts for the so-called neo-classical theism advocated by the process thought of Charles Hartshorne. This suggests that the main feature of Tracy's God-discussion is its eclectic character. Let us look at Coreth's arguments for the existence of God.

In his arguments, Coreth incorporates Thomas Aquinas' well-known five proofs (or ways) for the existence of God.[94] Coreth takes up, however, only three proofs out of the five proofs of Thomas Aquinas.[95] Coreth attempts to reformulate those three Thomistic proofs on the basis of his "transcendental-metaphysical *ontology*."

---

94     Thomas Aquinas' five ways to prove the existence of God are: (1) to prove by means of the argument concerning *motion*. Everything that is moved is moved by another, and we come in the end to an unmoved mover, 'and all understand that this is God.' (*S.Th.*, I, 2, 3, c); (2) to prove by means of the argument concerning *efficient causes*. A finite being cannot be the cause of itself. There must be a first efficient cause which is not caused, 'which everybody calls God.' (*S.Th.*, I, 2, 3, c); (3) to prove by means of the argument concerning a necessary being. Finite beings come into existence and perish, which shows they are contingent and not necessary. Then, there must be a necessary being, which is the reason why finite beings come into existence. 'This being we call God' (*S.Th.*, I, 2, 3, c); (4) to prove by means of the argument concerning the degrees of perfection, of goodness, truth, etc. The comparative judgment of things in the world in accordance with the degrees of perfection, of goodness, of truth (i.e., 'this is more beautiful than that') assumes something that is truest, best, noblest, etc., as an objective foundation. There must be a supreme Being which is the cause of being, goodness, truth, and every other perfection. 'This being we call God.' (*S.Th.*, I, 2, 3, c); (5) to prove by means of the argument concerning the teleological orientation of all natural things. We observe inorganic things operating for an end, although they are without intelligence. This shows the fact that they tend towards an end not by chance but by design. Whatever has no intelligence cannot tend toward an end, unless it is directed by some intelligent being by whom all inorganic things are directed to an end. 'This being we call God.' (*S.Th.*, I, 2, 3, c). For the explanation of the five ways of Thomas Aquinas, see Joseph K. Kockelmans, *The Metaphysics of Aquinas: A Systematic Presentation* (Leuven: Bibliotheek van de Faculteit Godgeleerdheid, 2001) 277–93; Frederick Copleston, *A History of Philosophy: Medieval Philosophy*, vol.II (New York: Doubleday, 1993) 336–46.

95     The three ways that Coreth takes up are Thomas Aquinas' second, third, and fifth proofs. Coreth puts them, however, in a different order in his own arguments.

*God as the Necessary Being in Fullness*[96]

In his doctrine of *being* (his "transcendental-metaphysical *ontology*"), Coreth affirmed that the necessity of *being* as such is co-affirmed and co-known in all of our questioning about beings. According to Coreth, the starting point of our knowledge of God is that basic knowledge and affirmation of *being* as the horizon of any knowledge and inquiry (including our knowledge of, and inquiry concerning God). This is to say that, for him, our unthematic knowledge and affirmation of *being* underlies all our understanding of God and is made explicit in that understanding. He explains that "the knowledge of God does not really represent a passage of our mind to something hitherto wholly unknown, but only an explicitation and development of our knowledge of the necessity of being."[97] As shown in his development of our knowledge of *being* as such, the nub of developing our knowledge of God also lies in our self-transcendence or "unthematic anticipation," through which we unconsciously reach out towards the absolute being of God. For him, our unrestricted metaphysical thrust towards *being* as such reaches its final destination when we get to the absolute being of God, that is, "the fullness of being and its ultimate foundation."[98] It is in God alone that human metaphysical restlessness can find satisfaction.

96    This argument is derived from the third proof of Thomas Aquinas. Aquinas finds the source of this proof in the argument formulated by Avicenna and Maimonides (See Kockelmans, *The Metaphysics of Aquinas*, 286; Copleston, *A History of Philosophy*, 341).

97    Coreth, *Metaphysics*, 175.

98    *Ibid.*, 194.

For this argument, Coreth uses the principle of causality according to which contingent beings do not possess the ground of their being in themselves. In order for every contingent being to be, it requires "a positive element, by which it is determined to the necessity of being" beyond its own contingent essence; "[h]ence the contingent being is the product of the activity of some other being. Its exterior cause is an efficient cause, a cause which actively brings it about [...] This is the law of the cause or the principle of causality."[100] Coreth states that this principle is "an application of the universal principle of sufficient reason to the being of the contingent being."[101] This causality principle is, for him, one more example of the dynamism of our self-transcending intellect. Owing to this dynamism, we are irresistibly propelled to pass beyond every contingent being (ens) towards the cause of its necessary being (esse). Hence, this principle is also "unthematically co-posited and co-affirmed in every act of inquiring or of knowing."[102]

Coreth discusses God in relation to this principle as follows. A finite and contingent cause is incapable of constituting beings as beings. Even if we suppose an infinite series of contingent causes, this series remains contingent, which directs us to a further cause. Hence, "to produce beings as beings supposes a cause whose formal object is being as being, which is therefore capable of producing absolutely all beings, of realizing all the possibilities of being. No finite cause is capable of this realization; only the infinite first cause possesses this power, this omnipotence."[103] For him, this first cause is none other than God as the Absolute and Infinite Being itself.

---

99    This argument is derived from the second proof of Thomas Aquinas. Aquinas finds the source of this proof in Aristotle's second book of *Metaphysics* (*Metaph.*, II, 2, 994a1–b31). See Kockelmans, *The Metaphysics of Aquinas*, 285; Copleston, *A History of Philosophy*, 341.

100   Coreth, *Metaphysics*, 97 (italics of being mine).

101   *Ibid.*, 98 (italics mine).

102   *Ibid.*

103   *Ibid.*, 177.

# God as the Final End of Human Spirit[104]

Coreth explains that whenever a finite existent acts, that activity has to do with a "self-actuation and self-realization of the existent."[105] And, in order to actuate and realize itself, every being strives, beyond its own being and essence, to put itself into a new reality, which is the purpose or goal of its activity. Therefore, "whenever a being acts, it acts for a certain end or goal. This is the *principle of finality*."[106] In the act of questioning, when it has reached a particular being, the dynamism of our intellect pushes past that finite being towards its ultimate ground, towards the absolute and infinite *being* as such. Here, the particular being is a partial goal and the absolute and infinite *being* is the final goal. This final goal is an "*a priori* condition of the possibility of the undeniable striving of the human spirit."[107]

According to Coreth, God is the final end of human spirit in its unquenchable metaphysical striving towards the unconditioned and infinite *being* as such: viz., God is the fullness of Being itself. Here, Coreth's essential argument is that God as the finality of human spirit must be at least *possible* and also necessarily *real*. Firstly, God must be at least *possible*, because our act of metaphysical striving towards the absolute and infinite *being* as such is possible "only if its content, *in casu*, absolute being itself, is possible; otherwise, the striving of the spirit, as it really is, would be contradictory."[108] Secondly, God is necessarily real if God is possible. As he already indicated, God is the infinite fullness of *being* itself. Hence, God is *possible* "only as *being itself*, which subsists no longer in the duality of being and essence, but whose essence it is to be, whose being is its essence."[109] That its essence is *being* itself means that by its very essence it cannot not be;

---

104    This argument is derived from the fifth proof of Thomas Aquinas. Aquinas makes use of ideas derived from Aristotle, and also the reflections of Damascene and Averroes (See Kockelmans, *The Metaphysics of Aquinas*, 290; Copleston, *A History of Philosophy*, 344).

105    Coreth, *Metaphysics*, 100.

106    *Ibid.*, 101.

107    *Ibid.*, 178.

108    *Ibid.*, 179.

109    *Ibid.*

therefore, it is the absolutely necessary being. Thus, the possibility here in question is "not a mere logical possibility, but the real possibility of being."[110] Coreth concludes, "since its essence is to be, it would no longer be possible if it were merely possible and not real. In that case, its very essence would be suppressed. Hence if the absolute being is possible, it is also real."[111]

## Some Critical Remarks on Coreth's Arguments for the Existence of God

As we have seen, Coreth's arguments for the existence of God basically follow Thomistic proofs. The only distinctiveness of Coreth's arguments is that he incorporates Thomistic proofs in the context of his "transcendental-metaphysical ontology." This means that, in effect, Coreth's arguments for the existence of God are doomed to the same critique that the Thomistic proofs are subject to. The most problematic point in Thomistic arguments for the existence of God (also in Coreth) is the fact that the metaphysical concept of (necessary) being as such (esse) is eventually inferred to (the Christian) God.[112] In other words, the question is how the equivalence between

110    *Ibid.*
111    *Ibid.*
112    In the foregoing discussion on Coreth's God, we did not deal with his understanding of God as a person who reveals himself to the world, namely, the God of Christianity (he deals with this part very briefly; see his *Metaphysics*, 186–96). In Coreth, it is clear that God, as the necessary, absolute being, is equated with God as the "*free personal God*" of Christianity (*Ibid.*, 196). He says that "philosophy can really reach a *personal God*." (*Ibid.*, 188). Concerning the problem of the Thomistic equation of *being* and God, Copleston points out that Aquinas develops his proofs in a context where people in general have a belief in God, which is quite different from ours. Copleston states that "it is not as though he [Aquinas] had in mind the composition of a treatise against professed atheists. If he had to deal with Marxists, he would doubtless treat the proofs in a different, or at least in a more elaborate and developed manner: as it is, his main interest is to give a proof of the *praeambula fidei*. Even in the *Summa contra Gentiles* the saint was not dealing primarily with atheists, but rather with the Mohammedans, who had a firm belief in God." (Copleston, *A History of Philosophy*, 343; see also Kockelmans, *The Metaphysics of Aquinas*,

being as such and God can be justified?[113] We regard this identification between the metaphysical concept of being as such and God
as problematic and unconvincing for two reasons.

Firstly, as Heidegger's well-known critique of "onto-theology"
shows, this identification can be understood in view of the western
metaphysical tradition that maintains the marriage of ontology and
theology since its beginning with the Greeks.[114] In other words, the
quest for the natural knowledge of God in Christianity finds an
objective warrant in such an "onto-theological" Greek metaphysical
system. According to Heidegger, western metaphysics is a science
inquiring after beings as such in their totality, that is to say, the Being
of beings. Western metaphysics, however, thinks of the Being of
beings in a twofold manner: "both in the ground-giving unity of what
is most general, what is indifferently valid everywhere, and also in the
unity of all that accounts for the ground, that is, of the All-Highest."[115]
The Being as the ground (the second modality) "is thought out fully
only when the ground is represented as the first ground."[116] This
means that "the Being of beings is represented fundamentally, in the

291–2). In short, in the religious culture of his time where the belief in God's
existence prevailed, the aim of Aquinas is to demonstrate by means of the
available metaphysical systems of his time that faith in the God of Christianity
is not irrational or unreasonable.

113 Louis-Marie Chauvet raises this question as follows: "Who establishes this
equivalence between the final term to which the [Thomistic] demonstration
(and thus rational discourse) tends and the God which 'all' are claimed to
discover there? [referring to Aquinas' refrain at the end of each proof, 'and all
understand that this is God']. Even if 'all' do, with what right do they? Who are
these 'all,' and how can they establish an equivalence which no theologian, no
philosopher has been able to establish, but an equivalence these 'all' build
upon?" (Louis-Marie Chauvet, *Symbol and Sacrament: A Sacramental Reinterpretation of Christian Existence* (Collegeville: The Liturgical Press, 1995) 39);
see also, Jan Van der Veken, "Ultimate Reality and God; The Same?," in Lewis
E. Hahn (ed.), *The Philosophy of Charles Hartshorne* (La Salle: Open Court
Publishing Company, 1991) 203–14.

114 Martin Heidegger, "The Onto-theo-logical Constitution of Metaphysics," in
John D. Caputo (ed.), *The Religious* (Oxford: Blackwell Publishers Ltd, 2002)
67–75. Hereafter, this work will be referred to as "Onto-theo-logical."

115 Heidegger, "Onto-theological," 69.

116 *Ibid.*, 70.

sense of the ground, only as *causa sui*. This is the metaphysical concept of God."[117] Hence, from its inception (with Plato and Aristotle) "the essential constitution of metaphysics is based on the unity of beings as such in the universal and that which is highest."[118] In short, "the fundamental character of metaphysics is onto-theologic."[119] In the Thomistic arguments, God is identified with that which onto-theological metaphysics represents as the necessary *being*, the first cause, or the finality of human spirit (or the final cause), etc. The problem of this identification is that it is, as Louis-Marie Chauvet points out, "simply postulated, not *demonstrated.*"[120] This is to say that it appeals to "a support *outside the demonstration proper*: that of common agreement" in the religious culture of Aquinas' time: namely, the prevailing faith in God's existence.[121] Chauvet writes that "at that time, such an identification imposed itself irresistibly as a cultural imperative, that is, as one of the numerous assumptions which appear within any culture as so naturally self-evident that they are impervious to questioning."[122]

Moreover, the so-called postmodern contemporary critiques of traditional western metaphysics (e.g., the critique of onto-theology in

---

117    *Ibid.*
118    *Ibid.* We already saw that this position is clearly evident in Coreth's statement that "metaphysics as the science of beings as beings finds its fulfillment only when it turns into a science of the divine Being. And metaphysics as the science of the divine Being is possible only when it derives from the science of beings as such. Both aspects are complementary, they posses – as Aristotle has said – their unity in metaphysics." (Coreth, *Metaphysics*, 170).
119    Heidegger, "Onto-theo-logical," 69–70. According to Heidegger, the onto-theological structure of metaphysics has to do with the oblivion of what he calls "the ontological difference" between Being (*Sein*) and beings (*seiendes*). According to him, the western metaphysical tradition, from Plato and Aristotle up to Nietzsche, has failed to consider Being itself (*Sein*) over against beings (entities). Instead, Being (*Sein*) has been defined as the common property of all entities and, thus, has been represented as a foundation-being (*Grund*) or a subsistent being (*sub-stratum*). Ultimately, the Being of beings, conceived as a foundation, is *causa sui*.
120    Chauvet, *Symbol and Sacrament*, 39
121    *Ibid.*
122    *Ibid.*, 40.

202

Heidegger, and the critiques of ontology in Emmanuel Levinas and Jean-Luc Marion) portray the Thomistic justification of God as the reduction of God to an "Ultimate Explainer" of human desire, and thereby of making the whole of reality intelligible by human measures.[123] In Chauvet's words, the God posited by Thomistic demonstration "appears only in the perspective of a *causality* working as a foundation. The entire discussion is distorted by the passion to master the truth."[124] He goes on to say that "such an ambition inevitably degraded the truth into an unfailingly available foundation, a substantial permanence, an objective presence."[125] The point here is that

123 More concretely, the expression, "Ultimate Explainer," is Heidegger's. See Heidegger, *The Principle of Reason*, trans. by Reginald Lilly (Bloomington: Indiana University Press, 1991); cf, Merold Westphal, "Divine Excess: The God Who Comes After," in *The Religious*, 261. For Levinas' critique, *inter alia*, see *Totality and Infinity*, trans. by Alphonso Lingis (Pittsburgh: Duquesne University Press, 1969) and *Otherwise Than Being or Beyond Essence*, trans. by Alphonso Lingis (Boston: Kluwer, 1991); for Marion's critique, *inter alia*, see *God without Being*, trans. by Thomas A. Carlson (Chicago: Chicago University Press, 1991). In the article mentioned above, Merold Westphal summarizes the central tenets of the three critics (Heidegger, Levinas, and Marion) with respect to overcoming the onto-theological representation of God as follows: Heidegger: *we must think God as the mystery that exceeds the wisdom of the Greeks*; Levinas: *we must think God as the voice that exceeds vision so as to establish a relation irreducible to comprehension*; Marion: *we must think God as the gift of love who exceeds not merely the images but also the concepts with which we aim at God*. These three tenets are cited from Westphal's formulations (See Westphal, "Divine Excess: The God Who Comes After," 261–5).
124 Chauvet, Symbol and Sacrament, 28.
125 *Ibid.* One thing to note here, however, is that a criticism like this is particularly relevant to the Thomistic proofs for the existence of God. There is a claim that we should not ignore another dimension of the Thomistic understanding of God that reflects a meditative and contemplative sense of the sacred and of the holy. For Aquinas and Coreth, God ultimately remains a mystery. For Aquinas, human intellect "does not and cannot by its own power apprehend God directly; but sensible objects, as finite and contingent, reveal their relation to God, so that the intellect can know that God exists [...]. the intellect can come to know something of God's nature, though this knowledge cannot (naturally) be more than analogical." (Copleston, *A History of Philosophy*, 393–4). Coreth states that "God remains a *mystery*. We reach him only by starting from finite beings,

the exposition of God based on such an objectivist, closed totality is irrelevant to the actual reality of the practice of faith and believers' lives.[126] John D. Caputo's remark is worth quoting in this context:

> The objectifying tendencies, the preoccupation with cognitive certainty, the confusion of religious life with assenting to certain propositions, prove to be almost completely irrelevant to anyone with the least experience of religious matters, which beg to be treated differently and on their own terms. The God of the traditional philosophy of religion is a philosopher's God explicating a philosopher's faith, to be found, if anywhere, only on the pages of philosophy journals, not in the hearts of believers or the practice of faith. This philosopher's God is a *creature* of scholastic, modernist, and Enlightenment modes of thinking that deserve nothing so much as a decent burial [...]. Let us leave the guns of metaphysics at the door and let God and religious faith feel free to speak for themselves.[127]

Our second consideration illustrating that the Thomistic demonstration of God's existence (Coreth's as well) is problematic today has to do with our concern with religious pluralism. The Thomistic

only in finite concepts, never in adequate, always only in analogous knowledge which, beyond all the finite, reaches out for the infinite. Even when known by us, God remains unknown. Even when we know him, we do not understand him. And thus the question stays with us." (Coreth, *Metaphysics*, 196). For an attempt to illuminate a more religiously animating aspect of Thomas Aquinas' metaphysics vis-à-vis Heidegger's criticism of Thomism, see John D. Caputo, *Heidegger and Aquinas: An Essay on Overcoming Metaphysics* (New York: Fordham University Press, 1982).

126    The following famous statement of Heidegger is relevant to quote here: God as *causa sui* is "the right name for the god of philosophy. Man can neither pray nor sacrifice to this god. Before the *causa sui*, man can neither fall to his knees in awe nor can he play music and dance before this god. The god-less thinking which must abandon the god of philosophy, god as *causa sui*, is thus perhaps closer to the divine God. Here this means only: god-less thinking is more open to Him than onto-theo-logic would like to admit." (Heidegger, "The Onto-theological," 74–5).

127    John D. Caputo, "Introduction: Who Comes After the God of Metaphysics?," *The Religious*, 2–3 (italics mine). For the irrelevance of Thomistic arguments for the existence of God today, see also Joseph J. Kockelmans, "Hermeneutic Philosophy and Natural Theology," in Eugene T. Long (ed.), *Prospects for Natural Theology* (Washington: The Catholic University of America Press, 1992) 92–112.

identification between (necessary) *being* as such and God is difficult to regard as self-evident especially in light of some of the major non-theistic Asian religious philosophies or traditions. Taoist philosophy and Buddhism are noteworthy here.

For example, in Taoist philosophy,[128] "Tao" (way), the most important concept in the teachings of its scriptures, *Tao-te-ching* and *Chuang-tzu* has a metaphysical and ontological meaning.[129] According to the teaching of Taoist scriptures, the essential notion of Tao is as follows. "As a primordial and eternal entity, the Tao exists before all visible things, including *ti*, the superior divinities of the official

---

128 Taoist philosophy (*Tao-chia/Daojia*: the fourth and third centuries B.C.) is generally distinghuished from Taoist religion (*Tao-chiao/Daojiao*: appeared in the second and third centuries A.D.). Taoist philosophy is concerned with the metaphysical and mystical understanding of the universe. Taoist religion is a Chinese religion which originated by incorporating the many local cults and beliefs into Taoist philosophy. Our concern in this discussion is only Taoist philosophy. For a general introduction to both areas of Taoism, see Farzeen Baldrian, "Taoism," in Mircea Eliade (ed.), *The Encyclopedia of Religion*, vol.14 (New York: Macmillan Publishing Company, 1987) 288–306; Julia Ching, *Chinese Religions* (London: The Macmillan Press, 1993) 85–118.

129 The concept of *Tao* is not a new concept that Taoist philosophy originated. It already existed in the ancient Chinese world as a basic philosophical concept designating "the correct or natural way something is done; verbally, it also meant 'show the way,' or 'guide,' hence 'teaching' or 'doctrine,' and so 'moral truth'." (David S. Nivison, "Tao and Te," in Mircea Eliade (ed.), *The Encyclopedia of Religion*, vol.14, 285). Thus, granted the fact that this concept, *Tao*, is most importantly expounded as the essential notion in Taoist philosophy, it is also commonly used as a basic concept in other major philosophical or religious traditions practiced in China, such as, in Confucianism and Buddhism (See W.E. Soothill, *The Three Religions of China* (London: Curzon Press, 1973) 15). Another thing to be noted is that Taoist scripture, *Tao-te-ching* begins with the famous line: "The way (Tao) that can be spoken of, is not the constant way (Tao)." In this line, there is a play on words. Tao is used as a noun meaning "way" and also used as a verb meaning "to speak": thus, "The Tao that can be articulated (Tao) is not the constant Tao." This Chinese word, Tao, having meaning both "way" and "to speak," is used in the Chinese translation of the New Testament as an equivalent of both the Greek words, *logos* (the Word) and *hodos* (the Way): i.e., "In the beginning was the Word (Tao)" (Jn 1: 1); "I am the Way (Tao), the Truth and the Life." (Jn 14: 6). For this, see Julia Ching, *Chinese Religions*, 88.

religion, such as Shang-ti ('lord on high') and T'ien-ti ('lord of heaven'). The Tao is beyond the grasp of the senses and is imperceptible. But from 'nothingness' (*wu*) the visible world (*yu*) is born and particularized phenomena are produced. Tao is formless, limitless, and nameless: the term *tao* is not a name but a practical referent" of the all-embracing first principle and the origin of the entire universe.[130] Our question here is whether Tao, the metaphysical and mystical principle of the universe, is also posited as a God? In Taoist philosophy, Tao is not posited as a personal or anthropomorphic deity, but as "the natural way as well as the human way, even the political way."[131] Taoist philosophy offers a vision which carries with it a mystical or religious impulse for communion not with a deity but with the hidden, self-actuating force of life, "a universal Tao, the *all*-inclusive Way."[132]

130    Farzeen Baldrian, "Taoism," 291; see also Aloysius Chang, "The Concept of the Tao," in Sebastian A. Matczak (ed.), *God in Contemporary Thought: A Philosophical Perspective* (New York: Learned Publications, 1977) 83. Chang explains that, "Everything that exists has its own *principium vitale*, but the all-embracing first principle from which all the other things are produced is the Tao." (Chang, *ibid.*).

131    Julia Ching writes that, in Taoist philosophy, "we discern a philosophical attempt to conceptualize an earlier, religious belief. In the Confucian classics, the 'Lord-on-high' has referred to a supreme deity, while 'Heaven' has at least the great ancestor's role, as that which gives birth to all things. The term Heaven did not completely disappear from Taoist philosophical writings, appearing especially in *Chuang-tzu* alongside the term Tao, but *Tao* has obviously taken over 'Heaven' in *Lao-tzu* [*Tao-te-ching*], as the natural Way as well as the human way, even the political way. And while the Tao is no longer a personal deity, it remains as a model for human behaviour." (Julia Ching, *Chinese Religions*, 88–9).

132    Julia Ching, *Chinese Religions*, 92. Richard C. Bush writes that "mysticism usually refers to the knowledge of, communion with, or perhaps even union with the divine. A Christian mystic, for example, is one who claims to have a vision of God or Christ leading on to an experience of oneness with God or of intimate communion with Christ. The early Taoist books say practically nothing about a god figure, and the few references to a 'Creator' should not be interpreted as meaning a personal, creator god." (Richard C. Bush, *Religion in China* (Niles: Argus Communications, 1977) 30).

Buddhism serves as another example of a non-theistic approach to metaphysical and ontological questions. With respect to the issue of God or the Absolute, the essence of Buddhist teaching is "the Middle Way" (*madhyama-pratipad*) which dissolves "the duality of theism and atheism." In his article, "[The] Buddhist Approach to the Problem of God," Charles Wei-hsun Fu explains that "the principle of the Middle Way leaves no room for any Buddhist speculation on or commitment to the existence or non-existence of God or Atman. That Buddhism does not assume the existence of God or the Absolute is logically very different from a flat *denial* of any divine existence. The latter violates the principle of the Middle Way, while the former only puts aside the notion of God as irrelevant to the Buddhist solution of *samsaric* problems."[133] In short, "Buddhism never assumes the existence of a creator-deity or a ruler of the world, the world is simply accepted as it is without any ultimate [or teleological] meaning."[134]

Now, our next concern is to examine Tracy's metaphysical validation of God. As we already indicated, Tracy relies on Coreth's transcendental method for presenting what he refers to as his "metaphysical or transcendental" reflection. Bearing in mind the foregoing critiques of the Thomistic justification of God, let us look at how far and in what way Tracy incorporates Coreth's method for his revisionist justification of God.

---

133   Charles Wei-hsun Fu, "[The] Buddhist Approach to the Problem of God," in Sebastian A. Matczak (ed.), *God in Contemporary Thought: A Philosophical Perspective*, 160. In connection to the idea that Buddhism is neither theistic nor atheistic, Kenneth Inada observes as follows: "It should be remembered that the denial of atheism does not bring forth theism just as the denial of theism does not bring forth atheism. These are not mutually identifiable or mutually refutable concepts; and thanks to this, Buddhism is neither of the two [...]. It has been argued that Buddhism is not monotheistic, atheistic, polytheistic, pantheistic, or agnostic. Then, what is it? To add another 'ism' to the list will not do. We have no alternative but to keep the challenge open and to continue to call it Buddhism." (Kenneth Inada, "Some Basic Misconceptions of Buddhism," *International Philosophical Quarterly* 9 (1969) 115).

134   Charles Wei-hsun Fu, *ibid.*, 159–60.

*Tracy's Metaphysical Validation of God*

*Tracy's Incorporation of Transcendental Thomism*

For Tracy, the eminence of the transcendental method is situated, firstly, in its ability to mediate the move from the transcendental conditions of human experience to the reality of God (or, in his revisionist terms, the move from "human religious experience" to "theism"). The transcendental method approaches the question of the transcendent (the God-question) "from below."[135] This means that incorporating the modern "turn to the subject" (especially Kant), the transcendental method takes human experience seriously to the degree that human experience grounds the metaphysical account of reality (including God's reality). In other words, the starting point of the metaphysical account of a transcendent is the human subject's reflectivity which possesses the "immanent source of transcendence."[136] In view of Tracy's prior analysis of human religious experience, it is fair to say that this "immanent source of transcendence" is compatible with the *religious dimension* ("limit-to" and "limit-of") operative in

---

135  Although this expression is not Tracy's himself, it is adequate to characterize "transcendental Thomism" in general. See Philip Clayton, *The Problem of God in Modern Thought*, 44–9.

136  Long, *Twentieth-Century Western Philosophy of Religion 1900-2000*, 356. Put differently, the "immanent source of transcendence" means the *a priori* conditions of human transcendentality. For example, among the transcendental Thomists, for Rahner, this *a priori* condition of human transcendentality can be his famous "supernatural existential": the natural orientation of the human spirit towards God which results from God's grace *a priori*. For Lonergan, it refers to the human quality of "self-transcendence" in intellectual, moral, and religious conversions. For this particular concern with the turn to human experience (or human subject) in transcendental Thomism, see Donald L. Gelpi, "The Turn to Experience in Transcendental Thomism," in idem, *The Turn to Experience in Contemporary Theology* (New York: Paulist Press, 1994) 90–120; John R. Sachs, "Transcendental Method in Theology and the Normativity of Human Experience," in *Ph&Th*, 7 (1992) 213–25; Carl J. Peter, "A Shift to the Human Subject in Roman Catholic Theology," in *Communio: International Catholic Review* 6 (1979) 56–72; John C. Robertson, "Rahner and Ogden: Man's Knowledge of God," in *HTR*, 63 (1970) 377–407.

common human experience. Hence, in light of the basic structure of the transcendental method, his prior analysis of the human religious experience is fully acknowledged as essential and fundamental for a metaphysical account of God. The following claim can be understood in this context: the "logical order" of dealing with the God-question is "from religion to theism, not vice versa."[137]

Secondly, for Tracy, another value of the transcendental method, as shown in Coreth, is that it can provide a metaphysically "constitutive" account of God's reality.[138] In other words, for him, Coreth's transcendental method can serve for validating the truth-status of his theistic claim and providing it with universal, objective foundations. As we saw before, for Tracy, the criterion for truth is "adequacy to experience."[139] More concretely, a theistic claim is true when transcendental or metaphysical analysis shows its "adequacy to experi-

---

137  *BRO*, 83 n.27. Here, Tracy means by "religion" the religious dimension, "a final dimension or horizon to all the experience of the self." He means by "theism" that God is the necessary existent as the objective referent of such a religious dimension (See *ibid.*, 71).

138  Here, "constitutive" means being able to "refer to an object and express actual positive content about it." Clayton, *The Problem of God in Modern Thought*, 19. This concept of "constitutive" needs to be understood over against that of "regulative." This distinction goes back to Kant. According to Kant, Clayton explains, "in attempting to understand and to unify our experience, we formulate general ideas that serve to guide our reflection, to help us attain greater consistency and to extend our comprehension further. Kant calls these ideas *transcendental concepts*. Such concepts do not express an existing but a 'projected' unity." (*Ibid.*, 18). For example, these *transcendental concepts* are such as "necessity," "infinity," "unity," "eternity" and "God." According to Kant, since these *transcendental* concepts "cannot ever be objects of knowledge, they remain merely *regulative* rather than *constitutive* concepts; they regulate the quest for knowledge rather than serving as actual items of knowledge themselves." (*Ibid.*, 19; italics mine). For example, the concept of God, which is a concept without empirical content for Kant, only serves in a regulative fashion to complete and crown the whole of human knowledge. Here, Clayton raises an important question which is directly relevant to Tracy's God-question. Clayton asks whether God must remain, as Kant argues, "an 'as if' concept, a useful fiction, or whether we can move beyond this point to a constructive theory of God." (*Ibid.*). Tracy's option is the latter position.

139  *BRO*, 71.

ence" by clarifying how the concept of God "functions as a fundamental 'belief' or 'condition of possibility' of all our experience."[140]
Tracy sees in Coreth's transcendental method the possibility to
validate theistic claims in accordance with this criterion for truth. To
understand how Tracy looks at such a possibility in Coreth's metaphysics, it is good to briefly recall Coreth's metaphysics of realism as
based on the human experience of reflectivity.

Coreth claims that his transcendental method does not deduce
reality with logical necessity from a mere principle or idea, but from a
lived experience of our reflectivity ("an intellectual experience").
More concretely, his transcendental method starts "from a real,
existential self-actuation of the spirit, which manifests itself to us as
endowed with a pre-reflexive metaphysical knowledge of being."[141]
Here, the pre-reflexive knowledge of being is the *a priori* or
transcendental condition of human reflection as such. In other words,
*being* as such is the necessary condition of possibility for the fact that
particular beings, regardless of what they are, can be questioned.
Insofar as the transcendental condition (the horizon of *being*) is co-
affirmed in the *act* of human reflection as such, which is a real, lived
experience, this condition is not merely possible, but real and
universal. In short, the realism of the transcendental condition (the
horizon of *being*) is derived from the dialectic of *act* and *content* (not
of *content* and *content*), which is concomitant with a real, lived
experience.

Tracy attempts to fulfill his criterion of truth by incorporating
Coreth's metaphysics of realism based on human experience. Tracy,
however, utilizes Coreth's metaphysics in a broader, more general
manner. Coreth's metaphysical system is a sophisticated one in that it
focuses upon the transcendental condition of an intellectual, reflective
experience (the act of human reflection itself). In this system,
methodologically speaking, the transcendental condition refers to the
condition of possibility of human reflection, or human intellectual
experience. Tracy reformulates this transcendental structure in a more
general way as explicating the transcendental conditions of *all* human

140   *Ibid.*
141   Coreth, *Metaphysics*, 42.

knowing and experience. Tracy's motivation for this would seem to be his conviction that "we do not, in fact, experience without some understanding of that experience and we do not understand *in vacuo*: we always understand some experience."[142] It can be presumed from this statement that, for Tracy, as far as understanding (reflection) and experience are concomitant, Coreth's transcendental condition of human reflection can be methodologically stretched to embrace all human knowing and experience.[143] Accordingly, Tracy delineates transcendental or metaphysical reflection as follows: it focuses upon certain *a priori* conditions which are "basic and universal for all human knowing and experience insofar as those conditions are conditions of possibility, i.e., they are so constitutive of any performance of cognition or experience that they can be reductively exhibited from it."[144] Tracy states that such constitutive *a priori* conditions "can be shown to be basic by demonstrating the self-contradictory character which their denial involves for any intelligent and rational ('reflective') inquirer."[145] As Coreth points out, the self-contradiction here is not to be perceived "between conflicting *concepts* but between the *performance* of the intelligent, rational, and responsible inquirer and the *concepts* he employs to thematize that performance."[146] Tracy accepts Coreth's realism with regard to the

142 *BRO*, 146.
143 We may conjecture another possibility of such a stretch for Tracy. The transcendental condition of the act of human reflection in Coreth's transcendental method is *being* as such. Philosophically speaking, *being* as such is that which makes any entity exist as an entity. Therefore, any entity cannot be reflected upon and experienced without the horizon of *being* as such. In short, it can be supposed that, for Tracy, the transcendental condition of human reflection, *being* as such, can be applied to all human knowledge and experience.
144 *BRO*, 67–8.
145 *Ibid.*, 159. This statement is reminiscent of Coreth's argument that "a rejection of the possibility of metaphysics implies a contradiction between that denial and the act by means of which one denies, between the thematic content of the act and the unthematically co-affirmed and presupposed conditions of its possibility [...] We do really start from an immediate evidence, but this evidence itself cannot be demonstrated, except by showing that whoever rejects it, affirms it in his very act of rejection." (Coreth, *Metaphysics*, 35).
146 *BRO*, 114 n.41.

transcendental condition as this is derived from the dialectic of act and content (in Tracy's terms, performance and concept). In other words, for Tracy, the dialectic of *performance* and *concept* of the transcendental method provides the decisive clue to the validation of the *a priori* conditions of all human knowing and experience as basic, real, and universal.

Now, Tracy's key question is how to demonstrate that God has a bearing upon the transcendental conditions of all human knowing and experience at all. He is convinced that if he can show this, he will be able to construct a *public* discourse of God (his revisionist goal) in such a way that that discourse rests upon *a priori* structures of all human knowing and experience which are real, universal, and, thus, objective. This is to say that, in view of his criterion of truth ("truth-as-adequacy-to-experience"), his discourse on God, constructed as described above, can be claimed to be *true* in the sense that it is adequate to all human experience. He also believes that as far as such a discourse on God is adequate to *all* human experience, it can be claimed as public to the extent that it can encompass even non-theistic religious experiences. Let us look at how Tracy deploys his vindication of God.

### God Is the Single Metaphysical Referent to Our Most Basic Faith

We have seen that, in Coreth's transcendental method, his ontology of realism (*being* as such is real) constitutes his philosophical theology. For him, God is "the fullness of being and its ultimate foundation."[147] In this understanding, as far as being is real, God is real too. This implies that Coreth's ontology and philosophical theology have the same basic and realistic structure: as shown in his ontology, Coreth's vindication of God's existence also starts from a real, lived experience (not a pure concept) of human reflection which unlimitedly strives towards the infinity of all that is knowable. For Coreth, God exists as real in the sense that God is co-posited in the real act of human

---

147  Coreth, *Metaphysics*, 194.

transcending reflection as its ultimate condition (as "the primordial realization of the necessity of absolute being") and as its finality.[148]

We can say that Tracy takes on the basic structure of Coreth's argumentation for God's existence in terms of the following two aspects. Firstly, for Tracy, God is being itself as real. Secondly, God functions as a transcendental condition or fundamental presupposition of all human experience. In order to substantiate these arguments, Tracy, however, utilizes another source, namely, Schubert Ogden's metaphysical analysis of God.[149] For Tracy, the use of Ogden's analysis offers an advantage. Firstly, Ogden's analysis allows Tracy to discuss the metaphysical validation of God in closer relationship to his prior investigation of human religious experience and religious language. Secondly, while incorporating the transcendental reflection as shown in Coreth's, Odgen advances his metaphysical argument of God by appealing to the Anglo-American philosophical tradition (i.e., the process thought of Alfred N. Whitehead and Charles Hartshorne). The so-called neo-classical theism advocated by process philosophy is the position that Tracy will defend in constructing his revisionist Christian theism. Hence, the use of Ogden's metaphysical discussion of God here facilitates Tracy's subsequent discussion of Christian theism. In what follows, we will look at the way in which Tracy uses Ogden's analysis for his argument.

---

148  *Ibid.*, 171. Recall Coreth's argument that "being as such cannot not be, being as such is absolute." This absolute being as such is the transcendental condition of every act of reflection (questioning) as its horizon. God is "the primordial realization" of the absolute being as such. Coreth writes that "whenever through reflection we make explicit the metaphysically transcendent nature of the human spirit, we have a proof of God's existence – or rather we have *the* proof of God's existence, which is the ground and foundation of all the other demonstrations." (*Ibid.*, 181).

149  Schubert Ogden, "The Task of Philosophical Theology," 55–84. Hereafter, this work will be referred to as "Task."

Embracing transcendental Thomism in general (especially that of Coreth, Rahner, and Lonergan), the starting point of Ogden's metaphysical discussion of God is also human experience (or the human subject).[150]

Being influenced by transcendental Thomism, Ogden starts his analysis by reflecting upon the transcendental condition of the possibility of human understanding and existing.[151] Ogden's distinctiveness, however, can be found in his portrayal of that transcendental condition as "faith." As we will see in this discussion, this portrayal has to do with the influence of Whitehead's thought.

150 More specifically speaking, the main source for Ogden's metaphysical discussion of God is the Anglo-American process thought. The focus on human existential experience in his God-discussion has to do with the influence of Whitehead's metaphysics which is based on the "reformed subjectivist principle" over against Descartes' subjectivism (See Whitehead, *Process and Reality: An Essay in Cosmology* (New York: The Free Press, 1978, first published in 1929) 157–67.) The key idea of Whitehead's "reformed subjectivist principle" is that human experience cannot be exhaustively explicated by external sense experiences and an isolated thinking substance. The more immediate to human being than sense experiences is the nonsensuous and existential awareness of oneself. This existential experience can be the basis for formulating metaphysical principles including God's reality. Taking on this position, Ogden claims that "the starting-point for a genuinely new theistic conception is what Whitehead speaks of as 'the reformed subjectivist principle'. According to this principle, we can give an adequate answer to the metaphysical question of the meaning of 'reality' only by imaginatively generalizing 'elements disclosed in the analysis of the experiences of subjects.' In other words, the principle requires that we take as the experiential basis of all our most fundamental concepts the primal phenomenon of our own existence as experiencing subjects or selves." (Ogden, *The Reality of God*, 57).

151 In order to attempt a metaphysical validation of God, one needs to explicate first what one refers to by a metaphysics. For Ogden, metaphysics "invariably involves the most basic and comprehensive questions that can occur to the human mind, and the procedure it follows in answering these questions always involves some form or other of what I, at least, would be willing to call the 'transcendental' method, by which I mean, in general, the raising to full self-consciousness of the basic beliefs that are the condition of the possibility of our existing or understanding at all." (Ogden, "Task," 64).

Concerning "faith," Ogden explains that "to exist in the characteristically human way is to exist by faith, for what is meant by 'faith' is fundamentally that elevation of animal feeling and vitality to self-consciousness which constitutes the distinctively human mode of being."[152] Animals also live by a certain faith, namely, "animal faith": "the instinctive confidence in its environment as permissive of its struggles to live and to reproduce its kind."[153] We, human beings, share such an animal faith to a certain extent (i.e., accepting one's life and its environment, and adjusting oneself to them). However, on a distinctively human level, "the acceptance and adjustment in question are not merely instinctive but are more or less self-conscious acts. Thus it has been well said that man not only lives his life but also leads it."[154] On a human level, in short, "faith" and "understanding" are coincidentally operative. Ogden claims that "if [...] to exist by faith is fundamentally to accept one's life and its setting and to adjust oneself to them in a self-conscious way, faith itself, as already involving self-consciousness, is a mode of understanding."[155] He calls such a faith (one involving self-consciousness) "existential faith."[156] Based on this argument, Ogden makes a further specification: existential faith is subject to a reflective understanding of a higher order. Here, the reflective reasoning of a higher order refers to an understanding "whereby what is presented existentially can be re-presented in an express, thematic, and conceptually precise way."[157] Existential faith is "constitutive of human existence as such," which always precedes reflective reasoning, not vice versa. Ogden explains that "the existential faith by which we live – which, in fact, we ourselves essentially are – neither needs justification nor can ever be justified.

---

152  *Ibid.*, 56.
153  *Ibid.* Ogden takes on this idea from George Santayana, *Scepticism and Animal Faith: Introduction to a System of Philosophy* (New York: Dover Publications, Inc., 1955, first published in 1923).
154  Ogden, "Task," 56.
155  *Ibid.*, 57.
156  *Ibid.* In different terms, Ogden describes this "existential faith" as our basic confidence that "our existence as such is finally meaningful." See Ogden, *The Reality of God*, 35.
157  Ogden, "Task," 57–8.

Rather, it is the very ground of justification, which pertains, therefore, to those re-presentations of itself in reflection which it belongs to human reason to provide."[158] This statement suggests his view on the relationship between existential faith and reflective reasoning (or philosophical reflection). Ogden claims that "the task of philosophy is to understand such existential faith at the level of full self-consciousness, in an express, thematic, and conceptually precise way."[159] Incorporating Whitehead's idea, Ogden argues that "precisely in meditating on the 'variety of expression' which makes up the history of human life and culture, philosophy always has aimed, and quite properly should aim, to lay bare the faith by which every man exists simply as a man, together with the structure of reality as revealed to such faith."[160] The central ideas of Whitehead that Ogden intends to highlight here are two elements. Firstly, what we appeal to in the development of philosophical thought is human experience. Whitehead states that "philosophy is limited in its sources to the world as disclosed in human experience."[161] The final aim of philosophy is an "elucidation" of the basic, ultimate, integral experience which is presupposed in the various activities of humankind.[162] Whitehead writes that "philosophy is the attempt to make manifest the fundamental evidence as to the nature of things. Upon the presupposition of this evidence, all understanding rests. A correctly verbalized philosophy mobilizes this basic experience which all premises presuppose."[163] Ogden understands such basic experience as that which is

158   *Ibid.*, 58.
159   *Ibid.*, 60.
160   *Ibid.*, 61.
161   Alfred N. Whitehead, *Modes of Thought* (New York: The Free Press, 1966, first published in 1938) 71. For Whitehead's transforming the concept of "experience" into a formal metaphysical category, see Donald L. Gelpi, "The Turn to Experience in Process Theology," in idem, *The Turn to Experience in Contemporary Theology*, 52–89.
162   Whitehead, *Process and Reality*, 208. Whitehead writes that "without doubt, if we are to go back to that ultimate, integral experience, unwarped by the sophistications of theory, that experience whose elucidation is the final aim of philosophy, the flux of things is one ultimate generalization around which we must weave our philosophical system." (*Ibid.*).
163   Whitehead, *Modes of Thought*, 48.

comprised in our basic "existential faith." Secondly, according to Whitehead, philosophy is a "secondary activity" that seeks to *meditate* on "the interfusion of modes of existence."[164] The idea here is that the vocation of philosophy is not omniscience. Rather, philosophy is a resolute attempt to make "the content of the human mind manageable; it adds meaning to fragmentary details; it discloses disjunctions and conjunctions, consistencies and inconsistencies. Philosophy is the criticism of abstraction which govern special modes of thought [...] all inference in philosophy is a sign of that imperfection which clings to all human endeavour. The aim of philosophy is sheer disclosure."[165] In this context, Whitehead states that "if you like to phrase it so, philosophy is mystical. For mysticism is direct insight into depths as yet unspoken. But the purpose of philosophy is to rationalize mysticism: not by explaining it away, but by the introduction of novel verbal characterizations, rationally coordinated."[166]

Now, Ogden deals with the question of God, basing himself on the philosophical task mentioned above. Ogden's thesis is that "the task of philosophical theology, which is integral to philosophy's central task as metaphysics, is so to understand our common faith to answer the basic question of the reality of God."[167] In other words, the task of philosophical theology is to elucidate that "faith in God as the ground of confidence in life's ultimate meaning is the necessary condition of our existence as selves."[168] The essential point of this

164   *Ibid.,* 71.
165   *Ibid.,* 48–9. Whitehead states that "philosophy is akin to poetry. Philosophy is the endeavour to find a conventional phraseology for the vivid suggestiveness of the poet [...]. understanding is not primarily based on inference. Understanding is self-evidence. But our clarity of intuition is limited, and it flickers. Thus inference enters as means for the attainment of such understanding as we can achieve. Proofs are the tools for the extension of our imperfect self-evidence. They presuppose some clarity; and they also presuppose that this clarity represents an imperfect penetration into our dim recognition of the world around – the world of fact, the world of possibility, the world as valued, the world as purposed." (*Ibid.,* 50).
166   *Ibid.,* 174.
167   Ogden, "Task," 65.
168   Ogden, *The Reality of God,* 43. In other terms, the task of philosophical theology is to verify that "the primary use or function of 'God' is to refer to the

thesis is that the question of God is eventually a philosophical or metaphysical (thus, universal) question which has bearing upon our *common* "existential faith." Accordingly, this question of God can be only adequately investigated by a metaphysical inquiry. He claims that "because 'God' is the metaphysical concept par excellence, the question of how this concept is to be understood and whether it refers to anything real can only be answered as a metaphysical question."[169] What is his rationale for this claim?

According to Ogden, "God's reality is the ultimate presupposition of religion."[170] In other words, God is a "constitutive concept" of religion, such as the concept of "physical object" in physics or that of "obligation" in ethics.[171] Religion, however, unlike science, morality, aesthetics, etc., cannot be considered as one of the diverse fields of human life and culture. Rather, "for all the obvious specificity of its beliefs, rites, and social organizations, it presents itself as having to do with the ultimate basis of man's entire existence and, therefore, as fundamental to, not merely coordinate with, all the other cultural fields."[172] Based on this view, Ogden relates religion to our basic "existential faith" which he presents as a transcendental condition for human existence. He states, "Religion in general is the primary and most direct reflection of the basic existential faith that constitutes human existence."[173] In this statement, we can see an interface between the nature of religion and that of philosophy (metaphysics): namely, both religion and philosophy have to do with reflecting upon our basic "existential faith." Ogden claims that, in the case of the world religions, although they maintain distinctive doctrines which originated in different backgrounds, they invariably put forward their doctrines as universally true and valid for every human being. In this sense, the doctrines of religion are, in the final analysis, metaphysical in nature. To highlight this relationship

objective ground in reality itself of our ineradicable confidence in the final worth of our existence." (*Ibid.*, 37).

169  Ogden, "Task," 67.
170  *Ibid.*, 65.
171  *Ibid.*
172  *Ibid.*, 66.
173  *Ibid.*

between religion and metaphysics, Ogden resorts to the following statement of Whitehead: "The doctrines of rational religion aim at being that metaphysics which can be derived from the supernormal experience of mankind in its moments of finest insight."[174] Ogden concludes that, "If the doctrines of developed religion aim at being metaphysics, the question of God's reality, which religion poses for philosophical understanding, is in its logic a metaphysical question."[175]

In the process of developing this argument, however, there is an element that is tacitly acknowledged but not explained. This is Ogden's presupposition that God's reality is the ultimate presupposition of religion as such. His position appears to be that the reality of God is a question in any religion, whether theistic or non-theistic. In fact, there is no serious approach to non-theistic religious traditions in his discussion of God's reality as universal. Instead, Ogden tacitly acknowledges the theistic reality as *the* reality of religion itself.[176] This position is confirmed in his next argument on the very concept of God.

Ogden claims that his thesis that the question of God is a metaphysical question can be vindicated by the very concept of God. He states that "when God is conceived radically, as in monotheistic religions such as Judaism and Christianity, he is clearly understood as metaphysically real."[177] More specifically, in these religions:

as 'the Father Almighty, Maker of heaven and earth, and of all things visible and invisible,' he is understood to be the ultimate creative ground of anything

174  Alfred N. Whitehead, *Religion in the Making* (New York: The World Publishing Company, 1972, first published in 1926) 31. Whitehead also writes that Christianity "has always been a religion seeking a metaphysic, in contrast to Buddhism which is a metaphysic generating a religion." (*Ibid.*, 50).
175  Ogden, "Task," 66.
176  Compare the following two statements: "is it not the case, rather, that God's reality is the ultimate presupposition of religion, that 'God' is its 'constitutive concept', [...]? "; "the religions which are in a broad sense 'theistic,' for which in one way or another 'God' is a 'constitutive concept' [...]" (both quotations from *ibid.*, 65). From these two statements, we rightly infer that the reference of his view that God is a "constitutive concept" of religion is to theistic religions.
177  *Ibid.*, 66.

that is so much as even possible, and hence to be in the strict sense necessary, not merely a being among others, but in some way 'being-itself.' In fact, the God of theism in its most fully developed forms is the one metaphysical individual, the sole being whose individuality is constitutive of reality as such and who, therefore, is the inclusive object of all our faith and understanding.[178]

Hence, for him, the very concept of God conceived as above testifies to the fact that the question of God can only be answered as a metaphysical question (by means of a metaphysical inquiry). Two points are relevant here. Firstly, Ogden's aforementioned concept of God indicates that he is referring to the Judaeo-Christian God. Consequently, his concept of God is an already limited and biased one. Secondly, his theism is based on the construal of the Judaeo-Christian God as Creator in terms of the classical western metaphysical concept (i.e., the necessary "being-itself"). The important point here is that, in developing this theism, he relies on the so-called western "onto-theological" (not necessarily with a pejorative sense) metaphysical system which represents the necessary being as such as the most fundamental and highest reality. Therefore, it is clear that, for him, the most appropriate discipline to verify his theism is the same kind of metaphysics that has always been used for this purpose. We see a circular reasoning operative here.

The metaphysics that he defends for verifying God's reality is, we can presume, the one in which "ontology itself must be theology, even as theology must be ontology."[179] In other words, what is at stake here is that metaphysics in which, as Charles Hartshorne explains, "the import of the word 'God' is no mere special meaning in our language, but the soul of significance in general, for it refers to the Life in and for which all things live."[180] Ogden finds in Hartshorne's metaphysics a proper metaphysical approach to the question of God. Hartshorne says that "the theistic question [...] is not one more

178    *Ibid.*, 67.
179    *Ibid.* More specifically, Ogden's option is the so-called neo-classical theistic metaphysics advocated by Charles Hartshorne.
180    Charles Hartshorne, *The Logic of Perfection and Other Essays in Neoclassical Metaphysics* (La Salle: The Open Court Publishing Company, 1991, first published in 1962) 297.

question, even the most important one. It is, on the fundamental level, and when all its implications are taken into account, the sole question [...]. Philosophy as a nonempirical study has no other subject matter."[181]

Concerning the nature of metaphysics, following Hartshorne, Ogden claims that if there is a metaphysics, it cannot get around the God-question.[182] Conversely, if there is a God-question, it can only be metaphysical.[183] Metaphysics and the God-question are interlocked. Ogden states that, "hence, while there may very well be a 'metaphysics' that is neutral on the question of God, this is only because its meanings are so indefinite that it does not really know anything, and so is hardly metaphysics after all."[184] In short, for him, there is no other way to explain human existence metaphysically without the category of God. Therefore, the question of God is, *par excellence*, a metaphysical question which is universally applicable to every human being. This view precludes non-theistic explanations of human existence as shown in Taoist philosophy and Buddhism.

---

181  *Ibid.*, 131–2.
182  Hartshorne writes that "If metaphysics knows anything, it must either know God, or know that the idea of God is meaningless. Neutrality as to God means no metaphysics." Hartshorne, *Reality as Social Process Studies in Metaphysics and Religion* (New York: Hafner Publishing Company, 1971, first published in 1953) 176; in his *A Natural Theology for Our Time* (La Salle: The Open Court Publishing Company, 1967), he states that "any metaphysical assumption implicitly either expresses or contradicts theism. It cannot be neutral toward it if it is on the metaphysical level of generality. Only empirical issues are thus neutral. Hence no theistic view can be criticized without at least implicit metaphysical commitments." (*Ibid.*, 32).
183  Ogden claims that "it follows from the strictly metaphysical character of the question of God that any argument for, or proof of, God's reality, as well as, of course, any conterargument or disproof, can only be metaphysical." (Ogden, "Task," 69).
184  *Ibid.*

For Tracy, Ogden's analysis is a good example for showing why theistic claims (or, the cognitive claims of religious experience and language) can only be adequately investigated by a metaphysical analysis. Tracy reformulates the essential question at stake in the following manner: "Why are the issues of religious theistic cognitive claims in the final analysis metaphysical questions?" Tracy fully endorses Ogden's approach to this question in terms of the relationship between religion and metaphysics. Tracy argues that "religion, in short, is basically a representative phenomenon whose cognitive claims can be investigated only by a mode of reflection (metaphysics) whose task is precisely the investigation of all claims to re-present our basic beliefs as the conditions of the possibility of all our existing and understanding."[185] Tracy follows Ogden's view that religion and metaphysics have a common task to reflect upon our basic, existential beliefs. Now, his question is how to explain why both religion and metaphysics demand the concept of God as their constitutive concept. Tracy's key claim is that "the concept of God is the central and the clearest expression of the general metaphysical character of religious language."[186] Tracy argues that:

> If religion be in fact the kind of re-presentative expression explicated by Ogden [religion as a re-presentation of our existential faith], or the kind of limit-experience and limit-language explicated in my own prior analysis, then we are logically impelled to ask whether the explicitly theistic representation of that

185  *BRO*, 155. Tracy indicates that he bases this argument on Ogden's two principal assumptions concerning religion. Firstly, religion is not a particular dimension coordinate with other fields such as science, art, morality, and politics, etc., but the ultimate dimension fundamental to all cultural fields (See Ogden, "Task," 66). Secondly, as we already examined in the previous chapter, religion is "one and all expressions or re-pesentations" of our fundamental confidence (or our existential faith) in the final worth of our existence (Ogden, *The Reality of God*, 33ff).

186  *BRO*, 155. In other words, God is "the objective referent in reality" for our basic, existential beliefs (*Ibid.*, 167 n.46). In Ogden's words, "faith in God as the ground of confidence in life's ultimate meaning is the necessary condition of our existence as selves." (Ogden, *The Reality of God*, 43).

[existential] faith is both possible and necessary. That latter issue is more systematic than historical. Historically it is not, of course, the case that all religious language is God-language. In systematic terms, however, one cannot but ask whether the cognitive character of *all* religious language does not imply the reality of God as the objective referent of that language.[187]

For Tracy, given the existence of our ineradicable existential faith in life's ultimate meaning, there opens up the possibility of its transcendental (or metaphysical) ground; given that a religious dimension is a limit dimension as shown in his prior analysis of the limit-experience and limit-language, that limit dimension may involve a metaphysically final, ultimate reality ("limit-of" dimension). According to Tracy, these general metaphysical dimensions of religion imply God's realty as the objective referent of those dimensions. In short, the metaphysical dimensions of religion, regardless of whether the religion is theistic or non-theistic, are interfaced with God's realty. Then, where does this supposed general principle come from? Following Ogden's approach, Tracy derives this principle from Judaeo-Christian theism. Tracy states that, "in Ogden's own language, which I see every reason to endorse, [the Judaeo-Christian] God is conceived as 'the ultimate creative ground of anything that is so much as even possible, and hence to be in the strictest sense necessary, not merely a being among others, but in some way 'being-itself.' In fact, the God of theism in its most fully developed forms is the one metaphysical individual, the sole reality whose individuality is constitutive of reality as such; the sole being who is, therefore, the inclusive object of all our faith and understanding'."[188] It is from this Judaeo-Christian theism that Tracy draws forth his thesis that God is the objective referent of the metaphysical dimension of religion in general. This means that his thesis is built on the same limited and biased basis as Ogden's. Accordingly, it is hard to claim that his thesis can serve as a general principle which is applicable to all human 'religious' experience (theistic, atheistic, and non-theistic).

Secondly, Tracy claims that since the question of God is a metaphysical question (as shown above), it can only be adequately

187    *BRO*, 155 (italics mine).
188    *Ibid*. The reference of Ogden, "Task," 67.

investigated by a metaphysical reflection. The metaphysical reflection that he advocates, however, is a theistic metaphysics. Following Ogden, for him, the concept of God is a "basic category for metaphysics itself."[189] Provided that the task of metaphysics is to reflect upon our basic faith (following Ogden), the concept of God is "*the single metaphysical referent to our basic faith.*"[190] Interestingly enough, the rationale for his argument that the concept of God is a basic category to metaphysics itself, is the Judaeo-Christian theism conceived as above. Tracy states that "If one recognizes the strictly metaphysical claims which the radically theistic concept of God [Judaeo-Christian concept of God] involves, one may recognize as well that precisely that concept also provides a basic category for metaphysics itself."[191] We see here the same kind of circular argument as Ogden's between his (Judaeo-Christian) theism and his defense of theistic metaphysics. A question raised here is whether the metaphysical reflection on his theistic claims, based on such a circular argument, can be considered as a scientific and critical investigation (his revisionist methodological aim) of the truth-status of his theistic claims. Can Tracy's metaphysical account of God be a public discourse which is adequate to all human experience, such as he desires? A comprehensive critique on these issues will be made in the conclusion of this chapter. In the following, we will deal with the final issue of Tracy's God-discussion, the Christian theism proposed for the revisionist model.

189   *BRO*, 156.
190   *Ibid.*
191   *Ibid.*

## II. The Search for an Appropriate Conceptuality for the Christian God

In the course of his methodological exposition, Tracy indicated that any metaphysical analysis which deals with religious and theistic claims must fulfill two general criteria: (1) it should be capable of explicating the ground or the fundamental conditions in common human experience for having any notions of religion (the ultimate, limit dimension of human existence) and God (the referent of such a limit dimension); (2) it should be capable of explicating how those religious and theistic claims are internally coherent and faithful to experience broadly and fairly understood.[192] When we reformulate the above criteria in terms of the God-question, we can lay them out in the following way. The first criterion is concerned with the question of verifying God's *existence* (that God is) in relation to human existential experience. In other words, it is concerned with a metaphysical valid-ation of God's existence as a way to the final understanding of human existence as such. We examined in the preceding section how Tracy attempts to undertake this first task by using transcendental Thomism (Coreth) and Schubert Ogden's analysis. In terms of the God-question, the second criterion is concerned with a metaphysical reflection on God's *nature* (who and what God is). The issue here is whether the cognitive content relative to God's nature that a metaphysical re-flection elaborates displays an internal coherence and an adequacy to human experience.

For Tracy, transcendental Thomism is an appropriate meta-physical system for fulfilling the first criterion, but not the second. Tracy claims that the theism of transcendental Thomism is "unwilling to break with the classical theistic concepts of Aquinas," and that this type of theism is "neither internally coherent nor adequate as a full account for our common experience and of the scriptural under-standing of the Christian God."[193] One thing to note here is that Tracy approached the first question (the question of God's *existence*) as a

---

192  See *ibid.*, 55 and 172.
193  *Ibid.*, 172.

general metaphysical question. For the second question (the question of who and what God is), however, Tracy's concern becomes theological, viz., to search for a proper conceptuality for Christian theism. In fact, Tracy's statement above suggests three criteria that are necessary to develop a proper conceptuality for Christian theism: (1) internal coherence; (2) adequacy to human experience (his first theological source); (3) appropriateness to the scriptural understanding of the Christian God (his second theological source).[194] In view of the fact that transcendental Thomism is not able to fulfill these three criteria, Tracy's key concern here is to search for a new mode of metaphysical reflection which can satisfy them. The aim of this final section is to examine Tracy's option in this context.

## 1. Process Thought as a Proper Metaphysical Conceptuality for Christian Theism

Tracy proposes process thought (mainly that of Whitehead and Hartshorne) as a proper metaphysical conceptuality for constructing Christian theism. Tracy claims that process thought "has developed categories which seem both more faithful to the kind of limit-concepts needed to explicate the religious limit-dimension of our common experience and more faithful to the actual related and temporal God referred to by the limit-language of the Christian scriptures themselves."[195] How, then, does Tracy deal with the value of process thought for Christian theism? Tracy explores two important elements of process thought in relation to the God-question.

---

194 Among the three criteria, for Tracy, what distinguishes most importantly a theological reflection from a purely philosophical one is the third one. Recall Tracy's statement that the major specific difference of a theological as distinct from a philosophical investigation is "the Christian theologian's responsibility to show how his or her present categories are *appropriate* understandings of the Christian understanding of existence" upheld by the Christian tradition (*Ibid.*, 72, italics mine).

195 *Ibid.*, 174.

*Experience as Process or Becoming*

Firstly, Tracy focuses on process thought's understanding of experience which is approached by means of the category of "process." As we already saw in Ogden's use of Whitehead's understanding of experience, process thought bases its metaphysical system upon experience. Whitehead states that "the whole universe consists of elements disclosed in the analysis of the experiences of subjects."[196] Put differently, "apart from the experiences of subjects there is nothing, nothing, nothing, bare nothingness."[197] This suggests that, for Whitehead, experiences and realities ("actual entities") are equated.

According to Whitehead, realities do not rest on the inherent quality described by the unchanging Aristotelian "substance." Rather, the ultimate factor pervading "actual entities" is a drive toward "creativity" (or "becoming"), that is, toward the endless production of novelty.[198] In other words, for him, "what is real is in process. The unchanging is either dead, or past, or abstracted from the real. What is living, real and concrete is a momentary event in a continual process

---

196 Whitehead, *Process and Reality*, 166. Donald L. Gelpi explains that when Whitehead mentions "the experiences of subjects," "he does not mean that the subject has the experience but that the subject is the experience; for Whitehead rejects the notion of substance and with it the idea that anything underlies experience." (Gelpi, "The Turn To Experience in Process Theology," 54).

197 Whitehead, *Process and Reality*, 167. Tracy points out that the process tradition is committed to the so-called modern "turn to the subject" as is transcendental Thomism. We can say that these two philosophical traditions (transcendental Thomism and process thought) influenced on Tracy's revisionist model which hinges on common human experience as a principal source and as shaping the criteria of truth ("truth-as-adequacy-to-experience").

198 See *ibid.*, 28. Whitehead states that "every ultimate actuality embodies in its own essence what Alexander terms 'a principle of unrest,' namely, its becoming." This "becoming" is a "creative advance into novelty. It is for this reason that the meaning of the phrase 'the actual world' is relative to the becoming of a definite actual entity which is both novel and actual, relative to the meaning, and to no other meaning of that phrase [...] An actual world is a nexus; and the actual world of one actual entity sinks to the level of a subordinate nexus in actual worlds beyond that actual entity." (*Ibid.*).

of change." [199] Hence, in Whitehead's metaphysical system, "the category of 'creativity' functions as the category of 'the ultimate.' By 'the ultimate' Whitehead means 'the universal of universals.' In other words, whatever exists must exemplify creativity [...] In effect, Whitehead is portraying all reality as self-creative." [200] Based on this principle of "creativity" or "becoming," Whitehead explains that "the final facts are, all alike, actual entities; and these actual entities are drops of experience, complex and interdependent." [201] As regards this identification of actual entities with experiences, Donald L. Gelpi's explanation is helpful. Gelpi explains that, according to Whitehead:

> experience consists in the interrelations of concrete, physical feelings and particular conceptual feelings. In Whitehead's universe, as experience grows, decision transforms particular ideas, or possibilities, into wholly determinate and concrete physical realities. The development of experience, its 'concrescence,' implies, therefore, both the harmonizing, the growing together, of concrete facts and abstract possibilities and the reduction of an instance of experience to physical concreteness. [202]

For Whitehead, an immediate experience in its living occurrence is, therefore, "a full fact, in comparison with which all other things are

---

199 David A. Pailin, "Process Theology: Why and What?," in idem, *Probing the Foundations: A Study in Theistic Reconstruction* (Kampen: Kok Pharos Publishing House, 1994) 73.

200 Gelpi, "The Turn to Experience in Process Theology," 58–9.

201 Whitehead, *Process and Reality*, 18.

202 Gelpi, "The Turn to Experience in Process Theology," 56. Victor Lowe points out that one can detect the anti-dualistic motive of *value* and *fact* in Whitehead's universe which undergoes its development in the interplay of concrete facts and abstract ideas. He writes that, "Whitehead does not wish to think that intrinsic value is an exclusive property of superior beings; rather it belongs to even 'the most trivial puff of existence.' In human life, he finds value not far off, but at hand as the living essence of present experience. If every puff of existence is a pulse of some kind of immediate experience, there can be no final dualism of value and fact in the universe." (Victor Lowe, "Whitehead's Metaphysical System," in Delwin Brown, Ralph E. James, Jr., Gene Revees (eds), *Process Philosophy and Christian Thought* (New York and Indianapolis: The Bobbs-Merrill, 1971) 5).

pale abstractions."[203] Whitehead, thus, contends that it is a mistake of philosophers to hold that they "begin with substances which appear solid or obvious to them, like the material body or the soul, and then, almost as if it were an afterthought, bring in transient experiences to provide these with an adventitious historical filling. The transient experiences [however] *are* the ultimate realities."[204]

In Whitehead's metaphysical system, experiences are equated with realities, and realities exemplify process (creativity). Therefore, it follows by the principle of coherence that experiences exemplify process (creativity). Whitehead states that *"experience* involves a *becoming,* that *becoming* means that *something becomes,* and that *what becomes* involves *repetition* transformed into novel immediacy."[205] Conversely, it is also the case that "process is the becoming of experience."[206] For Whitehead, therefore, "the subject which enjoys an experience does not exist beforehand, neither is it created from the outside; it creates itself in that very process of experiencing."[207] This suggests that the reality of the subject's experience is highly relational and dynamic; it is bound up with and interacts with everything else in the universe.

Tracy considers this a significant development in Whitehead's understanding of experience. According to Tracy, for Whitehead, "one might say that the 'turn to the subject' characteristic of modern metaphysics has been taken to its logical and liberating conclusion."[208] It is so in the sense that the experiencing self is understood in its full multi-dimensional radicality, namely, in the nexus of "a process which precisely as process involves both internal relations with all reality and the distinct temporal modes of present, past, and future."[209] This is

---

203   Victor Lowe, *Understanding Whitehead* (Baltimore: The Johns Hopkins Press, 1968) 38.
204   *Ibid.*
205   Whitehead, *Process and Reality,* 136–7.
206   *Ibid.,* 166.
207   Lowe, "Whitehead's Metaphysical System," 7.
208   *BRO,* 173. Concerning this assessment, Tracy notes that this insight is "my own value-judgment; that same insight can, I believe, be incorporated into the tradition of 'transcendental methods" of Rahner and Lonergan." (*Ibid.,* 193 n.14).
209   *Ibid.,* 173.

to say that "in place of the essentially non-temporal and non-relational categories of 'substance' and 'being' of the classical metaphysical tradition, the categories 'process,' 'sociality,' and 'time' emerge. The very meaning and hence reality of the self's full experience is intrinsically and systematically relational, social, and temporal."[210] Tracy points out that, more importantly, Whitehead's analysis of experience in terms of these new categories of process and becoming is co-extensive with his conception of the whole universe, including God.[211] In other words, the new central metaphysical categories in Whitehead – process, creativity, becoming, relation, sociality, and temporality – are developed and articulated "in direct dependence upon the metaphysical analysis of the experiencing self as the paradigm case of all reality."[212] Now, in relation to the God-question, Tracy reckons that process thought's development of these new metaphysical categories can significantly contribute to developing a new Christian theism. As we will see below, in the process tradition, as Whitehead puts it, "God is not to be treated as an exception to all metaphysical principles," but "their chief exemplification."[213] In what follows, as the second element of process thought that Tracy high-lights, we shall examine how process thought develops these meta-physical categories for God over against classical theistic categories.

### New Metaphysical Categories for God in Process Thought

Tracy regards as another crucial development in process thought its critique of classical theism, and reinterpretation of God's reality. The key characteristic of process thinkers' critique of classical theism can be described as follows. They affirm with the classical tradition that God's *existence* is the fundamental ground of, or horizon to, human

210   *Ibid.*
211   Tracy writes that, "As this process tradition, in the work of Whitehead and Hartshorne, metaphysically refined the categories appropriate to this under-standing of the self and of the self's multi-dimensional experience, a new set of metaphysical categories was developed to replace those of classical ration-alisms, empiricisms, and transcendental methods." (*Ibid.*).
212   *Ibid.*, 174.
213   Whitehead, *Process and Reality*, 343.

existence as such. However, they deny the classical understanding of God's *nature* by means of such monopolar concepts as "changeless," "non-relative," and "immutable," etc. Tracy explains that process thinkers "affirm that God is the supremely perfect one, but they deny that the concept of perfection excludes change and process in God himself. They affirm with the scriptural tradition that fundamentally God is love, but insist that Christians can only really *mean* this statement when they reject the concept of a changeless, non-relative being articulated by classical Christian theism."[214] Tracy assesses the process thinkers' critique of classical theism as a significant move towards a revision and clarification of God-talk in view of our modern and postmodern experiences and the scriptural understanding of God. From the theological point of view, most importantly, the classical Christian theistic understanding does not go with the scriptural understanding of God's relationship to human beings. Tracy puts it as follows:

> Is not the God of the Jewish and Christian scriptures a God profoundly involved in humanity's struggle to the point where God not merely affects but is affected by the struggle? Is Bonhoeffer's famous cry that only a suffering God can help merely a rhetorical flourish of a troubled man? Can the God of Jesus Christ really be *simply* changeless, omnipotent, omniscient, unaffected by our anguish and our achievements? Was the magnificent move of classical patristic and medieval Catholic Christianity from the *quoad nos* of the scriptural interest in

214  *BRO*, 176. Sterling M. McMurrin explicates Hartshorne's critique of the monopolar logic of classical theism as follows: according to Hartshorne, "the chief error of classical metaphysics and theology has been to treat contraries as if they were contradictories, to fail to recognize that the ultimate reality is both absolute and relative – absolute in some respects and relative in others – that God, who, contrary to the traditional theology, is essentially diverse rather than simple, is both absolute and relative or finite – absolute in some respects and finite in others." (Sterling M. McMurrin, "Hartshorne's Critique of Classical Metaphysics and Theology," in Lewis E. Hahn (ed.), *The Philosophy of Charles Hartshorne* (La Salle: Open Court Publishing Company, 1991) 434; for an illumination of Hartshorne's understanding of God over against the classical theistic understandings, see also, Jan Van der Veken, "Ultimate Reality and God: The Same?," 203–14.

God's relationship to humanity to the *quoad se* of the patristic and medieval interest in God-in-himself a fully positive move?[215]

Tracy argues that, on an existential level, all authentic Christians, in fact, live, speak, and pray as if God not only affects the world but also is *really* (not just notionally) affected by its suffering, struggle, and achievements. Tracy enquires whether, since Christians live and pray in this fashion, they can, then, articulate it in a conceptually coherent and meaningful by employing classical theistic concepts? In other words, "Can Christians mean the most fundamental religious affirmation of Christian self-understanding [i.e., God is Unbounded Love] if they simultaneously affirm the usual understanding of classical Christianity that God is the self-subsistent, changeless, omniscient, all-powerful one who is not really but only notionally affected by human actions?"[216] Tracy points out that this difficulty is one of the central questions that process thinkers pose to classical Christian theism. Fully endorsing process thinkers' challenge to classical theism, Tracy turns to one of the most eminent process thinkers, Charles Hartshorne. He focuses on Hartshorne's alternative approach to the question of God's nature, namely, the "dipolar" concept of God.

---

215  *BRO*, 177.
216  *Ibid*. In other words, the dilemma of classical theism consists in the fact that while God is Being-itself, the Ground of the whole reality, God is, at the same time, the Absolute in the sense that God does not stand in any relation to anything else, and is, therefore, independent of the world. The problem of this classical understanding is the lack of internal coherence. According to Tracy, the classical theist has usually described this lacuna as "mystery" in the Catholic tradition and "paradox" or "scandal" in the Protestant tradition.

*Charles Hartshorne's Dipolar Concept of God*

The "dipolar" concept of God is considered as Hartshorne's most distinctive and original contribution to the discussion of God's nature.[217] It can be said that Hartshorne's central concern in his development of this concept is the question of how to weave together the two seemingly paradoxical characteristics of God's nature, viz., transcendence and immanence, in an intellectually reasonable, logically coherent, and religiously appealing way. In short, the question is how to comprehend and explicate the paradoxical conjunction that God is both absolute and relative through our metaphysical insight and vision. For Hartshorne, religion, as "a live option," cannot be exhaustively tailored by "some standard metaphysical position of the past."[218] For him, God is, above all, the God of religion, a personal

217 Hartshorne developed this concept based on Whitehead's idea that God is the supreme exemplification of, rather than an exception to, the metaphysical principles of the universe (viz., the principles of process, creativity, becoming, and relativity). For this relationship, see Pailin, "Process Theology: Why and What?," 73; Santiago Sia, *God in Process Thought: A Study in Charles Hartshorne's Concept of God* (Dordrecht: Martinus Nijhoff Publishers, 1985) 46–9. It should be noted, however, that there is a difference between Whitehead's understanding of God and Hartshorne's. The major difference between them can be described as follows. Whitehead made a clear distinction between the God of religion and the metaphysical ultimate (for him, creativity). This means that, for Whitehead, the God of religion is not creativity itself, but its "primordial characterization." Hartshorne, on the other hand, identifies the God of religion with the metaphysical ultimate (all-inclusive creativity). Hartshorne's position finds its foundation in his understanding of God as panentheistic, viz., God is the ultimate locus of all creativity, "'the place' of all things, and all things are, in the most utterly literal sense 'in' him." (Charles Hartshorne, *Creative Synthesis and Philosophic Method* (La Salle: Open Court Publishing Company, 1970) 17). In his presentation, Tracy does not deal with the fundamental divergence between Whitehead's understanding of God and Hartshorne's. For this divergence, see André Cloots and Jan Van der Veken, "Can the God of Process Thought be 'Redeemed'?," in Santiago Sia (ed.), *Charles Hartshorne's Concept of God: Philosophical and Theological Responses* (Dordrecht: Kluwer Academic Publishers, 1990) 125–36.

218 Charles Hartshorne, *The Divine Relativity: A Social Conception of God* (New Haven and London: Yale University Press, 1967, first published in 1948) vi.

God who is the worshipful one.[219] Hartshorne's fundamental understanding of God as personal and worshipful explains his keen sensitivity to God's relationality to the world which classical theism, he claims, does not properly work out. He states that "a personal God is one who has social relations, really has them, and is thus constituted by relationships and hence is relative – in a sense not provided for by the traditional doctrine of divine substance wholly nonrelative toward the world [...]"[220]

Hartshorne's alternative approach to the understanding of God is "dipolar." The kernel of his dipolar approach is to conceive God's nature in terms of *both* poles of the classical ultimate 'contraries' such as being-becoming, actuality-potentiality, necessity-contingency, and unity-multiplicity, etc. For the development of his dipolar concept, the essential principle that Hartshorne appeals to is the so-called "Law of Polarity." According to this principle, Hartshorne explains, "ultimate contraries are correlatives, mutually interdependent, so that nothing real can be described by the wholly one-sided assertion of simplicity, being, actuality, and the like, each in a 'pure' form, devoid and independent of complexity, becoming, potentiality, and related contraries."[221] The key idea here is that the ultimate "contraries" are not necessarily "contradictories," but mutually interdependent "correlatives" and that both are necessary in order to conceive reality. Put differently, "categories run in contraries so related that neither of the contrary poles has meaning or application by itself."[222] This is to say that neither of the two contrary poles is "simply to be denied or

219  Hartshorne admits that the development of his conception of God could not be conceived without the Christian tradition. See "A Conversation between Charles Hartshorne and Jan Van der Veken," in *LS*, 8 (1980) 142. For Hartshorne's religious idea of God as personal and worshipful, see Charles Hartshorne, *A Natural Theology for Our Time*, 1–28. For an explanation of Hartshorne's religious idea of God, see Santiago Sia, *God in Process Thought*, 9–18.

220  Hartshorne, The Divine Relativity, x.

221  Charles Hartshorne and William L. Reese, *Philosophers Speak of God* (Chicago: The University of Chicago Press, 1953, reissued in 1976 in Midway Reprints) 2.

222  Charles Hartshorne, *Reality as Social Process: Studies in Metaphysics and Religion* (New York: Hafner Publishing Company, 1971) 86.

explained away, or called 'unreal'."[223] Hartshorne, therefore, denies taking the ultimate "contraries" as if they were unequal or invidious "excellent-inferior" contrasts as classical theism posits. He explains that, according to the traditional monopolar view of reality, for example, "'contingent' can only mean something bad by comparison with 'necessary.' Necessary and contingent are [however] not rivals in merit but complementary poles of a unity in which is all meaning and all value. Only if we distinguish carefully, contrasting, not the necessary as such with the contingent as such, but the necessarily existing individual with contingently existing individuals, have we a question of comparative merit."[224] With such polar contrasts as "one-many," "cause-effect," "active-passive," he attempt to explicate his view more clearly:

> There is good or superior unity and bad or inferior unity; but, equally, good complexity and bad or inferior complexity; and so it is with active-passive and the others. Good passivity we are likely to call by special names, such as sensitivity, responsiveness, adaptability, sympathy – but they all mean that other beings are influencing us. Similarly, good plurality we may call richness, or variety of functions and constituents; but merely 'simplicity' is radically excluded by these terms.[225]

Hence, it is improper to conceive ultimate contraries as "excellent-inferior" contrasts. Instead, the values of each pole of a pair of ultimate contraries should be equally affirmed, and Hartshorne characterizes this view as "dipolar." Hartshorne finds the ground for this possible shift of our view from the monopolar to the dipolar in our modern experience. Hartshorne says that "at the last all reasons reduce in some sense to experience."[226] For him, "a thought is an experience of a certain kind, it means through experience [...] A thought which does not mean by virtue of an experience is simply a thought which does not mean."[227] According to Hartshorne, our modern experience

223   Hartshorne, Creative Synthesis and Philosophic Method, 99.
224   Hartshorne, Philosophers Speak of God, 13.
225   Ibid., 4.
226   Ibid., 3.
227   Charles Hartshorne, Man's Vision of God and the Logic of Theism (Hamden: Archon Books, 1964) 311.

does not entertain the monopolar approach to reality any longer. He argues that according to our modern experience, for example, the good is "unity-in-variety, or variety-in-unity; if the variety overbalances, we have chaos or discord; if the unity, we have monotony or triviality. The one defect is in principle as serious as the other, for infinite triviality would be as bad as infinite chaos."[228] It is also the case that concerning one of the most fundamental metaphysical categories, being vs. becoming, modern philosophy holds a different view from previous philosophy. The conviction of modern philosophy is that "being and becoming must somehow form a single reality."[229] He explains that in modern philosophy:

> becoming is the more inclusive category. This does not mean that it is 'more real.' We can abstract from the stages of becoming various real common factors and call these 'being.' Redness 'is' in diverse stages of process. But the process includes redness and more – even if all qualities common to diverse stages are taken as represented by 'redness.' Process is not the mere identities of 'being'; it is the identities with the differences, or rather it is the diverse states with abstract aspects of identity [...] Questions about being arise in present experience and for present experience. 'This experience' [...] is the final reference to concreteness. And this experience is always something that becomes.[230]

Now, the question is how to apply this principle of dipolarity to the understanding of God. Hartshorne, following Whitehead, considers God not as an exception to metaphysical principles but their chief exemplification. According to Hartshorne, there is, however, a difference between the way that these principles apply to the world and the way that they apply to God. He says that "the difference is between a partial and a maximum realization of the principle."[231] In other words, *"whatever is at a maximum in God is present in some degree in every creature; whatever is present in some degree in every creature is maximally present in God* (excluding self-contradictions

---

228 Hartshorne, *Philosophers Speak of God*, 3.
229 *Ibid.*, 9.
230 *Ibid.*
231 Charles Hartshorne, "Redefining God," in *AJTP*, 22 (2001) 111. This article was originally published in *The New Humanist* 7 (1934).

like a maximum number, or like perfect evil)."[232] How, then, does Hartshorne elaborate God's dipolarity as the primordial exemplification of the metaphysical dipolar principle? In the following section, we will discuss three essential points of Hartshorne's conception of God's dipolarity.

*God's Existence and Actuality*

Firstly, Hartshorne maintains an important distinction in relation to his dipolar principle of God. According to him, God is always to be conceived in two aspects: (1) in God-self, or apart from the world; (2) God in relation to the world. He describes these two aspects as God "in his essential, and God in his accidental functions" respectively.[233] Put differently, the first aspect refers to God's abstract "essence" and the second to God's concrete "actuality."[234] This distinction can also be described as God's "existence" and "actuality." Following classical theism, Hartshorne regards God's essence as equivalent to God's existence because God's essence is to *be* necessarily. On the other hand, God's abstract existence must be *actualized* in some concrete, determinate state or other (actuality). The abstract pole of God's reality is independent from any other realities whatsoever, and can therefore truly be called Absolute; God has always existed and will always exist; God is, therefore, unbegotten, unchanging, and etern-

---

232  *Ibid.*, 112–13. Hartshorne writes that, "this formula has never been consistently followed out. For just as there has been a tendency to say that what is present finitely in the creatures is simply absent altogether from God, e.g., temporality, so there has been the converse tendency to say that what is present maximally in God is at an absolute zero in certain at least of the creatures [...] Again, if man is strictly determined, has a zero degree of creative choice, then God can have only a zero degree. We can never have the right to treat the gap between the finite and the perfect as though it were the gap between nothing and perfection. It is the gap between something and perfection, between 'some' and 'all'." (*Ibid.*, 113).

233  *Ibid.*, 111.

234  See Hartshorne, *Philosophers Speak of God*, 4–5. Hartshorne explains that "essence," for him, means "the individual in abstraction from all in him that is accidental, or without which he would still be 'himself'." (*Ibid.*, 4). "Actuality" refers to a concrete and determinate state or condition of an individual.

al.[235] However, without a concrete actuality, the abstract existence of God is empty and inconceivable. God's actuality is expressive of God's concrete reality. Therefore, God in this concreteness, is contingent, mutable, finite, and temporal in the ongoing interrelation with actual events of the world. What one should not forget here is that these two aspects point to different facets or poles (not two different substances) of the one and same God's reality. In other words, for Hartshorne, these polar aspects, abstract and concrete, "require each other," and are to be understood in terms of each other as constituents of God's reality.[236] David A. Pailin explains this view of Hartshorne as follows:

> All that the absolute and necessary character of God's existence implies for God's actuality is that there cannot not be some actuality that exemplifies God's mode of existence in some appropriate form. Consequently, it is fully consistent with holding that God's *existence* is absolute, necessary, unchanging, infinite and eternal, to hold that God's *actuality* is relative, contingent, changing, finite and temporal if and so far as this actuality appropriately exemplifies the nature of the divine mode of existence. In this way Hartshorne shows that so long as we observe carefully the distinction between abstract existence and concrete actuality, it is possible to talk about God in a way that both recognizes the essential 'Godness' of God and allows personal qualities to be attributed to the divine.[237]

In short, when we reflect Hartshorne's dipolar concept of God, the distinction between God's existence and actuality should be kept in mind as a primary condition.

235 Hartshorne writes that, "God must coincide with Being as such; for he cannot be without existence, and therefore equally existence cannot be without him, so that the very meaning of 'exist' must be theistic [...] God is thus the great 'I am,' the one whose existence is the expression of his own power and none other, who self-exists – rather than is caused, or happens, to exist – and by whose power of existence all other things exist." (*Ibid.*, 8).
236 Hartshorne, *Man's Vision of God and the Logic of Theism*, 15.
237 Pailin, "Process Theology: Why and What?," 75.

We already implicitly indicated in the foregoing that, in Hartshorne's understanding, God's existence and actuality stand apart from ours. This means that God's exemplification of metaphysical principles (here, dipolarity) is the primordial or supreme case. To explain, God's reality is:

> the union of supreme actuality and supreme potentiality, supreme activity and supreme passivity, supreme being and supreme becoming, the most strictly absolute and the most universally relative of all entities, actual or possible.[238]

God's existence is the supreme case in the sense that all creaturely existence is contingent, but only God's existence is necessary. God's contingent, relative actuality is also the supreme case and as such is distinct from ours. Whereas we are relative to some, God is relative to *all* other beings.[239] This means that God is the supreme individual "whose change is to be coextensive with all change, whose actuality is to be coextensive with all actuality, and whose power-to-become is to include all such power."[240] In effect, Hartshorne finds the absolute character of God's reality in this supreme mode of God's relativity, distinguishing it from the "idolatry of absoluteness" of classical theism.[241] Hartshorne expresses this

238 Hartshorne, Philosophers Speak of God, 14.
239 Hartshorne claims that "if we can speak of an actuality which includes or surpasses all actuality, why not also of a potentiality which embraces all potentiality? A power-to-become-actual which as such includes or surpasses all such powers? Or why not a relativity consisting in this: that a being is made what it is not simply by relationship to some but to all other entities? If the exclusion of all relations [God's abstract, independent existence] is a unique characteristic, perhaps the inclusion of all [God's relatedness to all other beings] is no less unique." (*Ibid.*, 5).
240 *Ibid.*
241 Hartshorne, *Creative Synthesis and Philosophic Method*, 104. For Hartshorne, the idea of God's absoluteness advocated by classical theism is the "idolatry of absoluteness" because it idolizes the idea of absoluteness in such a way that it does not react or interact. He asks, "How can we know God as causally related to the world, if he is not related at all, if he has no relative being?," (Hartshorne, *The Divine Relativity*, 15). He claims that if God is "wholly absolute, a term but

absolute character of God's reality as "excellence" as distinct from "aseity." Douglas Pratt explains that "Hartshorne makes a useful distinction between using the term 'absolute' to denote excellence and using it to denote aseity. The marks of aseity – independence, immutability, and so on – are not to be taken as *ipso facto* excellent in and of themselves. By thus separating excellence from absolute [as aseity] Hartshorne is able to propound a view of God as the supreme or 'excellent' being."[242] Put differently, Hartshorne tries to resolve the conflicting predication of absolute-relative in God by arguing that the absolute (aseity) is not identical with the supremacy of God (excellence) which is conceived in his supreme relativity. Hartshorne claims that the absolute (as aseity) "in a strict sense is infinitely less than the supreme, and in fact is a certain kind of constituent within it."[243] In other words, for Hartshorne, "God is not describable in terms of absolutes alone, but God is nonetheless describable 'absolutely' in terms of the relativity that contains the absolute as a factor within itself."[244] It is important to note that Hartshorne's view is based on his methodological principle that the relative, concrete pole takes conceptual priority over the absolute, abstract pole.[245] He explains that "the main thesis, called Surrelativism, also Panentheism, is that the 'relative' or changeable, that which depends upon and varies with varying relationships, includes within itself and in value exceeds the nonrelative, immutable, independent, or 'absolute,' *as the concrete*

---

never a subject of relations, it follows that God does not know or love or will us, his creatures." (*Ibid.*, 16).

242  Douglas Pratt, *Relational Deity: Hartshorne and Macquarrie on God* (Lanham and New York and Oxford: University Press of America, Inc., 2002) 6.

243  Hartshorne, *The Divine Relativity*, 16.

244  Pratt, *Relational Deity*, 6. Hartshorne claims that, "The idolatry of absoluteness which disfigures the history of metaphysics needs to be unmasked and if possible done away with. The real absolute is relativity itself, since its limitations are provided by its own reflexivity, or self-applicability, together with negation. And negation is a subordinate principle in the sense that finally we must affirm the conjunction of true positive and true negative propositions to state the whole truth." (Hartshorne, *Creative Synthesis and Philosophic Method*, 104).

245  See Hartshorne, *Creative Synthesis and Philosophic Method*, 89–90.

*includes and exceeds the abstract.*"[246] This is to say that, as Ralph E. James puts it, "actual doing is concrete becoming, and what 'is' after it has occurred is an abstraction."[247] Thus, the concrete is "ontologically prior to the abstract; precedes the abstract temporally; and that the changing concrete is superior to abstractions which do not change."[248] In short, "the concrete is greater than and includes all abstractions."[249] Hartshorne's doctrine of surrelativism, therefore, denotes that God is "super-relative" or has a "super-eminent type of relativity," in the sense that his relative concreteness includes and exceeds the absolute and the abstract.[250] In other words, God is "the supreme relativist; the supreme concrete reality."[251] In sum, Hartshorne's dipolar (abstract-concrete) God is, in a strict sense, neither absolute nor relative in the traditional sense, but a synthesis of

246 Hartshorne, *The Divine Relativity*, ix.
247 Ralph E. James, *The Concrete God: A New Beginning for Theology – The Thought of Charles Hartshorne* (Indianapolis and Kansas City and New York: The Bobbs – Merrill Company, Inc., 1967) 57.
248 *Ibid.*, 58.
249 *Ibid.*, 57. Hartshorne explains that his theory of concreteness is based on the metaphysical definition of "being" in terms of "becoming," which can be found in Bergson and Whitehead's metaphysics for the first time in metaphysical history. He states that "the effort had almost always been to define becoming in terms of being. This could only result in a fallacy of misplaced concreteness. Becoming is the richer, more concrete conception and includes within itself all needed contrasts with mere being. In each particular instance of becoming, what has previously become does not *then and there* become; yet it does constitute a causal factor in the new, and in all subsequent, instances of becoming. This cumulativeness of becoming is causality, the efficacy of the past in the present. And any eternal entity constitutes a factor in every becoming whatsoever [...]. It is the unique relatedness or relativity of becoming which makes it the inclusive or concrete form of reality. All else is abstraction." (Hartshorne, *Creative Synthesis and Philosophic Method*, 26–7).
250 Hartshorne, *Reality as Social Process*, 113.
251 Pratt, *Relational Deity*, 13. Hartshorne writes that "the surrelative actuality of God is the highest actualized level of concreteness, subject surveying all actual objects, event subsequent to all actual events not contemporaneous with it. In this aspect, God is not pure being but total actual being of a given moment, with all achieved determinations. Thus God is being in both its opposite aspects: abstract least common denominator, and concrete de facto maximal achieved totality." (Hartshorne, *The Divine Relativity*, 88).

absolute and relative, a higher unity, viz., the surrelative, supreme deity, which is primarily concrete, inclusive of all reality.

*God's All-Inclusiveness: The Doctrine of Panentheism*

Finally, we will briefly discuss Hartshorne's idea of panentheism. Hartshorne's dipolar God as surrelative (relative to *all* other reality that exists) is inclusive of all reality. For Hartshorne, God's all-inclusiveness and surrelativity are interchangeable ideas. This is why he uses the term of panentheism as another expression to specify his surrelativism.[252] The term, panentheism, specifies *how*, or *in what mode*, God is *related* to the world. It denotes the relationship between God and the world in such a way that the world – all that exists – is "in" God, who nevertheless is not coincident with the world.[253] According to Hartshorne, insofar as God as creator is the supreme cause or source for the world, "God's existence would make it inevitable that there be a world [as its effect] but only possible that there be just this sort of world."[254] This is to say that "deity would be independent of (would not require or necessitate) any particular world, but he *would not be independent of world-as-such*."[255] The essential idea here is that God is effect as well as cause vis-à-vis the world in his concrete reality. Put differently, God requires "other things than

---

252 Hartshorne states that, "I scarcely need to say that surrelativism and panentheism are logically the same doctrine with only a difference of emphasis." (Hartshorne, *The Divine Relativity*, 90). James indicates that the term "panentheism" did not originate with Hartshorne, as Hartshorne is aware. James explains that this term was perhaps first employed by Karl Christian Friedrich Krause (1781–1832), who belonged to the school of Fichte and Schelling. See Heinrich Schmidt, *Philosophisches Wörterbuch* (New York: Mary S. Rosenburg, 1945) 237.

253 Panentheism is Hartshorne's alternative to the classical options of theism and pantheism. Hartshorne explains that panentheism is distinguished from pantheism in that God is not identical with the world as such, while God is all-inclusive of the world. Panentheism is distinct from theism in that God is relative to the world, while God is independent of the world in its abstract existence.

254 Hartshorne, *Philosophers Speak of God*, 501.

255 *Ibid.*, (italics mine).

242

himself to be just what he concretely and in fact is. In this his [sic] concrete total actuality God may interact with the world, receiving as well as imparting influence."[256] More specifically, Hartshorne explains, "without us God would not be the same as he is. He would exist, and existence would be generically what it is now, namely, the self-identity of his all-participating life. But it is obvious that the details of the participations would be different if the things to be participated in were different, and that thus the divine dependence and independence are inseparable aspects of one mutual relationship."[257] The world depends on God, and God also depends on the world. In other words, God's all-inclusiveness of the world (panentheistic character) has to be understood in such a mutual relationship of divine dependence and independence.[258] Now, an important question needs to be clarified here. Provided that God as the perfect or supreme being includes within himself the world which involves imperfection, contingency, finiteness, and so on, do worldly imperfection and inferiority not mar God's perfection or supremacy? Apart from the abstract pole of his independence, does God's dependence on the

256  *Ibid.*, 502.
257  Hartshorne, *Man's Vision of God*, 282.
258  One thing to note here is that there is a difference in principle between God and creatures as regards the cause-effect relation. The way that God is cause and effect vis-à-vis the world is, in Hartshorne's own words, "categorically superior (or supreme)." (Hartshorne, *Philosophers Speak of God*, 10). This is to say that only God influences the *whole* of reality (cause) and is *universally* affected (effect) by it. Sia explains that "since the creatures' power and freedom are really their own, and not God's, there is a real plurality of powers. In the exercise of these powers, they are said to have an effect on God. This leads Hartshorne to say that God is an effect. But he is so in a truly distinctive way because only he is universally affected. He is influenced by everything that occurs with an intensity that no one else can rival. God, of course, is cause. He initiates activities and because he is supreme cause, he is always one of the agents of everything that takes place [...] No matter what creatures do, they cannot [however] challenge God's superiority for only God exercises universal influence. That God is both cause and effect is a further application of the doctrine of dipolarity." (Sia, *God in Process Thought*, 87) A key feature of panentheism, thus, is its claim that "creatures have influence on God. While creatures cannot effect the destruction of God, they determine how much each new event adds to God's concrete reality." (*Ibid.*).

world (being affected by all of reality) in his concrete actuality not impair his perfection? If God, however, does not include the totality of reality, God is still marred by imperfection. For if it is so, the totality of reality is greater than God, because the totality of reality consists of God *plus* all that is not included within him. Hartshorne's solution for this dilemma is a radical definition of God's "perfection." Hartshorne claims that the only way to escape the above dilemma is "to admit that the perfect-*and*-the-imperfect is something superior to the perfect 'alone'."[259] Here, the pivotal idea underpinning Hartshorne's definition of perfection is the notion of "self-surpassibility." He explains, "suppose we define the perfect, or supremely excellent or good, as that individual being [...] than which no *other individual* being could *conceivably* be greater, but which *itself*, in another 'state,' could become greater (perhaps by the creation within itself of new constituents)."[260] More specifically, he explicates:

> Let us define perfection as an excellence such that rivalry or superiority on the part of other individuals is impossible, but self-superiority is not impossible. Or again, let us say that the perfect is the 'self-surpassing surpasser of all.' This formula resolves the dilemma. For suppose the self-surpassing surpasser of all has the power of unfailingly enjoying as its own constituents whatever imperfect things come to exist. Then it will be bound to possess in its own unity

259  Hartshorne, *The Divine Relativity*, 19.
260  *Ibid.*, 20. Here, the distinction between "individual" and "state" is equivalent to his distinction between "essence" and "actuality." Hartshorne explains that "individual" refers to an identical entity, "an abstract determination in something still more determinate or concrete." (Hartshorne, *Creative Synthesis and Philosophic Method*, 185). "State" refers to the "the unit of concrete reality," "event," or "experience" without which the existence of the individual is empty (*Ibid.*, 23). Hartshorne claims that the Aristotelian tradition evidences a confusion. Here, the "states of an individual were taken as accidental predicates 'in,' and *therefore* dependent upon, the individual for their existence." (*Ibid.*, 104–5). Hartshorne calls this confusion a "fallacy of misplaced concreteness." Hartshorne contends that, according to the Aristotelian tradition, "a constituent depends upon its whole. Quite the contrary. Constituents may have to be in *some* whole, but the particular whole is accidental or contingent. [...] A whole depends upon its constituents, and one's past individuality is a constituent of one's present wholeness. States are *more* than identical individualities and contain them, not *vice versa*." (*Ibid.*, 105).

244

all the values which the imperfect things severally and separately achieve, and therefore it is bound to surpass each and every one of them. Thus it is certain of superiority to any 'other individual.' It must, in any conceivable state of existence, be the 'most excellent being'."[261]

The above statement implies that Hartshorne tries to resolve the problem of imperfection ascribed to God by challenging the traditional notion of perfection. Hartshorne describes Plato's definition of deity as the perfect in the following manner: deity is "possessed of value or worth so great that no increase or improvement would be conceivable, and no decrease either, since the possibility of such corruption would be a defect."[262] Hartshorne aims to discharge the idea of immutability which is pivotal to the classical Platonic notion of perfection. In his neo-classical definition of perfection, Hartshorne uses the same methodological strategy that is applied to his doctrine of surrelativism, viz., the relative or changeable *includes* and *exceeds* the nonrelative, immutable, independent. In his new definition of God's perfection, the key term to denote the relative, changeable aspect of God is "surpassibility." Hartshorne says that this term of "surpassibility" is a different expression of God's surrelativity while suggesting another feature of it.[263] The concept of "surpassibility" illumines a "reflexive" dimension of God's relativity: God surpasses *himself*, as well as everything else, viz., "self-surpassing surpasser of all."[264] For Hartshorne, God's perfection issues in the capacity for self-surpassability in his concrete "state," while his "being-itself" is unsurpassable by another. God's supreme mode of relativity (surrelativity) leaves open the door to self-surpassing or self-excelling. "Through such self-excelling the most excellent being changes, not into a more excellent being, but into a more excellent state of the *same*

261 Hartshorne, *The Divine Relativity*, 20.
262 Hartshorne, *Aquinas to Whitehead: Seven Centuries of Metaphysics of Religion* (Milwaukee: Marquette University Publications, 1976) 4.
263 Hartshorne writes that, "since the relativity of the all-surpassing [of God] is a unique and supreme case, it needs a special title. I propose the terms, Surrelative and Surrelativism, for this kind of relativity and the doctrine asserting it." (Hartshorne, *The Divine Relativity*, 21).
264 *Ibid.*, 20.

being."[265] According to this view, therefore, the fact that God is all-inclusive of the world of imperfection would not mar the self-identity of God as perfect. For God's self-surpassing and surpassing of all will always lead him into a more excellent state.[266]

Hartshorne claims that a God who cannot change cannot but be literally indifferent to whatever happens in the contingent world. "Such a being is totally 'impassible' toward all things, utterly in-sensitive and unresponsive. This is the exact denial that 'God is love'."[267] For him, God as love unmistakably implies the supremacy of God's relativity. He explains:

> To be relative is to take other things into account, to allow them to make a difference to oneself, in some sense to care about them. What else, then, can the ancient saying, *deus est caritas*, imply if not the supremacy of relativity? Yet nearly two thousand years have been partly wasted in the effort to make this deepest truth connote its opposite, the supremacy of absoluteness, i.e., of indifference to others."[268]

---

265  Hartshorne, *Philosophers Speak of God*, 10.
266  It can be said that one of the most difficult issues to handle in the God-discussion is the problem of evil. To mention briefly Hartshorne's approach to the problem of evil, he distinguishes evil in the sense of wickedness and evil in the sense of suffering. According to Hartshorne, evil in the former sense cannot be applied to God. "Evil, in the sense of wickedness, is not a universal category. For example, the animals are incapable of it, because of their unconsciousness of principles. And God is incapable of it [...] Thus wickedness is not in the divine 'character' at all. True, the contrast between God's goodness and the wickedness of various individuals does fall within God (whose total reality is more than his mere character or essential individuality) but not in such fashion that he could be called wicked, even in his particular states. A round stone may be within a square building – to use a crude analogy." (*Ibid.*, 15). However, evil in the sense of suffering can be applied to God because it is a universal category. Hence, "the dipolar view must hold not only that God contains suffering but that he suffers and that it is in his character to suffer, in accordance with the suffering in the world. Here the Christian idea of a suffering deity – symbolized by the Cross, together with the doctrine of the Incarnation – achieves technical metaphysical expression." (*Ibid.*).
267  *Ibid.*, 20.
268  Hartshorne, *Creative Synthesis and Philosophic Method*, 55–6.

According to Hartshorne, the classical monopolar conception of God gives us notions of sheer power and causation which are not understood in terms of their effects in the world. The neutrality of God in this conception, devoid of such values as divine responsiveness and love, is the price that monopolarity pays for metaphysical incompetence. His dipolar conception of God is, therefore, an attempt "to find a logical structure in our thinking about deity that makes room" for those divine values of responsiveness, relativity, love, etc.[269] Hartshorne argues that in a monopolar doctrine of God, the categories of "being" and "cause" are virtually the objects of worship, while the contrary poles of "becoming" and "effect" are degraded. Therefore, "we may speak of 'ontolatry,' worship of being, or similarly 'etiolatry,' worship of cause."[270] The antidote for these problems, however, is not to substitute the contrary pole, and to worship becoming and effect, while degrading being and cause. Instead, the remedy is:

> to recognize that both poles under each category apply in one way to God and in another to other individuals. God is neither being as contrasted to becoming nor becoming as contrasted to being; but categorically supreme becoming in which there is a factor of categorically supreme being, [...]. We worship [therefore] supreme-being-in-supreme-becoming, supreme-cause-in-supreme-effect; that is, we worship the supreme, not any polar category.[271]

269  Hartshorne, *Philosophers Speak of God*, 24.
270  *Ibid.*
271  *Ibid.* We can see in Hartshorne's conception a kind of confluence between God as the worshipful (personal) one and God as a metaphysical "being" (supreme-being-in-supreme-becoming). Elsewhere, he says that God is "*the*" being. God is the universally relevant, the definitive being, the being whose reality includes every other reality and defines its reality." ("A Conversation between Charles Hartshorne and Jan Van der Veken," 133). In short, for Hartshorne, God as the worshipful one is equivalent with (*the*) being or all-inclusive reality. In his discussion of Hartshorne's conception of God, André Cloots raises a question: "Should God and being be identified?" (André Cloots and Jan Van der Veken, "Can the God of Process Thought be 'Redeemed'?," 134). In other terms, is this identification of God and being or all-inclusive reality a "viable option" for today's natural theology? Cloots thinks that it is not. He notes two points. Firstly, God is unmistakably a "religious category, a category of interpretation." (*Ibid.*). Hence, one cannot be forced to perceive all-inclusive reality necessarily

For Hartshorne, God, as "supreme-being-in-supreme-becoming," is related to every event in human history because God is the inclusive whole in which history lives. God's supreme mode of relativity in his all-inclusiveness denotes God's love. Ralph James says that, "on Hartshorne's terms, there is one way finally to describe God's concrete wholeness [...] This is to say that God is love."[272] God's love is the quintessential aspect of his relativity and responsiveness towards the world. God's love involves even passivity in himself: "Passivity *is* activity in so far as it is receptive to, or engaged in taking account of, the activity of others; and the higher the activity the more comprehensive the receptivity."[273] God is "alive" only if God is changing in view of his surrelative love, with the changes of history. This means that in the dipolar conception, God and the world are interdependent and involved in concrete and actual interaction. This interaction serves as the basis upon which novelty is possible in God's concrete actuality, while God never ceases to be the one, all-inclusive reality outside which nothing exists.

as divine reality. He contends that "a believer who understands what Paul says to the philosophers at Athens ('In him we move and have our being.' Acts 17: 28) will recognize in all-inclusive reality some features of divine care. But he recognizes it as such precisely *because* he believes. A nonbeliever recognizes in all-inclusive reality *only* the ongoingness of the universe itself." (*Ibid.*, 135). Secondly, Hartshorne explains God's all-inclusive reality in terms of idealistic inclusion: namely, God is supremely knowing, and this means that he is supremely inclusive, because to know is to include. Cloots argues that "it is so difficult to identify God with all-inclusive reality because, without doubt, idealistic inclusion is for many of us not a viable concept. Perfect knowledge may include its objects, but contingent realities are too earthly, too bodily, too 'heavy' to be included by knowledge. The dark side of existence, the sphere of nonrealized possibilities, is not merely evil resulting from cross purposes [...]. Hartshorne's way of philosophizing, [...] seems somewhat limpid and ethereal. It is almost too logical to reflect our not-completely-logical world. It is too 'idealistic' for ordinary, not-completely-rational beings." (*Ibid.*). In short, it does not do justice to the otherness of the world.

272   James, *The Concrete God*, 122.
273   Charles Hartshorne, "A Philosopher's Assessment of Christianity," in Walter Leibrecht (ed.), *Religion and Culture: Essays in Honor of Paul Tillich* (London: SCM Press Ltd., 1959) 169.

248

*Tracy's Appropriation of the Dipolar Concept of God*

In this section, we will examine how Tracy appropriates Hartshorne's neo-classical dipolar concept of God as an alternative conceptuality for Christian theism. More specifically, Tracy attempts to illumine this new conceptuality for God in connection with his three criteria: (1) internal coherence; (2) adequacy to our common experience (his first theological source); (3) appropriateness to the scriptural understanding of God (his second theological source).

*The Dipolar Concept of God is an Internally Coherent Concept*

Tracy specifies that his criterion of "coherence" denotes both the narrower meaning of internal coherence in concepts, and the wider meaning of coherent with our experience. Tracy's central argument is as follows: "By means of the metaphysical employment of the analogy of the social and temporal self's own dipolar structure, this dipolar understanding of God presents one with what seems to be a coherent and thereby a meaningful concept for the reality of God."[274] Tracy explains that one of the persistent convictions of classical theism is that God is absolute in the sense of his aseity and immutability. "Indeed, only a freedom from history and from change really frees the classical mind for an authentic contemplative approach to God, the perfect and changeless one."[275] However, such a classical understanding of God, argues Tracy, does not seem to appeal to any modern mind which conceives all reality as being *constituted* by ongoing interrelations in the organic nexus of the universe, in which *change* and *relativity* are operative as ultimate principles.[276] He contends:

> Is not intelligent and responsible change a positive not a negative factor in all our experience? For example, does not Newman's famous dictum 'To live is to change and to be perfect is to have changed often' find resonance in our most fundamental outlook upon our lives? How then do we move from this modern

---

274   *BRO*, 183.
275   *Ibid.*, 178.
276   Here, it is clear that Tracy appeals to Whiteheadian process philosophy.

self-understanding to the insistence that God precisely as *the perfect one* must be changeless?[277]

Having recourse to the view of process thought, Tracy explains the modern understanding of self-as-relative as follows:

> We are authentic selves only in direct proportion to our ability to be affected by and related to other selves. The substance-self of the classical tradition is at best an abstraction. I am the person I am precisely because of my relationship to this history, this family, these friends, those mentors, these ideas appropriated and experiences shared. I am, in a word, a profoundly relative not substantial being [...]. We take it for granted that a person who cannot be reached, cannot be affected by the ideas of others, the experience of the historical moment, the love of other persons, the wonder and anguish of existence, is one closed, frightened, dead. Are we then to affirm with the ordinary understanding of classical Christian theology that God alone is in no real way affected by others?[278]

Tracy maintains that the dipolar understanding of God is a significant corrective to classical God-talk in light of our modern self-understanding. In other words, the dipolar understanding of God is an attempt to reconceive God's reality on the analogical basis provided by modern self-understanding. Tracy describes this analogical understanding in the following way:

> Dipolarity, in fact, is less difficult a concept if we consider first not God's but our own analogously dipolar structure. In one aspect of my person – that highly abstract aspect whereby I simply *exist* – I am not affected by others. I simply exist. Yet, in another aspect of my reality, my actual, concrete person, I am intrinsically and deeply related to others. As a feeling, thinking, willing, acting self, I am related to my own body (as my first environment), to other persons, to my historical moment, to such other historical moments as I can appropriate and so forth. In a word, I am myself dipolar.[279]

In short, "given the fact that the basic metaphysical analogy for reality is the self and the self's own experience as intrinsically social and temporal, God too – precisely *as real* – is to be understood as social

---

277  *BRO*, 178.
278  *Ibid.*
279  *Ibid.*, 179.

and temporal."[280] However, this is not to mean that God's dipolarity is to be thought of at the same degree as ours. Here, Tracy recognizes the important point of the classical analogy (of Thomas Aquinas): it enables us to conceive and speak of God's nature in meaningful concepts, while acknowledging that those concepts are applied to God in an eminent sense (in Hartshorne's terms, in a "categorically superior" sense).[281] Thus, Tracy delineates God's *eminent* dipolarity in the following way:

> God alone is related to all reality through immediate participation in a manner analogous to the self's immediate relationship to its own body. God, as social, both eminently affects and is affected by all reality. In a similar manner, the dipolar God as eminently temporal may be understood to be in a continual process of self-creation, again analogous to the self's own temporal creation. As eminently or supremely temporal, the divine process of self-creation is also genuine but only analogous to our process.[282]

For Tracy, the idea of God's *eminent* dipolarity provides a coherent conception of God's reality in the following sense. The dipolar conception incorporates all the metaphysical attributes of God's absoluteness that classical theism posits, i.e., eternal, independent,

---

280  *Ibid.*, 181.
281  As regards a key characteristic of Thomas Aquinas' principle of analogy, F. Copleston explains as follows: "If one reads what St. Thomas has to say of analogy, it may appear that he is simply examining the way in which we speak about God, the verbal and conceptual implications of our statements, and that he is not actually establishing anything about our real knowledge of God. But it is a fundamental principle with St. Thomas that the perfections of creatures must be found in the Creator in a super-eminent manner." (Copleston, *A History of Philosophy: Medieval Philosophy*, vol.II, 357). The basic idea behind the Thomistic analogy is that a certain likeness must exist between God, the Creator, and creatures, and this is the likeness of an effect to its cause (God is the First Cause). However, the practice of analogy consists in attributing to God to an eminent degree all the perfections found in creatures (i.e., life, intelligence, love, goodness, etc.). Otherwise, one may not avoid anthropomorphism, which pretends to know God as God knows himself. See G.P. Klubertanz, "Analogy," in Berard L. Marthaler and others (eds), *New Catholic Encyclopedia*, vol.I (Washington, DC: The Catholic University of America; Gale Group, Inc., second edition, 2003) 371–7.
282  *BRO*, 181.

immutable, impassive, etc. However, in the neo-classical dipolar approach, God is conceived not as merely identical with the absolute, but as the supremely relative reality which includes and exceeds the absolute. In other words, the genuinely absolute character of God's reality is construed by his supreme relativity. Tracy points out that the dipolar conception has significant consequences for the very formulation of the question of God's absoluteness. Now the concern is "to understand how the already personal (as social and temporal) God may also be understood as absolute – not the reverse."[283] In other words, as Hartshorne insists, in the dipolar conception of God, the relative and concrete reality takes conceptual priority over the absolute and abstract.[284] Tracy reckons that a significant value of neo-classical dipolar theism lies in its distinct form of *synthesis* concerning God's absoluteness. Put more specifically, dipolar theism attempts to provide a way to resolve the central problem of Christian theism, the seemingly contradictory conjunction of God's transcendence and immanence, by construing God as *supremely relative* (the synthesis of God's absolute and relative aspects). By conceiving God as supremely relative, as Ogden's puts it, "one can assert God's independence of the actual world (in his abstract identity) without saying he is wholly external to it, and one can affirm his inclusion of the actual world (in his concrete existence) without denying that the world as actual is completely contingent and radically dependent on him as its sole necessary ground."[285] A key claim of God's surrelativism here is that it conceives God's transcendence and immanence as *complementary*,

---

283  *Ibid.*, 182.
284  Tracy describes how God's concrete reality precedes his abstract state by means of an analogy with ours in the following way: "In the case of self-understanding, we best understand certain attributes of our own person (our passivity and mutability, for example) only after we have first understood as best we can the concrete social and temporal constitution of our own experience. Similarly, we best understand certain attributes of God's person (immutability and impassivity, for example) only after we have analogously understood God's concrete, eminently social and temporal person." (*Ibid.*).
285  Ogden, *The Reality of God*, 62. Recall Hartshorne's statement that the doctrine of panentheism (God is all-inclusive of the world) is another way to specify the doctrine of surrelativism (God is relative to *all* reality).

*interdependent*, not *contradictory*, poles of one and the same reality, i.e., of God. And, these complementariness and interdependence find their meaning in God's surrelativity.[286] In short, this neo-classical doctrine of God's surrelativity can serve as an alternative conception of God which remedies classical theism's dilemma of incoherence or antinomy, the dilemma that resulted from its monopolar approach to God's transcendental-immanent reality. Moreover, this dipolar conception of God's reality is able to do more justice to modern sensitivities which see in ongoing creative, interrelative becoming the "really real." Based on the foregoing argument, Tracy concludes that, "in terms of the first criterion for 'meaning,' internal coherence, the dipolar concept of God seems clearly meaningful."[287]

### The Adequacy of the Dipolar God to Human Religious Experience

Tracy's second criterion for a metaphysical conceptuality for God is its adequacy to human religious experience: viz., whether a metaphysical reflection of God enables one to explicate human existential, religious experience meaningfully. Tracy contends that the classical monopolar understanding of God's absoluteness ends up neutralizing both God's and our actual commitments to the ultimate worth of human existence. He claims:

> Can a Wholly Absolute God, unrelated internally to creatures and thus literally unaffected by their actions, seem anything other than an existentially intolerable burden for humanity? If the heart of our authentic secularity is its consistent insistence that our life here and now is that which is of ultimate significance, can we really hold that our ultimate commitment is to a God literally unaffected by that life? Is the real Christian belief one in a 'supernatural' world whose existential lure too often removes its believers from the struggle for truth and justice in this world?[288]

---

286  Ogden puts this aspect in the following way: "Just because God is the *eminently* relative One, there is also a sense in which he is strictly absolute. His being related to all others is itself relative to nothing, but is the absolute ground of any and all real relationships, whether his own or thóse of his creatures." (*Ibid.*, 60).
287  *BRO*, 183.
288  *Ibid.*, 180.

Tracy argues that the barren absoluteness of God in classical theism is, in a sense, responsible for making God's reality absurd or incredible to the modern mind. Tracy asserts that, "in terms of existential meaningfulness, at least, the 'wholly absolute' God of classical super-naturalism cannot but seem repugnant to the secular spirit."[289] He goes on to say that "that existential difficulty – probably far more than the possible incoherence of the concept of the Wholly Absolute itself – has rendered atheism a seemingly unavoidable option for some of the paradigmatic witness of the modern struggle for liberation."[290]

Tracy points briefly to the significance of the dipolar concept of God for the question of our existential meaningfulness. As we already have seen, in his earlier discussion of the question of God's *existence*, Tracy's central task was to portray God as the "objective referent" of human religious (limit) experiences and Christian religious (limit) language. In his own terms, the task was to validate that "the primary existential use of the word 'God' is to refer to the objective ground in reality itself for those limit-languages and limit-experiences of an ultimate worth of our existence, our commitment to the good, and our struggle to achieve it."[291] Now, for him, the dipolar concept of God serves to articulate *the concrete manner* in which that God exists and acts. For Tracy, the dipolar concept of God is a new metaphysical insight which resuscitates God as the richest concrete actuality in the world. Tracy states that "there is a God – the God of Abraham, Isaac, Jacob, and Jesus Christ – which a process metaphysics can aid us to understand in strictly conceptual terms."[292] More specifically, the dipolar concept of God articulates God's nature as an "eminently social and relative one." God is involved in the struggle "to persuade us to the good; to aid us by that immediate participation we call love to choose the true and right possibility; to be affected by the actual

---

289  *Ibid.*
290  *Ibid.* Tracy writes that the existential difficulty resulting from the classical barren understanding of God's absoluteness "can [also] be summarized in the cultural fact of the 'death of God' announced by the radical theologians." (*Ibid.*, 198 n.61).
291  *Ibid.*, 183.
292  *Ibid.*

choice made."[293] Hence, he argues, "no contemporary secular thinker with a real commitment to the ultimate significance of our actions for good or evil here and now need fear that this God – the only God, I believe, whom Christians know – is indifferent to or unaffected by that commitment or that struggle."[294] In short, for Tracy, the dipolar understanding of God can provide for a metaphysical discourse on the existential meaningfulness of Christian theism that articulates the central Christian insight that "a loving and related God alone is God."[295]

*The Dipolar Concept of God is Appropriate to the Scriptural Understanding of God*

Tracy's final criterion for a metaphysical reflection on God is its harmony with the scriptural understanding of God. This criterion addresses an important issue, the relationship between the meta-physical understanding of God and the scriptural understanding of God. According to Tracy, in classical theism, the gap or conflict between these two understandings (i.e., the independent, immutable, impassive God vs. the personal and loving God) tends to be positively expressed as a "mystery," or "paradox." In classical theism, the idea of "mystery" or "paradox" as regards the reality of the Christian God seems to trade on the concept of "Wholly Absolute." Tracy points out that such a classical approach, however, may induce a hermeneutical problem with regard to the scriptural symbolic or metaphoric attributes for God. For example, classical theism seems to consider "the original scriptural metaphor [as] a 'mere metaphor' (e.g., for Aquinas, an analogy of improper attribution), a 'mere symbol,' or a 'useful anthropomorphism' which should be eliminated when formulating a strictly conceptual understanding of the God-humanity relationship."[296] Tracy contends, "If all the 'attributes' of the classical Absolute – immutability, aseity, omnipotence, impassivity, etc. – are

293   *Ibid.*
294   *Ibid.*
295   *Ibid.*, 179.
296   *Ibid.*, 161.

interpreted as denying that God bears an internal [not just notional, but real] relationship to anything beyond divine Absolute being," the scriptural assertions of the God-humanity relationship (of which a primary metaphor is "God is love") become simply feeble attributes.[297] According to Tracy, the contribution of the neo-classical dipolar conception of God is that it renders conceptually explicit the symbolic meanings of the scriptural assertions without negating their original symbols by the use of new metaphysical categories for God, i.e., surrelativity, self-surpassibility, receptivity, becoming, etc. Thus, Tracy states that, "from a hermeneutical viewpoint, the interpreter of Hebrew and Christian texts seems on far more solid ground in appealing to the dipolar concept of God as more in harmony with scriptural meanings than any concept informed by the monopolar outlook."[298] Tracy contends that, in this sense, he does not agree to the fear that an employment of metaphysics in our understanding of the scriptural God will harm or eliminate the symbolic meanings that the scriptural religious language discloses. Instead, as shown in process thought, the proper use of metaphysical concepts genuinely allows the cognitive claims involved in the originating religious language to be conceptually intelligible. It is so in the sense that "the correct employment of metaphysics *can* eliminate incoherence and self-contradiction in the concepts used to explicate the 'disclosure' which the 'interaction' of the metaphorical statement is meant to evoke."[299] Hence, for him, the neo-classical dipolar conception of God contributes to bridge the chasm between the metaphysical understanding of God and the scriptural understanding of God. This means that, for him, the neo-classical conception of God can provide a third theological way which does not fall into the classical theological models of "rationalism" (overriding reason) and "fideism" (overriding faith).[300] In other words, the neo-classical conception of God shows a possibility to overcome the classical metaphysical inability to explicate the scriptural, divine values of love, responsiveness, etc. It

297   *Ibid.*, 180.
298   *Ibid.*, 184.
299   *Ibid.*, 161.
300   See *ibid.*, 161–2.

opens a new path for articulating God's scriptural values in a metaphysical system. In short, it weaves together the metaphysical and scriptural understandings of God in an intellectually reasonable, logically coherent, and religiously appealing way. In this sense, for him, it can provide a third alternative to the two extreme theological models of "rationalism" and "fideism."[301] In the conclusion of this chapter, we will comment on this observation of Tracy.

301 Tracy does not develop this issue further here. As a postscript, he briefly points out several limitations of process thought. Firstly, Tracy remarks that Hartshorne's critique of Thomas Aquinas' monopolar theism may be still sound, but it needs further reflection upon the subtle and complex position of Aquinas. He writes that, "Hartshorne and others are too often satisfied with accepting some outdated neo-scholastic interpretation of Aquinas' meaning when more accurate and more contemporary formulations can be found in the work of such diverse thinkers and traditions as Rahner, Lonergan, Preller, and Burrell." (*Ibid.*, 188). Secondly, Tracy indicates that process thought does not fully articulate the human existential (limit) situation of "the ambiguity, the tragedy, the sin involved in a truly contemporary as distinct from a modern model of humanity." Tracy states that "the seeming inability of process thought to have the wider existential impact which its revisionary concept of the Christian God's reality deserves may result from the presence of a kind of residual liberal optimism." (*Ibid.*). Finally, Tracy says that as his earlier analysis of Christian religious language as "limit-language" shows, the originating religious language's symbolic power of disclosure is immense. If the conceptual language of process thought were able to find expression in such symbolic language, it "may find the wider existential-religious impact which, in my judgment, its rich conceptual discoveries deserve." (*Ibid.*, 189). Tracy states that "such conceptual clarification of the disclosing Christian metaphor 'God is love' by means of process categories would be no small theological achievement. What would still seem badly needed, however, would be symbolic forms of expression that might allow that insight to resonate more fully to the deepest sensitivities of our present multi-dimensional cultural situation." (*Ibid.*).

## 2. Conclusion

In this chapter, we discussed the most essential concern of Tracy's revisionist theological project, the question of God. In relation to his methodological exposition, the chapter was concerned with examining how Tracy substantiates his fifth thesis: *to determine the truth-status of the results of one's investigations into the meaning of both common human experience and Christian texts the theologian should employ an explicitly transcendental or metaphysical mode of reflection.*

In Tracy, the God-question is dealt with not as an independent issue but in relation to his previous investigation of two theological sources: the religious (limit) dimension present in common human experience and in the life-world disclosed by the Christian texts. Put differently, the final truth of the religious dimension present in the both sources cannot be cognitively articulated until that dimension is reflected in a theistic perspective. Tracy writes that, "without religious meaningfulness, theism tends to become merely a dead and un-interesting issue. Without the truth of theism, religion tends to become an existentially useful but not cognitively serious question. The existential meaningfulness of the theistic question, to be sure, emerges only from an authentically religious base. But the final truth of religion, I believe, is in fact its objective ground in theism."[302] Tracy's fundamental assumption here is that the religious (limit) dimension present in both sources has a transcendental or metaphysical ground without which that dimension cannot be accounted for. In other words, this transcendental or metaphysical ground is the "objective referent" of that religious (limit) dimension, which is God. Here, God is metaphysically a "limit-concept" which can be validated only by a metaphysical reflection. Hence, Tracy interconnects two issues. He attempts to elucidate the truth of religion (or the religious dimension) by means of validating its transcendental or metaphysical ground (or referent), the reality of God. Conversely, he attempts to justify God's reality by means of demonstrating how God functions as a transcendental ground to (or condition for) our existence in which the religious dimension is fundamentally operative.

302    *Ibid.,* 163.

For him, the question at stake is how to rationally and critically conduct the above task by means of a scientific methodology (his revisionist project's aim). Tracy opts for three different metaphysical reflections to fulfill this task: the transcendental method of Emerich Coreth, Schubert Ogden's model of philosophical theology, and process thought. Tracy deals with the God-question at two levels: (1) the *existence* of God's reality as a transcendental condition for our existence as such and (2) the *nature* of God's reality (the manner in which God exists and acts vis-à-vis the world). For the former question, Tracy uses Coreth's transcendental method and Ogden's analysis, and for the latter, he uses process thought. In the following assessment, we will focus upon several elements in Tracy's position which seem problematic.

Firstly, according to Tracy, following Ogden's view, at the foundation of human existence is an undeniable basic "existential faith" (in life's ultimate worth) which is the necessary condition of the possibility of all our existing and understanding. Religion is a re-presentation of this basic faith, and we can posit God as its objective referent. In a similar manner, the religious (limit) dimension operative in human experience opens upon its objective referent which we may call God. However, here, Tracy does not offer any explanation concerning why this "existential faith" or religious (limit) dimension necessarily supposes its objective referent or ground. Without positing its objective referent or ground, can we not meaningfully think of "existential faith" or human religious (limit) experience in itself? Actually, it is not impossible to think of them without assuming their external objective referent or ground. Tracy takes it for granted that there is the objective referent of human religious experience. For Tracy, this assumption is necessary for explaining "the necessity of God's existence as a datum of fundamental theological anthropology."[303]

303 Mark I. Wallace, "Can God Be Named Without Being Known?: The Problem of Revelation in Thiemann, Ogden, and Ricoeur," in *JAAR*, 59 (1991) 303. This remark of Wallace is concerned with Ogden's position of philosophical theology. This comment can also apply to Tracy's position which accommodates Ogden's.

Secondly, we mentioned before in this chapter that a value of transcendental method (or transcendental Thomism) for Tracy is that it approaches the question of God's existence from "below," namely, the transcendental conditions of human existence as such. Here, the question at stake is whether one is able to formulate a sound argument that justifies the move from the transcendental conditions of human existence to God's existence. Tracy's strategy for this justification is to introduce the question of religion into this discussion. He approaches the question of religion in relation to the transcendental condition of human existence. For this approach, he has recourse to Ogden's analysis of religion. For Tracy, following Ogden, religion is not one of the diverse cultural fields of human life, but has to do with an ultimate, fundamental dimension of all human existence. Religion is a re-presentation of the "existential faith" (in life's ultimate worth) which is the necessary (transcendental) condition of the possibility of all our existing and understanding. In this sense, religion has a general metaphysical character. Now, Tracy tries to link God's existence to this metaphysical character of religion. He reformulates his question of God in the following way: is the concept of God an adequate representation of the metaphysical character of religion? Tracy's key claim is that God is a constitutive concept of religion as such. Let us recall Tracy's important argument:

> It may prove helpful to note that the argument [God is a constitutive concept of the general metaphysical character of religion] need not to be confined to the 'radically monotheistic' concept of Western religion. If religion be in fact the kind of re-presentative expression explicated by Ogden [religion as a re-presentation of our existential faith], or the kind of limit-experience and limit-language explicated in my own prior analysis, then we are logically impelled to ask whether the explicitly theistic representation of that faith is both possible and necessary. That latter issue is more systematic than historical. Historically it is not, of course, the case that all religious language is God-language. In systematic terms, however, one cannot but ask whether the cognitive character of *all* religious language does not imply the reality of God as the objective referent of that language.[304]

304   *BRO*, 155 (italics mine).

A problem with the above argument is, however, that Tracy does not provide any apodictic reason why a theistic experience is indispensable to "our existential faith" or "limit-experiences" as religious. Here, we need to pay attention to the crucial assumption by means of which he develops his argument. Tracy enquires, "granted the existence of 'basic beliefs' [or "existential faith"], [...] is explicitly theistic language an adequate re-presentation of those basic beliefs? To answer that question the analysis must turn to the question of the cognitive meaning of all religious, especially theistic, language."[305] This means that, for him, the datum of the argument that God is a constitutive concept of religion lies in the cognitive meaning of God developed in theistic (Judaeo-Christian) religion. Tracy asserts that, "where God is conceived radically (as in such monotheistic religions as Judaism, Christianity, and Islam), God is conceived metaphysically."[306] More specifically, in those religions, God is conceived as "the ultimate creative ground of anything that is so much as even possible, and hence to be in the strict sense necessary, not merely a being among others, but in some way 'being-itself' [...] the sole being who is, therefore the inclusive object of all our faith and understanding."[307] In short, for him, this cognitive understanding of Judaeo-Christian God is the rationale to affirm that God is a metaphysical reality universally true and valid for all human religious experience. It is clear that, here, Tracy appeals to a religious discourse developed in one particular religious tradition as a universal criterion. In this position, in fact, other religious traditions end up describing the Judaeo-Christian understanding of God, using only different languages to inadequately express it. In his justification of God's existence, Tracy appears to handle both concepts of "theistic" and "religious" in almost the same breath. In short, for him, the theistic reality is the reality of religion as such.

As we saw in his earlier methodological exposition, Tracy made clear that the revisionist theologian like himself appeals to public warrants available to fair-minded critics inside and outside Christ-

305   Ibid., 154.
306   Ibid., 155.
307   Ibid.

ianity for his or her truth claims. Hence, such a theologian does not allow "his own – or his tradition's – beliefs to serve as warrants for his arguments."[308] What we see in his justification above, however, does not seem to be in accord with his methodological proposition. In that justification, his religious tradition's belief in God (specifically here, Thomistic Christian theism: God is the ground of all reality as being-itself) serves as a warrant for his truth claim, something he wishes to avoid.[309]

Thirdly, for Tracy, since God is a constitutive concept of religion, and religion has a metaphysical character, the question of God can only be adequately investigated and justified by a metaphysical reflection. In relation to this issue, we need to point out two things. Firstly, Tracy claims that where God is conceived radically, as in the Judaeo-Christian religion, God is conceived metaphysically in such a way that God is "being-itself," or the ground of all reality, etc. Here, it should be noted that this conception of God itself is interpretive, resting upon a particular philosophical tradition (Thomistic metaphysics). For instance, in his later works in the 1990s, Tracy puts forward quite different conceptions of the Judaeo-Christian God aided by different philosophical categories under different contextual exigencies for theology: i.e., God as "the incomprehensible," God as "the Hidden." Here, Tracy employs no longer the Thomistic metaphysical category of "being-itself" (or "onto-theological category") for conceiving God. A problematic element in Tracy's earlier work is clearly his use of such a particular, context-bound conception of God as a universal criterion for justifying his theistic claim.

---

308   *Ibid.*, 7.
309   Here, Philip Clayton's critique of transcendental Thomism's way of validating God's existence from the transcendental conditions of human existence is relevant to Tracy's position. He writes that whatever Kantian terminology transcendental Thomists may employ, "one always detects that the choice for the transcendent has already been made at an earlier stage of their thought. If the Absolute is assumed from the outset to be built into human nature, it will be no surprise when anthropological or transcendental reflection 'discovers' it there [...] Perhaps this fact helps to account for the somewhat awkward tone of the Kantian terminology, which sometimes appears to be tacked on to a deeper-level Thomism." (Philip Clayton, *The Problem of God in Modern Thought*, 27).

Secondly, it should be mentioned that the metaphysical reflection that he defends for validating his theistic claims is a theistic metaphysics which is rooted in Christian theism. Endorsing Charles Hartshorne's metaphysics, Tracy asserts that "metaphysical inquiry itself is completed only when the concept of God is explicitly accepted or rejected. If one recognizes the strictly metaphysical claims which the radically theistic [Judaeo-Christian] concept of God involves, one may recognize as well that precisely that concept also provides a basic category for metaphysics itself: *the* single metaphysical referent to our most basic faith or trust."[310] In short, Tracy's metaphysical justification of theistic claims depends on a circular argument. His criterion (a conception of the Judaeo-Christian God) is universal because a particular metaphysical tradition that he relies on defines it as universal. And the metaphysical tradition that he relies on is rooted in Judaeo-Christian theism. This means that Tracy's metaphysical justification of God may convince the inner circle of Christianity which shares his metaphysical option, but hardly those outside as a public discourse.

Fourthly, concerning the question of God's nature (who God is or in what manner God exists and acts vis-à-vis the world), in his search for a mediating conceptuality, Tracy moves his attention from transcendental Thomism to process thought, more specifically, Charles Hartshorne's dipolar conception of God. For Tracy, the eminence of Hartshorne's dipolar conception of God is that it provides a new conceptuality which does better justice than classical theistic conceptuality to human religious experience and the scriptural understanding of God. One of the most essential issues addressed in this discussion is how to conduct a conceptual articulation of the scriptural understanding of God. In Ricoeur's terms, it is the issue that concerns "the dynamism of the transition" from religious discourse to theological discourse.[311] For Tracy, this issue is concerned with a use of metaphysical concepts for articulating the cognitive claims involved in the originating religious language. It is known that this issue has been associated with engendering two major theological pitfalls,

310   *BRO*, 156.
311   Ricoeur, "Outline," in *Semeia* 4 (1975) 35.

"rationalism" and "fideism" in the history of theology. When a philosophical or metaphysical speculation is unbalanced, it can lead to an intellectual mastery of the symbolic, revelatory meanings of the originating scriptural assertions by means of a rational system (the pitfall of rationalism). On the contrary, when it is claimed that the symbolic, revelatory meanings of scriptural assertions belong to a different order of intelligibility (i.e., the order of faith), and any philosophical or metaphysical conceptuality cannot genuinely serve to articulate them, it can lead to the danger of fideism.

Given the fact that Tracy insists on the necessity of the use of metaphysics for articulating the cognitive claims involved in scriptural language, the question at stake is how far Tracy's metaphysical account of God resists the danger of rationalism. Put differently, how far does his position do justice to the specificity of the scriptural language of God whose originating, evocative meanings cannot be subsumed under a metaphysical system. Tracy himself is aware of contemporary critiques of the use of metaphysics in a biblical hermeneutics of God. For instance, over against Ricoeur's critique of the classical onto-theological conceptualization of the scriptural God,[312] Tracy defends his own position by insisting that it is not dependent on the classical metaphysical approaches, i.e., the so-called "*hautes époques*" (the high times of dreaming of an intellectual completion of knowledge).[313] Instead, he claims that his position appropriates legitimate revisions of those earlier classical meta-

---

312  For this issue, see among others, Paul Ricoeur, *Figuring the Sacred: Religion, Narrative and Imagination*, trans. by David Pellauer (Minneapolis: Fortress Press, 1995); idem, "From Interpretation to Translation," 331–61; idem, "Specificity," 129–45. For the secondary materials on this issue, see Christina M. Gschwandtner, "Ricoeur's Hermeneutics of God: A Symbol That Gives Rise to Thought," in *Ph&Th*, 13 (2001) 287–309; Mark I. Wallace, "Can God Be Named Without Being Known?: The Problem of Revelation in Thiemann, Ogden, and Ricoeur," in *JAAR*, 59 (1991) 281–308.

313  The expression the "*hautes époques*" is from Ricoeur. Ricoeur means by this expression "the supreme moments when our culture dreamt of its complete integration and projected these dreams in systems where harmony had overcome war, at least in discourse. Such were the blessed times of the great Neo-Platonic onto-theologies, the Aristotelean-Thomistic synthesis, the Leibnizian theodicy, the Hegelian system." (Ricoeur, "Specificity," 132).

physical conceptualities (i.e., transcendental method and process thought). He asserts that his metaphysical position concerning God "may perhaps even meet the excellent demands for 'limit concepts' developed by Paul Ricoeur."[314] We have a problem with this claim of Tracy. We observe that there is a divergence between Tracy's position and Ricoeur's approach to the scriptural God based on "limit concepts." Here, Ricoeur's notion of "limit concepts" represents his philosophical position concerning the God-question which is opposed to an objectivistic approach to God based on classical onto-theological metaphysics.[315] What is more, the notion of "limit concepts" stands for a move to a new mode of conceiving God represented by Ricoeur's option for a philosophical hermeneutics. In this regard, the notion of "limit" involves two motifs: negative and positive.[316] Negatively, it functions to prohibit (puts a limit to) an objectivistic knowledge of God, but positively, it serves to point beyond that knowledge to a new way to look at God's reality.[317] Let us briefly examine Ricoeur's hermeneutics of God, based on his philosophy of the limits. Then, we shall discuss whether Tracy's position is in accord with Ricoeur's as he maintains.

314  *BRO*, 143 n.67.
315  Here, Ricoeur borrows the notion of "limit" from Kant. For the meaning of "limit" in Kant, see the section, *The Theistic Prospect Assumed in the Religious Dimension of Human Experience* in this chapter.
316  We already examined this double-meaning aspect of the notion of 'limit' in Kant, which Ricoeur adopts in his own analysis.
317  Ricoeur explains that "we may understand that a philosophy of the limits does not close the philosophical discourse, but breaks the claim of objective knowledge to close it at the level of spatio-temporal objects. The limit is an act which opens, because it is an act which breaks the closure. In that sense, it already belongs to hope, in spite of the fact that it is merely negative, as the destruction of an illusion and of claim." (Ricoeur, "Hope and the Structure of Philosophical Systems," in *Figuring the Sacred: Religion, Narrative, and Imagination*, 213).

*Two Important Assumptions Underlying Ricoeur's Distinctive Approach to the God-Question*

The most distinctive aspect of Ricoeur's approach to the God-question is that he deals with this issue by means of a biblical hermeneutics that utilizes modern literary and textual theories.[318] There are two assumptions underlying this distinctive approach. First, for Ricoeur, naming God does not arrive from either a vacuum or from a pure construction of our mind, but happens only within a particular, contingent context of faith-experiences. Moreover, faith-experiences (or religious experiences) always come to articulation within a language, a discourse. This is to say that faith, as a lived experience, is "formed, clarified, and educated" within texts.[319] He says, "This presupposition of the *textuality* of faith distinguishes *biblical* faith ('Bible' meaning book) from all others. In one sense, therefore, texts do precede life. I can name God in my faith because the texts preached to me have already named God."[320] Hence, God is, in a way, the ultimate referent of the world or the "issue" of biblical texts.

The second assumption is that, for him, a conceptual understanding of God is not concerned with an extrinsic encounter between the God-language of biblical texts and metaphysical concepts, but with a direct inquiry into that religious language "from the standpoint of its own conceptual potentialities."[321] The dynamics of the transition from the figurative mode of religious language toward the conceptual mode of that language must draw its strength from the hermeneutical potentialities of religious language itself. This dynamic transition is motivated by the symbolic power of religious language itself that "gives rise to thought."[322] He explains that this dynamism "belongs to the essence of a figurative [or symbolic] expression to *stand for*

---

318 Since we already extensively dealt with Ricoeur's literary hermeneutical theories of metaphor and symbol in the previous chapter, we will not discuss these at length here.
319 Ricoeur, "Naming God," in *Figuring the Sacred: Religion, Narrative, and Imagination*, 218.
320 *Ibid.*
321 Ricoeur, "Specificity," 132.
322 *Ibid.*, 133.

something else, to *call for* a new speech-act which would paraphrase the first one without exhausting its meaningful resources."[323] There-fore, a conceptual articulation of God is neither something super-imposed from the outside on a self-sufficient expression, nor some-thing issuing from the exhaustive absorption of the figurative in the conceptual. It has to do with the hermeneutical task of disentangling the world or the "issue" of the God-language of the biblical texts that is unfolded by that language's own dynamism. In the following, we will point out several essential characteristics of his hermeneutics of God.

### *The Word of "God" as an "Originary" Utterance*

Ricoeur characterizes the standing of the very word of God as follows: it "primordially belongs to a level of discourse I speak of as *originary* in relation to utterances of a speculative, theological, or philosophical type, such as: 'God exists,' 'God is immutable and omnipotent...,' 'God is the first cause,' and so on."[324] For him, in one's approach to the God-question, to enter into the nonspeculative, prephilosophical, and originary modalities of language where God is named implies a double-renouncement: objectivism and subjectivism. To get oneself involved with the world of the texts where God is named is "first of all to let go (*se depouiller*) of every form of onto-theological know-ledge."[325] This letting go of objectivistic knowledge about God has everything to do with a move away from the knowledge of God based on self-founding presuppositions. As one of the representatives of this type of knowledge, Ricoeur points to the transcendental reflection of Neo-Thomists. He claims that "this knowledge does not stand on the side of objects to be known but on the side of the conditions of possibility of knowing, therefore on the side of the subject. The idea of a subject that posits itself thus becomes the unfounded foundation, or better, the foundation that founds itself, in relation to which every rule of validity is derived. In this way, the subject becomes the

---

323   *Ibid.*
324   Ricoeur, "Naming God," 223.
325   *Ibid.*

supreme 'presupposition'."[326] According to Ricoeur, to enter into the most "originary" level of the scriptural God-language requires giving up (*dessaisissement*) an appeal to a self-founding presupposition, a pretentious claim to a total mastery of the thinking subject.[327] Thus, he claims that "it is the task of a philosophical hermeneutic to guide us from the double absolute of onto-theological speculation and transcendental reflection toward the more originary modalities of language by means of which the members of the community of faith have interpreted their experience to themselves and to others. It is here where God has been named."[328]

### The Philosophical Hermeneutics of God as a Poetics of Biblical God-Discourses

Ricoeur assimilates biblical texts to poetic texts. Here, "poetic," Ricoeur explains, does not refer to a "literary genre." Instead, it refers to a referential function of language which entertains a "semantic innovation" in the suspension of the meaning of the first-order

326 *Ibid.*, 224.
327 According to Ricoeur, human reflection is mediated by a universe of signs. This means that there is no immediate self-consciousness. All reflection is mediated "by the ideas, actions, works, institutions, and monuments that objectify it. It is in these objects, in the widest sense of the word, that the Ego must lose and find itself." (Paul Ricoeur, "Toward a Hermeneutic of the Idea of Revelation," in Lewis S. Mudge (ed.), *Paul Ricoeur: Essays on Biblical Interpretation* (Philadelphia: Fortress Press, 1985) 106). In other words, a thinking subject always finds itself in a relation to a language, a tradition, a culture, and a world that precedes it. For Ricoeur, since we only come to understand human being and human possibilities through an interpretation of symbols and texts which attest to that existence, self-understanding has to do with a hermeneutic task to understand oneself before signs, i.e., texts. "To understand oneself before the text is not to impose one's own finite capacity of understanding on it, but to expose oneself to receive from it a larger self which would be the proposed way of existing that most appropriately responds to the proposed world of the text. Understanding then is the complete opposite of a constitution for which the subject would have the key. It would be better in this regard to say that the self is constituted by the issue of the text." (*Ibid.*, 108).
328 Ricoeur, "Naming God," 224.

description.[329] The suspension entailed by poetic discourse is the negative condition for the emancipation of a nondescriptive reference to the world which is not exhausted in the first-order description of objects. Poetic discourse discloses the modalities of our rootedness in, and belonging-to (*appartenance*), the world that precede our object-ification of the world. In the crucible of semantic innovation, by breaking with everyday language, poetic language opens up the world of the text which "incites the reader, or the listener, to understand himself or herself in the face of the text and to develop, in imagination and sympathy, the *self* capable of inhabiting this world by deploying his or her ownmost possibilities there."[330] Ricoeur sees in this referential function of poetic language "a dimension of revelation in a nonreligious, nontheistic, nonbiblical sense of the word, yet a sense capable of furnishing a first approximation of what revelation in the biblical sense may signify."[331] In such a revelatory aspect of poetic discourse, Ricoeur looks at the emergence of another concept of truth than the one defined by the "adequation" of our mind to objects, regulated by the criteria of verification and falsification. Truth, here, no longer means adequation, but "*manifestation*, in the sense of letting be what shows itself."[332] Now, according to Ricoeur, biblical language is poetic in all these senses. It is poetic language but as a unique case. What makes it a unique case is that it contains the naming of God. This distinctive character adds to the revelatory trait of poetic language an overarching referent, God. Hence, Ricoeur states, "naming God, before being an act of which I am capable, is what the texts of my predilection do when they escape from their authors, their redactional setting, and their first audience, when they deploy their world, when they poetically manifest and thereby reveal a world we

---

329 For the meaning of "semantic innovation," see the section, *The Semantic Innovation of Metaphor* in chapter 2.

330 Ricoeur, "Naming God," 223.

331 *Ibid.*, 222. In other words, the revelatory function is "coextensive with the poetic function." (Ricoeur, "Toward a Hermeneutic of the Idea of Revelation," 102).

332 Ricoeur, "Naming God," 223 (italics mine); see also, idem, "Toward a Hermeneutic of the Idea of Revelation," 102.

might inhabit."[333] In sum, by placing "the originary expressions of biblical faith [in God] under the sign of the poetic [revelatory] function of language," Ricoeur attempts to deliver a hermeneutics of God from both objectivistic and subjectivistic approaches.

## *The Biblical Polyphony of God and its Theological Implications*

For shaping his philosophical hermeneutics of God, Ricoeur deals seriously with the fact that the naming of God in biblical texts involves a variety of discourses. Ricoeur points out that "the naming of God, in the originary expressions of faith, is not simple but multiple. It is not a single tone, but polyphonic."[334] More specifically, the originating expressions of naming God exhibit diverse forms of discourse such as "narratives, prophecies, laws, proverbs, prayers, hymns, liturgical formulas, and wisdom writings."[335] Each of these forms of discourse has a particular style of naming God. The various literary forms that we mentioned, however, are not mere rhetorical devices, but "instruments for producing discourse as a *work* [a wrought piece]."[336] In other words, "structure and kerygma accommodate each other in each form of narration. It is within this mutual accommodation of the form and the confession of faith that the naming of God diversifies itself."[337] The picture of God portrayed in such diversified ways is, therefore, neither transparent, nor always consistent, nor exhaustive in one particular form. Ricoeur explains that "throughout these [diversified] discourses, God appears differently each time: sometimes as the hero of the saving acts, sometimes as wrathful and compassionate, sometimes as the one to whom one

---

333 Ricoeur, "Naming God," 223. Here, Ricoeur's statement presupposes his theory of the semantic autonomy of the text. Owing to writing, a written text (work) obtains a new existence through three kinds of "distanciation": (1) distanciation from the situation of discourse; (2) distanciation from the author; (3) distanciation from the original audience. For this topic, see Thesis 4 in chapter 1.
334 *Ibid.*, 224.
335 *Ibid.*
336 Ricoeur, "Philosophy and Religious Language," in *Figuring the Sacred: Religion, Narrative, and Imagination*, 38.
337 Ricoeur, "Naming God," 224.

can speak in a relation of an I-Thou type, or sometimes as the one whom I meet only in a cosmic order that ignores me."[338] Hence, there are evoked tensions and contrasts among the multiple portraits of God. According to Ricoeur, such tensions and contrasts should not be resolved into any unifying philosophical abstraction. Instead, they should be taken into account as theologically significant. He claims that "the word 'God' cannot be understood as a philosophical concept, not even 'being' in the sense of medieval philosophy or in Heidegger's sense. The word 'God' says more than the word 'being' because it presupposes the entire context of narratives, prophecies, laws, wisdom writings, psalms, and so on."[339] Here, Ricoeur calls for our attention to a double-direction that the word 'God' leads to in the confrontation of the diverse forms of discourse. This is to say that the word 'God' exhibits two aspects at once: viz., it unites all partial discourses as their coordinator, and it escapes all of them like a vanishing point on their common horizon. In other words, "the referent God is not just the index of the mutual belonging together (*appartenance*) of the originary forms of the discourse of faith. It is also the index of their incompleteness. It is their common goal, which escapes each of them."[340] From a hermeneutical perspective, to understand the word of God is, thus, to recognize its dynamic power "to gather all the significations that issue from the partial discourses and to open up a horizon that escapes from the closure of discourse."[341] For Ricoeur, this is why no "metastory" about the God of scriptures is possible.[342] The dialectic of the naming of God, viz., God as the point

338  Ricoeur, "Philosophy and Religious Language," 41.
339  Ricoeur, "Naming God," 227.
340  *Ibid.*, 228.
341  Ricoeur, "Philosophy and Religious Language," 46.
342  Ricoeur writes that "the ineffability of the Name [of God] is the same thing as the inexhaustibility of the metastory. This close connection is clearly asserted in the episode of the burning bush, which at the same time proclaims the retreat of Yahweh in the incognito 'I am who I am' and Yahweh's partnership with Israel's journey: 'Thus you shall say to the Israelites, 'Yahweh, the God of your ancestors, the God of Abraham, the God of Isaac, and *the God of Jacob*, has sent me to you'." (Ricoeur, "Toward a Narrative Theology: Its Necessity, Its Resources, Its Difficulties," in *Figuring the Sacred: Religion, Narrative, and Imagination*, 243).

of intersection and the index of the incompleteness of all our discourse about him, resists being transformed into a closed form of knowledge.

In order to explain this dialectical aspect in a more effective way, Ricoeur appeals to the idea of "model" or "schema."[343] He claims that the biblical discourses about God "are not established at the level of the concept but at that of the schema [or model]."[344] This is to say that the multiple discourses about God serve as the multiple *"rules* for producing figures of the divine: models of the monarch, the judge, the father, the husband, the rabbi, the servant."[345] Moreover, these models do not express just figures of the divine as such, but figures of God's relationship with all of humanity. Here, his key point is that "these schemas or models remain diversified and heterogeneous and are incapable by themselves of forming a system."[346] For Ricoeur, the value of using the idea of "model" here is to keep alive the dialectic between "the Name and the idol."[347] In other words, the idea of "model" serves to protect the Names of God from becoming idols which we make for ourselves by employing fixed categories. Ricoeur states:

> The Name works on the schema or model by making it move, by making it dynamic, by inverting it into an opposed image. (Thus God assumes all the positions in the figures of the family: father, mother, spouse, brother, and finally 'Son of Man.') Just as, according to Kant, the Idea requires the surpassing of not only the image but also the concept, in the demand to 'think more,' the Name subverts every model, but only through them.[348]

For Ricoeur, the task of a philosophical hermeneutics of God is to unfold all the implications of the dialectical tension and dynamism 'contained' in the biblical naming of God.[349] The dialectical dyn-

---

343  We already examined Ricoeur's use of this idea of "model" in his theory of metaphor in the previous chapter.
344  Ricoeur, "Naming God," 233.
345  *Ibid.*, (italics mine).
346  *Ibid.*
347  *Ibid.*
348  *Ibid.*
349  Here, we cannot deal in a fully fledged form with the theological implications that Ricoeur's hermeneutics of God unfolds. This needs another extensive

amism of polyphonic discourses about God opens up the interpretative horizon for us and allows us to be challenged by the revelatory appeal of those poetic discourses. This is a way to get out of *both* a "misalignment between the philosophical and biblical names [i.e., God and Being]," and an opposite position that rejects the mediation of any philosophical conceptuality for understanding God.[350]

We have examined several essential characteristics of Ricoeur's hermeneutics of God, based on his philosophy of limits. With regard to the question of whether Tracy's position concurs with Ricoeur's as Tracy maintains, we will indicate three points in our assessment.

Firstly, in our examination above, we mentioned that Ricoeur's concept of "limit" (or his philosophy of the limits) represents his non-objectivistic conceptual *mode* for approaching the God-question. In Tracy, however, when the concept of "limit" is applied to the God-question, it is used as a conceptual *category* pointing to God as the *ultimate* reality. This is to say that, in Tracy, the meaning of "limit" and that of "ultimate" can be almost identified. The concept of "limit" is a metaphysical qualifier of God. In short, in Tracy, the concept of "limit" is not a mode of thinking as is the case with Ricoeur. Rather, it is an effective category that denotes God's *ultimate* reality without which the "limit" dimension of human existence and language cannot be accounted for. Moreover, for him, God as a "limit-concept" can be justified at the level of a metaphysical certainty through transcendental reflection.[351] However, as our examination of Ricoeur's

section. In this section, it suffices to point out its most fundamental theological implication.

350 Here, the latter position refers to a fundamentalist position that maintains "psychologizing interpretations of the inspiration of the scriptures in the sense of an insufflation of their words into the writers' ears." (Ricoeur, "Toward a Hermeneutic of the Idea of Revelation," 104).

351 Tracy writes that, "If it be proper to speak of God as the objective ground in reality itself for the limit-experience and limit-language of the Christian religion, then it also seems logically necessary to describe this concept 'God' as a limit-concept. One may then ask whether there is in fact a mode of analysis which can investigate the cognitive claims of that kind of limit-concept. Neither the disciplines of empirical science, nor ethics, nor aesthetics, nor general cultural analysis make any such claim. One mode of analysis, metaphysical or transcendental analysis, does." (*BRO*, 148).

hermeneutics of God shows, such a conviction about objective knowledge of God is exactly the one that Ricoeur intends to overcome. We need to recall here that the concept of "limit" in Ricoeur refers to putting a "limit" to the illusion of objective knowledge concerning God in the Kantian sense. It is clear that Tracy does not accommodate the concept of "limit" in this sense. Hence, Tracy's following claim is refutable: his conception of God "may perhaps even meet the excellent demands for 'limit-concepts' developed by Paul Ricoeur."[352]

Secondly, we already mentioned in this chapter that Tracy evaluates the value of the dipolar conception of God (of Charles Hartshorne) in terms of two elements. Firstly, the dipolar conception of God contributes to bridge the chasm between the God of metaphysics and the God of scriptures. Secondly, in this regard, the dipolar conception of God can provide a third alternative that overcomes the two major theological pitfalls of "rationalism" and "fideism." Our observation is that, from the perspective of Ricoeur's hermeneutics of God, this evaluation of Tracy has limitations.

The kernel of Hartshorne's dipolar conception of God is that "we *worship* supreme-being-in-supreme-becoming, supreme-cause-in-supreme-effect; that is, we worship the supreme, not any polar category."[353] This statement reflects an interesting confluence of the scriptural notion of God (a personal God who is the worshipful one) and classical western metaphysical categories (being vs. becoming; cause vs. effect). The central aim of Hartshorne's dipolar conception is to break through the metaphysical incompetence of the classical monopolar conception of God which cannot account for the scriptural divine values of love, responsiveness, etc. His unique contribution can be found in his new systematization of the classical metaphysical categories (thus, it is called "neo-classical") that makes room for the

352    *Ibid.*, 143 n.67.
353    Hartshorne, *Philosophers Speak of God*, 24 (italics mine). Hartshorne's other important statement that sums up his dipolar conception of God is the following: God is *"the* being. God is the universally relevant, the definitive being, the being whose reality includes every other reality and defines its reality." ("A Conversation between Charles Hartshorne and Jan Van der Veken," 133).

scriptural, divine values. However, in Ricoeur's perspective, this dipolar conception of God would still be a kind of onto-theology that reduces all the complexity of biblical polyphonic descriptions of God to a unifying metaphysical system. This rationalistic reduction completes or closes off the dialectical picture of God's reality into such a metaphysical scheme, God as the "supreme-being-in-supreme-becoming or supreme-cause-in-supreme-effect."[354]

Our final question here is whether this dipolar conception of God, which Tracy defends, can have a future in a Christian theism that would be viable in the contemporary context of religious plurality. It is clear that the dipolar conception of God is worked out by means of western-centric metaphysical categories (being vs. becoming, cause vs. effect, etc.) as a way of constructing a universal argument. However, if the biblical discourses about God are to be heard and read in any other world than the west, it seems unlikely that such a western-centric metaphysical account of God will be plausible to those living in different cultural, religious worlds. There is no doubt about the importance of providing rational accounts for religious beliefs that are publicly intelligible and free of fideism. However, as Ricoeur claims, the conceptuality that we need to find today is the one that seriously takes into account the radical "tension and paradoxes" that our epistemological and existential situations address.[355] Religious pluralism is certainly one of the tensions that calls for renewed intellectual integrity in theological reflection. Our contention is that Ricoeur's hermeneutics of God is more adequate to the religious

354 Here, André Cloots' comment on Hartshorne's position is helpful. Cloots says that, "Even when he [Hartshorne] recognizes the basically religious origin of the word 'God,' for him there is after all a rather quick transition from all-inclusive Reality to the all-inclusive God. For Hartshorne, the problem of God tends to become a metaphysical problem, i.e., a problem of how we *think*. That is a danger in all rationalistic and idealistic philosophies. Is the problem of God eventually a problem of how we think? Does the religious person mean by God all-inclusive Reality? Even if not the total meaning, is that after all the central meaning of the religious word 'God'? Religion is more than a pseudo-philosophy." (André Cloots, "Philosophical and Religious Backgrounds of Hartshorne's Panentheism," (unpublished paper, Faculty of Philosophy, K.U. Leuven, Leuven, 2001, 11).

355 See Ricoeur, "Specificity," 131–2.

pluralistic context as a useful conceptuality for Christian theism than the dipolar conception. The essential implication of Ricoeur's hermeneutics of God is that our understanding of God is not established at the level of a static form of certainty prescribed by a predominant culture's metaphysical categories. Rather, it has to do with an experience of an event of disclosure that challenges the recipient of Christian (biblical) discourses, whoever he or she might be, to new forms of life in diverse living contexts. In this regard, Ricoeur's hermeneutics of God allows room for an ongoing and open-ended recontextualization of an experience of God with novelty and alterity in different cultural and religious contexts. Such a possibility of recontextualization is proffered by the imaginative space that is opened up by the dialectic of the complex naming of God in biblical discourses. Hence, it challenges and resists any totalizing or monopolizing approach to God.

# Chapter Four
## Tracy's Fundamental Theology after His Revisionist Model: The Question of God Reformulated

Tracy's theological development reflects the transition between modernity and postmodernity. This chapter aims to explore the shifts and continuities in Tracy's method of fundamental theology since his *Blessed Rage for Order* up to the early 2000s. The central concern in this exploration is to enquire whether Tracy's revised view of fundamental theology during this period, if it exists, can provide better methodological frameworks and insights for our contemporary context of pluralities.

In his new preface to *BRO* (1996), Tracy says that the fundamental arguments developed in this book remain "as necessary now as then."[1] Those fundamental arguments are: "the need to focus in theology on an ever increasing pluralism; the need to develop a genuinely public theology – available, in principle, to all intelligent, reasonable, responsible persons; the usefulness of some form of a correlation method as a heuristic guide for theology; the signal importance of fundamental theology to the entire theological enterprise; the importance, therefore, of reason and its critical, self-correcting function for all theology."[2] Tracy, however, is not hesitant about indicating some necessary revisions of his positions in *BRO*. Two elements are noteworthy here.

Firstly, Tracy points out that in his revisionist model proposed in *BRO*, "hermeneutics" is used in a limited way and not as the very heart of his theological epistemology. As we examined in chapter 2, in *BRO*, Tracy deliberately limits the function of hermeneutics in the-

---

1    David Tracy, "Preface," in *Blessed Rage for Order: The New Pluralism in Theology* (Chicago and London: The University of Chicago Press, 1996) xiii.
2    *Ibid.*

ology to interpreting the Christian texts as an interpretation theory. He makes clear in *BRO* that hermeneutics cannot encompass the whole of theological reflection. In other words, a hermeneutical investigation is *a part* of a fundamental theological enterprise, and should be differentiated from a further, necessary task of truth-validation, namely, a metaphysical-transcendental analysis. However, Tracy explains that since his *The Analogical Imagination* (1981), hermeneutics has constituted his essential theological epistemology. He states that, "indeed, a hermeneutical understanding of reason, history, and theology has defined, for me, how to understand reality and thought most adequately. Inevitably, as all my subsequent work on hermeneutics argues, modern 'rationality' cannot be, therefore, as straightforwardly clear and controlled as 'rationality' frequently functions in *Blessed Rage for Order*."[3] He goes on to say that, "I still firmly believe in the self-correcting power of reason (as Bernard Lonergan nicely names it). However, I am not as sure as I once was that modern reason can produce so unproblematically the kind of uncomplicated metaphysical and transcendental arguments needed for fundamental theology."[4]

Secondly, Tracy indicates that *BRO* does not sufficiently deal with the complex cultural reality of postmodernity. Although his *BRO* involves a critique of the Enlightenment ideal of modernity, "still further qualifications and, beyond that, challenges to a good deal of modernity's self-consciousness and, above all, self-confidence are needed than *Blessed Rage for Order* provides."[5] Tracy's revisionist project in *BRO* aims to resolve a dual crisis: "the crisis of meaning of traditional Christianity in the modern 'post-Christian' period and the present crisis of traditional modernity in the contemporary 'postmodern' world."[6] Interestingly enough, even though Tracy addresses a dual crisis, his whole project is, in fact, far more oriented to the resolution of the former crisis, the modern challenge to traditional Christianity. His revisionist project does not focus on the latter crisis as much as on the former.

3     *Ibid.*, xiv.
4     *Ibid.*
5     *Ibid.*, xiv–xv.
6     *BRO*, 4.

For Tracy, the postmodern challenges that we need to consider more seriously than *BRO* had done are the two essential traits of the postmodern situation: "plurality" and "ambiguity."[7] Regarding "plurality," Tracy explains that today we are confronted with different and possibly conflicting claims to reality. No one person holds the truth. According to Tracy, the dream of romanticism and positivism to have direct access to reality has proved to be illusory. Their common fallacy lies in the view that language is instrumental and peripheral to reality. For the romantic and the positivist, reality is "purely prelinguistic: either my deep feelings or insights from within [romanticism] or my clear grasp of clear, distinct, scientific facts [positivism]."[8] Tracy claims that reality is, however, "neither out there nor in here."[9] Rather, "reality is constituted, not created or simply found, through interpretations" in and through language.[10] Truth consists in historical, contextual, plural, and possibly conflicting interpretations of reality. Tracy says that "truth is the reality we know through our best interpretations."[11] In other words, our claim to truth is, at best, our "relatively adequate" interpretations of reality.[12] This means that "we can never possess absolute certainty. But we can achieve a good –

---

7    For Tracy's analysis of these essential postmodern traits, see his book, *Plurality and Ambiguity: Hermeneutics, Religion, Hope.*

8    *PA*, 49.

9    *Ibid.*, 48.

10   *Ibid.*

11   *Ibid.*

12   *Ibid.* Tracy writes elsewhere that "unlike the later Hegel, none of [us: sic] believes that *we* possess an 'absolute knowledge' in regard to this process of discernment of either our historical situation or the tradition. Like Hegel and unlike the neo-scholastics, we do believe that even reason has a history (Gerrish, Toulmin, Habermas, Küng, Lash, Jüngel, Coleman, Geffré, Jossua), that the 'not-yet,' the negative, is part of tradition and situation alike and all our discernments of each. We believe that we pursue not certainty but understanding, and do so with the knowledge that our interpretations too will prove inadequate. For all is interpretation." (David Tracy, "Some Concluding Reflections on the Conference: Unity Amidst Diversity and Conflict?," in Hans Küng and David Tracy (eds), *Paradigm Change in Theology: A Symposium for the Future* (Edinburgh: T&T Clark Ltd., 1989) 463.

that is, a relatively adequate – interpretation."[13] Hence, this post-modern consciousness of "plurality" resists a premature or definitive closure for determining truth.

Concerning the issue of "ambiguity," Tracy focuses on the "ambiguity" of human history. What he means by "ambiguity" here is that our history has revealed the strange confluence of opposing values, such as "cognitively, the true and the false; morally, the good and the evil; religiously, the holy and the demonic."[14] He says that our history is not simply "contingent" but also "interruptive," having been afflicted by radical evil and distortions.[15] Tracy points out that his theological project in *BRO* does not sufficiently deal with this ambiguity of the human situation. Rather, in *BRO*, he stresses "the experience of fundamental trust" in our secular life.[16] This experience of trust is viewed "as the principal contemporary 'secular' clue for approaching the meaning of religion, God and Christ."[17] However, he doubts whether "the route from fundamental trust to religion and God can prove as direct or as unencumbered" as he once thought. He goes on to say, "Rather, the profound negativities of human existence – personal, societal and historical – seem so pervasive in this age that any route to fundamental trust must be far more circuitous, tentative and even potholed than I had once hoped."[18] In short, the "recognition of the need for both the negative and the positive as always already together in every religious journey has forced me onto a more unsteady route for every question of theology."[19]

According to Tracy, the ambiguity of human history can be more explicitly illuminated by the idea of a "systemic distortion." He

13   *PA*, 22.
14   *Ibid.*, 131 n.15. Tracy writes that "historical ambiguity means that a once seemingly clear historical narrative of progressive Western enlightenment and emancipation has now become a montage of classics and new speak, of startling beauty and revolting cruelty, of partial emancipation and ever-subtler forms of entrapment." (*Ibid.*, 70).
15   See *ibid.*, 68.
16   Tracy, "Defending the Public Character of Theology," 121.
17   *Ibid.*
18   *Ibid.*
19   *Ibid.*, 122.

differentiates this idea from the concept of an "error." He says that today our postmodern consciousness is more keenly aware that something more elusive and overpowering than "conscious errors" is at stake, that is, "unconscious systemic distortions" in our individual and communal lives.[20] He asserts that, "to understand the difference between an error and a systemic distortion is to understand a central difference between modernity and postmodernity."[21] Tracy explains that an "error" represents something that can be *consciously* handled or rectified by means of constructing better rational arguments or adjustments. A "systemic distortion," on the contrary, refers to something that *unconsciously* pervades and dispossesses the self's will to control, which no mere new argument or adjustment can eliminate. For example, every discourse of ours already carries "within itself the anonymous and repressed actuality of highly particular arrangements of power and knowledge."[22] In a sense, all interpretations of every culture, tradition, text cannot be free from unconscious, systematically functioning "material conditions that underlie both its production and its reception."[23] Such underlying conditions are responsible for the occurrence of systemic distortions. When we realize those unconsciously pervading power arrangements, we experience the terrifying, interruptive "otherness within our own discourse and within ourselves."[24] In short, according to Tracy, given that a central postmodern insight is that all experience and all understanding is interpretive, there is no innocent interpreter, no innocent interpretation, no innocent text, tradition, culture, etc.[25]

Tracy's new treatise on fundamental theology which updates his postmodern concerns and agendas in a full scale is not yet available.[26]

---

20    *PA*, 76.
21    *Ibid.*, 73.
22    *Ibid.*, 79.
23    *Ibid.*, 77.
24    *Ibid.*, 79.
25    See *ibid.*, 78–9.
26    In an interview with Scott Holland in 2002, Tracy said that his new book on God which is an essential theme of fundamental theology is forthcoming. See "This Side of God: A Conversation with David Tracy," in *CrCur*, 52 (2002) 54–9.

Because of this limitation of resources, we cannot conduct a thorough analysis concerning his later positions as we did of *BRO*. Our analysis will, therefore, focus on uncovering how Tracy tries to grapple with new methodological questions of fundamental theology addressed in new situations.

We divide into two phases Tracy's methodological development of fundamental theology after *BRO*: (1) the 1980s; (2) from the 1990s to the early 2000s. It can be said that *BRO* is the matrix of Tracy's fundamental theology from which his later revisions have emerged. Hence, our discussion of each phase shall focus on his revised positions in comparison to *BRO*. Prior to discussing the first phase, we need to discuss a pivotal methodological principle of Tracy's fundamental theology, the so-called correlational model.

# I. The Constant Methodological Principle of Tracy's Fundamental Theology: A Correlational Model

*1. Tracy's Correlational Model in Two (Broad and Narrow) Senses*

Since his *BRO* up to the present time, one of the most constant and essential methodological principles of Tracy's fundamental theology is the correlational model (or the method of correlation). In the 1980s, we can find Tracy's slightly revised view of the correlational model, one that nevertheless retains the basic idea of that model developed in *BRO*. We can lay out his revised view in two, broad and narrow, senses.

Firstly, for Tracy, in a broad sense, a correlational model refers to a mode of theological reflection which attempts a mutually critical correlation between an *interpretation* of the Christian tradition and an *interpretation* of the contemporary situation.[27] More concretely, it

---

27    For Tracy's correlational theological model in the 1980s, see David Tracy, "Particular Questions within General Consensus," in *JES*, 17 (1980) 33–9; *The Analogical Imagination* (1981); "Hermeneutical Reflections in the New

refs to a mutually critical correlation between the theologian's interpretation of the Christian event and tradition in a particular situation, and the theologian's interpretation of the situation by means of the event and tradition.[28] There is a slight difference between the correlational model proposed in *BRO* and the above formulation. In *BRO*, Tracy proposes that, "The theological task will involve a critical correlation of the results of the investigations of the two sources of theology," namely, the Christian tradition and common human experience.[29] The term, "investigations," in this proposal is transformed into "interpretation" in his new formulation. This transformation reflects Tracy's full attention to hermeneutics as an essential theological epistemology in the 1980s. Tracy explains that his new formulation of the correlational model can be shared by all contemporary theologians who take hermeneutics seriously: namely, the theologians who "have embraced a situated historical, practical understanding and have abandoned the illusion of a context-less certainty."[30] Tracy explains that, "In one sense, this hermeneutical formulation [of the correlational model] is simply a rendering explicit and deliberate of the fact which unites all forms of theology: that every Christian theology *is* interpretation of Christianity."[31]

According to Tracy, this hermeneutical formulation of the correlational model opens one to a pluralism of individual theologies at a substantive level. Precisely because we are dealing with *inter-*

Paradigm," in Hans Küng and David Tracy (eds), *Paradigm Change in Theology: A Symposium for the Future*, 34–62; "Some Concluding Reflections on the Conference: Unity Amidst Diversity and Conflict?," in idem, 461–71. On Tracy's correlational theology, see Werner G. Jeanrond, "Correlational Theology and the Chicago School," in Roger A. Badham (ed.), *Introduction to Christian Theology* (Louisville: Westminster John Knox Press, 1998) 137–53; idem, "Theology in the Context of Pluralism and Postmodernity: David Tracy's Theological Method," in David Jasper (ed.), *Postmodernism, Literature and the Future of Theology* (New York: St. Martin's Press, 1993) 143–63.

28    See *AI*, 405.

29    *BRO*, 45.

30    Tracy, "Some Concluding Reflections on the Conference: Unity Amidst Diversity and Conflict?," 464. Hereafter this work will be referred to as "Some Concluding Reflections."

31    *Ibid.*, 462.

*pretations* of the Christian tradition and the situation, there can be no theological claims to "immediacy nor to certainty."[32] There can be different, often conflictual, individual interpretations of the Christian tradition and situation, which may engender a pluralism of theologies.[33] This is to say that the hermeneutical formulation of the correlational model renders explicit "the [contemporary] need to interpret the plural and ambiguous tradition, the need to give up the quest for an illusory ahistorical certainty and live the quest for a situated understanding of the Christian tradition in a particular place at a particular time."[34] Basing himself on this hermeneutical character of the theological correlation, Tracy claims that the correlational model is, thus, "a general heuristic model – no more, no less."[35] This means that, as a heuristic and general method, the correlational model "can [only] *guide* discussions and assessments of concrete programmes of particular differing, arguing, conflicting theologies."[36] The correlational model does not determine the concrete program of a theological inquiry which "is always hermeneutically determined by the question, the subject matter."[37] Tracy explains that the concept, "correlation," is a "logical category" in the sense that it "allows for the full spectrum of logical possibilities from identity through continuity and similarity to paradoxical and dialectical relationships to radical (confrontational) non-identity" between two poles in correlation.[38] No theologian can decide before his or her actual theological inquiry which of these possibilities will emerge. As a method, a correlational model "is always and only a heuristic guide: a useful, critical guide which, if

---

32  *Ibid.*
33  Tracy writes that the particularity of theologies "is largely determined by the particular set of material questions and discernments of our contemporary situation which demand a theological response, and by the equally particular interpretations of certain symbols, doctrines, images and narratives, and so on, chosen from the Christian tradition to respond to those questions." (*Ibid.*, 461).
34  *Ibid.*, 463.
35  *Ibid.*
36  *Ibid.*, 463–4 (italics mine).
37  Tracy, "The Uneasy Alliance Reconceived: Catholic Theological Method, Modernity, and Postmodernity," 563. Hereafter, this work will be referred to as "Uneasy Alliance."
38  Tracy, "Particular Questions within General Consensus," 35–6.

allied to flexible criteria, can aid but never *replace* the actual theological inquiry."[39] In other words, it can never replace concrete material theologies "any more than the general and abstract can replace the concrete."[40]

Secondly, for Tracy, in a narrower sense, a correlational model refers to a theological method which attempts a critical dialogue between Christian understanding and other forms of rational thinking (such as, philosophy, history, anthropology, sociology, psychology, linguistics, literary theories, natural sciences, etc.). For him, this endeavor of correlation, in particular, is essential for constructing theology as a public discourse, a central task of fundamental theology. In hermeneutically-informed theologies, this correlational task refers to "the difficult, necessary exercise in the quest for some understanding of how all claims to meaning and truth in the revelatory and salvific manifestations of faith" cohere or does not cohere with what one otherwise holds as reasonable.[41]

According to Tracy, in this narrower sense as well, the correlational model serves only as a heuristic guide to a theological inquiry. For example, theologians such as Thomas Aquinas, Karl Rahner, Paul Tillich, Bernard Lonergan, Edward Schillebeeckx, and Langdon Gilkey all attempted some form of correlational theology, and were keen on this second sense of correlation. This was so despite the fact that these theologians' endeavors are distinguished by important differences in their respective theological motivations, objectives, and programs.

The correlational model in both senses that Tracy defends is not, however, shared by all contemporary theologians. Among others, we would like to focus on the so-called postliberal theologians represented by Hans W. Frei and George A. Lindbeck.[42] We will not deal

---

39    Tracy, "Uneasy Alliance," 563 (italics mine).
40    Tracy, "Some Concluding Reflections," 464.
41    Tracy, "Uneasy Alliance," 568.
42    For an extensive study on George Lindbeck's postliberal theological program with a wide-ranging bibliography relevant to this theme, see Jeffrey C.K. Goh, *Christian Tradition Today: A Postliberal Vision of Church and World* (Leuven: Peeters Press, 2000). Goh explains that "postliberal theology refers to the theological movement that began with Hans Frei's proposals for intratextual

with these postliberal theologians here. Our concern here is to briefly explain Tracy's perception of Lindbeck's anti-correlationalist position.


## 2. Tracy's Perception of George Lindbeck's
## Anti-Correlationalist Position

In order to explain Tracy's criticism of Lindbeck's position, we need to look at two important theses of Lindbeck's postliberal program developed in his *The Nature of Doctrine*.[43] The first is Lindbeck's claim that 'cultural-linguistic' model is appropriate for the study of religion. The second is that an intratextual theology is necessary for the survival of the distinctive Christian faith-tradition in contemporary pluralistic settings.

Lindbeck's "cultural-linguistic" model views religions "as comprehensive interpretive schemes, usually embodied in myths or narratives and heavily ritualized, which structure human experience and understanding of self and world."[44] According to this model, religion functions like a cultural or linguistic system that "shapes the entirety of life and thought."[45] In this view of religion, religious doctrines are approached "not as expressive symbols or as truth claims, but as communally authoritative rules of discourse, attitude, and action."[46] In other words, doctrines function as "regulative prin-

---

biblical hermeneutics and found its most forceful and systematic articulation in George Lindbeck. Lindbeck's postliberal theology is indebted, hermeneutically, to Frei rather than Ricoeur, theologically, to Barth rather than Schleiermacher, philosophically, to the later work of Wittgenstein and, culturally, Lindbeck's counterfashionable stance is closer to Alasdair MacIntyre [...] than to any form of the regnant 'liberal individualism' of the [sic] Western society." (Goh, *ibid.*, 7 n.19).

43    Lindbeck, The Nature of Doctrine: Religion and Theology in a Postliberal Age (Philadelphia: The Westminster Press, 1984).
44    *Ibid.*, 32.
45    *Ibid.*, 33.
46    *Ibid.*, 18.

ciples" directing members of a faith-community to speak and act in particular ways.

Lindbeck's "cultural-linguistic" proposal is set over against the liberal tradition's approach (in Lindbeck's terminology, the "experiential-expressive" model) according to which different religions are diverse representations or objectifications of a common, primordial, pre-reflective experience which can be named as religious. Lindbeck illustrates the problematic element in this liberal tradition's view as follows: because the primordial religious experience "is said to be common to a wide diversity of religions, it is difficult or impossible to specify its distinctive features, and yet unless this is done, the assertion of commonality becomes logically and empirically vacuous."[47] For Lindbeck, the liberal tradition's search for universally applicable foundations to ground religion, be they metaphysical, existential, phenomenological, or hermeneutical, is misplaced, because there are no neutral criteria outside a religion for evaluating its distinctive meaning. In relation to this criticism, Werner Jeanrond remarks that the "defenders of Lindbeck's model sometimes name the line taken by Tracy [especially in *Blessed Rage for Order*] or Lonergan as 'foundationalism', since for them religion rests on certain experiential and expressive foundations which are discussed in 'fundamental theology'. For Lindbeck, fundamental theology has thus become an impossible undertaking."[48] What Lindbeck finds problematic in the fundamental theology (and also in the correlational theology) developed in the liberal tradition is its contribution to the erosion of Christian identity and particularity. As liberal theology translates Christian categories into terms intelligible to the modern world, it measures the Christian distinctive claims by means of its chosen interpretive framework, be they transcendental Thomist, phenomenological, existential, or Marxist. All of these are extrabiblical in nature. In Lindbeck's view, this judgment of Christian claims by means of extra-biblical conceptualities is to the detriment of Christian identity and particularity. Repudiating any extrabiblical criteria or

47  *Ibid.*, 32.
48  Jeanrond, "Theology in the Context of Pluralism and Postmodernity: David Tracy's Theological Method," 156.

foundations, Lindbeck, therefore, intends to emphasize that "Christian theology, to be faithful, must be configured in terms that closely adhere to the normativity of the biblical world as it has been read and interpreted in the ecclesial community through the ages."[49] In other words, the task of theology, in keeping with his "cultural-linguistic" approach, is "to give a normative explication of the meaning a religion has for its adherents."[50]

For Lindbeck, one way of pursuing this task is an "intratextual" hermeneutics.[51] His plea for an "intratextual" hermeneutics is grounded in his standpoint that "religions, like languages, can be understood only in their own terms, not by transposing them into an alien speech."[52] An "intratextual" reading, accordingly, focuses on decoding the *immanent* meaning that is constituted by the *uses* of a specific (biblical) language in its own tradition. The meaning that an "intratextual" reading is concerned with is "not something behind, beneath, or in front of the text; not something that the text reveals, discloses, implies, or suggests to those with extraneous metaphysical, historical, or experiential interests. It must rather be what the text says in terms of the communal language of which the text is an instantiation."[53] Moreover, according to Lindbeck, this intratextual approach is attentive to the direction of interpretation: the scriptures

---

49     Goh, Christian Tradition Today, 175.

50     Lindbeck, The Nature of Doctrine, 113.

51     *Ibid.*, 114.

52     *Ibid.*, 129. Lindbeck explains that "the proper way to determine what 'God' signifies, for example, is by examining how the word operates within a religion and thereby shapes reality and experience rather than by first establishing its propositional or experiential meaning and reinterpreting or reformulating its uses accordingly." (*Ibid.*, 114).

53     *Ibid.*, 120. For example, Lindbeck claims that, "The believer, so an intratextual approach would maintain, is not told primarily to be conformed to a reconstructed Jesus of history (as Hans Küng maintains), nor to a metaphysical Christ of faith (as in much of the propositionalist tradition), nor to an abba experience of God (as for Schillebeeckx), nor to an agapeic way of being in the world (as for David Tracy), but he or she is rather to be conformed to the Jesus Christ depicted in the narrative. An intratextual reading tries to derive the interpretive framework that designates the theologically controlling sense from the literary structure of the text itself." (*Ibid.*).

provide the interpretive framework for 'extrascriptural' realities, never the other way around. He claims, "Intratextual theology redescribes reality within the scriptural framework rather than translating Scripture into extrascriptural categories. It is the text, so to speak, which absorbs the world, rather than the world the text."[54] In short, for Lindbeck, the primary theological responsibility lies in invigorating and preserving the distinctive Christian faith-tradition, and this calls for an intratextual strategy that eschews all foundationalist and correlational enterprises.

In his review article on Lindbeck's *The Nature of Doctrine*,[55] Tracy presents a critique of Lindbeck's "cultural-linguistic" program. Tracy's criticism can be summarized in two major points

Firstly, Tracy claims that Lindbeck's analysis of the liberal theological program, which Lindbeck categorizes as an "experiential-expressive" model, "is seriously, even fatally, flawed."[56] An interesting element in Tracy's criticism of Lindbeck's analysis is that Tracy does not object to Lindbeck's critical descriptions of the problems within the "experiential-expressive" model. Rather, Tracy's criticism focuses on the fact that Lindbeck ignores the efforts of thinkers in the liberal tradition to address precisely those issues that Lindbeck points out as problematic. For instance, one of the most problematic aspects of the liberal tradition, for Lindbeck, is that this tradition is grounded in the errant conviction that there is a unified essence to all religions. The liberals find this unified essence "in the prereflective experiential depths of the self and regard the public or outer features of religion as expressive and evocative objectifications (i.e., nondiscursive symbols) of internal experience."[57] In short, for Lindbeck, the liberal theologians "understand inner-pre-reflective experience as 'foundational' and all language and culture as merely 'expressive' of that foundational, non-discursive experience. They

---

54    *Ibid.*, 118.
55    Tracy, "Lindbeck's New Program for Theology: A Reflection," in *Thomist* 49 (1985) 460–72. Hereafter, this work will be referred to as "Lindbeck's Program."
56    Tracy, "Lindbeck's Program," 461.
57    Lindbeck, *The Nature of Doctrine*, 21.

possess a 'unilateral' understanding of the relationship of experience and language as well as of experience and culture when what we need is a 'dialectical' understanding of these complex relationships."[58] Tracy contends that this issue, however, has been reconsidered within the liberal tradition by the taking of two important turns: (1) the turn to a de-expressivist understanding of language and experience by means of hermeneutics, and (2) the turn to a radical "de-privatizing" of the liberal tradition by means of socio-political-cultural theories.

Tracy explains that, "The major argument of the hermeneutical tradition since Gadamer has been against Romantic 'expressivist' understandings of language's relationship to 'experience'. This work, in turn, has been what has allowed a major transformation of the Schleiermacher-Tillich-Rahner-Lonergan experiential paradigm into an explicitly hermeneutical one."[59] The hermeneutical understanding of the relationship between language and experience is no longer "unilateral," viz., language is merely expressive of pre-reflective, primordial experience. Instead, it is "dialectical," viz., we experience and understand *in* and *through* the languages available to us. Language in the Romantic 'expressivist' reading is instrumental. However, in a hermeneutical approach, Tracy explains, "language is not an instrument that I can pick up and put down at will; it is always already there, surrounding and invading all I experience, understand, judge, decide, and act upon. I belong to my language far more than it belongs to me, and through that language I find myself participating in this particular history and society."[60] Moreover, according to Tracy, this dialectical approach to language reintroduces society and history into our understanding of language. Modern socio-political-cultural theories (such as Freudian psychoanalytic theory, the Marxist critique of ideology, and the critical theories of the Frankfurt school) contribute to reveal that our discourse (language) bears within itself the anonymous, interruptive, repressed realities of history and society. This critical insight helps liberal theologians to be critical of the "privatist" accounts of the earlier liberal traditions (viz., language is instrumental

58    Tracy, "Lindbeck's Program," 462.
59    *Ibid.*, 463.
60    *PA*, 49–50.

to express or represent some deep, internal, primordial, nonlinguistic truth inside the self).

In sum, according to Tracy, Lindbeck's charge of "experiential-expressivism" is not applicable to the liberal theologians' position which has moved beyond earlier experiential formulations by developing hermeneutical-political theologies. Tracy asserts that "the label 'experiential-expressivism' does not fit as an accurate philosophical description of the alternative 'liberals' Lindbeck paints in such broad strokes."[61] In short, the label of "experiential-expressivism" is too restricted to characterize the whole range of the liberal theological tradition. Tracy states that Lindbeck seems to believe that:

> any theologian who agrees with the basic thrust of Rahner or Lonergan (as I clearly do) must also end up agreeing with Rahner's 'anonymous Christian' position or Lonergan's belief that F. Heiler had located a unified essence to all religions. If this material theological issue of the possible unity of essence of religion is the real theological problem for Lindbeck (he devotes considerable space to it), this one difference, at least, is easily resolved. For no one of their later hermeneutical-political descendents any longer agrees with the positions of their great predecessors on this 'unity of essence' issue: witness Gilkey vis-à-vis Tillich, Metz or Küng vis-à-vis Rahner, or Burrell or myself vis-à-vis Lonergan on these crucial issues of 'dialogue', 'essence' and 'unity-plurality'.[62]

Tracy claims that the turn to this hermeneutical-political understanding of language and experience is, however, distinct from Lindbeck's seemingly new 'unilateral' move from experience to language in his "cultural-linguistic" model. In other words, this hermeneutical-political turn in the liberal tradition does not suggest that "we should, in effect, abandon half the dialectic by simply placing all experience under the new guardianship of and production by the grammatical rules of the codes of language."[63] This statement of Tracy seems to point to the lack of a "correlation" between experience and (the Christian) language in Lindbeck's "cultural-linguistic" model. For Tracy, Lindbeck's "cultural-linguistic" model is another form of a "unilateral" approach to the relationship between experience and

61  Tracy, "Lindbeck's Program," 465.
62  *Ibid.*, 467–8.
63  *Ibid.*, 464.

language in such a way that language is a constitutive condition for experience, but not vice versa.[64]

According to Tracy, the distinctiveness of the liberal theologians who are hermeneutically and socio-politically informed vis-à-vis Lindbeck is that while the former are critical of their earlier tradition's expressivist-privatist accounts of language and experience, they maintain: (1) their tradition's discovery of a non-empiricist notion of "experience" and (2) the "correlational" enterprise of their tradition. Tracy claims that the liberals contributed to shape a non-empiricist, integrative notion of "experience": viz., experience cannot simply be identified as a collection of momentary sense-reports recorded within the human mind without reference to the social, cultural, and historical world which is its living context. The contexts of living and meaning belong to experience itself; experience is rendered as lived in the actual world and as including feelings, moods, attitudes, values, sociality, and historicality; in short, experience is intrinsically and systematically relational, social, and temporal. In their hermeneutical-political theologies, the liberal theologians take contemporary

---

64    The following statement of Lindbeck backs up Tracy's assessment of Lindbeck's position as unilateral, not correlational: "Religious change or innovation must be understood, not as proceeding from new experiences, but as resulting from the interactions of a cultural-linguistic system with changing situations. Religious traditions are not transformed, abandoned, or replaced because of an upwelling of new or different ways of feeling about the self, world, or God, but because a religious interpretive scheme (embodied, as it always is, in religious practice and belief) develops anomalies in its application in new contexts. This produces, among other things, negative effects, negative experiences, even by the religion's own norms. Prophetic figures apprehend, often with dramatic vividness, how the inherited patterns of belief, practice, and ritual need to be (and can be) reminted. They discover the concepts that remove the anomalies. Religious experiences in the sense of feelings, sentiments, or emotions then result from the new conceptual patterns instead of being their source. Thus, if one follows this account, Luther did not invent his doctrine of justification by faith because he had a tower experience, but rather the tower experience was made possible by his discovering (or thinking he discovered) the doctrine in the Bible [...] First come the objectivities of the religion, its language, doctrines, liturgies, and modes of action, and it is through these that passions are shaped into various kinds of what is called religious experience." (Lindbeck, *The Nature of Doctrine*, 39).

"experience" seriously in this integrative sense: namely, it serves as an important correlate with the Christian tradition in their mutually critical correlational enterprises. In sum, Tracy claims that hermeneutical-political theologians in the liberal tradition have challenged some of their tradition's earlier formulations "without abandoning the noble correlative enterprise of the great liberals and their self-critical successors, such dialectical or neo-orthodox theologians as Tillich, Bultmann, early Barth, Rahner, and Lonergan. To recognize an 'anomaly' is not necessarily to abandon completely a paradigm. It is to rethink the paradigm in such manner that its accomplishments are not rejected in the transformation of its problems."[65]

The second issue that Tracy's criticism exposes is "the 'cash-value' of Lindbeck's own 'cultural-linguistic' model for the crucial issue of 'truth-claims' in theology."[66] For Tracy, Lindbeck's "cultural-linguistic" program is not without worthwhile elements. Tracy explains that Lindbeck's approach to doctrines as "rules" or "regulative theories" seems to be "a way forward out of many propositional-confessional impasses."[67] Another illuminating element of Lindbeck's program is that it proposes "one way to formulate the grammatical aspect of theology's wider task."[68] This element refers to Lindbeck's formulation of the theological task as offering "a normative explication of the meaning" that a religious tradition (embodied in narratives, doctrines, practices, etc.) provides for its own community.[69] Tracy states that "no theologian should deny that one major task of all responsible theology is to show how it is the tradition itself that is being interpreted and not interpreted away or invented. Lindbeck's grammatical model for this task is illuminating."[70] In this context, Lindbeck's "intratextual" hermeneutics can be, to some extent, a useful theological strategy for being faithful to the tradition.[71]

65     Tracy, "Lindbeck's Program," 465.
66     *Ibid.*, 467.
67     *Ibid.*, 471.
68     *Ibid.*
69     Lindbeck, *The Nature of Doctrine*, 113.
70     Tracy, "Lindbeck's Program," 468.
71     Tracy says that correlational models of theology should be "fully open to all proposals for assuring an appropriately Christian identity, including the fruitful

However, Tracy's central question here is whether Lindbeck's formulation of the theological task as a grammatical analysis of the tradition (based on the notion of "intratextuality") can encompass the full range of that task. The issue Tracy has in mind is the question of whether Lindbeck's "cultural-linguistic" program offers adequate and sufficient criteria to legitimate truth-claims in theology. More theoretically put, can Lindbeck's "cultural-linguistic" approach, which wants theology to be worked out purely from *within* the confessing community, evade the charge of both relativism and fideism? Tracy says that, "I regret to say that I do not believe that he [Lindbeck] has solved the issues he has set for himself (viz. relativism and fideism)."[72] According to Tracy, it will be hardly persuasive to say that "Lindbeck's 'epistemological realism' is other than relativism with a new name or that his 'cultural-linguistic' grammatical model for theology is other than confessionalism."[73] In Tracy's view, "Lindbeck's substantive theological position is a methodologically sophisticated version of Barthian confessionalism."[74] In the conclusion of *The Nature of Doctrine*, Lindbeck portrays his "rule" theory of doctrine as a *new* and better paradigm in opposition to "propositional" and "experiential-expressivist" construals of doctrines which are thereby viewed as *old* and unhelpful.[75] Tracy does not agree with this position and remarks that, "Lindbeck's 'cultural-linguistic' model is, I fear, less a new paradigm which eliminates the anomalies of the old than a new paradigm which first ignores the accomplishments of the old and then develops new-old anomalies of its own (as on 'truth-claims')."[76]

---

intratextual studies of the anticorrelational theologians." (Tracy, "Uneasy Alliance," 557).

72    Tracy, "Lindbeck's Program," 468. Lindbeck claims that his intratextual approach implies neither relativism, viz., turning religions "into self-enclosed and incommensurable intellectual ghettoes," nor fideism, viz., where the "choice between religions is purely arbitrary, a matter of blind faith." (Lindbeck, *The Nature of Doctrine*, 128).

73    Tracy, "Lindbeck's Program," 469–70.

74    *Ibid.*, 465.

75    See Lindbeck, *The Nature of Doctrine*, 135.

76    Tracy, "Lindbeck's Program," 466.

In Tracy's view, the relativistic and fideistic dilemma of Lindbeck's "cultural-linguistic" program derives largely from the fact that it does not provide any methodological devices or criteria for a critique of one's own religious tradition. Lindbeck's intratextual strategy can hardly take into account the need to attend to the other, not only the other who is outside one's own religious tradition, but even the other within that tradition or even in the interpreter him/herself. For Tracy, in contrast to Lindbeck, a critical *and* self-critical mode of theologizing is necessary, and this is not possible unless Christian understanding engages in a dialogue with other forms of rational thinking. In other words, a mutually-critical correlational method is called for. Tracy claims that, "To abandon that critical correlational task of theology is to abandon, within theology, its reflective task and to abandon as well the claims of all the prophets and mystics to speak directly and purposively to the human search for meaning and truth."[77] Put differently, for him, a correlational model is "the only hope for a way forward for theological method," which does not claim "either control through purely neutral, a-historical notions of 'rationality', nor purely Romantic notions of 'inner feelings', nor deceptively 'economical' notions of the purely grammatical task of theology."[78]

Finally, Tracy wants to make clear that a correlational model should not be understood as a static or fixed methodological mould which is immune to any self-critique or self-revision. On the contrary, it is "always in need of re-examining its mode of inquiry" in ever-changing contexts. In what follows, we will examine Tracy's methodological views of fundamental theology in different phases (the 1980s and the 1990s). In the process of his methodological revisions, we shall see how Tracy consistently holds the need for "an ever revisionary and ever self-critical" correlational theology in new situations.[79]

77  Tracy, "Uneasy Alliance," 568.
78  *Ibid.*, 556 (the first quotation) and Tracy, "Lindbeck's Program," 470–1 (the second quotation).
79  Tracy, "Uneasy Alliance," 560.

## II. Tracy's Methodological View of Fundamental Theology in the 1980s

As we indicated earlier, the most important changes in Tracy's methodological approach to fundamental theology in this period can be summarized by two elements: (1) a concern to explicitly address the postmodern consciousness of the plurality and ambiguity embedded in human intellectual, cultural, political, and religious realities, thereby showing his keen concern with "otherness" and "difference"; (2) a concern to employ a hermeneutical model of "conversation" as the most adequate way to elucidate truth.

In his book, *Plurality and Ambiguity* (1987), Tracy attempts an analysis of the contemporary postmodern situation in relation to rationality, language, history, and religion. This book is not concerned with theology per se, but with a diagnosis of the new *context* of theology. Against the backdrop of this situational analysis, Tracy wrote an important article which specifically concerns the methodology of fundamental theology adequate to the postmodern situation.[80] This article shows how he attempts a first methodological revision after *BRO*. This article, however, does not offer a full treatment of his new position, but only proposes several new criteria for fundamental theology. In what follows, we will focus on these new criteria.

Tracy claims that, "If theology is to continue to have a systematically apologetic [or correlational] task, and if that task is to prove adequate to the contemporary postmodern situation, then new criteria for the task are needed."[81] For him, this need is made apparent by the self-critique that traditional fundamental theologies (including his own revisionist model) "relied too exclusively on transcendental inquiry – and, too often, models of that inquiry not explicitly related to the questions of language (and thereby plurality and historicity) and questions of history (and thereby ambiguity and postmodern suspicion, not merely modern critique)."[82] What Tracy proposes with his

---

80    Tracy, "Uneasy Alliance."
81    *Ibid.*, 560.
82    *Ibid.*

new criteria is, however, not to completely waive the transcendental reflection of the modern Catholic tradition. Rather, his aim is to revise "the kind of transcendental reflection proper to theological inquiry" such that it incorporates postmodern challenges and critiques. In other words, he tries to combine both modern and postmodern approaches in a methodological system. In this regard, Tracy's position at this stage (the late 1980s) is transitional between modernity and post-modernity.

In the above article, Tracy presents three new criteria for fundamental theology.[83] These new criteria are particularly concerned with the question of *truth*. They are as follows: (1) fundamental theology needs "the hermeneutical notion of truth as manifestation"; (2) it needs to show how a hermeneutical claim to truth "coheres or does not cohere with what we otherwise consider reasonable"; (3) it needs to show "the ethical-political implications" of hermeneutical truth-claims.[84] Tracy explains that these three criteria are (1) "not intended to be cumulative but demand a coherence of all three in order to function properly"[85]; (2) not supposed to "replace the actual task of theological inquiry on particular questions but only inform it with the

---

83    Tracy also mentions these new criteria in another article in which he looks back on his theological reflection during the decade of the 1980s. David Tracy, "God, Dialogue and Solidarity: A Theologian's Refrain," in *ChCent*, 107 (1990) 900–4.

84    Tracy, "Uneasy Alliance," 561. Tracy indicates that the source for these new criteria is William James' three criteria for assessing religious experience. He revised them for a more properly theological task. James' three criteria for assessing religious experience are as follows: religious experience can be evaluated by (1) spiritual judgments, judgments based on our own immediate feeling; (2) by its logical coherence with "the rest of what we hold as true"; (3) by its pragmatical relation to ethical consequences. In short, these three criteria can be summarized as "*immediate luminousness*," "*philosophical reasonableness*," and "*moral helpfulness*." (William James, *The Varieties of Religious Experiences: A Study in Human Nature* (London: Longmans, Green and Co., 1959) 19).

85    Tracy, "Uneasy Alliance," 561 n.48.

kind of questions and some general heuristic criteria for asking those questions."[86]

In the following, we will examine how Tracy attempts a methodological turn in fundamental theology from a monolithic transcendental reflection (*BRO*'s position) to a tripartite hermen-eutical-transcendental-pragmatic reflection. Let us look at each of the three criteria.

## 1. The First Criterion: Truth as Manifestation

### A Departure from the Foundationalist Stance of His Revisionist Model?

In the revisionist model of *BRO*, Tracy relies on a metaphysical-transcendental reflection for resolving the question of truth. In other words, for him, one's theological claims can be validated as true only when they are justified by a metaphysical-transcendental reflection. Hermeneutics is not included in this process for determining their truth-status. Now, Tracy changes his position to the extent that

86 *Ibid.*, 570. In order to properly understand Tracy's revised methodological position as expressed by these three criteria, we need to briefly compare these criteria with his five methodological theses proposed in *BRO*. The summary of the five theses are as follows: (1) There are two principle theological sources, common human experience and the Christian tradition (Christian texts); (2) The most suitable method for investigating the first source is phenomenology; (3) The most suitable method for investigating the second source is historical and hermeneutical inquiries; (4) The results of the investigation of these two sources ought to be critically correlated; (5) The truth status of the results of the investigation of the two sources should be validated by a transcendental or metaphysical mode of reflection. Among these five theses, the fifth one is concerned with the question of truth. As we will see in this section and also later, Tracy's important methodological revisions regarding fundamental theology have always to do with the fifth thesis, the question of truth. The first four theses have not been subject to a notable modification. Tracy's new criteria explain how he modifies his understanding of truth and the validation of the truth-status of theological claims. In addition to this adjustment, he brings an ethical-political element into his new criteria which is not found in his previous five theses.

hermeneutics serves as the primary philosophical reflection for elucidating truth. Here, the term, "primary," however, serves as a reminder that Tracy does not abandon a transcendental reflection completely but regards it as a secondary or complementary function. This complementary use of transcendental reflection will be examined in our discussion of his second criterion.

It might be said that Tracy's attempt at the validation of theological truth-claims in his revisionist model is "foundationalist" in character. This assessment does not accord with Tracy's own. As we already indicated in the preceding chapter, Tracy does not regard either transcendental Thomism or process thought as objectivistic and foundationalist.[87] However, our observation is that Tracy's revisionist pursuit of truth follows the strategy that is now commonly called "foundationalism."[88] A short explanation is in order.

At the heart of the classical foundationalist agenda is the quest for epistemological certainty in our claims to knowledge.[89] Foun-

---

87   Cf. *PA*, 30 and 122 n.9.
88   For the definition of "foundationalism," we refer to Stanley J. Grenz and John R. Franke, *Beyond Foundationalism: Shaping Theology in a Postmodern Context* (Louisville: Westminster John Knox Press, 2001) 28–32; W. Jay Wood, *Epistemology: Becoming Intellectually Virtuous* (Downers Grove: InterVarsity Press, 1998) 77–104; Jaegwon Kim, "What is 'Naturalized Epistemology'?," in Ernest Sosa and Jaegon Kim (eds), *Epistemology: An Anthology* (Oxford: Blackwell Publishers Ltd., 2002) 302. See also Richard J. Bernstein, *Beyond Objectivism and Relativism: Science, Hermeneutics, and Praxis* (Oxford: Basil Blackwell Publisher Limited, 1983) 16–20; Stanley Hauerwas, Nancey Murphy and Mark Nation, *Theology Without Foundations: Religious Practice and the Future of Theological Truth* (Nashville: Abingdon Press, 1994) 9–12.
89   John R. Franke explains that, "The problem of error and the quest for epistemological certainty – the quest for a means by which we can justify our claims to knowledge – dates at least to the ancient Greek philosophers. But in Western philosophical history, this difficulty became acute in the Enlightenment. Historians routinely look to the French philosopher René Descartes as the progenitor of modern foundationalism. In contrast to premodern Western philosophers who tended simply to assume the foundations for philosophical inquiry, Descartes began his philosophical work by attempting to establish that foundation." (Stanley J. Grenz and John R. Franke, *Beyond Foundationalism*, 31).

dationalists are convinced that the only way to fulfill this quest is "to find some means of grounding the entire edifice of human knowledge on invincible certainty."[90] These "means of grounding" refer to epistemological foundations which consist of "either a set of un-questioned beliefs or certain first principles on the basis of which the pursuit of knowledge can proceed."[91] More specifically, the foun-dationalist strategy requires two stages for its justification of truth. Firstly, it identifies "a set of beliefs that are 'directly' justified in that they are justified without deriving their justified status from that of any other belief."[92] Secondly, it explains "how other beliefs may be 'indirectly' or 'inferentially' justified by standing in an appropriate relation to those already justified."[93] The "directly" justified beliefs or "basic" beliefs in the first stage "constitute the foundation upon which the superstructure of 'nonbasic' or 'derived' beliefs is to rest."[94]

In Tracy's revisionist model, this foundationalist strategy is executed in the following way. Tracy regards human "existential faith" in life's ultimate worth as a "directly" justified or immediate belief. In other words, for him, this "existential faith" is "supposedly universal, context-free, and available – at least theoretically – to any rational person."[95] For him, a religious ("limit") dimension operative in common human experience has to do with this "existential faith." Out of the two modalities of the "limit" dimension, the "limit-of" dimension, in particular, is expressive of this "existential faith." For him, this "existential faith" represents the necessary or transcendental condition of the possibility of all our existing and understanding. Tracy attempts to validate God's reality as universal and true (in other words, the epistemic certainty of God's existence) by grounding this transcendental condition in God. God is the sole objective referent of this universal, context-free "existential faith." In short, our "existential faith," or "limit" experiences (or religious experiences) serve as an

90    *Ibid.*, 30.
91    *Ibid.*
92    Jaegon Kim, "What is 'Naturalized Epistemology'?," 302.
93    *Ibid.*
94    *Ibid.*
95    Grenz and Franke, *Beyond Foundationalism*, 30.

epistemological foundation or means for constructing our claim to God's reality.

*Truth as Manifestation in Conversation*

We may say that Tracy's first criterion expresses his intention to replace the above (foundationalist) stance with the hermeneutical approach to truth. Incorporating a Heideggerian understanding of truth, Tracy says that the question of truth no longer has to do with an epistemological certainty but with "manifestation" (*a-letheia*). For him, this shift refers to the transition from the quest for "certainty" to the recognition of "possibility." Here, the central hermeneutical category of "possibility" represents his fundamental postmodern insight that all experience and all understanding is interpretative. In other words, our claim to truth is, at best, our "possible" or "relatively adequate" interpretation of reality. Tracy states:

> Relative adequacy is just that: relative, not absolute, adequacy. If one demands certainty, one is assured of failure. We can never possess absolute certainty. But we can achieve a good –that is, a relatively adequate – interpretation: relative to the power of disclosure and concealment of the text, relative to the skills and attentiveness of the interpreter, relative to the kind of conversation possible for the interpreter in a particular culture at a particular time. Somehow conversation and relatively adequate interpretations suffice. As Hilary Putnam reminds us: in some situations, 'Enough is enough, enough is not everything.' Sometimes less is more.[96]

In order to illuminate this hermeneutical quality of truth, Tracy focuses on a key notion, "conversation." Tracy describes as "conversation" what happens in an act of interpretation. "Conversation" is the interaction between a phenomenon to be interpreted and an interpreter. He says, "Conversation accords primacy to one largely forgotten notion of truth: truth as manifestation."[97] Truth as manifestation means that truth manifests itself in the interaction (conversation) between "the object's disclosure and concealment and the

96    *PA*, 22–3.
97    *Ibid.*, 28.

subject's recognition."[98] In other words, through conversation, we experience truths made manifest by our willingness to dialogue and by a phenomenon's power to disclose. Tracy states that "the discovery of truth as manifestation is the first fruit of any dialogical life. Without genuine conversation, no manifestation. Without manifestation, no real dialogue."[99]

According to Tracy, in contrast to the objectivist quest for unequivocal certainty, the model of conversation involves "an exploration of possibilities in the search for truth."[100] The objectivist approach can be described as epistemological solipsism which reduces all reality to more of the same in the search for unitary certitude. Such a solipsism is "the enemy of conversation."[101] According to him, conversation is a kind of "game."[102] "To play a game demands that I be willing to allow the movement peculiar to this particular game to take over."[103] What makes a particular game peculiar is not the players but the movement of the play itself. It is generally observed that even with the same players, games themselves differ from one another because of the differently arranged movements of play. Play renews itself in a constant repetition. In fact, the players are not the subjects of game. Rather a game merely reaches its actualization through the players. In Gadamer's words, "Play fulfils its purpose only if the player loses himself in his play."[104] In short, "It is the game that is played – it is irrelevant whether or not there is a subject who plays. The play is the performance of the movement as such."[105]

---

98   *Ibid.*
99   *Ibid.*
100  *Ibid.*, 20.
101  *Ibid.*, 25.
102  Here, Tracy uses Gadamer's notion of "play." See Gadamer, *Truth and Method*, 91–119.
103  *PA*, 17.
104  Gadamer, *Truth and Method*, 92. Gadamer says that "the real subject of the game (this is shown in precisely those experiences in which there is only a single player) is not the player, but instead the game itself. The game is what holds the player in its spell, draws him into play, and keep him there." (*Ibid.*, 95–6).
105  *Ibid.*, 93.

According to Tracy, conversation is a game which is played by the movements of *questioning*. Here, it matters relatively little whether the conversation is "through person-to-person dialogue or through that peculiar form of dialogue we call close reading of texts, rituals, symbols, myths, or events."[106] The point is that conversation is "a game where we learn to give in to the movement required by questions worth exploring."[107] In a genuine conversation, the primacy of the movements of questioning (the movements of play) over subjectivity (the consciousness of players) is fundamentally acknowledged.[108] It is questioning itself, not pure subjectivity that must control every conversation. According to Tracy, the Gadamerian game theory helps us to see that in conversation we understand ourselves by losing ourselves in the movements of questioning itself. He explains:

> Real conversation occurs only when the participants allow the question, the subject matter, to assume primacy. It occurs only when our usual fears about our own self-image die: whether that fear is expressed in either arrogance or scrupulosity matters little. That fear dies only because we are carried along, and sometimes away, by the subject matter itself into the rare event or happening named 'thinking' and 'understanding.' For understanding *happens*; it *occurs* not as the pure result of personal achievement but in the back-and-forth movement of the conversation itself.[109]

What usually happens in the back-and-forth movement of conversation is that one is able to experience the other and the different in a fashion which may provoke, challenge, and upset one's present horizon of understanding. In other words, in a genuine conversation, we can understand ourselves "by facing something different, other, and sometimes strange," and which is encountered in the

---

106  Tracy, "Uneasy Alliance," 562.
107  *PA*, 18.
108  Tracy enquires, "What is authentic conversation as distinct from idle chatter, mere debate, gossip or nonnegotiable confrontation? As the classical model for conversation in the Western tradition, the Platonic dialogue, makes clear, real conversation occurs only when the individual conversation partners move past self-consciousness and self-aggrandizement into joint reflection upon the subject matter of the conversation." (*AI*, 101).
109  *Ibid.*

interaction of questioning.[110] The understanding that happens here is the fruit of attending to something different and other. This is the experience that something else might be the case or genuinely possible. In any serious conversation, Tracy claims, "to acknowledge the claim to attention of the other *as* other, the different *as* different, is also to acknowledge that other world of meaning as in some manner a genuine possibility for myself."[111] More specifically, he explains:

> In following the track of any question, we must allow for difference and otherness. At the same time, as the question takes over, we notice that to attend to the other as other, the different as different, is also to understand the different *as* possible. To recognize possibility is to sense some similarity to what we have already experienced or understood.[112]

However, Tracy is highly cautious about any misunderstanding that the central hermeneutical category of "possibility" here merely refers to a kind of domesticated or reduced "similarity." He makes clear that "similarity here must be described as similarity-in-difference, that is, analogy."[113] In short, to recognize possibility is "to think analogically, not reductionistically."[114]

*Conversation Retrieves the Contemporary Possibility of Analogical Imagination*

According to Tracy, the analogical imagination developed in Catholic thought is worth recapitulating, in admittedly new forms, for illuminating the hermeneutical exploration of "possibility" (or similarity-in-difference) in contemporary theological reflection.[115] Tracy

---

110  *PA*, 18.
111  Tracy, "Uneasy Alliance," 562.
112  *PA*, 20.
113  *Ibid.*
114  *AI*, 136 n.9.
115  Tracy's works that deal specifically with this idea of analogical imagination are: "Theological Pluralism and Analogy," in *Thought* 54 (1979) 24–36; *The Analogical Imagination*, 405–56; "The Analogical Imagination in Catholic Theology," in David Tracy and John B. Cobb, Jr., *Talking About God: Doing*

explains that analogical language, the creation of Aristotle, purports to find "an alternative language besides the usual candidates: a univocal language where all is the same and an equivocal language where all is different."[116] What analogical language attempts to do is, in a sense, "the nearly impossible: an articulation of real differences as genuinely different but also similar to what we already know."[117] Tracy explains that in theology, analogical language serves to preserve the tension of an original *symbolic* language employed for an originating religious event (i.e., the event of the self-manifestation of God) within the clarity of *concept*. In other words, analogical language is a theological reflective language that emerges from the "constantly expanding, never-ending *dialectical* relationship between authentically critical reflection and real participation in the negating, defamiliarizing, disclosing event."[118] Tracy claims that the dialectical relationship between *critique* and *participation* operative in analogical language implies its negation of full adequacy (i.e., exhaustive, univocal meanings in any analogue).[119] Put differently, the negations present in analogical relationships "function as principles of intensification constituted by the tensive event-character of the focal meaning to negate any slackening of the sense of radical mystery, any grasp at control of the event and the similarities-in-difference of the realities (God, self, world) focused upon and interpreted by that event."[120] Without this tensive power of the negative, Tracy asserts, all analogical concepts "produce not a believable harmony among various likenesses in all reality but the theological equivalent of 'cheap grace': boredom, sterility and an atheological vision of a deadening uni-

---

*Theology in the Context of Modern Pluralism* (New York: The Seabury Press, 1983) 17–38.

116   *PA*, 93.
117   *Ibid.*
118   *AI*, 410 (italics mine).
119   Tracy writes that "any claim to final adequacy masks a manipulative spirit which does justice to neither the irreducibility of the original religious event nor the real but finite powers of critical, discursive reason. Yet a relative adequacy for a particular theology in a particular situation can be hoped for." (*Ibid.* 421–2).
120   *Ibid.*, 409.

vocity."[121] In short, the analogical concepts released by the theologian's analogical imagination are always supposed to be intrinsically dialectical: negations are always operative in the very analogical, not univocal, expressions. Tracy states that "if we are not to domesticate the reality of conversation nor sentimentalize the ideal of an analogical imagination, we must remain sensitive to the need for new negations of present achievements – negations always needed for genuine analogy."[122]

To summarize, according to Tracy, the reality of self-exposure to the other and the different is a condition for the possibility of authentic conversation. The search for truth in conversation is the search for a relative adequacy, that is, the search for similarities-in-difference, such that "what once seemed merely other now seems a real possibility."[123] This hermeneutical model of conversation opens the theologian to the contemporary possibility of analogical imagination. For Tracy, analogical imagination can be used as one strategy for coping with the radical pluralism of the contemporary situation (i.e., the pluralism within the Christian tradition, the pluralism among the religious traditions, and the pluralism among the analyses of the situation, etc.). Tracy states that in our contemporary pluralist settings, "each of us understand each other through analogies to our own experience or not at all."[124] On an existential level, analogical imagination suggests that "to understand at all is to understand dif-

---

121  *Ibid.*, 413. According to Tracy, some misrepresentation of analogical imagination is found "in the Thomist tradition's later invention (in Cajetan) of a 'doctrine of analogy': a 'doctrine' historically unfaithful to the pluralistic uses of analogy and the sense for the importance of negations in Aquinas' own extraordinarily fruitful theological analogical imagination. For the later Thomistic 'doctrine of analogy' proved fateful in its consequences for Catholic theology by its antidialectical (and, finally its antianalogical) stance. That doctrine ultimately yielded in the neo-Scholastic manuals to the clear and distinct, the all-too-ordered and certain, the deadening, undisclosive and untransformative world of the dead analogies of a manualist Thomism committed to certitude, not understanding, veering towards univocity, not unity-in-difference." (*Ibid.*, 413).

122  *Ibid.*, 447.
123  Tracy, "Uneasy Alliance," 562.
124  *AI*, 451.

ferently. To understand at all is to understand for and within genuine dialogue allowing real manifestations of the other's truth and thereby mutual transformation."[125] For example, he says, "What little I understand of Buddhist 'compassion' I do not understand on inner-Buddhist grounds of enlightenment. Yet I can respond to that classic Buddhist notion with a resonance to the challenge it poses to my own Catholic understanding of love as *caritas*."[126] The analogical imagination that guides the self-exposure to the other and the different in conversation is "neither an earlier 'indifferentism' nor its modern correlate, the 'repressive tolerance' of a lazy pluralism."[127] In other words, the reality of analogical imagination can be a live option in our radically pluralistic situation "for all those thinkers, secular and religious alike, who cannot accept either the brittleness of self-righteous ideologies masking some univocal monism or the privatized sloth of an all too easy pluralism masking either a decorous defeatism or some equivocal rootlessness."[128] Tracy asserts that analogical imagination does not write off differences but clarifies them. It does not provide a ready theory by means of which one can predict or deduce the results of conversation in advance. Rather, analogical imagination enables each self-identity, in the self-respect of its own particularity, to "find itself anew by releasing itself to a self-exposure of conversation with the others."[129]

125  David Tracy, *Dialogue with the Other: The Inter-Religious Dialogue* (Louvain: Peeters Press, 1990) 44.
126  Tracy, "Uneasy Alliance," 563.
127  *AI*, 449.
128  *Ibid.*, 454.
129  *Ibid.*, 450.

## 2. The Second Criterion: Coherence of Truth-As-Manifestation with Reason

### The Necessity of Testing "Validity-Claims"

According to Tracy, the hermeneutical criterion for truth (truth as manifestation) is not sufficient for a fundamental theological reflection. This hermeneutical criterion needs a further methodological device, the second criterion, for clarifying the question of truth.[130] The second criterion is concerned with "the rough coherence of what truths-as-manifestations we may hermeneutically learn from revelation with what we otherwise know reasonably from science and all other uses of reason."[131] The question at stake is how our claims to true manifestations can measure up to "public" claims. In other words, how can we argue that our claims to true manifestations are not simply the claims born out of a mystification, privatization, or purely intuitive understanding of reality?

We can summarize Tracy's concept of "publicness" in this discussion in two senses: (1) "an argued consensus of warranted beliefs for a particular community of inquiry"; (2) "coherence" (a formal or logical consistency) of one's claim resulting from an interpretation.[132] Tracy explains that when one claims to recognize any manifestation as true, he or she implicitly claims "a relative adequacy for that interpretation."[133] Other interpreters may or may not agree with that interpretation. Our interpretations which lay claim to truth can be competing and possibly contradictory, so that truth appears difficult to account for. At this point, one needs to *argue* why other

---

130   In this regard, the second criterion is complementary to the first.
131   Tracy, "Uneasy Alliance," 566.
132   *PA*, 29. On the meaning of "coherence," Tracy explains that, "coherence can mean, first, the rough coherence implied in all manifestations and appropriate to all symbol systems, culture, languages, history, and life itself. Recall, for example, Aristotle in the *Poetics* on the role of plots, or modern appeals to how narrative or story provides the rough coherence proper to experience itself. Or coherence can also mean not strictly truth but validity, that coherence appropriate to all purely formal arguments." (*Ibid.*).
133   *Ibid.*

interpreters should agree to one's interpretation. Otherwise, one's interpretation remains as "the imagined joys of first naïveté," or as "the retreat into privacy."[134] Tracy writes:

> When challenged on an interpretation, do I have any evidence that my conversation partner could accept? Can we find those commonplaces (topoi) that constitute the right places for discussing our differences? Can we find commonplaces on what constitutes argument itself? Or shall I simply retreat into announcements arising from my intuitive sense? I may be right, but no one else, in principle, will ever know it [...] To give an interpretation is to make a claim. To make a claim is to be willing to defend that claim if challenged by others or by the further process of questioning itself.[135]

For example, in theology, "if an interpreter believes that religious claims about Ultimate Reality are non-sense, or sick, or meaningless, or purely epiphenomenal, then she should say so – and argue why others should agree. If the interpreter believes that religious claims are meaningful and true, or possible, even probable, again he should say so – and argue why others should agree."[136] In a sense, Tracy claims, the task of theologians is simply to render explicit "what is implicit in all interpretations of religion: some conscious or unconscious notions of what counts as true, as other or different, as similar or the same, as possible or impossible."[137]

In order to conduct this task, what one needs is a move from hermeneutical truth-claims to "further discursive reasoning," that is, "the further arguments on the implicit validity claims in all manifestation."[138] Tracy claims that, "The 'validity-claims' in religion, as in art, morality, and science, cannot be bracketed indefinitely for a relatively adequate interpretation of the phenomenon in question."[139] Put differently, what is necessary at this juncture is a move "from a

---

134  *Ibid.*, 31.
135  *Ibid.*, 25.
136  *Ibid.*, 99.
137  *Ibid.*
138  *Ibid.*, 121 n.2.
139  *Ibid.*, 140 n.48.

model of truth as primordial manifestation to truth as warranted consensus and truth as coherence."[140]

According to Tracy, what discursive reasoning (the moment of argument) purports to do is to *test* initial truth-claims resulting from the moment of manifestation *"on reasoned, public, communal grounds."*[141]

Firstly, concerning the function of *testing*, Tracy explains as follows. All interpretation *implicitly* contains validity-claims. However, when conflicts of interpretation emerge, arguments are called for. What Tracy means by *testing* is that the moment of argument functions to render *explicit* the *implicit* validity-claims made in the moment of manifestation by the aid of available rational forms of thinking. This means that the moment of argument is not supposed to replace or overrule the earlier moment of manifestation, but only to "discriminate and help to evaluate" it.[142] In other words, there a necessary *dialectical* relationship between the moment of manifestation and the moment of argument should be sustained. Tracy explains that, "to demand argument is not to disavow the intuitive skills necessary for conversation. To demand argument is not necessarily to think that we can find truth only through argument."[143] Put differently, argument "is not a replacement for exploratory conversation. Rather, argument is a vital moment *within* conversation that occasionally is needed if the conversation itself is to move forward."[144] In short, "arguments belong within conversation and not vice versa."[145]

Secondly, what does Tracy mean by his claim that the moment of argument tests validity-claims *"on reasoned, public, common*

---

140  *Ibid.*, 29.
141  *Ibid.*, 121 n.4 (italics mine). Tracy explains that, "arguments are by definition intersubjective and communal." (*Ibid.*, 29). This means that, "we humans must reason discursively, inquire communally, converse and argue with ourselves and one another. Human knowledge could be other than it is. But this is the way it is: embodied, communal, finite, discursive." (*Ibid.*, 27).
142  *Ibid.*, 121 n.2.
143  *Ibid.*, 23.
144  *Ibid.*, (italics mine).
145  *Ibid.*, 24.

*grounds*"? Tracy deals with this issue by presenting three refined forms of argument: "theories, methods, and explanations."[146] According to Tracy, all these forms of argument serve to "develop, correct, and challenge any initial understandings" obtained in the moment of manifestation.[147] When conflicts of interpretation occur, we can utilize these forms of argument which provide "a temporary distancing from more free-flowing movement of conversation."[148] In other words, methods, theories, and explanations enable us to distance (not alienate) ourselves from our primal participatory understanding. More specifically, these forms of argument "can clarify our initial understanding by making it firmer and more refined and thereby available to the wider community of inquiry. At other times a particular method or theory can correct or challenge our first understanding."[149] For example, Tracy explains:

> Historical critical methods have corrected all anachronistic interpretations of the classics. Literary critical methods have challenged all literalist readings of texts, including philosophical and scientific texts. Semiotic and structuralist methods have uncovered the codes present in all texts. Social scientific methods have demystified certain humanist categories, including the category of the Great Tradition.[150]

Although methods, theories, and explanations themselves are open to continual challenges and transformations, they can function to provide a reasoned and communal forum for clarifying, developing, and correcting one's initial validity-claims. Tracy notes, however, that

146   *Ibid.*, 30.
147   *Ibid.*, 34.
148   *Ibid.*
149   *Ibid.*
150   *Ibid.* For our interpretation of religion or religious texts especially, Tracy explains, "all the great hermeneutics of suspicion (Marxian, Freudian, Nietzschean) remain relevant methods of interpretation. Each develops a critical theory (psychoanalytic theory, ideology critique, genealogical method) to inform its hermeneutics of suspicion. These critical theories are employed to spot and emancipate the repressed, unconscious distortions that are also operative in the classic religious texts and in their history of effects through the classic religious traditions." Tracy, "Creativity in the Interpretation of Religion: The Question of Radical Pluralism," in *New Literary History* 15 (1984) 306.

such methods, theories, and explanations are "at the service of aiding" our conversation, but they never can take the place of conversation itself. Conversation should not be ruled out by these rational enterprises. Otherwise, in our conversation, the following dangers are possible: that "methods are hardened into methodologisms"; that "theory is reified into some new final truth mechanically applied to all interpretations"; that "explanations become replacements for the effort to understand."[151] This is why it is crucial to maintain a *dialectical* relationship between the moment of argument (discursive reasoning) and the moment of manifestation (an intuitive recognition of truth). Put differently, when discursive reasoning predominates, it may induce the danger of objectivism or scientism (i.e., a narrow scholasticism in theology). Conversely, when an intuitive approach to truth predominates, it may fall into romanticism, a "remystification" or "remythologizing" of reality.[152] In short, for Tracy, "explanation and understanding, method and truth, theory and common sense, concept and symbol," all are *dialectical* allies and partners that serve each other in the search for truth in our conversation.[153]

151   *PA*, 46.
152   *Ibid.*, 31.
153   *Ibid.*, 46. Concerning the relationship between "explanation and understanding" or "method and truth" in a hermeneutical reflection, a difference between Gadamer's and Ricoeur's positions is worth noting here. Tracy concurs with Ricoeur's position. Tracy explains that Gadamer, in his *Truth and Method*, is "so wary of the dangers of methodologism that he sometimes fears all method and all distancing through theory and explanation" in a hermeneutical quest for truth (*Ibid.*, 34). For Gadamer, truth is not something that we can infer by following some method. In other words, for him, "the happening of truth isn't a matter of methodological assurance; it manifests itself as a play in which we are involved." (Jean Grondin, "Hermeneutical Truth and Its Historical Presuppositions: A Possible Bridge between Analysis and Hermeneutics," in Evan Simpson (ed.), *Anti-Foundationalism and Practical Reasoning: Conversations between Hermeneutics and Analysis* (Edmonton, Alberta: Academic Printing & Publishing, 1987) 53). Standing against modern scientific methodologism, Gadamer claims that "what is clear is always something that is said, a proposal, a plan, a conjecture, an argument, or something of the sort. The idea is always that what is clear is not proved and not absolutely certain, but it asserts itself by reason of its own merit within the area of the possible and probable [...] The hermeneutical experience belongs in this sphere because it is also the event of a

*A Call for an Apologetical Task*

We have examined Tracy's two revised criteria for fundamental theology: (1) the hermeneutical notion of truth as manifestation; (2) the necessity for the coherence of truth-as-manifestation with reason. For Tracy, the theological task based on these criteria can be formulated as follows: the theologian (of fundamental theology) is supposed to be committed to the task "of rendering as explicit as possible an interpretation of the central Christian message for a

genuine experience." (Gadamer, *Truth and Method*, 441–2). Gary E. Aylesworth says that, for Gadamer, the hermeneutical experience of a disclosure of meaning in which his conception of truth consists, thus, "does not terminate in a moment of reflective knowledge *a posteriori*, nor is it ruled by a reflective concept *a priori*, but remains open to *further experience*." (Gary E. Aylesworth, "Dialogue, Text, Narrative: Confronting Gadamer and Ricoeur," in Hugh J. Silverman (ed.), *Gadamer and Hermeneutics* (New York and London: Routledge, 1991) 68). In contrast to Gadamer, according to Ricoeur, philosophical hermeneutics must incorporate the critical methods of the human sciences into its own discourse. This is to say that a valid interpretation must include an explanatory moment beyond our initial understanding of a first naïveté. Dan R. Stiver explains that, "Ricoeur sees virtue in testing our insightful understandings by critical methodologies at a second, explanatory stage. In Dilthey's terms, this is a shift from understanding to explanation. Unlike Dilthey, however, Ricoeur sees a place for the more analytical and critical mode of thought, even in the interpretation of texts. As he put it in later work, 'To explain more is to understand better'." (Dan R. Stiver, *Theology after Ricoeur: New Directions in Hermeneutical Theology* (Louisville: Westminster John Knox Press, 2001) 60. Ricoeur writes that, "As concerns the procedures of validation by which we test our guesses [our initial understandings], I agree with Hirsch that they are closer to a logic of probability than to a logic of empirical verification. To show that an interpretation is more probable in the light of what is known is something other than showing that a conclusion is true. In this sense, validation is not verification. Validation is an argumentative discipline comparable to the juridical procedures of legal interpretation. It is a logic of uncertainty and of qualitative probability [...] A text is a quasi-individual, and the validation of an interpretation applied to it may be said, with complete legitimacy, to give a scientific knowledge of the text." (Ricoeur, "The Model of the Text: Meaningful Action Considered as a Text," in *Paul Ricoeur, Hermeneutics and the Human Sciences: Essays on Language, Action, and Interpretation*, ed. and trans. by John B. Thompson (Cambridge: Cambridge University Press, 1981) 212).

concrete situation [the first criterion], and of showing why others should, in principle, agree with that interpretation [the second criterion]."[154] We can call the task that the second criterion informs in this formulation an apologetical task. In the following, we will further focus on this apologetical task that Tracy calls for. Two issues need to be discussed. Firstly, for Tracy, a fundamental condition for defending the necessity and possibility for apologetics is a defense of reason. We will look at Tracy's defense of reason. Secondly, Tracy mentions, although in a very brief form, the necessity and possibility for an apologetics based on his defense of reason. We will also deal with this issue.

*Tracy's Defense of Reason*

According to Tracy, it is a great challenge to find an adequate notion of reason which is readily available for the apologetical task of fundamental theology. He says that, "there is no *de facto* consensus among contemporary philosophers on what rational consensus is."[155] However, without a defense of reason, his insistence on the apologetical task cannot be plausible. Tracy's key concern here is where to find a notion of reason that is free from both "objectivism" and "relativism." Tracy finds this possibility in Lonergan's notion of reason. Tracy states that, "The most persuasive attempt in modern Catholic thought to defend the reality of reason without capitulating to foundationalist notions of rationality remains that of Bernard Lonergan."[156] In order to discuss this view of Tracy on Lonergan, we need, first, to look at Lonergan's cognitional theory in which he shows how human knowing is possible.

---

154   Tracy, "Some Concluding Reflections," 462.
155   Tracy, "Uneasy Alliance," 566.
156   *Ibid.*, 566–7.

*Lonergan's Cognitional Theory*

*The Threefold Cognitional Process*

In his *Insight*, Lonergan analyzes the process of human cognition in a threefold way: knowledge is what is to be achieved by the process of "experience," "intelligence" (or understanding), and "reflection" (or judgment), engaged in by an inquiring human subject.[157] These three levels are interrelated and cumulative: later stages presuppose and complement earlier contributions. Each level of this process has its own proper achievement and end. By "experience," one apprehends uncoordinated scraps of data; this level is concerned with providing "data, presentations, the empirical, the given."[158] By "intelligence," one grasps an intelligible order or form emergent in the apprehended data; this level is associated with "inquiry, insight, intelligence, definition, concept, formulation, law, function, correlation, hypothesis, supposition, consideration, theory, system, thought."[159] Finally, "reflection" concerns the acceptance or rejection of hypotheses, theories, and formulations produced at the level of "intelligence"; this level is related to "criticism, judgment, rationality, reasonableness, affirmation, knowledge, truth."[160] In short, at the level of "reflection," cognitional activities reach their total increment, and one whole process for achieving knowledge comes to a close. Hugo A. Meynell succinctly articulates this threefold cognitional process of Lonergan as follows: one comes to acquire knowledge "by the repeated process of putting questions to experience, arriving at theories which are answers to these questions, and then making reasonably-grounded judgments in terms of these theories."[161]

---

157 Lonergan, *Insight*, especially 252 and 272–8. In his *Method in Theology*, Lonergan uses the terms "understanding" and "judgment" instead of "intelligence" and "reflection" respectively. See *Method in Theology*, 101 ff.
158 Lonergan, *Insight*, 759.
159 *Ibid.*
160 *Ibid.*
161 Hugo A. Meynell, *An Introduction to the Philosophy of Bernard Lonergan* (London: The Macmillan Press, 1976) 142.

In this threefold cognitional process, Tracy's focus for his own argument is the final level, "reflection" (or judgment). At this level, Tracy's central concern is Lonergan's concept of a "virtually unconditioned."[162] Lonergan explains that the third level of "reflection" occurs when hypotheses, theories, and definitions produced at the preceding level of "intelligence" are posed a further question, such as 'Is it actually the case?' Such a (reflective) question elicits judgments on these activities of hypothesizing, theorizing, and defining. Lonergan says that, "it is within this third level that there is involved the personal commitment that makes one responsible for one's judgments. It is from this third level that come utterances to express one's affirming or denying, assenting or dissenting, agreeing or disagreeing."[163] The central task of this level is, therefore, to grasp "the sufficiency of the evidence for a prospective judgment."[164] What the inquirer grasps based on the sufficiency of evidence is what Lonergan terms a "virtually unconditioned." He says that, "To grasp evidence as sufficient for a prospective judgment is to grasp the prospective judgment as virtually unconditioned."[165] The question for reflection, 'Is it actually the case?,' positions a prospective judgment in need of sufficient evidence. A prospective judgment will become a virtually unconditioned, "if (1) it is conditioned, (2) its conditions are known, and (3) the conditions are fulfilled."[166] In short, a virtually unconditioned is a conditioned whose conditions (now available to the inquirer) are fulfilled. Lonergan explains that, "The function of reflective understanding is to meet the question for reflection [i.e., 'Is it so?'] by transforming the prospective judgment from the status of a conditioned to the status of a virtually unconditioned; and reflective understanding effects this transformation by grasping the conditions of the conditioned and their fulfillment."[167] For Lonergan, therefore, "all knowledge is [in fact] of the virtually unconditioned."[168] Meynell

162   See Bernard Lonergan's Model of "Self-Transcendence" in Chapter 2.
163   Lonergan, *Insight*, 273.
164   *Ibid.*, 279.
165   *Ibid.*, 280.
166   *Ibid.*
167   *Ibid.*
168   Meynell, An Introduction to the Philosophy of Bernard Lonergan, 50.

explains that, "Every matter of fact, everything that is the case, and can be found to be so by the process of experience, understanding, and judgment, is an example of the virtually unconditioned in Lonergan's sense."[169]

*The Nature of Human Knowing*

According to Lonergan, the aforementioned human cognitional process has a dynamic structure: it has both a self-correcting and cyclic character. Let us look at each of these characteristics.

Firstly, human knowing has a self-correcting character. As has been said, in Lonergan, everything that is deemed to be knowledge is an example of a "virtually unconditioned." A "virtually unconditioned" results from "the combination of a conditioned with the fulfillment of its conditions."[170] According to Lonergan, the fulfillment of conditions is achieved "when there are no further, pertinent questions" in relation to the subject matter and the evidence available to the inquirer.[171] Lonergan explains that, "when an insight meets the issue squarely, when it hits the bull's eye, when it settles the matter, there are no further questions to be asked and so there are no further insights to challenge the initial position."[172] Then, a prospective judgment becomes a virtually unconditioned. However, there is always an open possibility for the emergence of new questions that expose discontent or dissatisfaction with the accepted judgments. Lonergan states that, "it is only through further questions that there arise the further insights that complement, modify, or revise the initial approach and explanation."[173] In short, human knowing entertains "the self-correcting process of learning" in which the given insights and positions are put to test, complemented, or adjusted by further insights spawned by new questions.[174] In such a self-correcting process, "the

169   *Ibid.*, 49.
170   Lonergan, *Insight*, 344.
171   *Ibid.*, 284.
172   *Ibid.*
173   *Ibid.*
174   *Ibid.*, 346.

logical retinues of presuppositions and implications of each insight are being expanded either to conflict and provoke further questions or else to mesh into coherence."[175] A key idea here is that human knowing is a limited enterprise in the sense that "it is content to affirm some single conditioned that has a finite number of conditions which, in fact, are fulfilled."[176] Lonergan explains that the fulfillment of conditions:

> that is required for judgment is not the comprehensive coherence that is the ideal of understanding, that grounds answers to all questions of the first type [the questions for intelligence, i.e., what?, why?, how?]. On the contrary, it is a virtually unconditioned that results from the combination of a conditioned with the fulfillment of its conditions. Further, a judgment is a limited commitment; so far from resting on knowledge of the universe, it is to the effect that, no matter what the rest of the universe may prove to be, at least this is so."[177]

Secondly, human knowing is a cyclic process. According to Lonergan, the three cognitional activities, "experience," "intelligence," and "reflection" are the *invariant* features of human knowledge. This threefold process is a normative pattern of recurrent operations employed in every cognitional enterprise. This cyclic structure of human knowing is not subject to revision, "because this structure is the condition of the possibility of any revision."[178] In order to make any revision for a new judgment, the inquirer is "subject to the general conditions of beginning from presentations [experience], advancing through insights and formulations [intelligence], to terminate with reflections and judgments."[179] For Lonergan, even the sceptic cannot be free from engaging in this same cognitional process in order to rationalize his or her position, namely, the denial of the possibility of knowing. Otherwise, the sceptic can hardly be a knower about his or her denial. In short, our revision of knowledge cannot revise its own presuppositions. This means that "a reviser cannot appeal to data to deny data, to his new insights to deny insights, to his

175   *Ibid.*, 286.
176   *Ibid.*, 345.
177   *Ibid.*, 344.
178   Lonergan, *Method in Theology*, xii.
179   Lonergan, *Insight*, 277.

new formulation to deny formulation, to his reflective grasp to deny reflective grasp."[180] More specifically, Lonergan explains that a revision:

> contends that previous theory does not satisfactorily account for all the data. It claims to have reached complementary insights that lead to more accurate statements. It shows that these new statements either are unconditioned or more closely approximate to the unconditioned than previous statements. Now, if in fact revision is as described, then, it presupposes that cognitional process falls on the three levels of presentation, intelligence, and reflection; it presupposes that insights are cumulative and complementary; it presupposes that they head towards a limit described by the adjective, satisfactory; it presupposes a reflective grasp of the unconditioned or of what approximates to the unconditioned.[181]

According to Lonergan, an important distinction to be made is the distinction between the threefold normative pattern of the cognitional process and the objectifications of that pattern in concepts. There can be more adequate accounts of the dynamic cognitional structure, but the structure itself cannot be changed.[182] Where, then, does the normativity of this structure come from? Lonergan explains that the normative force of our cognitional structure lies:

> not just in its claims to authority, not just in the probability that what succeeded in the past will succeed in the future, but at root in the native spontaneities and inevitabilities of our consciousness which assembles its own constituent parts and unites them in a rounded whole in a manner we cannot set aside without, as it were, amputating [...] our own reasonableness, our own intelligence, our own sensitivity.[183]

---

180   *Ibid.*, 336.
181   *Ibid.*, 335–6.
182   Lonergan explains that, "Any theory, description, account of our conscious and intentional operations is bound to be incomplete and to admit further clarifications and extensions. But all such clarifications and extensions are to be derived from the conscious and intentional operations themselves. They as given in consciousness are the rock; they confirm every exact account; they refute every inexact or incomplete account." (Lonergan, *Method in Theology*, 19–20).
183   *Ibid.*, 18.

In other words, the dynamism of the threefold cognitional process is not a product of cultural advance, but due to the immanent nature of human consciousness which incessantly strives for a fuller and richer knowledge. In this sense, for Lonergan, this normative cognitional pattern is transcultural and universally relevant. In many fields of scientific enterprise, including theology, therefore, this pattern can serve as "common norms, foundations, systematics, and common critical, dialectical and heuristic procedures" of human rationality.[184]

One thing to note is that Lonergan's idea of the normative pattern of human cognitional process rests on his view that the human consciousness is a reliable substratum. Lonergan says that, "There is no revision of revisers themselves."[185] This is to say, "If rational consciousness can criticize the achievement of science, it cannot criticize itself. The critical spirit can weigh all else in the balance, only on condition that it does not criticize itself. It is a self-assertive spontaneity that demands sufficient reason for all else but offers no justification for its demanding."[186] For Lonergan, the invariability of the cognitional pattern is grounded in the invariability of the critical consciousness (as a "unity-identity-whole"[187]); and the invariability of the critical consciousness is grounded in the invariability of its self-assertive, spontaneous thrust for knowledge.

*Tracy's Defense of Lonergan's Notion of Reason*

Tracy considers Lonergan's analysis of human knowing as an important, retainable source for a "modest but real defense of reason."[188] In Tracy's view, Lonergan's cognitional theory presents a good model of a non-foundationalist quest for knowledge directed by human consciousness. Here, a non-foundationalist quest means a quest for relative adequacy, not for absolute certainty. Tracy interprets Lonergan's "virtually unconditioned" judgments as "judgments of relative

---

184    *Ibid.*, 24.
185    Lonergan, *Insight*, 277.
186    *Ibid.*, 332.
187    *Ibid.*, 319.
188    Tracy, "Uneasy Alliance," 567.

adequacy: adequate to the question at hand and relative to the evidence presently available."[189] In Lonergan's analysis of the "virtually unconditioned," Tracy perceives a possibility of human knowing without either foundationalist or relativistic strands; Lonergan shows this possibility "in recognizably empirical, Anglo-American terms."[190] Tracy states that, in Lonergan, human knowing is possible (beyond relativism) in such a way that "we reach, in every act of judgment, whether that of common sense, historical scholarship, or scientific theory, the point where, for the present inquirer faithful to the demands of the inquiry itself, no further relevant questions emerge [...] The judgment is unconditioned, since it answers the questions relevant to the subject, the criteria, and the evidence now available to competent inquirers."[191] However, such a judgment (a "virtually unconditioned") does not refer to a foundationalist judgment, because "every judgment [in Lonergan] is by definition open to further revision as further questions emerge. And further questions will always eventually emerge."[192]

We explained earlier Tracy's three rational forms of argument – methods, theories, and explanations – which can be utilized for testing one's hermeneutical validity-claims. For Tracy, Lonergan's notion of reason is useful to back up the possibility of constructing and operating these rational forms of thinking in theological reflection. Apologetics is, for him, nothing other than an attempt to make the *implicit* Christian validity-claims *explicit* by the aid of these rational forms of argument.

*Tracy's Apologetics*

Our next concern is to look at Tracy's position on the apologetics. What interests us is the fact that conceiving an apologetical discourse of God, Tracy intends to maintain a transcendental method. This means that, concerning this issue, he does not distance himself from

189   *Ibid.*
190   *Ibid.*
191   *Ibid.*
192   *Ibid.*

his revisionist stance in *BRO*. The difference between Tracy's present position and that of *BRO* is that he wants to draw on a transcendental method, while taking modernity's self-critique seriously. Tracy insists on the need of a transcendental method as follows:

> That some form of transcendental reflection is needed by theology seems as clear now as it was 20 years ago, and that for the same reason: if one understands the logic of the claim Jews, Christians, and Muslims make when they affirm their belief in a radically monotheistic God, transcendental reflection is that mode of rational inquiry appropriate to considering that claim.[193]

According to Tracy, his insistence on the need of transcendental reflection is not a purely philosophical concern to make a universal claim for God based on public conceptualities. Rather, having the anti-correlationalist's allegation against liberal theology in mind, Tracy asserts that, "this demand is formulated by the intratextual needs of the logic of the Christian understanding of God, and not only from modern situational needs [...] I can see no way, on purely inner-Christian grounds, to deny the universality and necessity of the Christian understanding of God. A lesser 'god,' for the Jew, Christian, and Muslim, is not God."[194] For him, the apologetics of God "must always be an intrinsic aspect of all Christian theology" on both intratextual and situational grounds.[195] And, transcendental reflection is appropriate to carry out this apologetical task. However, Tracy warns at the same time that any transcendental reflection will not function properly unless it acknowledges its own linguisticality and historicity. Transcendental reflection has its own historicity like any other mode of critical reflection. Tracy states that, "Insofar as all modes of reasoning are linguistically rendered (as they are), they are historically embedded. Any transcendental method needs to pay greater attention to that fact than many forms of theology, both classical and modern, characteristically do. If such attention is not forthcoming, theology will quietly but inevitably drift away from the

---

193   *Ibid.*, 559.
194   *Ibid.*
195   *Ibid.*, 568.

apologetic and situational elements of the correlation in fundamental theology."[196]

Now, our question is, 'What is, then, Tracy's option for a transcendental reflection which, being aware of its own historicity, provides a rational discourse of God's necessity and universality'? Tracy's option is the Lonerganian transcendental validation of God. In order to properly discuss some important methodological problems that Tracy's option raises, let us briefly recall Lonergan's transcendental validation of God by means of his model of the "self-transcendence" of human questioning.

According to Lonergan, humanity's unrestricted quest for knowledge has the character of self-transcendence.[197] This means that human inquiry is moving forward to a higher level of quest: "from experiencing to the effort to understand, from understanding to the effort to judge truly, from judging to the effort to choose rightly."[198] Lonergan claims that it is in this self-transcending quest for knowledge that the question of God unavoidably arises. In other words, the question of God is inevitably raised within this self-transcending process even without any religiously-motivated urge. He says, "In the measure that we advert to our own questioning and proceed to question it, there arises the question of God."[199]

More specifically, when we inquire into the possibility of fruitful inquiry at the level of "intelligence," we cannot but end up asking about the ultimate "intelligent ground" for our intelligence. When we reflect upon what we obtained from a fruitful inquiry, we may elicit "virtually unconditioned" judgments. Every "virtually unconditioned"

---

196  *Ibid.*, 559.
197  Lonergan explains that, "The transcendental notions, that is, our questions for intelligence, for reflection, and for deliberation, constitute our capacity for self-transcendence." (Lonergan, *Method in Theology*, 105).
198  *Ibid.*, 103. Lonergan's model of "self-transcendence" is developed on the basis of his cognitional theory. Note, here, that Lonergan adds one more level next to the level of "reflection," viz., the ethical level of "responsibility," "on which we are concerned with ourselves, our own operations, our goals, and so deliberate about possible courses of action, evaluate them, decide, and carry out our decisions." (*Ibid.*, 9).
199  *Ibid.*, 103.

raises further questions which continue until the mind reaches a "formally unconditioned," viz., an unconditioned which has no conditions to be fulfilled, standing outside the interlocked field of conditioning and conditioned.[200] When we deliberate on the ethical values of our intellectual discoveries, we are led to ask about the necessary ground of the possibility of our moral consciousness. For Lonergan, all these questions about the ultimate "intelligent ground," a "formally unconditioned," and the ultimate ground of our moral consciousness, are questions about God. For him, the objects of theology are not located outside the transcendental field that the self-transcending consciousness can ask about. As much as human questioning is unrestricted, the transcendental field is "unrestricted, and so outside it there is nothing at all."[201] In other words, "the transcendental field is defined not by what man knows, not by what he can know, but by what he can ask about [and which is unrestricted]."[202] For Lonergan, the question of God does not lie outside this transcendental field, and in this sense, this question is transcultural and universal.

For Tracy, this Lonerganian validation of God is a nonfoundationalist apologetical account of God in the sense that it does not rest on rationality for absolute certainty. Instead, it draws on the "self-correcting and unrestricted nature" of the human quest for knowledge, which inescapably poses the question of ultimate reality, unless it is willing to stop its inquiry arbitrarily; and this question of ultimate reality is the question of God. In the following, we will discuss some methodological problems that Tracy's hermeneutical-(Lonerganian) transcendental approach exposes.

---

200  Lonergan explains that in traditional terms, the "virtually unconditioned" refers to a contingent being and the "formally unconditioned" refers to a necessary being (See *ibid.*, 102).
201  *Ibid.*, 23.
202  *Ibid.*, 24.

We mentioned earlier that Tracy's two revised criteria indicate his methodological turn in fundamental theology from a monolithic transcendental approach (his revisionist model in *BRO*) to a twofold hermeneutical-transcendental approach to the question of "truth." In our assessment, we would like to focus on the question of whether the hermeneutical and transcendental approaches can be cohabited in a theological system of the kind that Tracy envisages. This question is associated with an important debate on methodological options for fundamental theology, especially in the Catholic circle. Some contend that these two approaches are alternative rather than complementary theological approaches, because "they are rooted in contradictory anthropological starting points and cannot be united in an inclusive hybrid."[203] Others claim that these two approaches can be used in a complementary or integrated manner in a theological reflection.[204] In

---

203  Jack A. Bonsor, "Irreducible Pluralism: The Transcendental and Hermeneutical as Theological Options," in *Horizons* 16 (1989) 316. Bonsor's other works in relation to fundamental theological issues include, "An Orthodox Historicism?," in *Ph&Th*, 4 (1990) 335–50; "History, Dogma, and Nature: Further Reflections on Postmodernism and Theology," in *TS*, 55 (1994) 295–313.

204  For this position, see Peter J. Drilling, "The Pyramid or the Raft: Francis Schüssler Fiorenza and Bernard Lonergan in Dialogue about Foundational Theology," in *Horizons* 13 (1986) 275–90; Francis S. Fiorenza, "Theology: Transcendental or Hermeneutical?," in *Horizons* 16 (1989) 329–41; Fred Lawrence, "On the Relationship between Transcendental and Hermeneutical Approaches to Theology," in *Horizons* 16 (1989) 342–5. One of the pressing contemporary concerns of fundamental theology is how to construct a rational account of God in both a non-relativist and a non-foundationalist way. For hermeneutical theologians, this concern can be formulated in the following way: how to account for the lasting value of the Christian truth-claim concerning God, while taking the historicity of its production and reception seriously. For these theologians, the major challenges in relation to the development of historical consciousness are historicism and relativism. As a way to deal with these challenges, some of these theologians seek to moderate the potential risk of historicism and relativism in hermeneutical theology with the stability of the transcendental (See Bonsor, "Irreducible Pluralism," 328).

For the relation between the transcendental and the hermeneutical, Francis S. Fiorenza presents his position in two theses: (1) "transcendental and

the following, we will discuss two crucial issues that this debate exposes, and clarify Tracy's position.

The first issue that the above debate addresses concerns the conflicting understandings of human consciousness (or the human subject) maintained in the hermeneutical and transcendental approaches. As we already saw, the hermeneutical notion of truth which Tracy's first criterion concerns, resists the Enlightenment model of consciousness: the consciousness invested with pure autonomy and transparency to itself. According to the hermeneutical perspectives of Heidegger and Gadamer, there is no transhistorical subjectivity shorn of the flux of its historical context. Heidegger's analysis of the pre-understanding of *Da-sein* (*Da-sein* always finds itself within a given context of involvement prior to the capacity to question) and Gadamer's theory of effective history (what is historically pre-given both prescribes and limits every possibility of self-knowledge) point up the historically-conditioned and determined character of subjectivity.[205] In

hermeneutical approaches are not equally appropriate for different areas of theology. The transcendental approaches have been more successful for the doctrine of God than for christology."; (2) "the transcendental and hermeneutical approaches cannot be successfully linked in one system, but form a complementary dialectic. They must remain two contrasting poles, both necessary for the theological task because they each bring distinctive perspectives and point to the limitations of the other perspectives." (Fiorenza, op. cit., 332 and 335). Fred Lawrence, an expert on Lonergan's theology, claims that Lonergan's transcendental method, as distinct from other transcendental Thomists such as Coreth and Rahner, is not contradictory to or incompatible with the hermeneutical approach to theology rooted in Heidegger and Gadamer's hermeneutics. He says that, "Lonergan's ideas about theology regard not a transcendental alternative to another, hermeneutical style of doing theology, but the clearest spelling out we possess as yet of the hermeneutical option as a radical rejection of idealist presuppositions about noetic *praxis*, including those still implicit in the work of Coreth and Rahner." (Lawrence, op. cit., 345). For Lawrence's defense of Lonergan's thought, i.e., that it meets postmodern concerns without yielding to postmodernist relativism and nihilism, see idem, "The Fragility of Consciousness: Lonergan and the Postmodern Concern for the Other," in *TS*, 54 (1993) 55–94.

205　See Bonsor, "Irreducible Pluralism," 322. For Heidegger's analysis of pre-understanding, see *Being and Time*, 91–145; for Gadamer's effective history, see *Truth and Method*, 267–74.

short, the human subject is "the creature of, and derived from" its context.[206] In Heideggerian words, "Dasein is no thing. It has no structure or nature, but is possibility for. For what? For whatever possibilities its there, its historically-conditioned world with others, make possible."[207] Basing himself on this hermeneutical perspective, Tracy is sympathetic to the postmodern position that disallows "any pretensions to full self-presence, any self-congratulatory Western resting in an untroubled, alinguistic, self-present, grounding ego."[208] Tracy states that the "ego is never fully present to itself – not even in Descartes's moments of certainty or Husserl's transcendental reduction [...] The ego is now de-centered. The dream of full presence is no more."[209]

Now, the question is how this postmodern understanding of the de-centered self can be compatible with the transcendental understanding of human consciousness shown in Lonergan which Tracy's second criterion defends. As indicated earlier, Lonergan's cognitional theory consists in the idea that human cognitional operations have a normative, recurrent pattern (such as experience, intelligence, and reflection) which is not subject to revision. Lonergan states that these operations "as given in consciousness are the rock [...] The rock, then, is the subject."[210] According to Jack A. Bonsor, in Lonergan's transcendental approach, "knowledge is the achievement of the subject in relationship to some other or itself."[211] In contrast to the hermeneutical approach which posits a phenomenon's power to disclose itself, for Lonergan, "the intelligible does not present itself as data. Knowledge is not taking a look. Rather, intelligibility is the achievement of the subject through its recurring operations [...] Knowledge, truth, occurs in judgment when the intellect attains the intelligibility of the known." [212] In short, Lonergan's cognitional theory "rests on its transcendental starting point, that the primary ground of knowledge is

---

206  Bonsor, *ibid.*, 324.
207  *Ibid.* See Heidegger, *Being and Time*, 239 and 321.
208  *PA*, 59.
209  *Ibid.*, 58.
210  Lonergan, *Method in Theology*, 20.
211  Bonsor, "Irreducible Pluralism," 320.
212  *Ibid.*

the achievement of a subject in relationship to the known. The transhistorical nature of subjectivity, *i.e.*, its recurrent operations, grounds the possibility of truth judgments that span historical flux."[213]

The difficulty in Tracy's twofold hermeneutical-transcendental approach is the confluence of these seemingly conflicting ideas on the human subject: the de-centered self which destabilizes the full self-presence of consciousness (or "the self as a reality-founding ego") *and* the transcendental subjectivity which is foundational for its know-ledge. What we cannot find in Tracy is in what way these two conflicting approaches can be theoretically or methodologically rec-onciled so as to be incorporated in a theological system. Rather than providing an explanation, Tracy simply expresses his twofold position as follows:

> It is indeed true that for postmodernity the purely autonomous ego is no more. And yet the subject, however chastened and transformed, has not been erased. As subjects we can resist our former illusions of pure autonomy by risking interpretations of all the classic signs and texts. The postmodern subject now knows that any route to reality must pass through the radical plurality of our differential languages and the ambiguity of all our histories. After such knowledge, what identity, what coherence, for what self? The coherent self attempted by the realistic and naturalist narrators of coherence is gone, to be replaced by a more fragile self – open to epiphanies.[214]

As a criticism on Tracy's juxtaposition of these conflicting approaches without explication, Richard J. Bernstein writes:

> It is not sufficient simply to tell us that the subject has been transformed but not erased. We want and need to understand how we can still speak of a subject and what this subject is after we take account of the multifaceted critiques of the subject in 'postmodern' discourses. What is disturbing here, and is unfor-tunately characteristic of Tracy's sensitive attempt to do justice to sharp oppositions is that just at the point where we look for further argumentation, explication, and probing, Tracy reassures us that we can do justice to both sides

213    *Ibid.*, 321.
214    *PA*, 82–3.

of what appears to be an irreconcilable opposition – without quite showing us how this is to be done.[215]

The second issue that we need to discuss in relation to the debate on the hermeneutical vis-à-vis the transcendental is a theological one. Our question is whether a theological reflection based on the hermeneutical model of conversation can be concordant with the Lonerganian transcendental reflection of God as Tracy envisions. We would like to discuss two problematic points in Tracy's twofold hermeneutical-transcendental approach.

Firstly, we must ask whether Tracy's view of the Lonerganian transcendental validation of God as non-foundationalist is reasonable. In contrast to Tracy's view, we suggest that the Lonerganian validation of God is close to a foundationalist approach. Lonergan attempts to validate God on the basis of the self-transcending process of human inquiry. Put differently, the invariable self-transcending operations of human cognition serve for "the rock," or the indubitable epistemological foundation from which God is inferred. A philosophical principle operative behind this inferential process is the coincidence of *being* and *intelligibility*.[216] When this principle is used in a transcendental method, it is applied as follows. When we question something, it is only possible when that something *exists*. We can never think, reflect, or question what *is* not. Therefore, if we can ask about the ultimate ground of our inquiry, the ultimate ground must exist. If the ultimate ground is God, God must exist. The problem in this approach, however, is that there is no theoretical justification of how God is identified with that ultimate ground. This is the same problem that we pointed out in other transcendental Thomists (i.e., Coreth and Ogden) in the preceding chapter. This identification is simply

215  Richard J. Bernstein, "Radical Plurality, Fearful Ambiguity, and Engaged Hope," in *JR*, 69 (1989) 89–90. See also Charles E. Winquist, "Analogy, Apology, and the Imaginative Pluralism of David Tracy," in *JAAR*, 56 (1988) 317–18.

216  Objectivism and foundationalism presuppose this undistorted correspondence between the "mirror" of the mind and reality. For criticism of this classical epistemology, see Richard Rorty, *Philosophy and the Mirror of Nature* (Princeton: Princeton University Press, 1979).

postulated, based on a cultural normality constituted in the Western-Christian community. Tracy takes for granted this identification. He seems to overlook that this tacit identification itself is a foundationalist move.

Secondly, we reckon that Tracy's twofold hermeneutical-transcendental approach to truth in a theological system exposes a contradictory element. In dealing with this element, we will particularly focus on the issue of religious plurality in fundamental theology.

As examined earlier, for Tracy, the heart of hermeneutical reflection is that truth emerges through conversation. In Gadamerian terms, this conversation is the "fusion" of horizons.[217] This means that conversation is "the setting for the encounter of disparate cultural and historical horizons which best guarantees that something will be learned rather than merely repeated."[218] For Tracy, one important imperative that a hermeneutical reflection calls for is to attend to the other which resists being translated into one's own. The hermeneutical model of conversation is one attempt "to give the other (whether person, event or text) our attention as other, not as a projection of our present fears, hopes and desires."[219] Tracy claims that this sense of otherness and difference occasions a de-centering of Eurocentric arrogance in dealing with contemporary intellectual, cultural and ecclesial situations. He writes, "At this time we all need to face the strong claims on our attention made by other cultures and by the other, subjugated, forgotten and marginalized traditions in Western culture itself."[220] In other words, "we no longer assume the cultural superiority of Western modernity. Anyone who continues to think and write (as many in the modern Western academy still do) as if other cultures either do not exist or exist only as steppingstones to or pale copies of Western modernity is self-deluding."[221] The contemporary ecclesial situation also asks for departing from a Eurocentric approach. Tracy explains:

217 Gadamer, *Truth and Method*, 273ff.
218 Thomas B. Ommen, "Theology and Foundationalism," in *SR*, 16 (1987) 164.
219 Tracy, "God, Dialogue and Solidarity: A Theologian's Refrain," 903.
220 *Ibid.*
221 *Ibid.*, 902.

The Eurocentric character of Christian theology surely cannot survive in a Christianity that is finally and irreversibly becoming a world church. That there are now more Anglicans in Africa than in Great Britain, more Presbyterians in South Korea and Taiwan than in Scotland, and that there will probably be more Roman Catholics at the close of this century in the Southern Hemisphere than in the Northern should give us all pause. No modern theologian can continue to assume that European and North American modes of Christian thought and practice can, even in principle, any longer suffice for an emerging world church."[222]

Another important part of the question of overcoming a Eurocentric approach is the Christian relationship to other religious traditions. Tracy warns by saying that "with the Jew and the so-called pagan, the Christian in dialogue (which demands, in practice, solidarity) needs to face the constant Christian temptation to project a Christian consciousness upon the other. Both the 'pagan' and the Jew have too often served as the projected other of 'Christian' self-understanding."[223] All these recognitions of the need to depart from a Eurocentric approach have to do with the development of the hermeneutical consciousness of otherness and difference. To summarize, the hermeneutical approach does not seek for the discovery of a privileged, universal, common, and neutral matrix which supposedly grounds knowledge and belief. Instead, given the renouncement of such a matrix, it appeals to the risky and open-ended conversation which allows the creative possibilities of incommensurate interpretations and discourses. In other words, its task is "not to find a common vocabulary which would end disagreement, but to further conversation."[224] In a hermeneutical approach, meaning and truth are dependent on warranted consensus attained in conversation. In short,

---

222  *Ibid.*
223  *Ibid.*, 903. Tracy writes that, for example, "when in dialogue with the Buddhist, Christians need to face not a projected other but this great other tradition with its profound vision of ultimate reality as emptiness (*sunnyata*). Buddhists speak and live that vision so persuasively that, in first meeting them, Christian theologians like myself are hurled into a state of such initial confusion that it bears all the marks of an experience of the *mysterium fascinans et tremendum*. Dialogue with Buddhists has forced me to rethink theologically the more radically apophatic mystics of the tradition, especially Meister Eckhart." (*Ibid.*).
224  Ommen, "Theology and Foundationalism," 164.

conversation cannot rest on an absolute standpoint in which contingent and different viewpoints are dissolved. Instead, for Tracy, conversation refers to, in Gadamer's words, "a transformation into a communion in which we do not remain what we were."[225]

Now, we return to our question: whether the Lonerganian transcendental approach to God is compatible with this hermeneutical stance that entails a de-centering of Eurocentrism. As indicated above, the normality of the identification of the (Christian) God with the necessary ground of our inquiry assumed in Lonergan is a cultural product in a particular religious (Christian) tradition. In other words, this identification is a Christian interpretation which would appeal only within the Christian community, but not within a wider, non-Christian setting. The problem in the Lonerganian approach is that this identification works as a 'universal' norm which renders possible a rational, transcultural validation of the (Christian) God. However, this point is exactly what Tracy wants to eschew by asserting that no contemporary theologian "can continue to assume that European and North American modes of Christian thought and practice can, even in principle, any longer suffice for an emerging world church."[226] In the Lonerganian transcendental approach to God, the hermeneutical consciousness of the contextuality and plurality of human religious experience, and the issues of the other and the different, are not worked out.[227] In this respect, we wonder whether the Lonerganian transcendental reflection, notwithstanding Tracy's option, is not ap-

---

225  Gadamer, *Truth and Method*, 341.
226  Tracy, "God, Dialogue and Solidarity: A Theologian's Refrain," 902.
227  Francis Fiorenza says that transcendental fundamental theology overlooks the contextualization of experience within a cultural situation. For example, when we experience contingency, some would experience it as a radical dependence on nature, while others would experience it as a radical dependence on God. "Thus, persons experience their contingency in relation to their notions of ultimacy according to the paradigms of the tradition affecting their own consciousness. When persons claim to have had an experience of God, this experience is not a pure experience, but is an experience mediated through the paradigms of cultural religious history as to what is the meaning of God and what counts as an experience of that meaning." (Fiorenza, *Foundational Theology: Jesus and the Church*, 300). Therefore, "transcendental standards are only available within a cultural and interpretative framework." (*Ibid.*, 289).

plicable to Tracy's own warning that any transcendental theology which does not consider historicity and plurality "will quietly but inevitably drift away from the apologetic and situational elements of the correlation in fundamental theology." [228] In relation to the limitation of Lonergan's transcendental reflection, Jack Bonsor's comment is relevant: "Lonergan's transcendental analysis seeks to get behind pluralism by identifying the universal operations of the subject which give rise to all theory, to all perspectives," including the doctrine of God.[229] The Lonerganian transcendental validation of God is hard to free from the general charge against objectivist (or foundationalist) forms of thinking, namely, that these forms of thinking "almost inevitably turn into vulgar or sophisticated forms of ethnocentricism in which some privileged understanding of rationality is falsely legitimated by claiming for it an unwarranted universality."[230] A similar accusation is made by Bonsor: a "foundationalist thinking legitimates the hegemony of a particular perspective. In doing so, it can mistake a historical perspective, with its inevitable limits and distortions, for the ontological structure of reality."[231]

In sum, our contention is that Tracy's twofold hermeneutical-transcendental approach contains a contradictory element in itself. On the one hand, Tracy asserts that the Eurocentric or Western-centric anthropology and theology cannot survive in an emerging world church any longer. In other words, they cannot function as the universal, normative criteria which ground a theoretical resolution of intellectual, cultural, religious, and theological plurality. On the other hand, however, Tracy appeals to the Lonerganian transcendental approach which posits the hegemony of a Western-centric and Christian-centric perspective on ultimate reality. At this point, we see a fundamental clash. For Tracy, however, these two approaches do not seem to be contradictory, because, contrary to our assessment, Tracy

---

228  Tracy, "Uneasy Alliance," 559.
229  Bonsor, "Irreducible Pluralism," 326.
230  Bernstein, *Beyond Objectivism and Relativism*, 19.
231  Jack Bonsor, "History, Dogma, and Nature: Further Reflections on Post-modernism and Theology," 297.

does not consider the Lonerganian transcendental approach to God as a foundationalist and, thereby, a Western-centric discourse of God.

Tracy's twofold hermeneutical-transcendental turn in fundamental theology represents his revised view in the 1980s. One of Tracy's major theological concerns in this period is interreligious dialogue.[232] Notwithstanding this involvement, we observe that his hermeneutical-transcendental approach in this period do not sufficiently reflect how the issue of religious plurality plays an essential part in constructing the methodology of contemporary fundamental theology.[233] His retention of a transcendental reflection (a constant element from his revisionist model) seems to be a limitation for him in constructing a methodological formulation of fundamental theology that does full justice to the reality of religious plurality.

232 See Tracy, "The Dialogue of Jews and Christians: A Necessary Hope," in *Christian Theological Seminary Register* 76 (1986) 20–8; "The Christian Understanding of Salvation-Liberation," in *Journal of Buddhist Christian Studies* 7 (1987) 129–38; "The Question of Criteria for Inter-Religious Dialogue: A Tribute to Langdon Gilkey," in Donald W. Musser and Joseph L. Price (eds), *The Whirlwind in Culture* (Bloomington: Meyer-Stone, 1988) 246–62; "Kenosis, Sunyata, and Trinity: A Dialogue with Masao Abe," in John B. Cobb and Christopher Ives (ed.), *The Emptying God: A Buddhist-Jewish-Christian Conversation* (Maryknoll: Orbis Books, 1990) 135–54; *Dialogue with the Other: The Inter-Religious Dialogue*. In the 1990s, see "Some Aspects of the Buddhist-Christian Dialogue," in James Byrne (ed.) *The Christian Understanding of God Today* (Dublin: The Columba Press, 1993) 145–53.
233 Unless we deny the fact that Christianity today situates itself within a religiously pluralistic context, we cannot but admit that religious plurality needs to be a point of departure for theological reflection. For this position, see, for example, Thomas B. Ommen, "Relativism, Objectivism, and Theology," 305; idem, "Theology and Foundationalism," 170–1; Lieven Boeve, *Interrupting Tradition: An Essay on Christian Faith in a Postmodern Context* (Louvain & Dudley: Peeters Press, 2003) 163–78; G. D'Costa, "The End of Systematic Theology," *Th*, 95 (1992) 324–34.

## 3. The Third Criterion: The Ethical-Political Implications of Hermeneutical Truth-Claims

This ethical-practical criterion is concerned with the final element of Tracy's tripartite (hermeneutical-transcendental-pragmatic) method-ological approach to fundamental theology. According to Tracy, any responsible theology today, for the fuller account of theological truth, must be both "mystical and prophetic; aesthetic and ethical-political; contemplative and committed to action." [234] This means that for dealing with the truth-question in theology, a model of truth as disclosure alone does not suffice. Hence, a model of "truth as trans-formative praxis" [235] needs to be taken as a dialectical counterpart to it. The necessity of this dual formulation for theological truth lies in the fact that our cognitive understanding of Christian truth-claims is not possible in a vacuum outside our concrete historical, cultural, social-political world. Christian truth-claims should not simply remain individualistic or privatist. These claims "can only live if they become explicitly historical and political." [236] They, theologically construed, must live as "mystical-prophetic." [237] Tracy states that:

> There is no more need to disparage the great liberal theologies than there is need to disown the achievements of the Enlightenment itself. The intentions of the liberal theologians were noble. Their accomplishments are real and retrievable, especially in the personal realm. But can personalism conquer in a culture ridden with possessive individualism? Can Christian hope be reduced to the ahistorical individual of modernity? Can reason be understood outside its historical, cultural, social context? Can resistance be active if the empty time of modernity relentlessly invades all consciousness to render all consolation merely private? [238]

---

234  *DO*, 122.
235  David Tracy, "Theoria and Praxis: A Partial Response," in *ThEd*, 17 (1981) 173. Hereafter, this work will be referred to as "Theoria and Praxis."
236  David Tracy, "On Naming the Present," (*Concilium* 1990) in *On Naming the Present*, 10.
237  *DO*, 7.
238  Tracy, "On Naming the Present," 10.

In short, the necessity of the ethical-political criterion in fundamental theology is grounded in the historical-social-political reality of Christian existence and faith. Fundamental theology should take into account not only the cognitive but also the transformative (ethical-political) dimension of Christian faith.

In dealing with this ethical-political criterion, Tracy's key point is that the Christian ethical-political imperative stands in a *dialectical* relationship with its cognitive, theoretical task. Tracy asserts that, "There is no manifestation disclosure that is not also a call to transformation. There is no revelation without salvation. There is no theological theory without praxis. There need be no hermeneutic without pragmatics. There need be no divisions between the mystical and prophetic strands of the great tradition unless we arbitrarily impose them."[239] In what follows, we will focus on Tracy's two important analyses which serve as rationales for the necessity of his ethical-political criterion in fundamental theology. Firstly, we will look at Tracy's analysis of the philosophical dialectic between theory and praxis. Secondly, we will examine his analysis of the religious dialectic between "manifestation" and "proclamation" in Christianity. Our examination of these two analyses will help us to understand Tracy's view of the ethical-political criterion.

*The Philosophical Dialectic of Theory and Praxis*

According to Tracy, in the contemporary theologies of praxis, "the positive proposals on the meaning of both praxis and theory and their interrelationships [...] are really diverse if not conflicting."[240] A central positive proposal that is the object of some consensus, however, is that praxis needs to be approached in terms of an authentic personal involvement in and commitment to the struggle for liberating transformation in the concrete life-world. According to this proposal, "any individual becomes who he/she is as an authentic or inauthentic

---

239  Tracy, "Uneasy Alliance," 569.
240  David Tracy, "Theologies of Praxis," in Matthew L. Lamb (ed.), *Creativity and Method: Essays in Honor of Bernard Lonergan* (Milwaukee: Marquette University Press, 1981) 35.

subject by one's *actions* in an intersubjective and a social-historical world with other subjects and in relationship to concrete social and historical structures and movements."[241] In view of this proposal, thus, any instrumentalist understanding of praxis as "mere practice (more exactly as mechanically and routinely applied theory)" or "technique" should be negated; "hence, the employment of the ancient Greek word praxis rather than the more familiar practice."[242] This is to say that praxis is not an application, afterbirth, or even goal of theory worked out elsewhere. Rather, "praxis is theory's own originating and self-correcting foundation since all theory is dependent, minimally, on the authentic praxis of the theorist's personally appropriated value of intellectual integrity and self-transcending commitment to the imperatives of critical rationality. In that sense, praxis sublates theory, not vice-versa."[243] In short, praxis must be related to theory in such a mode that theory "is grounded in the authentic praxis of intellectual integrity and cognitive self-transcendence."[244] Accordingly, "if we desire to determine criteria of adequacy for meaning and truth, [...] we must understand the foundational role of praxis in relationship to theory."[245] Basing himself on this relationship of theory and praxis

241 *Ibid.*, 35–6 (italics mine). Tracy's background works are: Nicholas Lobkowicz, *Theory and Practice: History of a Concept from Aristotle to Marx* (Notre Dame: University of Notre Dame Press, 1967); Richard Bernstein, *Praxis and Action* (Philadelphia: University of Pennsylvania Press, 1971); idem, *The Restructuring of Social and Political Theory* (New York: Harcourt, 1976); Matthew Lamb, "The Theory-Praxis Relationship in Contemporary Christian Theology," in *CTSAP* (1976) 147–78; Johann Baptist Metz, *Faith in History and Society* (New York: Seabury, 1979) 48–88; Hermut Peukert, *Wissenschafts-theories-Handlungstheorie-Fundamentale Theologie* (Frankfurt: Suterkamp, 1978).

242 Tracy, "Theologies of Praxis," 35 and "Theoria and Praxis," 168–9. Concerning this view, Tracy refers to Matthew Lamb's analysis (Lamb, "The Theory-Praxis Relationship in Contemporary Christian Theology," 150–2).

243 Tracy, "Theoria and Praxis," 169.

244 Tracy, "Theologies of Praxis," 49.

245 *Ibid.*, 36. Tracy portrays the scriptural warrants for this foundational role of praxis in relation to theory in the following manner: "Is it not the clear and consistent teaching of the scriptural and later Christian tradition, for example, that 'conversion' is central to the Christian life, including the life of thought? Is it not the case that Christian faith, hope, and love are first praxis-realities for a

(praxis as the foundation of theory), Tracy suggests several dialectical principles which need to be operative in it

Firstly, the foundational role of praxis in relation to theory does not point up an exclusive emphasis on praxis for truth. Tracy states that, "any exclusive emphasis upon praxis for truth needs other checks than the strictly theological ones [i.e., philosophical theories and critiques] as much as alternative theological models of truth need, as they do, the checks provided by models of truth as transformative praxis."[246] Secondly, any tendency to separate or dichotomize theory and praxis in dealing with truth is mistaken. Tracy states that, "the very notion of praxis is grounded in a distinction, not a separation."[247] He explains:

> 'Saying the truth' is distinct from, although never separate from, 'doing the truth.' *Fides quae* is distinct from, though never separate from *fides qua*. Cognitive claims are distinct from, though never separate from, their grounding in particular historical concrete situations and social structures. More concretely, there is never an authentic disclosure of truth in authentic praxis without also discerning some disclosure of what is now recognized as the case (i.e., true).[248]

Thirdly, a shift of emphasis to praxis in the contemporary theologies of praxis should not be misconstrued "as an entirely novel, rev-

---

transformed agent and community before they are expressed in cognitive claims or right beliefs? In that sense, is it not the case that orthopraxis does in fact ground orthodoxy? The scriptural and traditional warrants for a transformation model of religious and theological truth, therefore, seems to back the kind of praxis-emphasis desired by both the distinct Aristotelian and Hegelian-Marxist modern formulations." (*Ibid.*, 46).

246    *Ibid.*, 50.
247    *Ibid.* Tracy writes that, "Any real distinction (like that between disclosure and transformation, like that between theory and praxis, like that between faith and faith working through love, like that between liberation-emancipation and redemption) is never a separation. Distinctions remain distinctions, serving the cause of clarity and a need for emphasis through a process empowered by the necessary and enriching power of abstraction grounding all proper intellectual distinctions. As the too easily despised Scholastics correctly insisted, sometimes '*debemus distinguere*'." (*Ibid.*, 49).
248    *Ibid.*, 49.

olutionary notion of truth itself."[249] For example, since the Enlightenment, the cognitional crisis regarding the truth-status of Christian claims has been a serious dilemma for theologians. In that situation, a shift of emphasis from theory to praxis for handling the truth-question "can be and is emancipating, *even for theory*."[250] However, this shift of emphasis does not serve as a revolutionary dissolution of the cognitional dilemma. Tracy claims that, "cognitive claims are not simply validated through authentic praxis any more than causes are validated through the presence of martyrs; the crisis of cognitive claims dose not simply dissipate when the shift of emphasis to the social-ethical crisis of a global humanity comes more clearly into central focus."[251] This means that the theoretical enterprises of constructing "argument, criteria, warrants, evidence" and "the [hermeneutical] need for the ideal of conversation" remain in force as necessities.[252] For Tracy, among many, an important contribution of the contemporary theologies of praxis (i.e., liberation, feminist, and political theologies) is to aid theologians to recognize the fact that modern theologies have been concerned (even obsessed) too exclusively with the crisis of Christian cognitional claims, ignoring the social-political crisis of the world. These theologies of praxis help to refocus theological attention on "the social-ethical crisis of massive suffering and widespread oppression and alienation in an emerging global culture" as the major question in our situation.[253] Consequently, "the emergence of theologies of praxis in our time has aided the

---

249  *Ibid.*
250  *Ibid.*, 50. Tracy explains that, "For many theologians of liberation, for example, it follows that the major problematic of most forms of fundamental theology, the problem of the truth-status of the cognitive claims of both Christianity and modernity, cannot in principle be resolved by better theories. For the norms of all theories are, in fact, grounded in the value of theorizing. Those norms include a non-objectified reality which is not theoretical (viz., the theoretician's own emancipated or alienated subjectivity). Norms are ultimately grounded not in the self-evident axioms of further theories but in the concrete intellectual, moral, and religious praxis of concrete human beings in distinct societal and historical situations." (*Ibid.*, 37).
251  *Ibid.*, 50.
252  *Ibid.*, 50–1.
253  *Ibid.*, 50.

search for criteria of truth for all theologians by their emphasis upon truth as transformation."[254] Finally, Tracy cautions against the following danger resulting from the instrumentalist understanding of praxis. When praxis is identified with "some particular cause, movement, program" in a technical sense, "[it] soon becomes uncritically mediated practice of whatever form. And any theories daring to be critical of the cause [movement, and program] [...] are too quickly dismissed as pre-revolutionary, 'bourgeois,' or 'academic'."[255] In this case, the cause, movement, or program "may become yet another hardened ideology more than open to conflict, yet closed to the actuality of critique and even the ideal of conversation."[256]

In sum, Tracy takes the view that "praxis is theory's own originating and self-correcting foundation" on condition that the aforementioned dialectical principles are operative in it. For him, this view of praxis is a *philosophical* rationale for the need of the ethical-political criterion as complementary to the hermeneutical-transcendental criterion for truth in fundamental theology.

## The Religious Dialectic of Manifestation and Proclamation

Tracy's analysis of the religious dialectic of "manifestation" and "proclamation" provides a *religious* rationale for the need of his ethical-political criterion. According to Tracy, in most of the great religions, there are two major paradigms of the intensification of their religious particularity: "manifestation," released by the tradition of the mystics, and "proclamation," released by the tradition of the prophets.[257] The intertwinement of these two paradigms in a particular

---

254  *Ibid.*, 51.
255  *Ibid.*, 50.
256  *Ibid.* Tracy writes that, "The 'eschatological proviso' of most political theologies, to be sure, provides a good theological check upon these temptations (not inevitabilities) of any praxis-oriented theology. The internal developments of most forms of liberation theology seem to be providing the same kind of theological check on the same temptations." (*Ibid.*).
257  For this primordial religious dialectic, Tracy is indebted to Paul Ricoeur's article, "Manifestation and Proclamation," in *The Journal of the Blaisdell Institute* 12 (1978) 13–35.

religion reflects the complexity of a religious symbol system which resonates with the complexity of human religious experience. Tracy's essential point here is that these two paradigms, "manifestation" and "proclamation," must be approached in a *dialectical* distinction, not in an unrelated dichotomy. Tracy states that, "Each needs the other [...] exclusivity must be resisted."[258] It is clearly observed that this primordial religious dialectic of "manifestation" and "proclamation" is at the heart of Christianity. Tracy says that, "Christianity does not live by means of any 'only.' Christianity lives in and by the paradigmatic power of both manifestation and proclamation."[259]

The paradigm of "manifestation" in Christianity is discerned, *par excellence*, in the Christian affirmative understanding of the world as God's creation. More specifically, Christianity embraces and cele-brates the world in and through its doctrines of creation and incarnation. The world, as God's creation, is the locus of hierophany, namely, the place in which God as the power of "the whole" is manifested.[260] An essential principle operative in this religious para-digm is, in Ricoeur's words, "a law of *correspondence*."[261] Ricoeur states that a "law of correspondence constitutes the logic of mani-festation."[262] This means that the religious experience of "mani-festation" consists in the sense of the correspondence between the profane world (or elements) and religious or divine symbolism. Owing to this correspondence, the profane world becomes saturated by sacred meanings: the profane world signifies something other than itself, while still remaining itself. For example, "the burning bush" (Ex 3: 4) is the symbol of God's presence; the temple in Jerusalem symbolizes God's dwelling place (Jn 2: 16, "Stop making my Father's house a market-place"); the water in baptism is the symbol of purification, etc. Based on this law of correspondence, the religious experience of "manifestation" involves a radical sense of "belonging to, partici-

---

258  *AI*, 205.
259  *Ibid.*, 214.
260  *Ibid.*, 207.
261  Ricoeur, "Manifestation and Proclamation," 20.
262  *Ibid.*, 21.

pating in, even saturation by the power of the cosmos, of the whole, as a sacred power."[263]

As a dialectical counterpart to this paradigm of "manifestation," the paradigm of "proclamation" breaks away from the consecrated world invested with religious symbolism. In other words, in the religious paradigm of "proclamation," the language of radical participation is suspect as "extravagant, sometimes even idolatrous."[264] The paradigm of "proclamation" focuses on God's prophetic words and deeds which disturb and upset our complacent sense of participation in the world of our divinization. In view of this paradigm, God's proclamatory words occur "to disconfirm any complacency in participation, to shatter any illusions that this culture, this priesthood, this land, this ritual is enough, to defamiliarize us with ourselves and with nature, [...] to expose all idols of the self as projections of ourselves and our mad ambitions."[265] Tracy explains that this paradigm of proclamation, in fact, makes us "recognize that Judaism and Christianity disclose a radical world-affirmation only because they have first undergone a radical, decentering experience of world-negation in the kerygmatic, proclamatory word of address of prophetic religion." [266] In other words, proclamatory words, like 'kerygma,' demand some kind of "distanciation" from a saturated participation in the sacred world, and draw attention to the individual and communal conscience in concrete historical-social-political life: "The existence of a participating-nonparticipating, ethically and politically responsible self: responsible to conscience and to others, responsible for this world and this history, responsible to the words and deeds of this God."[267] In this paradigm of "proclamation," the world is, however, not deprived of religious meanings, but endowed with new and different religious meanings. This is to say that, "The realities once considered merely profane – time, history, the individual

263  *AI*, 207. Tracy writes that this sense of radical participation in the whole is what "Schleiermacher named 'the feeling of absolute dependence,' which others name a fundamental trust in the very worthwhileness of existence." (*Ibid.*, 215).
264  *Ibid.*, 211.
265  *Ibid.*, 209.
266  *Ibid.*
267  *Ibid.*, 209.

as individual – now become saturated with the religious meaning and truth proclaimed in the word's call to obedience, action, and freedom."[268] In other words, "the secular now emerges not as the realm of nonreligion but the realm where the power of word must be constantly expressed in new action for justice and radical neighbor-love, the realm of faithful historical religious meaning."[269]

For Tracy, as already indicated earlier, these two distinct religious paradigms should be understood as dialectical partners of interplay. This dialectical necessity rests on the fact that the reality of the world is ambiguous and religiously dialectical. This means that we live "*simul iustus et peccator* in and for the world": we live in a world endowed with "the significance and goodness of history, the estrangement and sin in self and society, the ultimate incomprehensibility of self, society and history," etc.[270] According to Tracy, an exclusively proclamation-oriented Christianity is always in danger of "self-righteousness and moralistic rigorism choking the manifestation powers of the religion itself."[271] The religious power of manifestation should not be suppressed in the paradigm of proclamation, because "manifestation is always the enveloping presupposition of the emergence and, at the limit, the eruption of the defamiliarizing word of proclamation."[272] In other words, without manifestation, "there is no

---

268  *Ibid.*, 211.
269  *Ibid.* Basing himself on this view, Tracy claims that, "the affirmation of the secular in contemporary Jewish and Christian theology, therefore, is not properly understood as some collapse of Christianity and Judaism in the face of contemporary secularism. Rather a secular Christianity and a secular Judaism are, in fact, faithful to the paradigmatic eruption of a proclaimed and addressing word-event which founds these traditions and drives them on as their religious focal meaning. *Some* desacralization of the claims of participation via manifestation must occur whenever this kind of world-shattering and world-affirming paradigmatic religious experience of proclamation happens." (*Ibid.*).
270  *Ibid.*, 213.
271  *Ibid.*, 228 n.72.
272  *Ibid.*, 215. In a similar manner, Ricoeur states that, "In truth, without the support and renewing power of the sacred cosmos and the sacredness of vital nature, the word itself becomes abstract and cerebral. Only the incarnation of the ancient symbolism ceaselessly reinterpreted gives this word something to say, not only to our understanding and will, but also to our imagination and our

place for the word to be heard and perform its shattering and affirmative tasks."[273] Ricoeur's following utterance is helpful for highlighting Tracy's point: "Would the word conversion continue to signify anything if we absolutely lost sight of what was expressed in these symbols of regeneration, new creation, and the advent of a new being and a new world?"[274]

Conversely, an exclusively manifestation-oriented Christianity is liable to fall into "a too easy humanism or [...] [a] hardened priest-craft" or "ritualism."[275] When only manifestation (world-affirmation) prevails, Christianity loses its religious vigor and poignancy, and its churches are likely to become "only psychological counseling centers or resources for societal causes."[276] In other words, without the world-shattering power of proclamation, Christianity "becomes another decent, ethical vision living in, by and for a world which sets its agenda and writes the words for its decent, ethical, but ultimately irreligious tunes."[277] The religious power of proclamation should not be neglected in the paradigm of manifestation, because manifestation is, in a way, reinterpreted in the light of proclamation. In the light of world-negating proclamation, the world is "truly affirmed without being canonized; the world's real ambiguity – its possibilities for both good and evil – is recognized on religious grounds."[278] More specifically,

---

heart; in short, to the whole human being." (Ricoeur, "Manifestation and Proclamation," 35).

273   *AI*, 211. Tracy remarks that some theologians in the evangelical or neo-orthodox Protestant tradition seem "so alive to the paradigmatic power of that word, some Christians become, so afraid of any claim to radical participation, any language of 'divinization,' any reality of *eros*, any 'point of contact' between the utterly transcendent, the hidden and revealed God who proclaims that liberating word that they, like Dietrich Bonhoeffer, are tempted to want to remove all manifestation from this paradigmatically word-centered Christianity, remove all mysticism, all metaphysics and finally all 'religion' itself from the stark and obedient faith of a 'religionless' secular Christianity come of age and living in and for the world." (*Ibid.*, 213).

274   Ricoeur, "Manifestation and Proclamation," 35.

275   *AI*, 212.

276   *Ibid.*

277   *Ibid.*

278   *Ibid.*

the Christian doctrine of creation becomes fully meaningful in the light of its doctrines of redemption and eschatology; the Christian doctrine of incarnation becomes fully meaningful in the light of disrupting, disorienting cross and resurrection.[279] Tracy says that to speak Christian prophetic-eschatological language is, therefore, to proclaim that God's power of immanence (manifestation) has entered time and history. This ongoing and vital dialectic between world-affirming *manifestation* and world-negating *proclamation* continues to empower "Christians to enter the struggle of history and time, to search for, work for, think for the *new* of a future which is an empowered *adventum* and a hoped-for, paradigmatic *promissio* in the always-already, not yet reality of the present."[280]

In sum, for Tracy, Christianity is a religion which embraces "both a prophetic-ethical-historical defamiliarizing focus and power and a mystical-metaphysical-aesthetic transformed and transformative enveloping ground."[281] Accordingly, Christian theology necessitates a methodological strategy which can cope with this religious dialectic. Tracy finds the religious rationale of his ethical-political criterion for fundamental theology in this primordial dialectic of proclamation and manifestation in Christianity. For Tracy, just as his first hermeneutical criterion "has genuine affinities with the [Christian] mystical orientations and their emphasis on revelation," his ethical-political criterion

---

279  See *ibid.*, 214. Tracy says that the paradigmatic Christ-event itself reveals the religious dialectic of manifestation and proclamation: namely, Christ is "the decisive re-presentation in both word and manifestation of our God and our humanity." (*Ibid.*, 218). According to Tracy, a dialectical (not juxtapositional or dichotomous) structure is, in fact, present in the entire Christian symbol system: "word and sacrament; the transcendence and immanence of God; operative and cooperative grace; creation and eschatology; prophet-reformer and mystic-sage-priest; incarnation and cross-resurrection; nature-grace and grace-sin; aesthetics and ethics; nature and history; the centering, encoding myth and the decoding, decentering kerygma; epiphany and historical event; analogy and negative dialectics; metaphor and metonymy; ontic event and ontological structure; world-negation and, through that negation, a real release to world-affirmation." (*Ibid.*).

280  *Ibid.*, 216.

281  *Ibid.*, 215.

has "clear affinities to the [Christian] prophetic emphasis on salvation as demanding both justice and love."[282]


## III. Tracy's Methodological View of Fundamental Theology from the 1990s to the Early 2000s


The principal characteristic of Tracy's theological development in the 1990s (up to the early 2000s) is his focal (almost exclusive) concern with the question of *God*. The key feature of Tracy's theological reflection on God in this period can be summarized by two elements. Firstly, Tracy makes a criticism of a comprehensive range of modern discourses on God (including his own previous positions). And, he pays attention to the "return of God" in contemporary postmodern theology and philosophy as the uncontrolled, shattering Other (e.g., Martin Heidegger's God as the mystery beyond Greek onto-theology, Emmanuel Levinas' God as glimpsed in the face of the other, Jean-Luc Marion's God as the gift of love) which disallows any modern totalitarian, objectivist discourse on God. Secondly, Tracy attempts to search for alternative forms for naming and thinking this God returned. Tracy characterizes this attempt not as a search for "a rival set of propositions to modern theology," but says that "it is something else: a search for entirely alternative forms."[283] More specifically, according to Tracy, most postmodern critiques of modern discourses on God involve a concern for how to liberate the reality of God from the captivity of modern controlling, totalitarian intellectual systems.

---

282  *DO*, 103.
283  David Tracy, "The Return of God in Contemporary Theology," (*Concilium* 1994), in *On Naming the Present*, 45. Hereafter, this work will be referred to as "The Return of God." Tracy's book, *On Naming the Present*, is a compilation of his articles published in *Concilium* in different years. On the topic of God, his three articles, all published in the 1990s, are included in this book. In the following footnotes, whenever we refer to one of these articles, we will put its year of publication in *Concilium* in a bracket next to the article's title.

However, since today's postmodern searches for alternative forms are still underway, no one knows where postmodern critiques and searches will finally lead. Tracy states that, "this much is clear: amid all the shouting of the present, the reality of God has returned to the center of theology. This is not the time to rush out new propositions on the reality of God. This is rather the time to allow wonder again at the overwhelming mystery of God."[284] He goes on to say, "this is the time for theologians to learn to disallow the *logos* of modernity to control their thoughts on God as we learn anew to be attentive to God. We must learn somehow, in God's absent presence, to be still and know that God is God."[285]

In what follows, we will discuss the aforementioned two elements of Tracy's reflection on God in the 1990s (up to the early 2000s). One thing to note is that the only available sources for Tracy's reflection on God in this period are his several articles and published interviews. His new book on God is forthcoming and not yet available. What we can get from these available sources is his brief critique of modern discourses on God and a sketchy proposal for a postmodern reflection on God. Hence, we can only present a short description on these in this section.

*1. Tracy's Criticism of Modern Discourses on God*

According to Tracy, the history of theology is, in a sense, the history of the ever-shifting correlation between *theos* and *logos*. In other words, the history of theology consists in the continuously renewing formulation of the "relationship between the reality of God and that divine reality as experienced and understood from within a *logos*, i.e., a particular horizon of intelligibility."[286] Tracy says that there can be little doubt that in modern theology, the *logos* of modern intelligibility overpowers and domesticates the reality of *theos* in this correlation. This is to say that theology in the modern period is "obsessed with

284   *Ibid.*
285   *Ibid.*
286   *Ibid.*, 36.

finding the exactly right method, the irrefutable modern argument, the proper horizon of intelligibility for comprehending and perhaps controlling God."[287] According to Tracy, this modern obsession with controlling intelligibility in relation to God's reality has spawned a series of modern 'isms' since the late seventeenth century: e.g., deism, pantheism, modern theism, atheism, agnosticism, and panentheism. In other words, all these diverse 'isms' are the invention of modernity. Tracy claims that "the modern God became the captive of one or another modern 'ism' [...] On the question of God, the modern mind had choices, to be sure. But all the modern choices were principally determined not by the reality of God but by the *logos* of modernity."[288] The *logos* of modernity operative in these 'isms' assumes the pure, clear and distinct presence of God to an alinguistic, ahistorical, self-present, and self-grounding consciousness. In Merold Westphal's words, in this modern totalitarian optimism, "as possessors of a system of thought which is adequate to grasp or to mirror the divine reality, we have both God and the world at our cognitive disposal." [289] In short, the modern intellectual confidence in a totalitarian understanding of God has produced "a series of seemingly endless debates on the correct ism, that is the correct set of abstract propositions which name and think God."[290] However, Tracy asserts, "despite modernity's belief, there is no set of abstract propositions, no rational, clear, and distinct ideas, no sublating concept, no rational propositional doctrine – in a word no *ism* – that is ever adequate for naming and thinking God."[291] For Tracy, the key problem in these well-known modern 'isms' is that God is rendered "a conceptual prisoner" of intellectual systems of totality "with no real moment of *infinity* allowing God to be God."[292] In other words, the modern series

---

287   *Ibid.*
288   *Ibid.*, 41.
289   Merold Westphal, *Transcendence and Self-Transcendence: On God and the Soul* (Bloomington: Indiana University Press, 2004) 93.
290   David Tracy, "Literary Theory and Return of the Forms for Naming and Thinking God in Theology," in *JR*, 74 (1994) 307. Hereafter, this work will be referred to as "Literary Theory."
291   *Ibid.*, 309.
292   "The Return of God," 41.

of 'isms' for naming God "had very little if anything to do with God as a religious phenomenon and religion as a saturated sacred phenomenon."[293] Tracy goes on to contend that, "Those 'isms' were intended rationally to control the discussion of the ultimate religious other in any radically monotheistic reflection on God. But can the question of God really be controlled as a religious question by the modern discussion of deism, pantheism, modern atheism, modern theism or even, in the best achievement of modern Western religious thought, panentheism from Bruno to Hegel to Whitehead?"[294]

An important change in Tracy's view on the question of God in the 1990s from his positions in the 1970s and the 1980s is, as the above statement implies, that Tracy does not consider panentheism (in Tracy's revisionist model, process thought) and transcendental reflection as adequate and viable reflections on God any longer. These two philosophical traditions, his revisionist options, are still constantly maintained in his 1980s' theological perspective. In our preceding discussion of Tracy's theological position in the 1980s, we saw that Tracy's approach is hermeneutical-*transcendental*-pragmatic. In this approach, Tracy incorporates the Lonerganian transcendental reflection on God. Tracy does not specifically mention panentheism in his revised view of fundamental theology in the 1980s. However, we can find in his *Plurality and Ambiguity* (1987) that Tracy still considers Charles Hartshorne's metaphysics (panentheistic process thought) as a useful resource for validating a Christian discourse on God. Tracy's defensive position concerning Hartshorne's metaphysics is seen in his claim in *Plurality and Ambiguity* that, "Critics of 'metaphysics' often miss the care with which modern metaphysical claims are claims to relative, not absolute, adequacy: careful claims like those in Aristotle and careful claims like those in one of the foremost metaphysical thinkers of our period, Charles Hartshorne."[295]

---

293    David Tracy, "Fragments: The Spiritual Situation of Our Times," in John D. Caputo and Michael J. Scanlon (eds), *God, The Gift, and Postmodernism* (Bloomington and Indianapolis: Indiana University Press, 1999) 171. Hereafter, this article will be referred to as "Fragments: The Spiritual Situation."
294    *Ibid.*, 171–2.
295    *PA*, 122 n.9.

More specifically, in the same book, Tracy expresses his method-ological position on the question of God as follows. In his in-corporation of hermeneutical reflection, to abandon the modern conviction about the transparency of consciousness to itself is not to discard:

> the demand for such transcendental analysis – whether linguistically and sociologically and analogically informed discourse analysis like that of Habermas or the necessarily metaphysical character of theological claims as in Hartshorne. In sum, the need to reformulate all earlier transcendental analyses which are based on a philosophy of consciousness seems clear and difficult. The need, however, to demand that kind of analysis for all the implicit validity claims in all our discourse and, even more so, for the logically unique claims of theology on the strictly necessary individual, God, seems equally clear.[296]

In the 1990s, however, Tracy leaves behind this view. Firstly, concerning transcendental reflection, he shows a different position by claiming that the modern concept of the transcendental self (in which God is epistemologically grounded) cannot any longer be adequate. Tracy says that what we need to recognize is that:

> none of the models of the modern self and the present time of modernity can any longer suffice: neither the purely autonomous self of the Enlightenment, nor the expressionist self of the Romantics, nor the anxious self of the existentialists, nor *the transcendental self of the transcendental philosophers and theologians of consciousness.* All such models are inadequate, for all are too deeply related to the embattled and self-deluding self of modernity. We need a new theological understanding of both self and modernity as 'the present.' We need historical subjects with memory, hope, and resistance.[297]

For Tracy, the criticism of modern discourses of God has to do with debunking the foundationalist pretensions of the modern self (including the self of transcendental reflection) to mastery and certainty in its pursuit of knowledge. For the critique of the modern self's delusions, Tracy takes notice of postmodern (more specifically, "poststructuralist") critiques of language which unmask the illusory character of the self portrayed by the Western logocentric belief: a

296    *Ibid.*, 134 n.40.
297    "Literary Theory," 305 (italics mine).

350

self-present user of language, and thereby, the self as a meaning-grounding ego. In other words, according to the poststructuralist claim (of which a representative is Jacque Derrida), it is an illusion that "we language-sated beings can ever be fully present to ourselves or that any other reality can be fully present to us either."[298] Our understanding of reality is rendered in and through language. However, when we use language, we must defer any claims to a full "presence" of meaning of it in conscious thought. According to the Derridean view, there is no unitary referential relationship between signifier and signified in the system of our language: there is no one-to-one fixed correspondence between them.[299] In metaphysical terms, word and thing (or being) never become coincidental. Instead, we must notice the arbitrary, pluralistic, non-identical, and continually dispersing character of this relationship between signifier and signified. This is because, in the Derridean account, the meaning of "signified" is not such that it preexists the signifier, being independent of it in its pure ideality or universality. Meaning is never conceivable as an absolutely identical, univocal, or immediately present one, held in abstraction from its linguistic, socio-political, religious-cultural, or historical context in which it is entangled. More precisely, each such context refers to "a system of reference," or "a system of signifiers,"[300] whose function includes the differentiating, equivocal, arbitrary, or disseminating configuration of meaning. Put differently, our understanding of meaning in and through language is never free from the play of "the dialectic of presence and absence in which anything (partially) present is a trace that points beyond itself to what is not present."[301] In short, "there is no meaning, no signified content, that stands above and is free from this play of differences. Nor could meaning withstand the continuous shifting of differences, the continuous sedimenting of traces, as some ideal *identity*. For Derrida,

298  *PA*, 59.
299  See Madan Sarup, *An Introductory Guide to Post-Structuralism and Post-modernism* (Hertfordshire: Harvester Wheatsheaf, 1993) 33.
300  David B. Allison, "Translator's Introduction," Jacque Derrida, *Speech and Phenomena: And Other Essays on Husserl's Theory of Signs* (Evanston: Northwestern University Press, 1973) xxxviii.
301  Westphal, *Transcendence and Self-Transcendence*, 104.

there is only a likeness or sameness to meaning, which is constituted across the history of ever-changing usage. Absolute objectivity, therefore, could never be claimed for meaning."[302] For Tracy, an important philosophical implication of this Derridean view is that neither in the mode of immediacy nor totality is the whole of reality (including God's reality) present to our cognition. Thus, he makes clear that the "self-grounding, self-present modern subject is dead: killed by its own pretensions to grounding all reality in itself. That subject, I believe, should be unmourned by all along with the modern totalized systems [including modern totalitarian God-talk] built upon it."[303] In sum, Tracy states his suspicion of the intellectual complacency of the modern self as follows:

> As the post-moderns make clear, the modern self, unfortunately for its foundationalist pretensions, must also use language. And the very self-deconstructing, non-grounding play of the signifiers in all language will assure that no signified, especially, *the great modern transcendental signified* (theism or ego-ism...) will ever find the pure identity, the clear and distinct self-presence it seeks or the totality it grasps at.[304]

Secondly, with regard to panentheism, Tracy expresses his position in the 1990s as follows. He still believes that panentheism, whose process version he defended in his *BRO*, is "the most original move of modernity for naming and thinking God."[305] In other words,

---

302 Allison, "Translator's Introduction," xxxviii.
303 David Tracy, "The Post-Modern Re-Naming of God as Incomprehensible and Hidden," in *CrCur*, 50 (2000) 241.
304 *Ibid.*, (italics mine).
305 "Literary Theory," 307. Tracy summarizes the achievements of panentheism as follows: "First, it maintains the highest standards of modern rationality from the scientific revolution of the nineteenth century forward, without yielding to either modern empiricism or historicism. Second, panentheism allows for the move that premodern thought could not make but which any proper naming of God in relationship to the world fundamentally needs: the insistence that the world affects God and therefore that history and, more broadly, action (not only contemplation) are constitutive of one's understanding of God. Third, on this reading the central Christian metaphor, 'God is Love' (1 John 4: 16), can be rendered coherent by articulating in panentheistic terms the intrinsically relational character of the Divine reality as indeed of all reality. Fourth, the

panentheism is "the best way to render in modern concepts God's relationship to us [God's relationality] as described in the Bible."[306] Tracy finds its most noticeable achievement in its ability to bridge the chasm between the God of metaphysics and the God of Scriptures. In other words, it contributes to breaking through the incompetence of the classical metaphysical (monopolar) conception of God in accounting for the scriptural divine values of love, responsiveness, companionship, taking part in human suffering, etc. Tracy says that most of contemporary theology which is keen on the issues of evil and suffering, "will be, in some sense, an heir of the panentheistic articulation of the biblical vision of the suffering of God."[307] This is to say that:

> The suffering God of process thought who persuades and lures us on to the Good is an honorable attempt to rethink earlier modern theodicies in a form more resonant to the central biblical imagery of the God who suffers along with all creation as well as more intelligible to a modern sensibility where change, becoming, process are so central to our scientific and historical understandings of all reality.[308]

However, Tracy does not believe that panentheism can "provide the way to approach the question of God now."[309] The panentheistic form "for naming and thinking God, by its usual lack of attention to the possible limits of its own form, may find itself in a series of

traditional confusions on Divine impassibility can be resolved in favor of an understanding of 'God's suffering.' Any panentheistic understanding of the suffering of God resonates not only with scriptural portraits of God but with modern religious sensibilities, as instanced by Bonhoeffer's famous cry that 'only a suffering God can help'." (*Ibid.*, 308).

306    An interview with David Tracy made by Malcolm Lois, "The Impossible God," http://www.file:///A/Malcolm-Christian Century-2002.htm (access 10 September 2002). Hereafter, the page numbers for quotations from this interview will follow those on this internet source. The above quotation is on p.1 on that source.

307    David Tracy, "Evil, Suffering, Hope: The Search for New Forms of Contemporary Theodicy," in *CTSAP*, 50 (1995) 25. Hereafter, this work will be referred to as "Evil, Suffering, Hope."

308    *Ibid.*, 25–6.

309    Tracy, "The Impossible God," 2.

impasses."[310] For Tracy, the category of history is vital to approach the impasses of panentheism, including other modern 'isms.' Let us briefly look at Tracy's explanation of the inadequacy of modern 'isms' of God for contemporary God-talk by analyzing this category, history.

According to Tracy, one of the eminent discoveries and achievements of modernity is historical consciousness. However, this modern historical consciousness too often includes "a not-so-secret narrative history of its own: a social-evolutionary schema whereby all history leads to 'the Western moderns'."[311] In other words, "history, in the modern schema, is too often a linear, continuous, teleological schema with a single *telos* – Western modernity."[312] According to Tracy, the God of modern 'isms' is a part of such a schema of continuity and confidence: "a sometimes important part (modern theism and panentheism) or a sometimes missing part (atheism and agnosticism), but a part nonetheless."[313]

Tracy presents two essential elements which have contributed to wreck this modern Eurocentric, imperialist, and teleological sense of history: "the interruption of massive global suffering in modern history and the eruption of all those others set aside, forgotten, and colonized by the grand narrative of modernity."[314] For Tracy, these two elements represent "the 'unthought' aspects of modernity" which we should now honestly acknowledge.[315] Put differently, the modern 'isms' of God find themselves in impasses when facing these unassimilable realities. Tracy claims that, "The history of modern

---

310  Tracy, "Literary Theory," 308.
311  David Tracy, "The Hidden God: The Divine Other of Liberation," 7. Hereafter, this work will be referred to as "The Hidden God."
312  *Ibid.*
313  *Ibid.*
314  *Ibid.*
315  *Ibid.* For Tracy, liberation, political, and feminist theologies have contributed a great deal to recognizing these "unthought" aspects of modernity. He writes that, "Surely the great liberation movements and theologies of our period are the theologies that best teach us all the dangerous truth of the God of history [...] In the liberation, political, and feminist theologians, Christian theology articulates anew its faith in the God of concrete history." (David Tracy, "God of History, God of Psychology," (*Concilium* 1993) in *On Naming the Present*, 50).

progressive theologies of history is too often a history without radical interruption, without a memory of the victims of history, without a consciousness of patriarchy, or racism or classism or Eurocentrism, without Auschwitz, Hiroshima, or the Gulag."[316] In these modern progressive theologies, God is projected as an objective referent or guarantor of a "modern social-evolutionary narrative that may comfort modern religiousness but seems incapable of manifesting any dangerous God of concrete history."[317] More specifically, the God active in the interruptive history of suffering is not identical to the God of existentialist and transcendental historicity. The entry of this interruptive God can occur through neither "the estranged and alienated self of the existential theologians, those admirable and deeply troubled moderns,"[318] nor through an analysis of the transcendental conditions of possibility of the modern historical subject. The God of existentialist and transcendental historicity "seems far removed from the dangerous and disruptive God of the history narrated in Exodus and in the history of Jesus."[319] Tracy asserts:

> God enters contemporary history not as a consoling 'ism' but above all as an awesome, often terrifying, hope-beyond-hope. God enters history again not as a new speculation – but as the unpredictable, liberating, Hidden God. For this God reveals Godself in hiddenness: in cross and negativity, above all in the suffering of all those others whom the grand narrative of modernity has too often set aside as non-peoples, non-events, non-memories, in a word, non-history.[320]

Regarding the panentheistic view of the suffering God, Tracy points out that it will not suffice to provide an acute focus on the horror of disruptive evils and ponderous suffering in human history. A reason for this limitation is that although the key idea, "process," in process thought is not simply identical with "progress," a process understanding of history "seems too dependent upon social evolutionary models" to lay bare the horror of disruptive evils and pon-

---

316  Tracy, "God of History, God of Psychology," 51.
317  *Ibid.*, 50.
318  Tracy, "The Return of God," 43.
319  Tracy, "God of History, God of Psychology," 51.
320  Tracy, "The Hidden God," 7–8.

derous suffering in human history. Tracy sums up two actualities that process thought seems either reluctant to confront or is incapable of addressing: "first, radical historical evil both destructive of all social evolutionary schemas for understanding history and disruptive of all assumed continuities in process; second, a God who acts in history as the prophets and Jesus of Nazareth insisted God does in fact act actively on behalf of the poor and oppressed."[321] For Tracy, insofar as process thought's vision of God does not sufficiently handle these actualities, it will be implausible as today's intellectual option. He states that, "The reality of evil is too deep in our histories, the all-pervasiveness of suffering too real, the activity against evil so insisted upon in the Bible too central to find sufficient, on inner-Christian grounds and on postmodern grounds alike, this kindly, perhaps all too kindly, modern liberal process vision of the great companion, the fellow sufferer [God] who understands and lures us on to the Good."[322] In sum, the modern existentialist, transcendental, or pan-entheistic envisioning of God does not suffice to reveal penetratingly the God active in the interruptive history of suffering, which needs to be the departure point for today's God-reflection.

## 2. A Search for Alternative Forms for Naming and Thinking God: The Apocalyptic and the Apophatic

In the wake of postmodern criticism of modern 'isms' of God, Tracy focuses on the emergence of an attempt across the philosophical and theological spectrum to free God from the stranglehold of modernity's controlling, self-complacent *logos*. Tracy indicates that this attempt is "a historical challenge that is as difficult, as conflictual, as painful as the earlier (equally necessary) attempt in early modernity to free thought from the then suffocating embrace of premodern modes of thought."[323] In his search for alternative forms for naming and thinking God, Tracy turns his attention to "a thought that modern

---

321    Tracy, "Evil, Suffering, Hope," 25.
322    *Ibid.*, 26.
323    Tracy, "The Hidden God," 6.

theology cannot think without yielding its *logos* to *theos* in ways it does not seem to know how to do."[324] In other words, he seeks for a new thought where "God returns to remove the '*theos*,' at once grounding and domesticated, in modernity's onto-*theo*-logy. God returns to demand that modernity disown once and for all its speculative ambitions to control the divine reality in order to let God be God again."[325] Here, for Tracy, the God beyond onto-theology refers to the God who is beyond such categories as "being," "transcendentality," and even "relationality" (in a panentheistic sense).[326] We saw in chapter 3 that these categories are pivotal for his revisionist reflection on God (in *BRO*). In the following, we will examine how Tracy attempts to search for new forms for God, overcoming these modern, onto-theological categories. We will focus on three major issues that Tracy touches on: (1) the new starting point for our contemporary theological reflection on God; (2) the importance of recovering the form of "fragments" for contemporary God-talk; (3) the retrieval of two fragmentary traditional forms for contemporary God-talk, the apocalyptic and apophatic forms.

*The New Starting Point for Contemporary Theological Reflection on God*

*Starting From God's Identity, Rather Than God's Existence and Nature*

According to Tracy, the starting point of our contemporary reflection on God needs to be the question of God's *identity*, rather than the question of God's *existence* and *nature* (or *essence*). Tracy says that, "In Judaism, Christianity, and Islam, monotheism is a religious before it is a philosophical category. Indeed, even within theology itself, soteriological monotheism is older than and grounding to all dogmatic monotheism. For the Jew, the Christian, and the Muslim monotheistic

---

324   Tracy, "The Return of God," 44
325   *Ibid.*
326   See *ibid.*, 44.

357

faith is fundamentally a gift of God: God's gift of self-revelation."[327] As we saw in chapter 3, in his revisionist model, Tracy holds a different position, namely, that the question of God (in theology) is a *metaphysical* question. This position is grounded in the view that "where God is conceived radically (as in such monotheistic religions as Judaism, Christianity, and Islam), God is conceived metaphysically."[328] For him, in *BRO*, the God of monotheistic religions is conceived as "the one metaphysical individual, the sole reality whose individuality is constitutive of reality as such."[329] In this revisionist approach, the philosophical categories, God's *existence* and *nature* (or *essence*), crucially serve for directing and constructing his theological discourse on God. Tracy says now that, for the modern (such as himself in *BRO*), to think God is to try to find the abstract, conceptual sets of propositions or ideas for articulating, on modern rational grounds, the *existence* and *nature* of God.

Now, according to Tracy, the quintessential turn of postmodernity, particularly, the turn to the other necessitates disowning this approach. Tracy says that, "God's shattering otherness, the neighbor's irreducible otherness, the othering reality of 'revelation,' not the consoling modern communality of 'religion,' all these expressions of otherness come now in new postmodern *and* post-neoorthodox forms to demand the serious attention of all thoughtful theologians."[330] Indeed, he says, "the other and the different come forward now as central intellectual categories across all the major disciplines, including theology."[331] What, then, can be a more adequate entry-point or starting point of our reflection on God in this new and demanding situation? Tracy says that, "intensity and transgression are frequent entry-points into this unsettling, new reality [of otherness] where sameness dissolves" into frightening differences

---

327 Tracy, "The Paradox of the Many Faces of God in Mono-Theism," (*Concilium* 1995) in *On Naming the Present*, 31. Hereafter, this work will be referred to as "The Paradox in Mono-Theism."

328 *BRO*, 155.

329 *Ibid.*

330 David Tracy, "Theology and The Many Faces of Postmodernity," 108. Hereafter, this work will be referred to as "Many Faces of Postmodernity."

331 *Ibid.*

or disruption.[332] According to him, the postmodern turn to otherness contributes to return biblical Judaism and Christianity to the entry-point of a theological reflection on God. This is to say, an intensity, transgression, excess, and non-closure for thinking God are *par excellence* found in biblical renderings of God's reality. Retrieving the Barthian approach, Tracy takes the view that, in biblical narratives, the question of God is not the question of God's *existence* and *nature*, but primarily the question of God's *identity*, from which we need to start our contemporary reflection on God.[333] Tracy does not, however, seem to rule out completely the usefulness of philosophical discussions concerning God's *existence* and *nature*, saying that, "Philosophical discussions of monotheism are indeed welcome and often relevant (e.g., for issues of credibility and intelligibility) in strictly theological analyses of religious monotheism."[334] In short, his point is that, "the Christian understanding of the 'existence' and 'nature' of the radically monotheistic God must be grounded in the 'identity' of the God disclosed" in and through the biblical renderings.[335] Then, a subsequent question will be, how to approach the identity of God?

332 *Ibid.*
333 Tracy writes that, "What might be called the second coming of Karl Barth in Christian theology is largely the result of this discovery of the centrality of the narrative form for Christian self-understanding. The question of God for Karl Barth is primarily the question not of God's nature but of God's identity. And that identity is affirmed in and through the central form of the great narratives of the Bible." (Tracy, "Literary Theory," 310).
334 Tracy, "The Paradox in Mono-Theism," 31.
335 *Ibid.*, 34.

In response to the question of how to approach the identity of God, Tracy utilizes Hans Frei's theological study of biblical narratives.[336] The key idea in Frei's study that Tracy intends to incorporate is that God's identity is definitively revealed in and through the unsubstitutable identity of Jesus Christ. And this identity of Jesus Christ is principally disclosed in and through the "plain sense" of the common passion narrative of the gospels. Here, the "plain sense" refers to the obvious, direct or literal sense of the biblical narratives as it is read by and for the Christian community.[337] According to Frei, this plain sense "has traditionally been, is, and should be both realistic and history-like."[338] More specifically, we can perceive the identity of Jesus Christ in a "plain," or "realistic and history-like" sense by means of a "close attention to the narrative interactions of an unsubstitutable character (Jesus) and the highly specific circumstances of all the events constituting the gospel accounts of the passion and resurrection."[339] In other words, for Frei, the plain sense of the common passion narrative is the key to understand theologically the unsubstitutable identity of Jesus Christ in the most explicit and fullest sense. Put differently, the interplay operative in the biblical narratives between the character of Jesus and circumstances "allow[s] both for an identity-clarification of

336    The representative works of Hans Frei that Tracy draws on are Hans Frei, The Eclipse of Biblical Narrative: A Study in Eighteenth and Nineteenth Century Hermeneutics (New Haven: Yale University Press, 1974); idem, The Identity of Jesus Christ: The Hermeneutical Bases of Dogmatic Theology (Philadelphia: Fortress Press, 1975); idem, "The 'Literal Reading' of Biblical Narrative in the Christian Tradition: Does It Stretch or Will It Break," in Frank McConnell (ed.), The Bible and the Narrative Tradition (New York: Oxford University Press, 1986) 36–78.

337    See, David Tracy, "On Reading the Scriptures Theologically," in Bruce D. Marshall (ed.), *Theology and Dialogue: Essays in Conversation with George Lindbeck* (Notre Dame: University of Notre Dame Press, 1990) 38. Hereafter, this work will be referred to as "Reading Scriptures." See Hans Frei, "The 'Literal Reading' of Biblical Narrative in the Christian Tradition: Does It Stretch or Will It Break," 41.

338    Tracy, "Reading Scriptures," 38. See Frei, *ibid.*, 61–75.

339    Tracy, "Reading Scriptures," 38.

the agent's (Jesus) intentions and actions and, through that narrative identification, a manifestation of the agent as present to the Christian community as Jesus Christ."[340] According to Tracy, Frei's substantive contribution is a theological clarification of the identity of Jesus Christ (and through that identity, the further identities of both God and the Christian community) which "neither symbol *alone*, nor doctrine *alone*, nor historical-critical reconstruction of the original apostolic witness *alone*, nor conceptual theology *alone*, nor confession *alone*, can achieve."[341]

Incorporating Frei's narrativist approach, Tracy sums up his position concerning the question of God's identity as follows:

> The fact that the Christian understanding of the one God is grounded not in a general philosophical theory of monotheism but in this concrete passion-narrative history of God's self-disclosure as Agent in the cross and resurrection of Jesus of Nazareth is *the primary theological foundation* of all properly Christian understandings of God and the many faces of God.[342]

An important implication of this statement is that our reflection on God, *from the outset*, needs to be grounded in Christology. Tracy says that, "It is impossible to separate theo-logy and Christology."[343] This theological stance is distinct from his revisionist one. In *BRO*, as we saw, Tracy's validation of God's reality (as a metaphysical reality) does not base itself on a Christological foundation. Instead, it starts from *common human experiences* (limit-experiences as religious) from which (1) the notion of religion in general is inferred (religion as the representative expression of limit-experiences), and, (2) from this notion of religion, God is inferred as its objective referent. In this process of validation, a Christological concern is not involved. In his revisionist reflection, Tracy makes clear that the theologian's own, or his or her tradition's beliefs should not serve as warrants for his or her theological arguments.[344]

---

340  *Ibid.*
341  *Ibid.*, 42.
342  Tracy, "The Paradox in Mono-Theism," 32.
343  *Ibid.*, 34.
344  See *BRO*, 7.

However, now, Tracy's approach to God is, from the starting-point, 'Christianly' or Christologically determined. Tracy claims that the Christian naming and thinking of God cannot but be "christomorphic."[345] This means that "it is the *form* of Christ that allows for the naming Christianly of God, of humanity, of cosmos."[346] Tracy writes that, "There is no serious form of *Christian* theology that is not christomorphic. This is a more accurate designation of the christological issue, I believe, than the more familiar but confusing word 'christocentric.' For theology is not christocentric but theocentric, although it is so only by means of its christomorphism."[347]

While Tracy takes the Freinian view that the 'plain sense' of the passion narrative is the foundation and focal point of all adequately Christian understanding of God, he is very keen on the following issue. The centrality of the 'plain sense' of the passion narrative should not downplay many other theological readings of this narrative in other genres and texts of the New Testament and the wider Christian tradition. In other words, this centrality "should define but should not confine the possible range of Christian construals of the common [passion] narrative."[348] Tracy asserts that this "plain" reading:

> should be open both to further questioning of its coherence with the 'Jesus-kerygma' of the original apostolic witness as well as to further reflections on the theological implications of the diversity of readings of that plain sense in the New Testament itself and indeed, in all biblically sound readings of the common narrative in the great Christian tradition.[349]

In short, the contemporary Christian community, no less than its predecessors in the New Testament communities, need not limit its

---

345 David Tracy, "Form and Fragment: The Recovery of the Hidden and Incomprehensible God," Tracy's Lecture at the Center of Theological Inquiry in Princeton in 1999. http://www.ctinquiry.org/publications/tracy.htm (access 13 September 2002). Hereafter, this work will be referred to as "Form and Fragment." The above quotation is from on p.6 in the web text.
346 *Ibid.*
347 Tracy, "Many Faces of Postmodernity," 111.
348 Tracy, "Reading Scriptures," 46.
349 *Ibid.*, 37.

attention to only one "plain" reading. Instead, we should acknowledge many faces of God experienced and portrayed in different readings for a fuller substantive view of God, given that these diverse readings are in essential harmony with the plain sense of the passion narrative.[350] Tracy indicates that his insistence on this need to embrace a diversity of theological readings in the wider spectrum of Christian tradition is based on his more Catholic interpretation of Frei's "plain sense" proposal. Moreover, for him, this Catholic perspective that we need to be open to diverse readings of the passion narrative in *the Christian tradition*, given that these readings cohere with the "plain" reading, clarifies the central role of the Scripture in relation to tradition as follows. Tracy says, "the central theological principle is 'Scripture in tradition,' not either the older Roman Catholic 'Scripture *and* tradition,' nor the Reformation's 'Scripture alone'."[351] In the sections to come, we will see how this principle is applied to Tracy's attempt to search for alternative forms for naming and thinking God.

350 Tracy explains the danger that can be occasioned by a resting in "realistic and history-like" reading alone as follows. He says that for example, Luke is the gospel that holds the closest affinity to the "realistic and history-like" sense of the common passion narrative. And, it will be not too wrong to sense that "Luke's relatively sanguine and sometimes all-too-continuous salvation-history narrative (as well as Luke's muted theology of the salvific power of the cross) can lend itself too easily to an undesirable degree of abstraction from the painful negativities, interruptions, and sufferings of history as viewed in the light of the cross." (*Ibid.*, 47–8). In other words, a theological emphasis on an exclusively 'realistic' reading of the common narrative will have the danger that may it "accord all too well with a culturally Anglo-Saxon reading of Christianity: clear, reasonable, moral, firm, and realistic. There is much to honor in this Anglo-Saxon tradition of moral realism. But there are alternative cultures, alternative spiritualities and theologies that also honor the realistic narrative in other and (for the Anglo-Saxon sensibility) often disturbing ways: apocalyptic and mystical readings, for example [...] We should take pains to assure that this Anglo-Saxon penchant for moral realism does not become synonymous, albeit unconsciously, with the truly disturbing realism of the passion narrative itself." (*Ibid.*, 48).

351 *Ibid.*, 37–8.

According to Tracy, the problem of modern discourses on God is associated not only with their totalitarian rationality and self-present subjectivity, but also with their *forms* for articulating God's reality. Tracy explains the principal dilemma of modern discourses on God in relation to this question of *forms* as follows:

> The central problem is this: modernity's pervasive lack of interest in traditional forms for naming God and thinking God has become an unacknowledged part of the present malaise of modern theologies and philosophies of religion. Modernity, in fact, does use and develop its own characteristic form for naming and understanding God. Indeed, modernity believes that only its form can name and think God responsibly, that is, rationally. To produce an acceptably rational form, modern thinkers decontextualize and denaturalize all discourse in order to constitute the only form that can pass muster with modern rationality: a set of abstract propositions arrived at through rational argument. Only thus can a modern theorist claim to be able to abstract the essential attributes of God and thus name and think God in properly modern terms.[352]

The form he envisions now over against the modern decontextualized and denaturalized forms for articulating God is the form of "fragments." In what follows, we will briefly look at what the form of "fragments" means for Tracy. However, prior to discussing the form of "fragments," one important concept needs to be explained: God as "Impossible."

## God as "Impossible"

Tracy uses the category, God as "Impossible," to condense the postmodern sense of God's uncontrolled otherness. For him, this category, God as "Impossible," symbolizes a resistance against modern totalitarian approaches to God. Tracy claims that today "the real conversation about God intellectually should be with the category of the impossible. I have in mind the sense in which Soren Kierkegaard used this term: it is impossible to have a direct communication with God. God cannot be known by way of persuasion and argument; one

---

352  Tracy, "Literary Theory," 305–6.

either believes in or is offended by this God."[353] An interesting point is that Tracy contrasts this category, God as "Impossible," with the modern categories for God, God as "Actual" and God as "Possible," which are maintained in his revisionist theology and his hermeneutic theology in the 1980s respectively. Tracy explains:

> For moderns, the debate over God has been about what is actual and possible. Modern God-talk reflects concrete experiences [for example, in his revisionist theology, "limit-experiences"], either actual or possible. When God is linked with concrete experiences, God can be understood by way of persuasion and argument – in an appeal to experience, reason or the imagination. Empirical or process theologies stress what is actual, and hermeneutic theologies deal with the possible.[354]

Tracy says that in modernity, the category of the "impossible" is a purely negative or embarrassing category: "for modern thinkers like Weber, Dewey and Habermas, to introduce the category of the impossible was to provoke laughter."[355] However, now, this category is "a deeply meaningful category" in need of appropriation when we shift our God-talk to "God-centeredness" (the return to *theos* from the domination of *logos*), and thereby to God's otherness as hidden and incomprehensible.[356] For him, this category is meaningful today in the sense that it can serve, as a positive category, to highlight and affirm God's realty as non-reductive to anything whatsoever (neither to "being," nor to "transcendentality," nor to "relationality"). In other words, Tracy wants to retrieve this category to speak for the post-modern manifesto that God is a radically religious phenomenon which cannot be subject to modern smothering onto-theological strategies. Moreover, this category can serve to promote the postmodern concern with the notions of excess, transgression, and the extreme for thinking God.

Now, Tracy's concern is with the kind of *form* that is most adequate to speak about the reality for which one uses the category of the "impossible." According to Tracy, the form of "fragments" is best

353 Tracy, "The Impossible God," 2.
354 *Ibid.*
355 *Ibid.*
356 *Ibid.*

suited for illuminating such a reality. The reason why Tracy speaks about the question of form as such here is that he thinks that it is one way to begin to address new theological challenges. According to him, one of the fatal separations that modern Western intellectualism brings about is the separation between form and content.[357] Tracy says that an important insight that we learn from theologians such as Karl Barth and Hans Urs von Balthasar is that the question of form is a vital issue in theology. What we learn from these theologians is that we need to understand "form not as some extra aesthetic addition to content but form as that which renders the content so that the search for the right theological form is at the very same time the search for the right theological content."[358] In other words, content obtains its meaning in and through form. Basing himself on this view, Tracy insists on the necessity to consider the form of "fragments" for illuminating God as "Impossible."

*The Form of "Fragments"*

Tracy explains that the form of "fragments" first originated with the German Romantics Schlegel and Novalis in their books named *Fragments*.[359] This form was conceived as a literary and philosophical strategy by the Romantics to illuminate "the 'sparks' of the divine."[360] Over against the religious certainties in modern holistic, totalitarian views (religion as, at best, ethics or bad science or pseudo-meta-physics), the Romantics, through this form of "fragments," attempted to make the divine "sparks" explosive. Even Kant calls this realm of the divine sparks "the intuitions of the divine-or" and for the great literary modernists like James Joyce, Virginia Woolf, and T.S. Eliot, it

---

357 Tracy points out three separations that modern Western culture is responsible for: (1) the separation of thought and feeling; (2) the separation of theory and practice; (3) the separation of form and content. Tracy says that "each is based on an originally helpful distinction that became, in modernity, an unbridgeable separation." (David Tracy, "Traditions of Spiritual Practice and the Practice of Theology," in *ThT*, 55 (1998) 235.

358 Tracy, "Form and Fragment," 2.

359 Tracy does not give the specific bibliographical information on this work.

360 Tracy, "Form and Fragment," 2.

is called "epiphanies," "lucid moments" and "unexpected moments" respectively.[361] In these thinkers, the form of "fragments" was forged to disrupt or interrupt the continuities and similarities masking the deadening sameness of the modern worldview. In other words, this form serves to transgress or disturb the present order and calls it into question. Tracy explains that in Baudelaire, for example, a poetic form of "fragments" is created to reveal "the brokenness and falseness of modern experience and the obfuscation of all singularities in the nineteenth century's deceptively continuous modern bourgeois experience."[362] Kafka, not less luminously, discloses "in his fragmentary parabolic, not symbolic, forms how one may be able to feel one's way to some slight hint of redemption, even if that redemption is neither understood [...] nor even fully experienced save through the unsettling fragments in Kafka's strange parables."[363] Kierkegaard tried to show that Christianity in the mode of a triumphant totalitarian system cannot survive any true experiment with authentic Christian existence. His literary efforts were focused on shattering the reified ideal of Enlightenment and totalitarian Christendom alike. He wrote under pseudonyms and attempted "any genre – diaries, music, exercises, dialogues, edifying discourses, narratives" in order to disrupt "any claim to adequacy of direct discourse in the idealist version of totality [...] He will try anything except a system."[364] Nietzsche, a more acrimonious opponent of Christendom and Enlightenment modernity, devised "style after style from his early essays to the quasi-gospel genre of *Thus Spoke Zarathustra* to genealogical analysis through aphorisms piled upon aphorisms to fragments juxtaposed with fragments in an increasingly desperate attempt" to undo the modern system.[365] Walter Benjamin, another significant unveiler of modernity's secret dream for continuity in history, through his fragmentary form of writings, exposes the fragmentary character of history. Tracy explains:

361  *Ibid.*
362  "Fragments: The Spiritual Situation," 179.
363  *Ibid.*
364  *Ibid.*, 172.
365  *Ibid.*

What Benjamin attempted was not a representation of history but a re-constellation of historical images to show the diachronic relationship of certain fragments as images from a past epic to related images that proliferate for us in every present moment. Even the category of the historical context so central to the historiographer can become a kind of totality that should be first respected and then dissolved to allow for the present to experience the historical event as a radically unique saturated fragment of time. The fragment, especially the marginal fragment that recalls forgotten, even repressed memories of the suffering of the victims of history, are privileged by Benjamin over any conception of an historical totality.[366]

Tracy says that Benjamin's fragmentary form of writings is "an attempt to let the fragments speak for themselves and thereby generate new tension and meanings as they work with and against every other fragment in a new constellation of fragments, or at times phantasmagoric collage."[367] Moreover, Benjamin is one of the representatives of those who regard fragments "as saturated and auratic bearers of infinity and sacred hope, fragmentary of genuine hope in some redemption, however, undefined."[368] According to Tracy, insofar as today we are situated in the welcome collapse of the modern domesticating view of religion and Infinity (or God), it is worth joining these literary and philosophical discussions of fragments, and reflecting on them in uniquely theological ways. Put differently, if we admit that no totality, no domestication, and no "isms" are still viable for thinking God today, we can say that "fragments are our spiritual situation [for thinking about God]. And that is not so bad a place to be."[369] This is so because "fragments" can be a sign of hope for bringing back the uncontrollable Infinity of God in force anew in our theological reflection. Tracy asserts:

> Let go of the hope for any totality system whatsoever. Focus instead on the explosive, marginal, saturated and, at times, auratic fragments of our heritages [...] Blast the marginalized fragments of the past alive with the memory of suffering and hope; remove them from their seemingly coherent pace in the

366  *Ibid.*, 178.
367  *Ibid.*, 179.
368  *Ibid.*, 173.
369  *Ibid.*

grand narratives we have imposed upon them. Learn to live joyfully, not despairingly, with and in the great fragments we do indeed possess.[370]

In sum, for contemporary God-reflection, what Tracy envisions is not a move to inventing brand-new forms, but a move to retrieving or recovering the fragmentary forms in the Christian tradition that have been forgotten, repressed, and neglected by modernity.[371] In what follows, we will look at Tracy's option for two traditional fragmentary forms for thinking God.

### The Retrieval of Two Fragmentary Forms: The Apocalyptic and The Apophatic Forms

It can be said that Tracy's "christomorphic" starting point for a reflection on God is a first step in his non-onto-theological move for contemporary God-talk. In this section, we will look at what Tracy specifically suggests, grounded in this "christomorphic" foundation, as the proper, alternative forms for naming and thinking God over against modern 'isms' for God.

As indicated earlier, the principal characteristic of Tracy's strategy for this task is a *retrieval* or *re-appropriation* of traditional forms that modernity has disregarded or marginalized as unreal or irrational according to its rational, totalitarian standards. Tracy says

---

370  *Ibid.*, 179
371  For Tracy, this move to retrieving traditional resources concurs with the move shown in some of the eminent postmodern thinkers such as Lyotard, Kristeva, and Foucault (although these thinkers' move is philosophical). Tracy explains that Lyotard attempted a "move from a radical rejection of modernity (here read Habermas) to an almost ecstatic rediscovery of certain fragments of pre-modernity. Consider for example Lyotard's retrieval of fragments of early modernity as distinct from Enlightenment modernity. Consider Kristeva's recovery of the Christian love mystics from Bernard of Clarvaux to Jeanne Guyon [...] Or consider Foucault's last radical turn in his history of sexuality when he discovered, despite his own earlier denials of the very possibility of a self, a new notion of caring for the self aided by fragments of the ancients available to him through the fine scholarship on ancient philosophy of Pierre Hadot and Peter Brown. These historians of the ancient world helped Foucault, the quintessential postmodern, to reconsider how to think anew with the fragments left by ancient Greeks and Romans." (*Ibid.*, 176).

that "most forms of postmodernity are explosions of once-forgotten, marginalized, and repressed realities in Enlightenment modernity": the marginal other and the uncannily different in modernity.[372] On these lines of thought, Tracy suggests recovering two traditional theological forms for illuminating God: the apocalyptic and the apophatic forms. For modern theology, these two forms might be the forms of theological "otherness." The principal reason why Tracy wants to pay attention to these two forms is that he believes that, in them, the form of "fragments," *par excellence*, lives in its full Christian sense. In what follows, we will look at Tracy's introduction to each of these two forms. Tracy discusses each of these forms in basic continuity with its biblical root and the later Christian tradition.

*From the Prophetic Tradition to the Apocalyptic Form*

Tracy begins his discussion of the apocalyptic form with reference to its biblical root, the prophetic tradition. He explains that in the Bible, the prophets speak not because of their wishes but because of God's command on behalf of the other, especially the poor, the oppressed, and the marginal other. He says, "Jesus is the eschatological prophet bespeaking the Other for the sake of all others. There is no way around the prophetic core of Christian self-understanding. Even our earliest christologies come in prophetic form."[373] According to Tracy, this prophetic tradition can move in two directions in its developmental trajectory. First, it can be developed in a *generalizing* direction wherein its religious core is seen as an ethics. Representative examples are found in liberal Protestantism, Reformed Judaism, and liberal Catholicism which, following Immanuel Kant, generalize the prophetic tradition and tend to accentuate the ethical. Among postmodern thinkers, Tracy takes Emmanuel Levinas as a good example in this direction, although indicating that Levinas develops the prophetic tradition in a quite different fashion from the modern liberal one. Tracy explains that, for Levinas:

372  *Ibid.,* 171.
373  Tracy, "Many Faces of Postmodernity," 112.

370

ethics is first philosophy and that true ethics is grounded in the face of the other. The other – the biblical neighbor – is what no ontological totality can ever control. The temptation to totalizing modes of thought is disrupted once and for all by the glimpse of the Infinite in the face of the other and its ethical command, 'Do not kill me.' Is it really so surprising that Levinas' work has become so central not only for Jewish thought but also for Christian liberation theology with its instinctive prophetic-ethical sense for the other, especially the preferred other of the prophets – the poor, the marginal, and the oppressed [?: sic][374]

The second direction that the prophetic tradition can take is a move of *intensification* or transgression into a radically disruptive, fragmentary form, the apocalyptic form. The apocalyptic here means a vision for "a reign of God on earth that can be established only as a result of a divine irruption into the present order that overthrows its evil."[375] In a general scope, the apocalyptic vision in the Jewish tradition consists of three elements: (1) the adverse situations of the present world inflicted by oppressive rules or catastrophic deprivation; (2) God's imminent interruptive and sovereign judgment of the wicked and adversaries at hand; (3) the vindication of the righteous in God's new order of prosperity and peace.[376] This radical vision emerges especially when the prophecies of God's promises and blessings fail in the time of socio-political, cultural, religious crises. The emergence of the apocalyptic was the Judean scribes' creative response to these crises, diverting the attention from the powerless and intolerable present to the assurance of God's decisive intervention for ushering in a new era. This move of diversion, however, "should not be seen as a flight from reality. Rather it is a way of coping with reality by providing a meaningful framework within which human beings can make decisions and take action."[377] In this apocalyptic vision, the time of God's intervention is completely in God's control,

---

374 *Ibid.*
375 Tracy, "The Impossible God," 3.
376 See "Apocalypses and Apocalypticism," in *The Anchor Bible Dictionary*, I (New York: Doubleday, 1992) 280–8; *The Encyclopedia of Apocalypticism*, vol.1, *The Origins of Apocalypticism in Judaism and Christianity*, ed. John J. Collins (New York: The Continuum, 1998).
377 "Apocalypses and Apocalypticism," 287.

and it is never subjected to or subsumed under human beings' projected goal.

This apocalyptic vision is detected throughout the New Testament: e.g., Thessalonians, Mark's gospel, the Book of Revelation, and others.[378] Tracy briefly focuses on Mark's gospel in which the apocalyptic vision of the Hidden-Revealed God is best portrayed among the gospels. He says that, "In Mark the God of history is present through absence – as in the seeming absence of his Father to Mark's Jesus on the cross, the Jesus who cries from the cross the cry of all the victims of history: 'My God, my God why have you forsaken me?'"[379] One of the most notable elements in Mark's gospel in comparison with other gospels is the reticence about Jesus' resurrection (Mk 16: 1–8). The brief Markan account of Jesus' resurrection ends with terror, amazement, fear, and uncertainty in non-closure (no explicit sense of joy of Jesus' victory in resurrection). In Mark, along with his insistence on the centrality of cross, suffering, and conflict, his vision of human salvific history is rendered by the open-ended conclusion, which symbolizes "the complexity of his apocalyptic vision of history as interruption, not continuity."[380] With a keen postmodern sensitivity to otherness, difference, marginality, and suffering, Tracy rereads in historical-political terms the Markan renderings of uncertainty, fear, and hesitation in its vision of God's hidden intervention. He explains:

> Mark's God of history is disclosed in genuine hiddenness: the hiddenness of the conflict, struggle, negativity, suffering, cross which *is* history to the victims of history. This is the history which Mark shows to all those clear-headed enough to view history not with the eyes of the victors, who always write the official

---

378 Tracy writes that, "Ernst Kaeseman may well have exaggerated, as many New Testament scholars would now say, in detail. But in principle surely he was on to something provocative and important for all theologians to remember in his famous statement: 'Apocalyptic is the mother of all Christian theology.' It is impossible, as far as I can see, to understand the New Testament without apocalyptic, and thereby Christianity." (Tracy, "Form and Fragment," 7).

379 Tracy, "The Hidden God," 14–15.

380 *Ibid.*, 15.

histories we all have learned, but with the new apocalyptic vision provided by the God who vindicated this Jesus.[381]

In short, the uncanny interruptions throughout Mark's gospel (including the reticence about Jesus' resurrection): e.g., the inability of the Markan disciples to understand Jesus' words and actions at crucial points, the pervasive motif of betrayal (Judas) and failure (Peter), "consistently reveal both the apocalyptic sensibility and the strong spirituality of suffering as endurance of radical negativity."[382] For Tracy, this Markan apocalyptic vision of God are valuable resources for contemporary theologians to embrace for reflecting on God's uncontrolled infinity.

However, in relation to the retrieval of the apocalyptic vision in the New Testament, Tracy notes two elements to be cautiously treated. Firstly, we should be keenly aware of the fact that when apocalyptic language is literalized, it will have a deadly effect. He explains that, "if apocalyptic language so fragmentary of continuity in history, does not also fragment itself through, for example, deliteralization as Augustine already insisted in *The City of God* and as such theologians as Bultmann, Reinhold Niebuhr and Karl Rahner following Augustine also insisted, it is totalizing and deadly."[383] More specifically:

> if apocalyptic does not also fragment itself, all could be lost. For all one would then possess is a fragmentary form that tries to avoid the void in the terror of history as that history is experienced by marginalized and oppressed peoples only by literalizing when the end will occur and by dualistically, even violently, separating all reality on behalf of its own all too certain sense of injustice, hardened into a sense of a community's finally fundamentalist self-righteousness.[384]

In short, Tracy's point is that the literalization of apocalyptic language is another kind of totalitarian (or fundamentalist) approach to the reality to come, which is exactly what apocalyptic language as a fragmenting language aims to disrupt.

---

381   *Ibid.*
382   Tracy, "Reading Scriptures," 49.
383   Tracy, "Form and Fragment," 7.
384   *Ibid.*

Secondly, according to Tracy, in reconsidering the apocalyptic vision in the New Testament, we need to recover the symbol of the "Second Coming" of Christ.[385] For him, the apocalyptic symbol of the "Second Coming" is as central as incarnation, cross or resurrection for understanding Christ (thereby God). He explains that, "for the fuller already/not yet dialectic of redemption, Christian theologians need to try to keep alive the inherent fragmenting tension present in the great Christological symbols, incarnation, cross, resurrection by increasing the tension through adding more explicitly (as the New Testament does) the fourth great Christological symbol – the Second Coming."[386] Tracy says that the New Testament begins chronologically with Mark's apocalyptic gospel and ends with, even after the resurrection, the apocalyptic exclamation of "Come Lord Jesus, come." According to the New Testament's vision, "Christ has come for us as Christians, but in an important sense he still has not come yet. We don't know who or what Christ will be or when his coming will happen."[387] In short, the symbol of the "Second Coming" indicates that there still remains a 'non-occurrence' concerning the full revelation of Christ's economy. Granted that one needs to bear in mind the particular historical and social settings which produced the New Testament's apocalyptic texts (e.g., the fall of the Jerusalem temple), what Tracy attends to is "what that non-occurrence might mean for a reading of the New Testament itself."[388] In this symbol of non-occurrence, the "Second Coming," Tracy reads the vision that history is a series of

---

385   Tracy indicates that this position is a shift from his christological view in *The Analogical Imagination* (1981). He writes that, "In *The Analogical Imagination*, the main symbols were incarnation-cross-resurrection. Now I would add apocalyptic. When I was young, no progressive theologian would dare speak about the apocalyptic. Talk of the apocalyptic was handed over to fundamentalism. Bultmann, Rahner and others preferred to speak of the 'eschatological.' In *The Analogical Imagination*, I spoke of the apocalyptic as an important 'corrective.' I no longer say that. For me, the Second Coming is as critical a symbol as incarnation, cross and resurrection. The Bible for Christians ends with 'Come, Lord Jesus.' We are still messianic." (Tracy, "The Impossible God," 4).

386   Tracy, "Form and Fragment," 6.

387   Tracy, "The Impossible God," 4.

388   Tracy, "Form and Fragment," 7.

ruptures and fragments rather than a pure continuity ending in the victors, and the disclosure of the never-controlled, hidden God in that history. Tracy asserts that, "Without the symbol of the Second Coming, without apocalyptic, Christianity can settle down, into a religion which no longer has a profound sense of the not-yet, and thereby no longer a profound sense of God's very hidden-ness in history."[389]

In the later Christian tradition, Tracy considers Martin Luther as the most eminent resource for providing the apocalyptic vision of God. For him, in Luther, the notion of God's hiddenness (*deus absconditus*) was first articulated with intellectual intensity and theological clarity in the full sense. What Tracy focuses on is Luther's *twofold* vision of God's hiddenness.[390] Luther's reflection on the Hidden God is carried out with great consistency through his theology of the cross. The nub of Luther's insight is that God's revelation is principally through the hiddenness of the cross: in Luther, "God discloses Godself to sinful humans *sub contrariis*: life through death; wisdom through folly; strength through abject weakness. A hidden God is not merely humble but humiliated: *deus incarnatus, deus absconditus in passionibus*."[391] In a sense, in Luther's vision of God, revelation (*deus revelatus*) and hiddenness (*deus absconditus*) appear to be not opposed, but coincidental.

In Luther, however, there is a second sense of God's hiddenness (Hiddenness II) which is distinct from and even seemingly contradictory to his notion of God's hiddenness *sub contrariis* in the cross (Hiddenness I).[392] This second sense is an insight into God's hiddenness as *behind* or even *beyond* the revelatory Word. This is to say that a distinction needs to be made between the Word of God and God

---

389   *Ibid.*
390   For Luther's twofold vision of God's hiddenness, Tracy uses B.A. Gerrish's work, "To the Unknown God: Luther and Calvin on the Hiddenness of God," in idem, *The Old Protestantism and the New* (Chicago: University of Chicago Press, 1982) 131–49. The same article is also found in *Journal of Religion* 53 (1973) 263–92. We will use the latter in what follows.
391   Tracy, "The Hidden God," 9.
392   Among others, both these forms of God's hiddenness can be found in Luther's treatise, *On the Bondage of the Will* (1525).

himself which remains unknown (or inscrutable) outside revelation.[393] Luther sees a certain awesome, unapproachable realm of God's hiddenness which does not completely coincide with what is revealed in Jesus Christ, his Word. Faith cannot penetrate this terrifying mysterious realm, but can only lose itself in a dark, threatening abyss. For Luther, this horror of God's hiddenness symbolizes, in a sense, God's absolute, indestructible, irreducible transcendence which is not restricted even by his revelatory Word. For him, to deny this distinction between the word of God and God himself is to make God an idol, depriving him of his free sovereign will.[394] Faith does not prevail over this frightening otherness of God. However, faith takes on an urgency before this realm of God's hiddenness which fissures any self-confident, self-complacent, and self-triumphant faith in a God of nature and history.

For Tracy, along with B.A. Gerrish, however disruptive and inharmonious the notion of God's hiddenness II may be vis-à-vis that of God's hiddenness I, its theological seriousness needs to be retrieved in today's reflection on God. Tracy says that Luther's notion of God's radical hiddenness "must be heard principally in political and liberationist ways and not merely the personalist ways."[395] Tracy sees Luther's vision of God's terrifying, unplumbed hiddenness as apocalyptic, which interrupts modernity's sense of history as continuity and progress towards victors' projected *telos*. In this version of history, the rule of the same reigns over otherness (even God's otherness), difference, particularity, marginality and suffering which are merely a moment to be subsumed under its integral grand narrative of progress. In this schema, "the victims, often made up of those who suffer under the remorseless implementation of such ideologies, are forgotten from the outset or reduced to a function of the evolutionary process."[396] What Tracy wants to retrieve in Luther's radical apoc-

---

393 See Martin Luther, D. Martin Luthers Werke: Kritische Gesamtausgabe (Weimar, 1883–) 18.685.26, recited from Gerrish, "To the Unknown God," 273.

394 See *Martin Luther, ibid.*, 18.706.15, recited from Gerrish, *ibid.*, 273.

395 Tracy, "The Hidden God," 13.

396 Lieven Boeve, "God Interrupts History: Apocalypticism as an Indispensable Theological Conceptual Strategy," in *LS*, 26 (2001) 210.

alyptic vision of God is that God is not sheer timeless infinity, but some reality who interrupts in concrete human history as hidden, awesome force which is sometimes experienced even as horror or violence or abysmal chaos (as portrayed in the Book of Job, the Lamentations, the Paslms, Mark's gospel).[397] According to Tracy, our postmodern sensitivity acutely reckons today that the principal self-disclosure of this hidden power of God as envisioned in Luther is most compellingly mediated in the voices and struggles of the forgotten, the oppressed, and the marginalized of all history. Tracy claims that, the entry of God as Hidden "now comes to us principally through the interruptive experience and the memory of suffering of whole peoples, especially the suffering of all those ignored, marginalized, and colonized by the grand narrative of modernity."[398] In these interruptive experiences, God enters "not as a consoling 'ism'," but above all as the unfathomable, but liberating "hope-beyond-hope."[399]

In sum, for Tracy, negatively, Luther's notion of God's hiddenness can serve to debunk "the superficiality of so much modern talk about God (including Lutheran talk) – indeed any theological talk which refuses to face the radical hiddenness often present in both the biblical portrait of God and in much human experience of God."[400] Positively, Luther's notion of God's hiddenness allows for a new theological recovery of apocalyptic as a vital option for today's exigency to 'let God be God again.'

---

397  Tracy writes that it is this second sense of God's radical hiddenness, "I believe, which inspired the great Lutheran phenomenologist Rudolf Otto to his brilliant description of religion and the reality of God as both numinous and holy. It is this radical sense of God's hiddenness which one senses in Paul Tillich at his most dialectical in his pleas for a 'God beyond God,' and in such artists, inspired by Swedish Lutheran culture, as Ingmar Bergman in his early films of ministers losing faith – i.e. moving, one might say, from the hiddenness of the cross to the radical sense of Hiddenness 'beyond the Word'." (Tracy, "Form and Fragment," 8).

398  Tracy, "The Hidden God," 8.

399  *Ibid.*, 7–8.

400  *Ibid.*, 11.

Another fragmentary form of naming God in the Christian tradition, which Tracy considers as highly resourceful today, is the *apophatic* form. Tracy situates the root of the apophatic form in the biblical meditative tradition. The central concern of the meditative tradition in the bible (e.g., John's gospel in the New Testament, wisdom literature in the Old Testament, etc.) is to disclose human participatory relationships to the beauty and glory of the whole of reality in creation. In this tradition, even the cross is a disclosure of glory (e.g., John's gospel). This meditative tradition may also move in the same two directions in its theological development as the prophetic tradition shows. First, when it moves in a *generalizing* direction, it moves toward the aesthetic realm. More specifically, Tracy explains, when the meditative traditions make generalizing moves:

> they are more likely to develop profound participatory metaphysics (like Platonism in all its splendid forms). When more ethically oriented, a wisdom ethics will prove an aesthetic ethics of appreciation of the good and of beauty (like Whitehead and Hartshorne). When more historically conscious, these meditative positions will develop into a hermeneutical philosophy disclosing the dialogical character of all reality. A wisdom-grounded metaphysics (never totalizing, if hermeneutically faithful to its biblical core) and an aesthetics will unite to relate themselves to some form of prophetic ethics, more likely in these traditions an ethics of the good, as in Iris Murdoch.[401]

Another direction that the meditative tradition can take is an *intensification* "to the point of becoming transgressive of all participation – as typically with postmodern recoveries of the more radical mystical traditions."[402] In this direction of intensification, the apophatic form emerges with a mystical quality. Here, without any specific discussion on the apophatic forms detected in the Bible, Tracy moves directly to the later Christian tradition.

As a counterpart of Luther in the apocalyptic form, Tracy takes Dionysius the Areopagite (*circa* sixth century) as a valuable apophatic resource in the Christian tradition. Tracy points out that it is surprising

---

401   Tracy, "Many Faces of Postmodernity," 113.
402   *Ibid.*, 114.

that although Dionysius was influential on medieval theology, his theology has long been neglected even by theologians who admire medieval theology, such as the neo-Thomists of the twentieth century. Tracy contends that the Dionysian theology is, contrary to the common accusation that it is neo-Platonist, not Christian, grounded in biblical revelation (especially the wisdom traditions). He writes:

> Dionysius, as much as Karl Barth, would allow no cataphatic namings of God which are not biblically, that is revelatorily, based. From the sensible, biblical images for God like 'rock,' to wisdom-oriented intellectual images that he found either explicit in or clearly implied by the biblical revelation like wisdom or sophia, word or logos, being, the one, and especially the Good, *ton agaton.* [sic].[403]

In terms of etymology, "*apophasis* is a Greek neologism for the breakdown of *speech*, which, in face of the unknowability of God, falls infinitely short of the mark."[404] The conception of 'unknowability' here, however, does not refer to "a naïve *pre*-critical ignorance" but to a kind of intellectually "acquired ignorance" (*docta ignorantia*).[405] Thus, *apophatic* theology is, in a sense, a theological attempt of paradox: to speak about God in the failure of speech.

In the same manner of his introduction to Luther's vision of God (God's Hiddenness I and II), Tracy highlights Dionysius' vision of God developed in several steps. The key characteristic of Dionysius' aphophaticism lies in his dialectical process of approaching God's absolute transcendentality: affirmation, negation, and the negation of

---

403   Tracy, "Form and Fragment," 10. Tracy's "Form and Fragment" was prepared for a lecture and some of the sentences in the text are not complete in form. Tracy writes that, "In the history of Western theology and philosophy, no greater change occurred in the naming of God, than when Thomas Aquinas read Exodus 3: 14 in the Latin translation of the *Deus sum qui sum* 'I am who I am,' and developed what Etienne Gilson nicely named Thomas's metaphysics of Exodus 3: 14. Thomas thereby insisted that God's principal name was not, as it was for his contemporary Bonaventure and the whole Dionysian thought prior to him, the Good, but Being [...] That is a brilliant metaphysical insight, but it shifts everything theologically." (*Ibid.*).

404   Denys Turner, *The Darkness of God: Negativity in Christian Mysticism* (Cambridge: Cambridge University Press, 1995) 20.

405   *Ibid.*, 19.

the negation. As one step in his apophatic process, Dionysius strains his efforts to name God in an affirmative (*cataphatic*) way. The captaphatic naming of God accounts for the *expressive* element in theology, utilizing all the resources available in God's creation by analogy. Dionysius' *The Divine Names*,[406] above all, is meticulously designed to articulate God's names as much as his intellectual reasoning can provide based on both scriptural source and others. For Dionysius, this abounding cataphatic description of God is based on the ontological affirmation that God is "the Cause of all things" as creator; hence, "the songs of praise and the names for it [God] are fittingly derived from the sum total of creation."[407]

However, in Dionysius' vision, this verbosity of cataphatic utterances does not fail to address its own limit. When our language is stretched to its full extent in the profusion of affirmation, there comes a language-defeating moment under the recognition that the whole resource of creation falls infinitely short of describing who and what God is like. Then, language naturally takes the form of paradox, namely, the negation of all the attributes to God. At this stage our theological language "is subjected to the twin pressures of affirmation and negation, of the cataphatic and the apophatic. We must both affirm and deny all things of God."[408] Tracy explains, for Dionysius, "every cataphatic name for God must be both affirmed as revealed – that is to say as God's own self naming in biblical revelation, and yet *negated* [or/and] *fragmented* by us with our finite minds, that is to say, as always intrinsically inadequate for naming the ultimately un-nameable, Incomprehensible God."[409] However, Dionysius' apophatic process does not stop here. There occurs a double negation or fragmentation in Dionysius' mystical vision of God. In this second or double negation, Dionysius attempts even to go beyond both affirmative and negative namings of God. Put differently, this strategy is differentiated from merely letting affirmative utterances fall away

---

406   *Pseudo-Dionysius, The Complete Works*, trans. Colm Luibheid (London: SPCK, 1987) 47–131.

407   *Ibid.*, 56.

408   Turner, The Darkness of God, 22.

409   Tracy, "Form and Fragment," 10 (italics mine).

into *negative* ones; it has to do with the *negation* of any utterance beyond the distinction between our language of similarity and dissimilarity about God. In front of God's transcendentality, what falls away is the distinction itself between similarity and dissimilarity to an ineffable degree. Dionysius says that, God "falls neither within the predicate of nonbeing nor of being [...] Darkness and light, error and truth – it is none of these. It is beyond assertion and denial. We make assertions and denials of what is next to it, but never of it."[410] It is to this double nature of negation in the Dionysian dialectic that Tracy wants to draw our attention for our contemporary reflection on God; namely, the apophatic sense of the incomprehensible otherness of God as an excessive reality which is glimpsed only through the clefts opened up in the breakdown of our language. In this breakdown, we are forced "now as worshiper, to enter the language not of predication but of praise and prayer."[411] Tracy explains:

> Experience of God, by what Dionysius calls a mystical union, is not a knowledge about God. We stutter God's name in such a state of an experience which cannot be experienced on the usual criteria of experience, by oscillating back and forth in praise, in hymn, in prayer, in contemplation between positive and negative namings of God in the ever more fragmentary language of the disclosure or manifestation that Dionysius believes is fragmentarily present in mystical union with the Incomprehensible God.[412]

In the Dionysian contemplative and doxological vision of God, Tracy sees a possible way out from the totalitarian "onto-theo-logical form of modernity's naming of God."[413] In short, for Tracy, the apophatic vision of God can serve to develop the postmodern category of the radical incomprehensibility of God which not merely unmasks the modern illusory belief in the reality-grounding self (the finitude of

410  Pseudo-Dionysius, "The Mystical Theology," in *Pseudo-Dionysius, The Complete Works*, 141.
411  Tracy, "Form and Fragment," 10. Westphal says that, "When we are content to let God's being remain a 'mystery' rather than a 'theorem', onto-theology is replaced by doxology." (Westphal, *Transcendence and Self-Transcendence*, 119).
412  Tracy, "Form and Fragment," 10.
413  Tracy, "Post-Modern Re-Naming of God," 240.

our intelligence), but also accentuates "Incomprehensibility as a positive affirmation of God's very reality."[414]

To sum up, for Tracy, in both the apocalyptic and apophatic forms, the realm of God as the "Impossible" which resists any totality system of naming and thinking God is *par excellence* opened up. Tracy writes that in these two forms, "we are finally freed from the role of the actual, or even the possible into what Kierkegaard was the first to see as what is really needed, namely, the realm of the Impossible [for naming and thinking God]. Today such thinkers as Levinas, Marion, Derrida, Caputo, myself, and many others, are attempting, in different even conflicting ways, to work out this meaning of the category 'the Impossible'."[415] Just as the apocalyptic vision disorients any triumphalist theodicies and releases the fragments of the interruptive memories of suffering and evil, so too, the apophatic vision breaks up any intellectual or linguistic totality system and releases the fragments of liturgical and contemplative (mystical) experiences. Where the apocalyptic form shows a way to naming God as *Hidden*, understood as the liberating 'hope beyond hopelessness,' the apophatic form shows a way to naming God as *Incomprehensible*, understood as the transgressive excess of sheer love.

Finally, we need to make several necessary remarks. Firstly, Tracy himself asks whether it is plausible "to affirm both Dionysius' naming of God as the incomprehensible one and Luther's radically hidden God without either having finally to choose between them or merely juxtapose them."[416] Tracy answers positively. He asserts that, "Surely, it must be [possible to affirm both forms], if Christian theology is to prove genuinely ecumenical and learn finally, as I think any Christian theologian today must from all our traditions generically, from the Orthodox, the Catholic, and the various Reformation traditions."[417]

Secondly, in an interview (2002), when he was asked whether we are simply left with fragments for our God-talk, Tracy answered that

---

414   *Ibid.*, 243 (italics mine).
415   Tracy, "Form and Fragment," 10–11.
416   *Ibid.*, 11.
417   *Ibid.*

his theological reflection on the forms of "fragments" would be comprehensive enough to deal with his subsequent concern: how to gather or order the fragmented forms.[418] He says that he is envisioning a three-volume work on Christian theology in postmodern situation. The first volume (provisionally entitled *This Side of God*), to which what we have examined in this whole section is related, focuses on, as a major concern, the two fragmentary forms of the Christian tradition, the apocalyptic (with Luther) and the apophatic (with Dionysius the Areopagite). In the second volume (provisionally entitled *The Gathering of the Fragments*), Tracy will study the forms of ordering or gathering fragments, drawing on biblical or liturgical resources. He says that, "In this effort, I will draw explicitly on biblical and liturgical metaphors. Though you can't have a totality of symbols, you do need to order and gather them – without losing the sense that religious expressions are simply fragments."[419] He will discuss three principal "gathering forms" developed in the Christian tradition: narratives, doctrines, and liturgy. This volume will be concerned with Christology and Trinity. The third volume will deal with the Spirit and Christianity in view of the other religions.

Thirdly, as we have already seen, in Tracy's view, Luther's apocalyptic and Dionysius' apophatic visions emerged in the history of Christian theology, being grounded in the biblical prophetic and meditative traditions. Moreover, these two biblical root-traditions will continuously generate new theological possibilities in response to new challenges and demands in history. Tracy writes that the fuller spectrum of a seemingly endless series of new prophetic and meditative forms of new possibilities in new theologies across the globe will surely increase. As both cross-cultural sensibilities and inter-religious dialogue take further hold on serious Christian theology, moreover, this prophetic-meditative spectrum will increase yet again.[420]

---

418  Tracy, "The Impossible God," 4.
419  *Ibid.*
420  Tracy, "Many Faces of Postmodernity," 114. For example, Tracy says that the inter-religious dialogues with Buddhism and Taoism may contribute to vital-izing apophatic theology.

Reflecting the above argument, in the interview that we previously mentioned, Tracy very briefly alluded to his options for naming God. His options are God as "Void" and "Open." For him, these two options are the ways to name God as the *Impossible*. Tracy briefly explains that in our reflection on God, "the 'void' has to do with experiences of extreme suffering, injustice, terror, despair or alienation."[421] Following Luther's apocalyptic vision, the category of "void" takes the view of history and nature as a series of openings into the abyss. The category of God as "open" is related to "experiences of the sheer giftedness of life – the sense of awe and wonder one might have about the beauty of the natural world or the sheer happiness one might find in human relationships."[422] He says that the experience of God as "open" "happens when you 'let go'."[423] In other words, this experience is "the 'let-go' aspect of faith."[424] Presumably, we can see his theological development of these categories in more detail in his forthcoming book.

---

421  Tracy, "The Impossible God," 4.
422  *Ibid.*
423  *Ibid.*
424  *Ibid.*

# Conclusion

In this book, we have explored the methodology of Tracy's fundamental theology since the 1970s (*Blessed Rage for Order*) up to the early 2000s. The focal concern in our exploration was the question of whether Tracy's methodologies, developed in the last three decades, are viable in our contemporary context of cultural, philosophical and religious pluralities. Since we already made extensive critical assessments of Tracy's revisionist model (see the conclusions of chapters 2 and 3), and of his theological revision in the 1980s (see chapter 4), in this general conclusion, we will only present a number of key implications that the development of Tracy's fundamental theology exposes.[1]

Firstly, Tracy's theological development in the last three decades shows itself as a *self-critical* and, thereby, *self-correcting* process. As we have seen, Lonergan understands human knowledge as "the self-correcting process of learning" in which the given insights and positions are put to test, complemented, or adjusted by further insights spawned by new questions and challenges. There is no doubt that theology is also a human knowledge which entertains and demands the continuous, self-correcting process of learning and revising. We may delineate the self-correcting process of Tracy's theological development in response to different problems and challenges as in the following table. The table focuses on the development of Tracy' reflection on God which is the central theme of his fundamental theology (see next page).

---

1    Regarding Tracy's theological reflection in the 1990s up to the early 2000s, we
     will only raise an important question at the end of this conclusion.

| The 1970s | The 1980s | The 1990s |
|---|---|---|
| *1. Naming God* | | |
| God as Actual: God as the objective referent of the religious ("limit") dimension present in common human experience and the Christian texts | God as Possible: God as the hermeneutically manifested | God as Impossible: God as the Hidden ("Void") and the Incomprehensible ("Open") |
| *2. Methodology* | | |
| A transcendental (together with process thought) approach | A hermeneutical-transcendental-ethical approach | An apocalyptic-apophatic approach |
| *3. Starting point* | | |
| Human religious experience (or religion as such) on the basis of which God's existence and nature are validated | The notion of God's revelation as the Heideggerian *a-letheia* | The biblical and Christological rendering: God's identity as disclosed in Jesus Christ |
| *4. The principal theological crises to be overcome and methodological searches* | | |
| Modern positivist secularism (not secularity) and supernaturalism | Objectivism (or foundationalism) and relativism | Modern onto-theological "isms" for God |
| The search for a universal ground, religious commonality, transcultural rationality, epistemological certainty | The cohabitation of contextuality, plurality, ambiguity, otherness and difference *with* a universal ground (the human subject's self-correcting and transcending reason) | A focus on fragments, interruptive otherness, radical difference, sheer excess, transgression |
| *5. The correlation* | | |
| Between faith in the Christian God and modern secular faith in the ultimate worth of existence | Between God as the hermeneutically manifested and the ultimate ground of self-transcendental reason | Between an apocalyptic and apophatic God *and* God as interruptive Other and unbounded Love active in the history of suffering and evils, and in liturgical prayers |

386

Secondly, the most important impetus driving Tracy's self-correcting theological development as shown above was his consistent theological objective: to construct a *public theology*. Being firmly grounded in the liberal tradition, Tracy has always been keen on the commitment to produce a theological language that is reasonable and responsible for the public realm. For him, fundamental theology is a theological discipline that addresses and deals with this task of establishing publicness at the most radical level. For him, publicness means, succinctly put, intelligibility "available, in principle, to all intelligent, reasonable, responsible persons."[2] Tracy's main concern in his fundamental theological project is to develop continuously and renew the substantive analyses of, and the mutually critical correlation between two principal theological sources, viz., the contemporary situation (or experience) and the Christian tradition. These activities need to be conducted in dialogue with ever-changing intellectual, cultural, religious, and social-political challenges and demands. These endeavors aim to bring Christian discourse up to date, not only for the Christian communities but also for the wider public. For Tracy, these theological efforts are fundamentally grounded in Christianity's own claim to universal truth, and its concern with all of humanity's salvation as attested in the New Testament. These endeavors are not the invention of modernity; in other words, they do not simply originate from the modern intellectual exigency in the accomplishment of universality, intelligibility, and communicability in theological discourse. These theological efforts have consistently been made in the history of Christianity and theology from the New Testament communities up to contemporary theologians.

The question at stake concerning the theological task of establishing intelligibility is the use of conceptuality to mediate Christian truth-claims to our understanding. We pointed out that, for the contemporary context of cultural, philosophical and religious pluralities, the limitation of Tracy's revisionist model (the 1970s) and his method in the 1980s lies in his use of Western-centric conceptualities as universal criteria to validate God's reality.

---

2    Tracy, "Preface," in *BRO* of the 1996 edition, xiii.

In his revisionist model, Tracy's central hypothesis is that the question of God, as a metaphysical question, can only and adequately be validated by a metaphysical reflection. Tracy's strategy for a metaphysical justification of God is to introduce the question of religion as such into his discussion. He approaches the question of religion in relation to the transcendental condition of human existence. Religion is a re-presentation of the "existential faith" (in life's ultimate worth) which is the transcendental condition of the possibility of all our existing and understanding. For him, God is the objective referent or, a constitutive concept, of religion understood as above. Tracy, however, finds the rationale for justifying this argument in a radically theistic, Judaeo-Christian conception of God, that is, God is the ground of all reality as "being-itself." In other words, for Tracy, this cognitive understanding of the Judaeo-Christian God, which rests upon Thomistic metaphysics, is the datum to affirm that God is a metaphysical reality universally true and valid for all human religious experience, whether theistic or non-theistic. It is on the basis of this Judaeo-Christian theism that Tracy also claims that the concept of God is a basic category of metaphysics itself. Therefore, metaphysics is theistic in nature. We pointed out that Tracy's metaphysical justification of God depends on a circular argument. His criterion (a conception of the Judaeo-Christian God) is universal because a particular metaphysical tradition that he relies on (Thomistic metaphysics) defines it as universal. And this Thomistic metaphysical tradition is (Christianly) theistic in character. Hence, we concluded that Tracy's metaphysical justification of God in his revisionist model may convince the inner circle of Christianity which shares his metaphysical option, but hardly those outside as a public discourse.

In the 1980s, the mediating conceptuality that Tracy relies on for validating God's reality is not free from Western-centrism, despite his acute concern with contextuality, plurality, otherness, and difference in his comprehensive incorporation of hermeneutics. In this period, what Tracy attempts is to combine the hermeneutical approach to truth as manifestation with a Lonerganian transcendental reflection. The problematic we pointed out in relation to this method of combination is a clash between seemingly incongruous conceptualities. More pointedly, the clash is between the quest for the epistemic certainty of

God's universal existence grounded in transcendental subjectivity *and* the quest for an understanding of God in terms of a "relatively," not absolutely, adequate interpretation. Here, a 'relatively adequate' interpretation means "relative to the power of disclosure and concealment of the text, relative to the skills and attentiveness of the interpreter, relative to the kind of conversation possible for the interpreter in a particular culture at a particular time."[3] What is at stake here is a clash between the quest for an objectivist certitude which is able to reduce all reality to more of the same *and* the quest for a 'possibility' within which to acknowledge the other world of meaning as a genuine possibility (similarity-in-difference) for oneself. Our observation is that Tracy's twofold hermeneutical-transcendental approach to God contains a contradictory element in itself. On the one hand, embracing the hermeneutical consciousness of contextuality, plurality, otherness and difference, Tracy asserts that the Eurocentric or Western-centric anthropology and theology cannot survive in an emerging world church any longer. In other words, they cannot function as the universal, normative criteria which ground a theoretical resolution of intellectual, cultural, religious, and theological plurality. On the other hand, however, Tracy appeals to the Lonerganian transcendental approach which posits the hegemony of a Western-centric and Christian-centric perspective on ultimate reality. The normality of the identification of the (Christian) God with the necessary, ultimate ground of the human subject's self transcending quest for knowledge assumed in Lonergan is a cultural product in a particular religious (Christian) tradition. The problem in the Lonerganian approach is that this identification works as a 'universal' norm which renders possible a rational, transcultural validation of the (Christian) God. At this point, we see a fundamental clash in Tracy's twofold hermeneutical-transcendental approach to God. One of Tracy's major theological concerns in the 1980s is interreligious dialogue. We pointed out that, notwithstanding this involvement, his hermeneutical-transcendental approach in this period does not sufficiently reflect how the issue of religious plurality plays an es-

3    *PA*, 22–3.

sential part in constructing the mediating conceptuality for a public discourse on God.

In the 1990s, we saw that Tracy left behind modern mediating conceptualities for thinking and naming God, including his own previous options, viz., transcendental reflection and process metaphysics. The principal reason for this shift is his awareness that modern discourses on God no longer function in proffering intelligibility or plausibility to contemporary human experience and thought. More specifically, for him, the modern conceptual renderings of God based on a social-evolutionary, Eurocentric, imperialist narrative for history and humanity no longer appeal to today's heightened consciousness and counter-experiences of the interruptions of social-political, economic, and religious evils and massive global, innocent suffering: violence, wars, partriarchy, racism, classism, etc.[4] As he indicated in an interview (2002), one of the most influential factors for shaping Tracy's theological development in the 1990s is "suffering, and especially innocent suffering."[5] Tracy says that, "The death of the self is not as important as the death of the other, especially those who have been devastated by the history of triumph, including the triumph of Christian churches. Attentiveness to such suffering – and hearing and learning from those who suffer – is crucial."[6]

Tracy's strategy to find alternative conceptualities for thinking God in response to today's contextual challenges is to *retrieve* or *reappropriate* the most marginalized or neglected conceptualities, or to use Georges De Schrijver's words, the conceptualities of "the repressed 'trace'"[7] in the past Christian tradition: the apocalyptic (with Martin Luther) and the apophatic (with Dionysius the Areopagite) traditions. In short, Tracy chooses to return, with postmodern sen-

---

4   Lieven Boeve says that, "theological plausibility is always also contextual plausibility." (Lieven Boeve, "The Particularity of Religious Truth Claims: How to Deal with it in a So-Called Postmodern Context," in Christine Helmer and Kristin De Troyer (eds), *Truth: Interdisciplinary Dialogues for a Pluralist Age* (Leuven: Peeters, 2003) 184.

5   Tracy, "The Impossible God," 5.

6   *Ibid.*

7   Georges De Schrijver, "The Use of Mediations in Theology Or, the Expanse and Self-Confinement of a Theology of the Trinity," 64.

sitivity, to the Christian tradition as the resources for mediating conceptualities for contemporary God-discourse.

Granted that we can make a proper assessment of Tracy's new theological proposal only after studying his forthcoming book, here we would nevertheless like to address one issue that his proposal exposes. Our key question is how Tracy's new proposal will avoid the problem of "traditionalism" or "self-confinement" in one's own tradition with regard to mediating Christian truth-claims to our understanding. In other words, how will Tracy's post-modern or post-metaphysical theological proposal distinguish itself from some contemporary postmodern theologies that "covertly or overtly turn back to pre-modern thinking, and opt for a ghettoizing type of church life [?]"[8] One of the serious problems of "traditionalism" is its inability to critique one's own tradition, or to "reflexively account for its truth claim."[9] "Traditionalism" is always in danger of taking "a self-proclaimed observer's position,"[10] which would give rise to a monological or solipsistic discourse in articulating the truth-claims of one's tradition. For example, the conceptualities, the apocalyptic and the apophatic, in Tracy's proposal are embedded, although traditionally in a marginalized way, in the Christian tradition, which would not be self-evidently available or immediately intelligible to the world outside (postmodern) Christian circles. An important question is how Tracy, if he is not to attach himself to any form of "traditionalism" or "self-confinement," will creatively reinterpret and develop these conceptualities to the end that they are able to mediate Christian truth-

---

8    *Ibid.*, 63. A good example of this type of theology is John Milbank's Radical Orthodoxy. See J. Milbank, C. Pickstock, and G. Ward (eds), *Radical Orthodoxy: A New Theology* (London and New York: Routlege, 1999); J. Milbank, *Theology and Social Theory: Beyond Secular Reason* (Oxford: Blackwell, 1994). For critiques of Milbank's position, see Georges De Schrijver, "The Use of Mediations in Theology Or, the Expanse and Self-Confinement of a Theology of the Trinity," esp. 19–41; Lieven Boeve, "(Post) Modern Theology on Trial?: Towards a Radical Theological Hermeneutics of Christian Particularity," in *LS*, 28 (2003) 240–54.

9    Boeve, "The Particularity of Religious Truth Claims," 191.

10   Boeve, "(Post)Modern Theology on Trial," 252.

claims as plausible and intelligible discourses to the multi-cultural, multi-religious world today.

To sum up, the pivotal characteristic of Tracy's theological proposal in the 1990s is his heightened focus on otherness: God's shattering otherness and the neighbor's irreducible otherness. His theological objective is to break through "any form of intellectual foundationalism and its institutional counterparts, cultural imperialism and ecclesial triumphalism" in theological practices.[11] He makes clear that, "The emerging world church is newly anxious to be freed of Eurocentrism – freed by the theologies of the new Europe that struggles to find a new intercultural and interreligious theological identity for itself."[12] Tracy strongly stresses the imperative that the contemporary Western theological discussion needs to expand its philosophical, cultural, religious horizons beyond a Western sense of centeredness, and of its own pluralism "toward a new global sense of polycentrism."[13] This need is urgent because "there is no longer a Western cultural center with margins. There are many centers now, of which the West is merely one. Moreover, once one drops the Western grand narrative, the continuities in that narrative begin to dissolve."[14] In his new theological venture, Tracy intends to explore a path for this objective (theology of "otherness") in a post-metaphysical or post-onto-theological form, which he finds *par excellence* in the fragmentary traditions of the apocalyptic and apophatic. Tracy asserts that, "Theology will never again be tamable by a system – any system – modern or premodern or postmodern. For theology does not bespeak a totality. Christian theology, at its best is the voice of the Other through all those others who have tasted, prophetically and meditatively, the Infinity disclosed in the kenotic reality of Jesus Christ."[15] How to successfully carry out this painstaking venture seems to be the burden of his new book on God that is now in preparation.

---

11  David Tracy, "Beyond Foundationalism and Relativism: Hermeneutics and the New Ecumenism," (*Concilium* 1992), in *On Naming the Present*, 139.
12  *Ibid.*
13  Tracy, "Fragments: The Spiritual Situation," 170.
14  *Ibid.*
15  Tracy, "Many Faces of Postmodernity," 114.

# Bibliography

## I. David Tracy's Works (Selective)

### 1. Books

*On Naming the Present.* Maryknoll: Orbis Books, 1994.

*Dialogue with the Other: The Inter-Religious Dialogue.* Leuven: Peeters Press, 1990.

*Plurality and Ambiguity: Hermeneutics, Religion, Hope.* San Francisco: Harper & Row, 1987.

*A Catholic Vision.* With Stephen Happel. Philadelphia: Fortress, 1984

*A Short History of the Interpretation of the Bible.* With Robert Grant. Philadelphia: Fortress, 1984.

*Talking about God: Doing Theology in the Context of Modern Pluralism.* With John Cobb, Jr. New York: Seabury, 1983.

*The Analogical Imagination: Christian Theology and the Culture of Pluralism.* New York: Crossroad, 1981.

*Blessed Rage for Order: The New Pluralism in Theology.* San Francisco: Harper & Row, 1975, 1996.

*The Achievement of Bernard Lonergan.* New York: Herder and Herder, 1970.

### 2. Articles

"Form and Fragment: The Recovery of the Hidden and Incomprehensible God." *The Concept of God in Global Dialogue.* Ed. Werner G. Jeanrond and Aasulv Lande. Maryknoll: Orbis Books, 2005. 98–114.

"Simone Weil and the Impossible." *The Critical Spirit: Theology at the Crossroads of Faith and Culture: Essays in Honour of Gabriel Daly.* Ed. Andrew Pierce and Geraldine Smyth. Dublin: The Columba Press, 2003. 208–22.

"The Post-Modern Re-Naming of God as Incomprehensible and Hidden." *Cross Currents* 50 (2000): 240–7.

"Fragments: The Spiritual Situation of Our Times." *God, The Gift, and Post-modernism.* Ed. John D. Caputo and Michael J. Scanlon. Bloomington and Indianapolis: Indiana University Press, 1999. 170–84.

"A Theological View of Philosophy: Revelation and Reason." *The Question of Christian Philosophy Today*. Ed. Francis J. Ambrosio. New York: Fordham University Press, 1999. 142–62.

"Traditions of Spiritual Practice and the Practice of Theology." *Theology Today* 55 (1998): 235–41.

"Fragments of Synthesis? The Hopeful Paradox of Dupré's Modernity." *Christian Spirituality and the Culture of Modernity: The Thought of Louis Dupré*. Ed. Peter J. Casarella and George P. Schner. Grand Rapids: William B. Eerdmans Publishing Company, 1998. 9–24.

"The Hidden God: The Divine Other of Liberation." *Cross Currents* 46 (1996): 5–16.

"Evil, Suffering, Hope: The Search for New Forms of Contemporary Theodicy." *Catholic Theological Society of America Proceedings* 50 (1995) 15–36.

"Modernity, Anti-Modernity and Post-Modernity in the American Setting." *Knowledge and Belief in America: Enlightenment Edition of a Modern Religious Thought*. Ed. William M. Shea and Peter A. Huff. New York: Cambridge University Press, 1995. 328–34.

"Literary Theory and Return of the Forms for Naming and Thinking God in Theology." *Journal of Religion* 74 (1994): 302–19.

"Theology and the Many Faces of Postmodernity." *Theology Today* 51 (1994): 104–14.

"Some Aspects of Buddhist-Christian Dialogue." *The Christian Understanding of God Today*. Ed. James M. Byrne. Dublin: The Columba Press, 1993. 145–53.

"Truthfulness in Catholic Theology." *Hans Küng: New Horizons for Faith and Thought*. Ed. K. Küschel and H. Häring. London: SCM Press, 1993. 81–192.

"Theology, Critical Social Theory, and the Public Realm." *Habermas, Modernity, and Public Theology*. Ed. D. Browning and Francis S. Fiorenza. New York: Crossroad, 1992. 19–42.

"The Word and Written Texts in the Hermeneutics of Christian Revelation." *Archivio Di Filosofia* 60 (1992): 265–80.

"The Hermeneutics of Naming God." *Irish Theological Quarterly* 57 (1991): 253–64.

"Approaching the Christian Understanding of God." *Systematic Theology: Roman Catholic Perspectives*. Vol.I. Ed. Francis S. Fiorenza and John P. Galvin. Minneapolis: Fortress, 1991. 133–48.

"God, Dialogue and Solidarity: A Theologian's Refrain." *Christian Century* 107 (1990): 900–4.

"On Reading the Scriptures Theologically." *Theology and Dialogue: Essays in Conversation with George Lindbeck*. Ed. Bruce D. Marshall. Notre Dame: University of Notre Dame Press, 1990. 35–68.

"Kenosis, Sunyata, and Trinity: A Dialogue with Masao Abe." *The Emptying God: A Buddhist-Jewish-Christian Conversation*. Ed. John B. Cobb, Jr., and Christopher Ives. Maryknoll: Orbis Books, 1990. 135–54.

"Hermeneutical Reflections in the New Paradigm." *Paradigm Change in Theology: A Symposium for the Future*. Ed. Hans Küng and David Tracy. Edinburgh: T&T Clark Ltd., 1989. 34–62.

"Some Concluding Reflections on the Conference: Unity Amidst Diversity and Conflict?" *Paradigm Change in Theology: A Symposium for the Future*. Ed. Hans Küng and David Tracy. Edinburgh: T&T Clark Ltd., 1989. 461–70.

"The Uneasy Alliance Reconceived: Catholic Theological Method, Modernity, and Postmodernity." *Theological Studies* 50 (1989): 548–70.

"Afterword: Theology, Public Discourse, and the American Tradition." *Religion and Twentieth-Century American Intellectual Life*. Ed. Michael J. Lacey. Cambridge: Cambridge University Press, 1989. 193–203.

"On Hope as a Theological Virtue in American Catholic Theology." *The Church in Anguish: Has the Vatican Betrayed Vatican II?*. Ed. Hans Küng and Leonard Swidler. San Francisco: Harper & Row, 1987. 268–72.

"Religious Studies and Its Community of Inquiry." *Criterion* 25 (1986): 21–4.

"Lindbeck's New Program for Theology." *Thomist* 49 (1985): 460–72.

"Tillich and Contemporary Theology." *The Thought of Paul Tillich*. Ed. James L. Adams, Wilhelm Pauck, and Roger L. Shinn. San Francisco: Harper & Row, 1985. 260–77.

"Is a Hermeneutics of Religion Possible?" *Religious Pluralism*. Ed. Leroy S. Rouner. Notre Dame: University of Notre Dame Press, 1984. 116–29.

"Creativity in the Interpretation of Religion: The Question of Radical Pluralism." *New Literary History* 15 (1984): 289–309.

"The Analogical Imagination in Catholic Theology." *Talking About God: Doing Theology in the Context of Modern Pluralism*. Ed. David Tracy and John B. Cobb, Jr. New York: The Seabury Press, 1983. 17–38.

"The Foundations of Practical Theology." *Practical Theology*. Ed. Don S. Browning. San Francisco: Harper and Row, 1983. 61–82.

"The Questions of Pluralism: The Context of the United States." *Mid-Stream: An Ecumenical Journal* 22 (1983): 273–85.

"Religious Values After the Holocaust: A Catholic View." *Jews and Christians After the Holocaust*. Ed. Abraham J. Peck. Philadelphia: Fortress, 1982. 87–106.

"Defending the Public Character of Theology." *Theologians in Transition*. Ed. James M. Wall. New York: Crossroad, 1981. 113–24.

"The Question of Pluralism in Contemporary Theology." *The Chicago Theological Seminary Register* 71 (1981) 29–38.

"Theologies of Praxis." *Creativity and Method: Essays in Honor of Bernard Lonergan*. Ed. Matthew L. Lamb. Milwaukee: Marquette University Press, 1981. 35–51.

"Theoria and Praxis: A Partial Response." *Theological Education* 17 (1981): 167–74.

"Particular Questions within General Consensus." *Journal of Ecumenical Studies* 17 (1980): 33–9.

"Theological Pluralism and Analogy." *Thought* 54 (1979): 24–36.

"Metaphor and Religion: The Test Case of Christian Texts." *On Metaphor.* Ed. Sheldon Sacks. Chicago: University of Chicago Press, 1979. 89–104.
"Christian Faith and Radical Equality." *Theology Today* 34 (1978): 370–7.
"Theological Table-Talk: Modes of Theological Argument." *Theology Today* 33 (1977): 387–95.
"Theology as Public Discourse." *The Christian Century* 92 (1975): 280–4.
"Religious Language as Limit-Language." *Theology Digest* 22 (1974): 292–6.
"Response to Professor Connelly–II." *Catholic Theological Society of America Proceedings* 29 (1974): 67–75
"The Task of Fundamental Theology." *Journal of Religion* 54 (1974): 13–34.
"God's Reality: The Most Important Issue." *Anglican Theological Review* 55 (1973): 218–24.
"Method as Foundation for Theology: Bernard Lonergan's Option." *Journal of Religion* 50 (1970): 292–318.

## 3. Interviews and Internet Sources

Interview with David Tracy by Scott Holland. "This Side of God: A Conversation with David Tracy." *Cross Currents* 52 (2002): 54–9.
Interview with David Tracy by Lois Malcolm. "The Impossible God." http://www. file:///A/Malcolm-Christian Century-2002.htm (access 10 September 2002).
"Form and Fragment: The Recovery of the Hidden and Incomprehensible God." Tracy's Lecture at the Center of Theological Inquiry in Princeton in 1999. http://www.ctinquiry.org/publications/tracy.htm (access 13 September 2002).
Interview with David Tracy by Todd Breyfogle and Thomas Levergood. "Conversation with David Tracy." *Cross Currents* 44 (1994): 293–315.

# II. Works By Other Authors (Consulted)

## 1. Books

Adorno, Theodor. W., *Metaphysics: Concepts and Problems*, trans. Edmund Jephcott and Ed. Rolf Tiedemann. Stanford: Standford University Press, 2000.
Beardslee, William, A. *Literary Criticism of the New Testament.* Philadelphia: Fortress, 1970.
Bernstein, Richard, J. *Beyond Objectivism and Relativism: Science, Hermeneutics, and Praxis.* Oxford: Basil Blackwell Publisher Limited, 1983.

Black, Max. *Models and Metaphors*. Ithaca: Cornell University Press, 1962.

Boeve, Lieven. *Interrupting Tradition: An Essay on Christian Faith in a Postmodern Context*. Louvain & Dudley: Peeters Press, 2003.

Boodoo, Gerald, M. *Development and Consolidation: the Use of Theological Method in the Works of David Tracy*. Unpublished doctoral dissertation. Faculty of Theology, K.U. Leuven, Leuven, 1991.

Bush, Richard, C. *Religion in China*. Niles: Argus Communications, 1977.

Caputo, John, D. *Heidegger and Aquinas: An Essay on Overcoming Metaphysics*. New York: Fordham University Press, 1982.

Chauvet, Louis-Marie. *Symbol and Sacrament: A Sacramental Reinterpretation of Christian Existence*. Collegeville: The Liturgical Press, 1995.

Ching, Julia. *Chinese Religions*. London: The Macmillan Press, 1993.

Clayton, Philip. *The Problem of God in Modern Thought*. Grand Rapids and Cambridge: William B. Eerdmans Publishing Company, 2000.

Copleston, Frederick. *A History of Philosophy: Medieval Philosophy*, vol.II. New York: Doubleday, 1993.

Crossan, Dominic. *In Parables*. New York: Harper & Row, 1973.

Desmond, William. *God and the Between*. A forthcoming book. Faculty of Philosophy, K.U. Leuven, Leuven, 2002.

Dewey, John. *A Common Faith*. New Haven and London: Yale University Press, 1934, 1970.

Dodd, Charles, H. *The Parables of the Kingdom*. London: Nisbet & Co. Ltd., 1935.

Emerich Coreth. *Metaphysics*, trans. and Ed. Joseph Donceel. New York: Herder & Herder, 1968.

Ferguson, Sinclair, B. and Wright, David, F. (eds). *New Dictionary of Theology*. Downers Grove: Inter-Varsity Press, 1988.

Fiorenza, Francis. *Foundational Theology: Jesus and the Church*. New York: Crossroad, 1985.

Frei, Hans. *The Identity of Jesus Christ: The Hermeneutical Bases of Dogmatic Theology*. Philadelphia: Fortress Press, 1975.

—— *The Eclipse of Biblical Narrative: A Study in Eighteenth and Nineteenth Century Hermeneutics*. New Haven: Yale University Press, 1974.

Gadamer, Hans-Georg. *Truth and Method*. New York: Crossroad, 1975, 1982.

Gilkey, Langdon. *Naming the Whirlwind: The Renewal of God-Language*. New York: Bobbs-Merrill, 1969.

Goh, Jeffrey, C.K. *Christian Tradition Today: A Postliberal Vision of Church and World*. Louvain: Peeters Press, 2000.

Grenz, Stanley, J., and Franke, John, R. *Beyond Foundationalism: Shaping Theology in a Postmodern Context*. Louisville: Westminster John Knox Press, 2001.

Hartshorne, Charles, and Reese, William, L. *Philosophers Speak of God*. Chicago: The University of Chicago Press, 1953, reissued in 1976 in Midway Reprints.

Hartshorne, Charles. *The Logic of Perfection and Other Essays in Neoclassical Metaphysics*. La Salle: The Open Court Publishing Company, 1962, 1991.

—— *Aquinas to Whitehead: Seven Centuries of Metaphysics of Religion.* Milwaukee: Marquette University Publications, 1976.

—— *Reality as Social Process Studies in Metaphysics and Religion.* New York: Hafner Publishing Company, 1953, 1971.

—— *Creative Synthesis and Philosophic Method.* La Salle: Open Court Publishing Company, 1970.

—— *A Natural Theology for Our Time.* La Salle: The Open Court Publishing Company, 1967.

—— *Man's Vision of God and the Logic of Theism.* Hamden: Archon Books, 1964.

Harvey, Van A. *The Historian and the Believer.* New York: Macmillan, 1966.

Hauerwas, Stanley, Murphy, Nancey & Mark Nation. *Theology Without Foundations: Religious Practice and the Future of Theological Truth.* Nashville: Abingdon Press, 1994.

Heidegger, Martin. *Being and Time,* trans. by John Macquarrie and Edward Robinson Oxford: Basil Blackwell, 1967.

Hick, John. *An Interpretation of Religion.* New Haven and London: Yale University Press, 1989.

Husserl, Edmund. *Experience and Judgment: Investigations in a Genealogy of Logic,* originally published as *Erfahrung und Urteil: Untersuchungen zur Genealogie der Logik* trans. James S. Churchill and Karl Ameriks. London: Routledge & Kegan Paul, 1973.

—— *The Crisis of European Sciences and Transcendental Phenomenology,* originally published as *Die Krisis der europäischen Wissenschaften und die transzendentale Phänomenologie: Eine Einleitung in die phänomenologische Philosophie* trans. by David Carr. Evanston: Northwestern University Press, 1970.

James, Ralph, E. *The Concrete God: A New Beginning for Theology – The Thought of Charles Hartshorne.* Indianapolis and Kansas City and New York: The Bobbs – Merrill Company, Inc., 1967.

James, William. *The Varieties of Religious Experiences: A Study in Human Nature.* London: Longmans, Green and Co., 1959.

Jay, Martin. *The Dialectical Imagination: A History of the Frankfurt School and the Institute of Social Research 1923–1950.* London: Heinemann Educational Books, 1973.

Jeanrond, Werner, G. and Rike, Jennifer, L. (eds). *Radical Pluralism and Truth: David Tracy and the Hermenetics of Religion.* New York: Crossroad, 1991.

Jeremias, Joachim. *Die Gleichnisse Jesu.* Zürich: Leemann & Co., 1947.

Jülicher, Adolph. *Die Gleichnisreden Jesu.* Tübingen: J.C.B. Mohr, 1888, 1910.

Kant, Immanuel. *Critique of Practical Reason and Other Writings in Moral Philosophy,* Chicago: University of Chicago Press, 1949.

—— *Critique of Pure Reason,* trans. by Paul Guyer and Allen W. Wood, Cambridge: Cambridge University Press, 1997.

—— *Religion Within the Limits of Reason Alone,* New York: Harper & Row, 1960.

Kaufman, Gordon. *God the Problem.* Cambridge: Harvard University Press, 1972.

—— *Relativism, Knowledge and Faith*. Chicago: University of Chicago Press, 1960.

Knasas, John, F.X. *Being and Some Twentieth-Century Thomists*. New York: Fordham University Press, 2003.

Kockelmans, Joseph, K. *The Metaphysics of Aquinas: A Systematic Presentation*. Leuven: Bibliotheek van de Faculteit Godgeleerdheid, 2001.

—— *Phenomenology: The Philosophy of Edmund Husserl and Its Interpretation*. New York: A Doubleday Garden City, 1967.

Latourelle, René and O'Collins, Gerald (eds). *Problems and Perspectives of Fundamental Theology*. New York: Paulist Press, 1982.

Levinas, Emmanuel. *Otherwise Than Being or Beyond Essence*, trans. by Alphonso Lingis. Boston: Kluwer, 1991.

—— *Totality and Infinity*, trans. by Alphonso Lingis. Pittsburgh: Dquesne University Press, 1969.

Lindbeck, George. *The Nature of Doctrine: Religion and Theology in a Postliberal Age*. Philadelphia: The Westminster Press, 1984.

Lonergan, Bernard. *Insight: A Study of Human Understanding*. New York: Philosophical Library, 1957, 1970.

—— *Method in Theology*. Toronto: University of Toronto Press, 1971, 1990.

Maréchal, Joseph. *Le point de départ de la métaphysique: Leçons sur le développement historique et théorique du problème de la connaissance*, 5 volumes. Louvain: Museum Lessianum, 1926–1947.

Marion, Jean-Luc. *God without Being*, trans. by Thomas A. Carlson. Chicago: Chicago University Press, 1991.

Martinez, Gaspar (Ed.). *Confronting the Mystery of God: Political, Liberation and Public Theologies*. New York: Continuum, 2001.

McCool, Gerald, A. *The Neo-Thomists*. Milwaukee: Marquette University Press, 1994.

Merleau-Ponty, Maurice. *Phenomenology of Perception*, originally published as *Phénoménologie de la Perception* trans. by Colin Smith. London: Routledge, 1962, 1996.

Metz, Johann Baptist. *Faith in History and Society*. New York: Seabury, 1979.

Meynell, Hugo, A. *An Introduction to the Philosophy of Bernard Lonergan*. London: The Macmillan Press, 1976.

Muck, Otto. *The Transcendental Method*. New York: Herder & Herder, 1968.

Nygren, Anders. *Method and Method: Prolegomena to a Scientific Philosophy of Religion and a Scientific Theology*. London: EP Worth Press, 1972.

O'Collins, Gerald. *Retrieving Fundamental Theology: The Three Styles of Contemporary Theology*. New York: Paulist Press, 1993.

Ogden, Schubert, M. *The Reality of God and Other Essays*. San Francisco: Harper & Row, 1977.

Peerbolte, L.J. Lietaert. *Paul the Missionary*. Leuven: Peeters, 2003.

Perrin, Norman. *Jesus and the Language of the Kingdom: Symbol and Metaphor in New Testament Interpretation*. Philadelphia: Fortress Press, 1976.

399

—— *The New Testament: An Introduction*. New York: Harcourt, Brace Jovanovich, 1974.

Pratt, Douglas. *Relational Deity: Hartshorne and Macquarrie on God*. Lanham and New York and Oxford: University Press of America, 2002.

Ramsey, Ian. *Models and Mystery*. London: Oxford University Press, 1964.

—— *Religious Language: An Empirical Placing of Theological Phrases*. London: SCM Press Ltd., 1969.

Rescher, Nicholas. *Kant's Theory of Knowledge and Reality*. Washington: University Press of America, Inc, 1983.

Richardson, Alan (Ed.). *A Dictionary of Christian Theology*. London: SCM, 1969.

Richardson, William, J. *Heidegger: Through Phenomenology to Thought*. The Hague: Nijhoff, 1967.

Ricoeur, Paul. *Figuring the Sacred: Religion, Narrative and Imagination*. trans. by David Pellauer. Minneapolis: Fortress Press, 1995.

—— *From Text to Action*. London: Northwestern University Press, 1991.

—— *Interpretation Theory: Discourse and the Surplus of Meaning*. Fort Worth: The Texas Christian University Press, 1976.

—— *The Symbolism of Evil*. trans. by Emerson Buchanan. Boston: Beacon Press, 1969.

Rorty, Richard. *Philosophy and the Mirror of Nature*. Princeton: Princeton University Press, 1979.

Schoof, Mark. *A Survey of Catholic Theology 1800–1970*. New York: Paulist Newman Press, 1970.

Schrag, Calvin, O. *Experience and Being: Prolegomena to a Future Ontology*. Evanston: Northwestern University Press, 1969.

Sia, Santiago. *God in Process Thought: A Study in Charles Hartshorne's Concept of God*. Dordrecht: Martinus Nijhoff Publishers, 1985.

Smith, John, E. *Experience and God*. New York: Oxford University Press, 1968, 1974.

Soothill, W.E. *The Three Religions of China*. London: Curzon Press, 1973.

Spiegelberg, Herbert. *The Phenomenological Movement: A Historical Introduction*. 2 vols. The Hague: Nijhoff, 1969.

Stiver, Dan, R. *Theology after Ricoeur: New Directions in Hermeneutical Theology*. Louisville: Westminster John Knox Press, 2001.

Tillich, Paul. *Systematic Theology. I*. Digswell Place: James Nisbet, 1951, 1964.

—— *Systematic Theology. II*. Digswell Place: James Nisbet, 1957, 1964.

Toulmin, Stephen. *An Examination of the Place of Reason in Ethics*. Cambridge: Cambridge University Press, 1950, 1958.

Van Buren, Paul M. *The Secular Meaning of the Gospel*. New York: Macmillan, 1963.

Via, Dan, O. *The Parables: Their Literary and Existential Dimension*. Philadelphia: Fortress, 1967.

Warnke, Georgia. *Gadamer: Hermeneutics, Tradition and Reason*. Cambridge: Polity Press, 1987.

Wheelwright, Philip. *Metaphor and Reality*. Bloomington: Indiana University Press, 1962, 1975.

Whitehead, Alfred, N. *Modes of Thought*. New York: The Free Press, 1938, 1966.

—— *Process and Reality: An Essay in Cosmology*. New York: The Free Press, 1929, 1978.

—— *Religion in the Making*. New York: The World Publishing Company, 1926, 1972.

Wilder, Amos, N. *Early Christian Rhetoric: The Language of the Gospel*. New York: Harper & Row, 1964.

Wood, W. Jay. *Epistemology: Becoming Intellectually Virtuous*. Downers Grove: InterVarsity Press, 1998.

## 2. Articles

Allison, Henry, E. "Kant, Immanuel." *The Oxford Companion to Philosophy*. Ed. Ted Honderich. Oxford: Oxford University Press, 1995, 435–8.

Aylesworth, Gary, E. "Dialogue, Text, Narrative: Confronting Gadamer and Ricoeur." *Gadamer and Hermeneutics*. Ed. Hugh J. Silverman. New York and London: Routledge, 1991, 63–81.

Baldrian, Farzeen. "Taoism." *The Encyclopedia of Religion*. Ed. Mircea Eliade, vol.14. New York: Macmillan Publishing Company, 1987, 288–306.

Beardslee, William, A. "The Uses of the Proverb in the Synoptic Tradition." *Interpretation* 24 (1970): 61–76.

Beardsley, Monroe. "The Metaphorical Twist." *Essays on Metaphor*. Ed. Warren Shibles. Whitewater, Wisc: The Language Press, 1972, 73–93.

Bedford, Errol. "Empiricism." *The Concise Encyclopedia of Western Philosophy and Philosophers*. Ed. J.O. Urmson and Jonathan Rée. London: Unwin Hyman, 1960, 88–90.

Bernstein, Richard, J. "Radical Plurality, Fearful Ambiguity, and Engaged Hope." *Journal of Religion* 69 (1989): 89–90.

Boeve, Lieven. "The Particularity of Religious Truth Claims: How to Deal with it in a So-Called Postmodern Context." *Truth: Interdisciplinary Dialogues for a Pluralist Age*. Eds. Christine Helmer and Kristin De Troyer. Leuven: Peeters, 2003, 181–95.

—— "(Post) Modern Theology on Trial?: Towards a Radical Theological Hermeneutics of Christian Particularity." *Louvain Studies* 28 (2003): 240–54.

—— "God Interrupts History: Apocalypticism as an Indispensable Theological Conceptual Strategy." *Louvain Studies* 26 (2001): 195–216.

—— "Critical Consciousness in the Postmodern Condition: A New Opportunity for Theology?" *Philosophy and Theology* 10 (1997): 449–68.

Bonsor, Jack, A. "An Orthodox Historicism?" *Philosophy & Theology* 4 (1990): 335–50.

—— "History, Dogma, and Nature: Further Reflections on Postmodernism and Theology." *Theological Studies* 55 (1994): 295–313.

—— "Irreducible Pluralism: The Transcendental and Hermeneutical as Theological Options." *Horizons* 16 (1989): 316–28.

Chang, Aloysius. "The Concept of the Tao." *God in Contemporary Thought: A Philosophical Perspective.* Ed. Sebastian A. Matczak. New York: Learned Publications, 1977, 79–95.

Cloots, André, and Van der Veken, Jan. "Can the God of Process Thought be 'Redeemed'?" Charles Hartshorne's *Concept of God: Philosophical and Theological Responses.* Ed. Santiago Sia. Dordrecht: Kluwer Academic Publishers, 1990. 125–36.

Cloots, André. "Thinking Things Together: The Concept of Metaphysics." *Framing a Vision of the World: Essays in Philosophy, Science and Religion in Honor of Professor Jan Van der Veken.* Eds. André Cloots and Santiago Sia. Leuven: Leuven University Press, 1999. 67–84.

Connelly, John. "The Task of Theology." *Catholic Theological Society of America Proceedings* 29 (1974): 1–58.

D'Costa, G. "The End of Systematic Theology." *Theology* 95 (1992): 324–34.

De Schrijver, Georges. "The Use of Mediations in Theology Or, the Expanse and Self-Confinement of a Theology of the Trinity." *Mediations in Theology: Georges De Schrijver's Wager and Liberation Theologies.* Eds. Jacques Haers, Edmundo Guzman and others. Leuven: Peeters, 2003, 1–64.

Dreyfus, H.L. and Todes, S.J. "Discussion: The Three Worlds of Merleau-Ponty." *Philosophy and Phenomenological Research* 22 (1961–1962): 559–65.

Drilling, Peter, J. "The Pyramid or the Raft: Francis Schüssler Fiorenza and Bernard Lonergan in Dialogue about Foundational Theology." *Horizons* 13 (1986): 275–90.

Fiorenza, Francis, S. "The Crisis of Hermeneutics and Christian Theology." *Theology at the End of Modernity: Essays in Honour of Gordon Kaufman.* Ed. Sheila G. Davaney. Philadelphia: Trinity Press International, 1991, 117–40.

—— "Theology: Transcendental or Hermeneutical?" *Horizons* 16 (1989): 329–41.

Frege, Gottlob. "On Sense and Reference." *Translations from the Philosophical Writings of Gottlob Frege.* Ed. Peter Geach and Max Black. Oxford: Basil Blackwell, 1970, 56–78.

Frei, Hans. "The 'Literal Reading' of Biblical Narrative in the Christian Tradition: Does It Stretch or Will It Break?" *The Bible and the Narrative Tradition.* Ed. Frank McConnell. New York: Oxford University Press, 1986, 36–78.

Fu, Charles, Wei-hsun. "[The] Buddhist Approach to the Problem of God." *God in Contemporary Thought: A Philosophical Perspective.* Ed. Sebastian A. Matczak. New York: Learned Publications, 1977, 155–78.

Geffré, Claude. "Recent Developments in Fundamental Theology: An Interpretation." *Concilium* 46 (1969): 5–27.

Gelpi, Donald, L. "The Turn to Experience in Transcendental Thomism." *The Turn to Experience in Contemporary Theology*. New York: Paulist Press, 1994. 90–120.

Gerrish, B.A. "To the Unknown God: Luther and Calvin on the Hiddenness of God." *The Old Protestantism and the New*. Chicago: University of Chicago Press, 1982, 131–49.

Grondin, Jean. "Hermeneutical Truth and Its Historical Presuppositions: A Possible Bridge between Analysis and Hermeneutics." *Anti-Foundationalism and Practical Reasoning: Conversations between Hermeneutics and Analysis*. Ed. Evan Simpson. Edmonton, Alberta: Academic Printing & Publishing, 1987, 45–58.

Gschwandtner, Christina, M. "Ricoeur's Hermeneutics of God: A Symbol That Gives Rise to Thought." *Philosophy & Theology* 13 (2001): 287–309.

Guarino, Thomas. "Between Foundationalism and Nihilism: Is *Phronesis* the *Via Media* for Theology?" *Theological Studies* 54 (1993): 37–54.

——"Revelation and Foundationalism: Toward Hermeneutical and Ontological Appropriateness." *Modern Theology* 6 (1990): 221–35.

Hartshorne, Charles and Van der Vaken, Jan. "A Conversation between Charles Hartshorne and Jan Van der Veken." *Louvain Studies* 8 (1980): 129–42.

Hartshorne, Charles. "Redefining God." *American Journal of Theology and Philosophy* 22 (2001): 107–13. Originally published in *The New Humanist* 7 (1934).

—— "Can We Understand God?" *Louvain Studies* 7 (1978) 75–84.

—— "A Philosopher's Assessment of Christianity." *Religion and Culture: Essays in Honor of Paul Tillich*. Ed. Walter Leibrecht. New York: Harper, 1959, 167–80.

Harvey, Van A. "The Alienated Theologian." *The Future of Philosophical Theology*. Ed. Robert A. Evans. Philadelphia: The Westminster Press, 1971. 113–43.

Heath, P.L. "Logical Positivism." *The Concise Encyclopedia of Western Philosophy and Philosophers*. Ed. J.O. Urmson and Jonathan Rée. London: Unwin Hyman, 1960, 182–7.

Heidegger, Martin. "The Onto-theo-logical Constitution of Metaphysics." *The Religious*. Ed. John D. Caputo. Oxford: Blackwell Publishers, 2002, 67–75.

Holland, Scott. "How Do Stories Save Us?: Two Contemporary Theological Responses." *Louvain Studies* 22 (1997): 328–51.

Inada, Kenneth. "Some Basic Misconceptions of Buddhism." *International Philosophical Quarterly* 9 (1969): 101–19.

Jeanrond, Werner, G. "Correlational Theology and the Chicago School." *Introduction to Christian Theology*. Ed. Roger A. Badham. Louisville: Westminster John Knox Press, 1998, 137–53.

—— "Theology in the Context of Pluralism and Postmodernity: David Tracy's Theological Method." *Postmodernism, Literature and the Future of Theology*. Ed. David Jasper. New York: St. Martin's Press, 1993, 143–63.

Jones, Gareth. "Tracy: Halting the Postmodernist Slide." *Critical Theology*. Cambridge: Polity Press, 1995, 113–34.

Kant, Immanuel. "What is Enlightenment?" *Critique of Practical Reason and Other Writings in Moral Philosophy*. Ed. Lewis W. Beck. Chicago: University of Chicago Press, 1949, 286–92.

Kim, Jaegwon. "What is 'Naturalized Epistemology'?" *Epistemology: An Anthology*. Ed. Ernest Sosa and Jaegon Kim. Oxford: Blackwell Publishers Ltd., 2002, 301–13.

Kockelmans, Joseph, J. "Hermeneutic Philosophy and Natural Theology." *Prospects for Natural Theology*. Ed. Eugene T. Long. Washington: The Catholic University of America Press, 1992, 92–112.

Lamb, Matthew. "The Theory-Praxis Relationship in Contemporary Christian Theology." *Catholic Theological Society of America Proceedings* (1976): 147–78.

Lawrence, Fred. "On the Relationship Between Transcendental and Hermeneutical Approaches to Theology." *Horizons* 16 (1989): 342–5.

—— "The Fragility of Consciousness: Lonergan and the Postmodern Concern for the Other." *Theological Studies* 54 (1993): 55–94.

Lints, Richard. "The Postpositivist Choice: Tracy or Lindbeck?" *Journal of the American Academy of Religion* 61 (1993): 655–77.

Lonergan, Bernard. "Metaphysics as Horizon." *Gregorianum* 44 (1963): 307–18.

Long, Eugene, T. "Neo-Thomism." *Twentieth-Century Western Philosophy of Religion 1900-2000*. Dordrecht: Kluwer Academic Publishers, 2000, 338–48.

Lowe, Victor. "Whitehead's Metaphysical System." *Process Philosophy and Christian Thought*. Ed. Delwin Brown, Ralph E. James, Jr., and Gene Revees. New York and Indianapolis: The Bobbs-Merrill, 1971, 3–20.

MacNabb, D.G.C. "Hume, David." *The Concise Encyclopedia of Western Philosophy and Philosophers*. Ed. J.O. Urmson and Jonathan Rée. London: Unwin Hyman, 1960, 139–44.

McMurrin, Sterling, M. "Hartshorne's Critique of Classical Metaphysics and Theology." *The Philosophy of Charles Hartshorne*. Ed. Lewis E. Hahn. La Salle: Open Court Publishing Company, 1991, 431–43.

Meerbote, Ralf. "Kant." *A Companion to the Philosophers*. Ed. Robert L. Arrington. Oxford and Malden: Blackwell Publishers, 1999, 338–52.

Nash, Jesse. "Tracy's Revisionist Project: Some Fundamental Issues." *American Benedictine Review* 34 (1983): 240–67.

Nivison, David, S. "Tao and Te." *The Encyclopedia of Religion*. Ed. Mircea Eliade, vol.14. New York: Macmillan, 1987, 283–6.

O'Donnell, John. "Transcendental Approaches to the Doctrine of God." *Gregorianum* 77 (1996): 659–76.

Ogden, Schubert, M. "What is Theology." *Journal of Religion* 52 (1972): 22–40.

—— "The Task of Philosophical Theology." *The Future of Philosophical Theology*. Ed. Robert A. Evans. Philadelphia: The Westminster Press, 1971, 55–84.

Ommen, Thomas, B. "Theology and Foundationalism." *Studies in Religion* 16 (1987): 159–71.

—— "Relativism, Objectivism, and Theology." *Horizons* 13 (1986): 291–305.

Pailin, David A. "Process Theology: Why and What?" *Probing the Foundations: A Study in Theistic Reconstruction.* Kampen: Kok Pharos Publishing House, 1994, 66–81.

Perrin, Norman. "The Modern Interpretation of the Parables of Jesus and the Problem of Hermeneutics." *Interpretation* 25 (1971): 131–48.

Peter, Carl, J. "A Shift to the Human Subject in Roman Catholic Theology." *Communio: International Catholic Review* 6 (1979): 56–72.

Ricoeur, Paul. "From Interpretation to Translation." *Thinking Biblically: Exegetical and Hermeneutical Studies.* Trans. by David Pellauer, ed. by André LaCocque and Paul Ricoeur. Chicago: The University of Chicago Press, 1998, 331–61.

—— "Word, Polysemy, Metaphor: Creativity in Language." *A Ricoeur Reader: Reflection and Imagination.* Ed. Mario J. Valdés. Hertfordshire: Harvester Wheatsheaf, 1991, 65–85.

—— "The Model of the Text: Meaningful Action Considered as a Text." *Paul Ricoeur: Hermeneutics and the Human Sciences.* Ed. John B. Thompson. Cambridge: Cambridge University Press, 1988, 197–221.

—— "The Hermeneutical Function of Distanciation." *Paul Ricoeur: Hermeneutics and the Human Sciences.* Ed. John B. Thompson. Cambridge: Cambridge University Press, 1988, 131–144.

—— "What is a Text?: Explanation and Understanding." *Paul Ricoeur: Hermeneutics and the Human Sciences.* Ed. John B. Thompson. Cambridge: Cambridge University Press, 1988, 145–164.

—— "Toward a Hermeneutic of the Idea of Revelation." *Paul Ricoeur: Essays on Biblical Interpretation.* Ed. Lewis S. Mudge. Philadelphia: Fortress Press, 1985, 73–118.

—— "From Existentialism to the Philosophy of Language." *The Philosophy of Paul Ricoeur: An Anthology of His Work.* Ed. Charles E. Reagan and David Stewart. Boston: Beacon Press, 1978, 86–93.

—— "Listening to the Parables of Jesus." *The Philosophy of Paul Ricoeur.* Ed. Charles E. Reagan and David Stewart. Boston: Beacon Press, 1978, 239–45.

—— "Manifestation and Proclamation." *The Journal of the Blaisdell Institute* 12 (1978): 13–35.

—— "The Metaphorical Process." *Semeia* 4 (1975): 75–106.

—— "The Specificity of Language." *Semeia* 4 (1975): 107–48.

—— "Philosophy and Religious Language." *Journal of Religion* 54 (1974): 71–86.

—— "Structure, Word, Event." *The Conflict of Interpretations: Essays in Hermeneutics.* Ed. Don Ihde. Evanston: Northwestern University Press, 1974, 27–61.

—— "The Problem of Double Meaning." *The Conflict of Interpretations: Essays in Hermeneutics.* Ed. Don Ihde. Evanston: Northwestern University Press, 1974, 62–78.

——— "New Developments in Phenomenology in France: The Phenomenology of Language." *Social Research* 34 (1967): 1–30.

Robertson, John, C. "Rahner and Ogden: Man's Knowledge of God." *Harvard Theological Review* 63 (1970): 377–407.

Sachs, John R. "Transcendental Method in Theology and Normativity of Human Experience." *Philosophy and Theology* 7 (1992): 213–25.

Sanks, T. Howland. "David Tracy's Theological Project: An Overview and Some Implications." *Theological Studies* 54 (1993): 698–727.

Shea, William, M. "The Stance and Task of the Foundational Theologian: Critical or Dogmatic?" *Heythrop Journal* 17 (1976): 273–92.

Shen, Philip. "Theological Pluralism: An Asian Response to David Tracy." *Journal of the American Academy of Religion* 53 (1985): 735–51.

Sheveland, John. "Interreligious Momentum in David Tracy's Postmodern Christian Theology." *Studies in Interreligious Dialogue* 12 (2002): 207–25.

Stell, Stephen L. "Hermeneutics in Theology and the Theology of Hermeneutics." *Journal of the American Academy of Religion* 61 (1993): 679–703.

Strawson, P.F. "Metaphysics." *The Concise Encyclopedia of Western Philosophy and Philosophers.* Ed. J.O. Urmson & Jonathan Rée. London: Unwin Hyman, 1960, 202–8.

Van der Veken, Jan. "Ultimate Reality and God: The Same?" *The Philosophy of Charles Hartshorne.* Ed. Lewis E. Hahn. La Salle: Open Court Publishing Company, 1991, 203–14.

——— "Toward a Dipolar View on the Whole of Reality." *Louvain Studies* 7 (1978): 102–14.

Vanhoozer, Kevin, J. "Philosophical Antecedents to Ricoeur's *Time and Narrative.*" *On Paul Ricoeur: Narrative and Interpretation.* Ed. David Wood. London: Routledge, 1991, 34–54.

Wallace, Mark, I. "Can God Be Named Without Being Known?: The Problem of Revelation in Thiemann, Ogden, and Ricoeur." *Journal of American Academy of Religion* 59 (1991): 281–308.

Westphal, Merold. "Divine Excess: The God Who Comes After." *The Religious.* Ed. John D. Caputo. Oxford: Blackwell Publishers, 2002, 258–76.

Wiles, Maurice, F. "Can Theology Still Be About God?" *Theology at the End of Modernity: Essays in Honour of Gordon Kaufman.* Ed. Davaney, S. Greeve. Philadelphia: Trinity, 1991, 221–32.

Winquist, Charles, E. "Analogy, Apology, and the Imaginative Pluralism of David Tracy." *Journal of the American Academy of Religion* 56 (1988): 307–19.

# Index

# Religions and Discourse

Edited by James M. M. Francis

*Religions and Discourse* explores religious language in the major world faiths from various viewpoints, including semiotics, pragmatics and cognitive linguistics, and reflects on how it is situated within wider intellectual and cultural contexts. In particular a key issue is the role of figurative speech. Many fascinating metaphors originate in religion e.g. revelation as a 'gar-ment', apostasy as 'adultery', loving kindness as the 'circumcision of the heart'. Every religion rests its specific orientations upon symbols such as these, to name but a few. The series strives after the interdisciplinary ap-proach that brings together such diverse disciplines as religious studies, theology, sociology, philosophy, linguistics and literature, guided by an international editorial board of scholars representative of the aforementioned disciplines. Though scholarly in its scope, the series also seeks to facilitate discussions pertaining to central religious issues in contemporary contexts.

The series will publish monographs and collected essays of a high scholarly standard.